VOLTAIRE

By the same author

MARIE ANTOINETTE

YOUNG MR PEPYS

Voltaire in old age
Bust by *Houdon*

John E. N. Hearsey

VOLTAIRE

BARNES & NOBLE

BOOKS

10 East 53d St., New York 10022
(a division of Harper & Row Publishers, Inc.)

Published in the U.S.A. 1976 by
HARPER & ROW PUBLISHERS, INC.
BARNES & NOBLE IMPORT DIVISION
ISBN 0-06-492780-6
Printed in Great Britain

CONTENTS

CONTENTS

ILLUSTRATIONS

DEDICATION

To all those, like Jean Calas, who through
the centuries have suffered from the evils
of fanaticism and falsehood.

ACKNOWLEDGEMENTS

I should like to express my thanks to Professor Asa Briggs B.SC., M.A., Vice Chancellor, for permission to use the Library of the University of Sussex for research, and to the Librarians for their assistance.

I should also like to thank the Director of the Victoria and Albert Museum and the Radio Times Hulton Picture Library, London, for permission to use reproductions of paintings, prints and sculpture as illustrations.

Lastly, I should like to thank all those who have helped bring the book itself into being.

J.E.N.H.

INTRODUCTION

All the encyclopedias, reference books and history books agree that Voltaire was one of the great figures of the eighteenth century. But what is it that makes him great in the eyes of the twentieth century, nearly two centuries after his death? Wit and a flamboyant life do not make for greatness, and these are his best remembered characteristics. If he were such a brilliant writer, why has so little of his vast output survived, at least so far as the general reader is concerned? Where does that greatness lie, and what is his relevance to the twentieth century?

Voltaire made men think for themselves. He infuriated them either by challenging accepted beliefs, or by questioning political and social conventions. He stimulated his readers by expressing what many secretly thought but dared not utter. Today, only the individual reader can decide for himself whether Voltaire was more important as a writer or as a catalyst in the minds of others. To posterity he can be all things to all people, as indeed he was inclined to be in life.

Voltaire's wide-ranging and profound study of history marked the beginning of a new chapter in historical research. No longer was it simply a matter of dates, kings and battles, set out in the form of a chronicle, but an interpretation of events seen from a political, economic and social standpoint. Above all, he did not see history as something in which man's destiny was guided by a Divine Providence. His most celebrated imitator was Edward Gibbon, whose *Decline and Fall of the Roman Empire* was modelled on such books as Voltaire's *Le Siècle de Louis XIV* and *Charles XII* (of Sweden).

The Frenchman's greatest and lifelong feud was with the Church. There was much that needed saying with regard to the corruption and intolerance of the Church in eighteenth-century

France, but to represent Voltaire as a basically orthodox Christian who merely quarrelled with his Church does him no service. He did not believe in a specifically Christian God, but in *a* god. Therein lies the difference between *Credo in unum Deum, Patrem omnipotentem* . . . and the Supreme Being of the Deists, who in the eighteenth century included many thinkers and writers among their numbers.

Voltaire's early fame rested on his abilities as a playwright, but even in his own day he was writing in accordance with a tradition which was already out of date. It is curious that so forward-looking a man of the theatre should not have broken with tradition, and given much needed life to the French drama, instead of casting most of his serious plays in the rhymed couplets of Alexandrine verse.

Like Goethe, Voltaire could claim to be a universal man: poet, philosopher, historian, playwright, author of short novels (properly described as *contes philosophiques*), encyclopedist, scientist, courtier, journalist, champion of the grossly wronged, humanist, businessman, correspondent and critic. It was he who was the first on the Continent to appreciate the scientific and philosophical genius of Isaac Newton, and to introduce Shakespeare to a French public. If that public had ever considered Shakespeare before, it was to dismiss him as a barbarian. Indeed, Voltaire considered him a barbarian too, but one with genius.

What Voltaire did for Shakespeare he also did for Newton. He was among the first to support the Newtonian theory of gravity, as opposed to the theory evolved by Descartes that the planetary system had been set in motion by "whirling vortices" stirred up by the Creator. Also, he defended the Englishman's theories on optics at a time when many of his countrymen still adhered to the view of Descartes, in whose opinion light was composed of a mass of infinitely tiny globules.

It was Voltaire who openly supported a rational and scientific explanation of much of what until then had been regarded as miraculous in origin. Today it is difficult to realise just how radical and dangerous such thinking was in France, particularly in the first half of the eighteenth century, and above all for those writers of whom the Church disapproved. If they escaped with the burning of their books and pamphlets they were lucky. The same applied to the monarchy, the government, and that most reactionary and sensitive of bodies, the judiciary.

As a man Voltaire had his shortcomings: they were considerable, but so too was his genius. Only when he was on the threshold of old age did he direct his anger against his most worthwhile targets, and he could weep real tears for the sufferings of innocent and defenceless people who had neither the power nor the influence to combat the powers of fanaticism.

The most endearing contribution to fiction made by Voltaire are his *contes philosophiques*: short fantastic tales, sometimes in dialogue form, with a strong undercurrent of philosophy. The most famous is, of course, *Candide*. Wickedly funny, it is also deadly serious, and the work of *un rieur plein des larmes*—which is what Voltaire was, when maturity and old age caught up with him. If a parable is timeless, so too is *Candide*. It is a shaft of wit which has winged its way round the world for more than two hundred years, and will surely last as long as civilisation itself. A big stumbling-block to the understanding of Voltaire's turn of thinking is his use of irony, and the consequent literal interpretation of some of his remarks and written statements. It is a medium beloved by the ancient Greeks and French men of letters alike. Voltaire's comment in *Candide* on the execution of Admiral Byng, that it was done "to encourage the others", is neither flippant nor heartless, but an excellent example of his use of irony when dealing with a deeply serious matter.

In his own day Voltaire's most important achievements must have been his contributions to the *Encyclopédie* being produced in Paris, and its offshoot the *Dictionnaire Philosophique*. It has been pointed out that the latter is neither a dictionary nor philosophical, but consists of his observations on a vast range of subjects, including religion, government and justice. Inevitably it was banned by the authorities, and it would not be an exaggeration to say that it was one of the fuses which helped to touch off the explosion of the French Revolution.

Although he is regarded as a philosopher, Voltaire's writings are very different from those of such thinkers as Spinoza, Bayle, or Locke. He never leads his reader into the cloudy world of metaphysics, which he himself admitted was not for him. His philosophy—admittedly an incomplete one—is rationalist, based on what can be proved, and what common sense dictated to him as being reasonable.

He stood the whole world on its head. Popes, kings, ministers, savants, pedants, critics, self-important nonentities, as well as genuine evil-doers and hypocrites, all squirmed with fury or discomfiture at the wit of this physically insignificant little man. There were as many others, including kings, empresses, nobles, statesmen, men of letters, philosophers and people who would otherwise be unknown to history who were proud to be his friends, or at least in correspondence with him; and Voltaire was one of the most prolific letter-writers ever born.

If he helped a decaying era into its grave, he did so with no other weapons than his intellect and wit: no bombs, no knives, no incitement to rebellion. In *Childe Harold*, Byron was less than fair to Voltaire's passion for justice, which formed the crowning achievement of his life, but otherwise the portrait is recognisable:

> The one was fire and fickleness, a child
> Most mutable in wishes, but in mind
> A wit as various—gay, grave, or wild—
> Historian, bard, philosopher, combined:
> He multiplied himself among mankind,
> The Proteus of their talents. But his own
> Breathed most in ridicule—which as the wind
> Blew where it listed, laying all things prone—
> Now to o'erthrow a fool, now to shake a throne.

Chapter 1

MAÎTRE AROUET'S SON

"Arouet, son of a notary, who was employed by my father and me until his death, was exiled and sent to Tulle at this time [the early part of 1716], for some verses very satirical and impudent. I should not amuse myself by writing down such a trifle, if this same Arouet, having become a great poet and academician under the name of Voltaire, had not also become—after many tragical adventures—a manner of personage in the republic of letters, and even achieved a sort of importance among certain people."

In the voluminous memoirs of the Duc de Saint-Simon, covering the close of the seventeenth and the beginning of the eighteenth centuries, that is the only reference made to Voltaire. Yet, in one paragraph, the nobleman who was close to Louis XIV and afterwards the Regent managed to convey all the lofty disdain felt by many of the *ancien régime* for this disconcerting gadfly. While undoubtedly clever, the very fact that he was not the scion of an ancient and illustrious family precluded many such as the Duc de Saint-Simon from having to take him too seriously. Yet the whole life of the Parisian notary's son was to prove one long paradox. He would call Frederick the Great a friend—though it was admittedly a somewhat stormy relationship—correspond with Catherine the Great, and become the welcome guest of some of the most distinguished families in France and the German states. At the same time he would stretch out a protecting hand towards obscure victims of injustice, and speak up for those oppressed by the ruthless self-interest of others.

Although he was to die eleven years before it began, Voltaire was the senior architect of the principles which inspired the French Revolution. The course that upheaval took is another matter, and it would undoubtedly have filled him with despair that a nation so gifted could overthrow one tyranny merely to replace it with another ten times worse.

While the reign of Louis XIV still had a quarter of a century to run, by 1690 the glory of the *Grand Siècle* was fast departing. Ahead for France lay a series of wars which would bleed the nation and lead to the imposition of higher and higher taxes. If the times could be said to be changing at all, it was not for the better. Intellectual life was far from vigorous. The Church was bedevilled with controversy involving Jansenism. Relations with the Vatican were bad—in fact they were strained to breaking-point by the king's policies, which resulted in his being described as Caesar-Pope. The Estates General, the French political assembly, had not been called together since 1614 (nor indeed would they meet again until 1789, on the eve of the Revolution itself), while the law was a mass of technicalities which had never been clari-fied, with the result that for most of the time it could be inter-preted exactly as the authorities wished, with little regard for the true meaning of justice.

At Versailles Louis XIV lived in his cocoon of etiquette in a palace that was still unfinished. For all its magnificence and splen-dour, the corridors could and did become so noisome with refuse that the court had to move elsewhere—to Marly—in search of fresher smelling air. Behind that great façade the courtiers emp-tied their chamber-pots straight out of the windows on to the flower beds. If it was the age of the Fables of La Fontaine and the music of Lully and Charpentier, it was also an age of sophisticated coarseness.

In the years gone by Louis XIV had been advised by such men as Mazarin, Turenne, Le Tellier, Colbert and Condé. But now all were dead, some bequeathing him their relatives and associates, such as Colbert's brothers, but not their genius. Such power as was not still in the king's hands was in those of his one-time mistress and now morganatic wife, Mme de Maintenon. She was the widow of Scarron the poet, who had been tutor to the king's bastards. Molière and Corneille were dead, and Racine was nearing the end of his career as a playwright. The wars of religion were only remembered by an older generation, but the revocation of the Edict of Nantes in 1685 reverberated through the life of the nation. More than 200,000 Protestants left the country to avoid savage persecution, moving to the Low Countries, England, Protestant Germany and even to Orthodox Russia, taking with them their intellect and their skills. While France could claim to be the most cultured nation in Europe, with a traditional interest in classical studies that survives to the present day, it is doubtful if at the end of the seventeenth century she could also claim to be the most civilised. Her social structure was rigid, her monarchy absolute, her church corrupt and her criminal laws were barbaric. England persecuted Roman Catholics with equal zeal, but by 1700 inflicted far less appalling physical suffering in the name of the law, less arbitrary arrest, and far less savage repression of the written and spoken word.

But in France it was not all stagnation and failed harvests. If the sun which was the king's personal emblem was already beginning to set on his reign, there were also signs of regeneration, born of the demise of the "classic period" of seventeenth-century French history. The first of the new generation of thinkers was Richard Simon, who belonged to the Oratorian Order, and who in 1678 found himself in trouble for writing his *Histoire Critique de l'Ancien Testament*. Not only did the king order the destruction of his book, but it was placed on the Index by the Vatican. Despite expulsion from his Order, Simon went ahead with a similar work exposing the corrupt text on which the New Testament was based. There were a few other brave spirits who were not attacking Christianity itself, but the accretions of centuries, such as the acceptance of comets as heavenly portents, and belief in witchcraft and oracles. Most important of all was the *Dictionnaire* compiled by Pierre Bayle, the philosopher and lexicographer who incurred the displeasure of the Church by holding that morality was independent of religious beliefs, and that an atheist was no less capable of possessing all the moral virtues than a devout Christian. Among those who shared Bayle's attitude, though they arrived at their opinions quite separately, were the Jesuits. In the course of their missionary work they had travelled to the four corners of the known world, and they had now pointed out that it was presumptuous to regard those who knew nothing of Christianity as being in every sense beyond the pale.

Already, in the early 1690s, there were to be found the stirrings of that intellectual upheaval which would find its fullest expression in the following century: first in the many-faceted genius of François Marie Arouet, who under the name of Voltaire "even achieved a sort of importance among certain people"; and finally in the death and rebirth that was the French Revolution.

The child who would one day call himself Voltaire came into the world on 21 November, 1694, the third and last surviving child of a successful notary, François Arouet. The two other children, Armand and Marguerite-Catherine, were respectively ten and nine years older. Three other children had died in infancy, and it looked at first as though this baby would share their fate. In fact his chances of surviving seemed so slight that he was christened the very next day. For godfather he had the Abbé Châteauneuf, a friend of the family, and his mother's sister-in-law as godmother. Doubt has been cast upon Voltaire's paternity, and no less an authority than Theodore Besterman is convinced that the philosopher was not joking or being deliberately misleading when he referred to Rochebrune (a minor poet and friend of his mother) as his real father.

Despite his puny frame and far from robust constitution—or perhaps because of it, for he became a great hypochondriac— Voltaire lived to the age of eighty-four. His mother, who was never strong, died when he was only seven, and maybe it was from her that he inherited his delicate constitution. François Arouet may or may not have been his father, but as the years passed Voltaire's appearance came to resemble that of the traditional notary, in fiction if not necessarily in fact.

At the time of this child's birth, in a now unidentifiable house not far from the Pont Saint-Michel in the parish of Saint-André-des-Arts, the forty-six-year-old François Arouet could feel with justification that he was making a success of his life. A century and a half before an ancestor had been a tanner in Poitou. The family prospered, became drapers and land-owners and married into the legal profession. Maître Arouet's own father had been a successful draper in the capital, and for a wife the lawyer chose Marie-Catherine d'Aumard, also from Poitou, and by all accounts a charming and gentle girl. In spite of reputed lapses later on, their marriage would seem to have been a love match, and it must have been gratifying to someone as ambitious as François Arouet that she was related to the leading Poitou families.

In his professional life Arouet could claim as clients three dukes—Praslin, Sully and Saint-Simon. Maître Arouet was of some consequence in the legal world, first as notary in the Department of Justice at the Châtelet, and later (when the future Voltaire was seven years old) as Receiver of Court-Fees, Fines and Taxes, of the Chamber of Accounts. The latter position entailed a move to a larger house in the Palais de Justice itself, that complex of buildings which has as its heart the old medieval palace of the kings of France on the Ile de la Cité.

Through his official position Maître Arouet came into contact with some of the great families of the day, and through his wife more doors were opened socially. Marie-Catherine d'Aumarde's father was Record Keeper to the *Parlement de Paris*: an institution which was not the French legislative assembly but the equivalent of the High Court of Justice in England; while her brother was Controller-General of the Royal Guard. Through the latter she gained access to the world of the courtiers at Versailles, and made a number of friendships, one of which was to influence the whole course of Voltaire's life.

Mme Arouet made her husband's house the meeting-place of an intelligent and worldly circle, including the Abbé de Châteauneuf, who became the tiny François Marie's godfather. Almost from the moment the child could talk he took his education in hand—which in the long run was to prove devastating for the Church he professed to serve. But since Châteauneuf cheerfully admitted that he was only in the Church for the benefices (*qui n'était d'église que pour les bénéfices*) serious religious instruction was hardly to be expected. The Abbé was in fact a cultivated and witty freethinking man of the world. He could claim a place in the life of another of Maître Arouet's clients, Ninon de Lenclos. Born in 1620 she already belonged to an earlier age. Though famous for her lovers, she had far more in common with Mme Récamier than with La Dame aux Camélias, and her literary salon had been honoured by Racine, Molière, La Fontaine and the Marquise de Maintenon. It was the Abbé de Châteauneuf who claimed the distinction of becoming her last lover, though this claim was disputed by another Abbé, Nicolas Gédoyn. The latter was a canon attached to the

Sainte Chapelle, and he was perhaps the first to perceive the future Voltaire's literary talents, which were to manifest themselves at a very early age. For some time Châteauneuf had been enamoured of Ninon de Lenclos, but she kept him at arm's length. Then at last she informed the delighted Abbé that on a certain date he could become her lover. When he asked what was the significance of the date he was informed that it was her sixtieth birthday. Many others had known her charms, among them the learned Dutch astronomer Huygens, who also invented the pendulum. He wrote:

> *Elle a cinq instruments*
> *dont je suis amoureux.*
> *Les deux premiers ses mains,*
> *Les deux autres ses yeux.*

It was indeed a worldly circle into which François Marie Arouet had been born, and one to which he would soon become accustomed.

Chapter 2

"LITTLE WILFUL"

Among those celebrated in the history of French literature who were also known to Maître Arouet and his wife were the playwright Corneille and the poet Boileau (Nicolas Boileau Despéraux). For some years before his death in 1684 the author of *Le Cid* was a drinking companion of François Arouet, though many years later Voltaire was to declare that his father had once stated, "the great man was the most boring mortal he had ever seen, and his conversation the driest." Evidently Boileau must have been a more agreeable companion, inviting the parents and the very young François to enjoy the pleasures of his country home, which Voltaire later recalled in his *Epistle to Boileau*. But if Corneille had bored the Maître, it was the elderly poet who was tedious to his wife. In a near-epigram Marie-Catherine dismissed him as "a good book but a silly man".

In the family circle those nearest to the child who would one day become Voltaire were not necessarily the closest. His mother would die at the age of forty when he was only seven, and perhaps by his very temperament the boy could never be very close to his father. His brother Armand, ten years his senior, had been educated at the seminary of Saint-Magloire, where the teaching was heavily influenced by the doctrines of Jansenism. Its followers believed implicitly in predestination, and that salvation could only be obtained through grace, which could and did lead to a life of futile austerities and the rejection of anything that could be described as personal relationships. Perhaps a parallel could be drawn by comparing Jansenism within the Catholic church to Calvinism in the Protestant fold. Its bitterest enemies were the Jesuits: those missionaries, brilliant educators of the young and skilled manœuvrers in the world of politics who rightly or wrongly had a reputation for worldliness, and who also could hold surprisingly broad views. With the example before him of what had happened to his elder son, who had become something of a fanatic and killjoy, when the time came Maître Arouet chose to send François to the Jesuit College of Saint Louis-le-Grand. Not only was it the most fashionable school in France but it also had the best teachers. Whatever Voltaire's attitude was to become towards the Church, he retained a very real affection and respect for all but one of his tutors at the college behind the Sorbonne. His official education, however, did not begin until his tenth year, and until he was seven François lived on the Left Bank, near the Pont Saint-Michel.

A figure who remained shadowy in his life, right up to her death in 1726, was his sister Marguerite-Catherine. She married François Mignot, an official in the Chamber of Accounts, and it was their daughter (the future Mme Denis) who was to play a considerable part in Voltaire's later life. There was also a nephew, the Abbé Mignot, who would one day become senior clerk of the *Parlement*, and eventually ensure Christian burial for his uncle.

Armand Arouet could claim the Duc de Richelieu and the mother of the Duc de Saint-Simon as his godparents, while those who acted as sponsors for François were the Abbé de Châteauneuf and his mother's sister-in-law, Marie Dumard. Ironically enough it would be the Abbé's own brother, the Marquis de Châteauneuf, who would take the young man with him as a page when he became ambassador to The Hague, in an attempt to remove him from the undesirable circle of friends and acquaintances to whom he had been introduced by his godfather.

In seventeenth- and eighteenth-century France it was more often than not the benefices a man received which attracted him to become an Abbé rather than a sense of vocation which took him into the Church. In fact many holders of the office were either laymen or only in minor orders. Two such individuals were the Abbé de Châteauneuf and the Abbé Gédoyn (though the latter was primarily a canon of the Sainte Chapelle), and it was they who would have the greatest influence on the childhood of François, setting him on the inevitable course his life would take.

As a child François possessed two nicknames: Zozo and "*Le*

petit volontaire", which might be translated as "Little Wilful". From a very early age at least one characteristic had made itself apparent. As much as anyone it was Châteauneuf who instructed the child, whom he soon realised was of above average intelligence. While not exactly inculcating a respect for religion it seems unlikely that the story that he taught François a long and irreligious poem called the *Moïsade* is anything but a fiction of later years. The Abbé's chief influence on his godson was to be indirect, for it was he who introduced the boy to his own circle of friends at the Temple, and they formed the most worldly and corrupt group in Paris. The part played by the Abbé Gédoyn in moulding the child's character was less pernicious. He was a frequent visitor to the Arouet house, which was like a second home to him. Châteauneuf may have been the first to notice the boy's intelligence, but it was Gédoyn who first realised his literary potential, and it may well have been his own almost excessive enthusiasm for writers such as Horace and Virgil (in preference to the 'moderns' at that time considered far superior by educated Frenchmen) that first sparked off the child's interest in the written word.

Education started in earnest for François late in 1703 when he was nearly ten. Although the college was within a short distance of home he was sent as a boarder to Saint Louis-le-Grand. By then his mother was dead and his sister married, while his father was wholly taken up with his career. It was a small, sickly child who now found himself in the lowest form in the Jesuit College. As an adult Voltaire only reached a height of five foot three inches. Around him he found the sons of almost all the leading French families, and it says all that need be said for Voltaire's undoubted charm that despite the rigid social conventions of the age the notary's son made lifelong friends of such as Louis de Plessis, at that time Duc de Fronsac, who later inherited the title of Duc de Richelieu, and was in fact a great-nephew of the famous Cardinal. Others were René de Palmy, the future Marquis d'Argenson, and his younger brother Marc-Pierre, Comte d'Argenson; as well as Charles Feriol, Comte d'Argental—probably the most loyal of all Voltaire's friends. His brother, the Comte de Pont-de-Veyle, could also call himself a friend, while others the new pupil made at this time included Jean de Longueuil, Marquis des Maisons, and Pierre Cideville, who became a respected legal figure in

Rouen, and who one day would hope, vainly, to marry one of Voltaire's nieces.

There were other good friends who were much older than the schoolboy, such as Louis de Caumartin, Marquis de Saint-Ange, who first was acquainted with Maître Arouet. It was through Caumartin's anecdotes of life at court, and as a result of letting him use his library, that François first became fired with the desire to write a verse epic, which finally took shape as the *Henriade*.

While the Jesuits made excellent school-teachers, the classical bias of the curriculum was such that their pupils probably wrote better Latin than French. Nearly three-quarters of a century later Voltaire wrote in his *Dictionnaire Philosophique* that as a boy he learnt "neither the constitution nor interests of my country: not a word of mathematics or of sound Philosophy. I learnt Latin and nonsense". His real education began after he left school, and it was a case of his teachers having a more lasting effect than what they taught. In particular there were three who helped mould his character: Father Porée, who commented of his pupil's inquiring mind: "that boy wants to weigh the great questions of Europe in his little scales." Then there was Father Tournemine, who later became a friend and counsellor at a difficult time, and whose good opinion he was always anxious to have. The third was Father Thoulier, who was destined to give up an active life in the church to devote himself to scholarship, taking the name of Abbé Olivet. From all three François learnt different aspects of classical studies. Father Porée taught him Latin and a little Greek, while it was Thoulier who gave him a love of Cicero. Another for whom he felt deep affection was Father Paullon, his confessor, who commented: "this child is consumed with a thirst for fame." In later years Voltaire was to revel to the full not only in being famous but also notorious.

There seems to have been only one among his tutors whom François actively disliked, and that dislike was mutual. Father Le Jay's chief function at Saint Louis-le-Grand was to compose suitable plays, in Latin of course, which were usually performed by the pupils before a privileged audience drawn from the salons of Paris and the court at Versailles. What is certain is that Le Jay thought young Arouet just a little too clever, and he is reputed to have made a highly unlikely remark which smells of apocryphal hindsight: "Wretch! One day you will be the standard-bearer of Deism in France."

If anecdotes are reliable, François' attitude to religion already showed signs of incipient scepticism: such as the occasion during the bitterly cold winter of 1709 when his otherwise enviable position meant that he sat at the front of the class and not at the back, next the stove. "Get out," he told the boy who was warming himself, "or I will send you to warm with Pluto!" The boy whose lack of intelligence had given him the most desirable place in the whole room asked: "Why don't you say hell?" "Bah, the one is no more a certainty than the other," retorted the future philosopher. But in the years ahead, however much he might enjoy sending his barbed shafts against the Church, he never wanted to hurt the good fathers of Saint Louis-le-Grand personally. Eighteen years after he had left school he could send a copy of the *Henriade* to Father Porée with an anxious covering letter. "If you, my reverend Father, recall a man who will remember you all his life with tenderest gratitude and fullest respect, accept this work with some indulgence, and regard me as a son who after an absence of several years presents his father with the fruit of his labours in an art his father first taught him. If there is anything in it objectionable on religious grounds please tell me that I may amend it, for I want your approval not only as an author, but as a Christian." Still later, in 1738, he could write to Father Tournemine about his play *Mérope*, "My very dear and most reverend Father, is it true that my *Mérope* has pleased you? Have you found in it any of the exalted feelings you inspired in me in my youth? If you like it, it is yours. I always say that when I talk of Father Porée."

As a pupil at Saint Louis-le-Grand François had preferred asking questions and talking with the fathers to playing games and exercising in the courtyard with the other boys. It was one of the rules that however severe the weather the boys must take their exercise and recreation out of doors, unless the water in the font in the chapel was frozen. The future philosopher assisted the natural process by adding ice.

Almost from the start François attracted the attention of his tutors by his ability to produce verses that were quite remarkable for their precocity. One day he was caught playing with a snuff-box instead of attending to his lessons. The box was confiscated, and it would only be returned if he composed verses on the subject. The story goes that within a quarter of an hour he turned out a charming piece of juvenilia beginning:

> Farewell, my poor snuff-box;
> Farewell, I shall never see you more;
> Neither care, nor tears, nor prayer
> will give you back to me;
> My efforts are for nothing.
> Farewell, my poor snuff-box;
> Farewell, sweet fruit of my shillings—
> were I able to buy you back
> I'd rifle Pluto's treasure,
> But he is not the God I must beseech,
> To see you again I must, alas, pray to Phoebus,
> and what a barrier is set between us!
> Verses are asked of me, but alas, I have no more.
> Farewell, my snuff-box,
> Farewell, I'll never see you more.

It was a beginning, and ransomed the box for its owner. Indeed, such was the prestige in which François was held as a versifier at school that when an old soldier, a would-be pensioner, came to Father Porée asking for a petition in verse which he could present to Monseigneur le Dauphin the busy Jesuit referred him to the notary's son.

> *Noble sang* [or *Digne fils*] *du plus grand des Rois,*
> *Son amour et notre espérance,*
> *Vous qui, sans régner sur la France,*
> *Régnés sur les coeurs des François.*

In fourteen lines François piped his plea for the old soldier to present to the king's son, piling flattery upon flattery with all the conventional classical allusions of the day in elegantly turned verses. He claimed that Mars had given courage to the Dauphin, while Minerva had bestowed wisdom, and Apollo had favoured him with his god-like features. Not only did the rhyming petition achieve its object for the old soldier, but its young author found himself talked about at Versailles. The tale even reached the ears of the eighty-four-year-old Ninon de Lenclos. She told the Abbé de Châteauneuf that she wished to meet the precocious son of Maître Arouet, and the boy was taken to her house. Evidently what Ninon de Lenclos saw met with her approval, and in her will she bequeathed him 2,000 *livres* to buy books. It was a legacy he was to receive the following year, 1705. While she left him an unexpected legacy, for his part Voltaire repaid her kindness years later by likening her to a blackened mummy.

During those years at school, secure and on the whole happy ones for the boy, much was happening beyond the walls of Saint Louis-le-Grand which was almost uniformly bad for France. Louis XIV was no longer fortunate in his wars. His luck had turned, and the man responsible for an astonishing series of disasters was John Churchill, Duke of Marlborough. The cause of the war was the fact that Louis XIV had placed his grandson, Philip V, on the Spanish throne, which meant that France had either direct or indirect control of the Iberian Peninsula, a large part of northern Italy and the Spanish Netherlands, together with the powerful kingdom of Bavaria as an ally. It was a situation which was looked on with alarm by England and Austria. In 1704 Bavaria was knocked out of the conflict at the Battle of Blenheim; two years later the battles of Ramillies and Oudenarde cleared the French from the Spanish Netherlands, while Prince Eugene of Savoy conquered Milan and Naples (the Austrians were to remain masters of northern Italy for a century and a half). By 1709 France was fighting to preserve her own frontiers intact, and it was a high price that Marlborough had to pay to defeat a desperate army at Malplaquet. But by then Austria and England had achieved their goal of reducing French influence throughout Europe, though the war dragged on until it was finally ended by the Peace of Utrecht in 1713.

Of course these events only affected François indirectly. It was the adult population of France who suffered from ever-mounting taxes and a decline in the standard of living. The *Grand Siècle* had departed and there was open criticism of the king's military campaigns which would have been unthinkable twenty years earlier. If François had no direct part in the War of the Spanish Succession it affected him in so far as he grew up in an atmosphere of disillusion and growing discontent with the nation's leaders.

In the same year as Malplaquet the Abbé de Châteauneuf died, but not before he had introduced his godson to his circle of friends at the Temple. However, that contact would not be renewed until after he had left school at the age of seventeen. The year before François said goodbye to the fathers at Saint Louis-le-Grand the poet Jean-Baptiste Rousseau was present at a prize-giving at which he received two awards. When the poet (not to be confused with the much younger Jean-Jacques Rousseau) asked who the youth was he was informed that he was a pupil with "an astonishing aptitude for poetry". According to the story, Rousseau heartily embraced the sixteen-year-old, though in later years he might have felt with some justification that he was cherishing a serpent in his bosom. By then the two men had quarrelled with all the venom of which only savants and scholars are capable.

Now, in 1711, even if François was not yet out in the world, he was at least out of school. His father hoped that like his elder brother Armand he too would enter the law. But the idea of spending his life in an office surrounded by massive law books, bonds, deeds and wills was far less attractive than the company of the late Abbé de Châteauneuf's friends at the Temple, formerly the headquarters in France of the Knights Templar. It was to form the basis of the first clash between father and son.

Chapter 3

PRINCES AND POETS

Whatever François' attitude to the Church in France might become his gratitude to the Jesuit Fathers at Saint Louis-le-Grand never diminished with the passing of time. Years later, in April 1746, he was to write to La Tour, the then head of the College, in glowing terms. For seven years, he declared, he had been brought up by men who took immense pains to form the minds and morals of the young. It had been his good fortune to be taught by more than one such as Father Porée, and he (Voltaire) knew the Father had his successors. Those he had known, he continued, divided their time between their educational and religious duties, and of all the pupils they had had no one would deny the truth of that statement. "This is why I never cease to be astonished that they can be accused of teaching a corrupting morality."

But in the summer of 1711 François had troubles of his own: the first of many brushes with authority, though at this point it was only parental. Maître Arouet had hoped, indeed expected, his younger son to enter the legal profession. No, the seventeen-year-old youth announced, he wanted to become a writer. "Literature," he was informed by his father, "is the profession of a man who wishes to be useless to society, a burden to his relatives, and to die of hunger." The Maître was not a man to be argued with, and François was not in a financial position to make a grand gesture by walking out of the house. Unwillingly he entered his father's office, but although he was to reveal a very shrewd business sense, amass a considerable fortune, and possess a vision sharp enough to pierce through the most complicated argument, he had not the slightest intention of putting that mind into the straitjacket of a legal training.

François was evidently one of those highly-strung individuals who may become physically ill on finding themselves in a distasteful situation. Though he complied with his father's desire that he should study law, he suffered from headaches which may or may not have been genuine, and his work deteriorated. Lectures fell on deaf ears, and there was just a touch of intellectual arrogance in his reply, transmitted through a well-meaning intermediary, when his father offered to buy him a place as Royal Attorney in Paris.

"Tell my father that I don't care for honoured positions which can be bought; I shall earn respect without having it bought for me."

Years later he wrote in a letter to his old school-friend the Marquis d'Argenson: "Money can make one State Recorder of Petitions, but money cannot write a poem, and I wrote one."

At the age of eighteen François Arouet knew exactly where he wanted to go, and he did not want any assistance from his father. Forced as he was to spend so much of his time studying and attending tedious lectures, his thoughts turned more and more to the amusing company of those he considered kindred spirits, and who regarded pleasure and the gratification of the senses as the prime object of existence.

The Temple stood about half a mile north of the Seine and the the Ile Saint-Louis. Within its walls it was like a small town, dominated by a tall medieval keep, before which stood the house of the Prince de Conti. At the end of the eighteenth century the royal family was to be rigorously confined in that keep: Louis XVI only leaving it to go to his death, and Marie Antoinette to an even worse cell in the Conciergerie. But of those buildings nothing now remains. In 1711 Philippe de Vendôme, brother of the Duc de Vendôme, was the Grand Prior, though from 1706 to 1714 he was exiled from Paris because of his excesses. In a sense he and his circle were part of that other Court whose centre was Philippe d'Orléans, the nephew of Louis XIV, and future Regent after the old king's death in 1715. By then the Sun King had outlived two generations and was in fact succeeded by his great-grandson Louis XV. As Louis XIV grew older the Court came under the influence of the Marquise de Maintenon, who was nothing if not devout. As a result many of the younger generation found Versailles unbearably dull, and they polarised about Philippe d'Orléans at the Palais Royal. Those with literary and poetic pretensions allied themselves with the Grand Prior at the Temple.

Philippe de Vendôme could claim descent from Henri IV and Gabrielle d'Estrés. According to Saint-Simon he was charming, witty and intelligent, but also "dishonest to the core which, by the way, was rotted with venereal disease." During the years of exile his place was taken by yet another quasi-cleric, the Abbé Chaulieu, a lyric poet known as "the Anacreon of the Temple". At the time François joined the circle he was over seventy. Another poet was the Marquis de la Fare, while others who were welcome at the Temple included the Duc d'Aremburg, the Duc de Sully, the Marquis de Saint-Ange and several Abbés. One of the latter was the Abbé Servier, uncle of the Duc de Sully, who eventually "died in the company of a male dancer at the Opera".

This was the famous (or infamous) "Anacreontic" group at the Temple who now astonishingly enough accepted the seventeen-year-old notary's son as an equal at their witty but drunken dinner parties. François found favour in their eyes no less for his pre-cociously sharp and witty tongue as for his ability to write good light verse.

Such was his audacious charm that during a dinner party given by the Prince de Conti he could exclaim: "Here we are all princes or poets!" and no one snubbed him. In an atmosphere in which those who scoffed loudest at religion were also its nominal servants it is hardly surprising that the impressionable youth should seek to emulate them. The Abbé Chaulieu, who acted as deputy for the banished Philippe de Vendôme, could write verses in which he described holy oils and Latin as the passport to Heaven, while François is reputed to have written the following verses to cheer up the Abbé de Bussy (the future Bishop of Luçon) on the death of his mistress.

> Your mistress is no more; and, captivated by her eyes,
> Your soul is ready to fly off with hers!
> How constant is the love of a Churchman!

Small wonder that Maître Arouet was seriously worried at the new friends his son was making. Encouraged by the good opinion of Chaulieu and others, François decided to try his hand at a tragedy. Already he was aiming high, for there was a well-known play by Corneille on the Oedipus legend which still held its place in the theatre. But the Maître, concerned by his son's habit of regularly coming home in the small hours, now took to locking him out. It had not the slightest effect on François. His father decided to send him to Caen. It would be the first of many exiles, voluntary and enforced, which were to punctuate the poet's long career.

The Norman town was delighted to have such a witty and educated young man in its midst, and one who was evidently intimate with the most distinguished people in the capital. François was a success in every drawing-room into which he was invited. The leader of fashion in Caen was a Mme d'Osserville, who took him under her wing and showed him her own efforts at poetry. But this enjoyable and rather lazy existence did not last for long. Whispers reached Caen that not all the verses written by the clever young man from Paris were suitable for the ears of delicate-minded ladies. Mme d'Osserville withdrew her patronage, and soon the remainder of local society closed its doors to him. Ironically enough it was Father Couvrigny, a Jesuit of doubtful reputation, who championed his new friend and asserted that he had great talents.

Back once again in the house of the Ile de la Cité life could hardly have been pleasant. Even now Maître Arouet hoped his son would settle down and become a lawyer like himself. But François had decided that he could not fight his destiny—not that he had ever intended to try—and in desperation his father enlisted the aid of the Marquis de Châteauneuf, the brother of his god-father, now dead, who was indirectly responsible for much of the trouble with François and his friends. The Marquis, who had served as Ambassador at Constantinople and Lisbon, and had now been appointed to The Hague, agreed to take François with him as a page. But inevitably matters did not work out as the Maître hoped. Where his son was concerned nothing was likely to go right. Before many weeks had passed François was involved in a love affair which had a plot that would have made an excellent libretto for a comic opera.

Many of the Huguenots who had been forced to leave France as a result of the revocation of the Edict of Nantes had settled in The Hague, forming a tight-knit community. Among them was a Mme Dunoyer and her daughter Olympe. Before long François found himself drawn into this circle of expatriates. It is less likely that Mme Dunoyer was attracted by his poetic gifts than his fund of racy and amusing stories about notable personages, for she edited a scandal sheet called *La Quintescence*, which retailed gossip about the Court and the salons of Paris for those who wished to keep abreast of such news. She was in fact a very dangerous woman to cross, as the Marquis de Châteauneuf was soon to discover. She had succeeded in marrying her elder daughter to a well-to-do army officer, but Olympe's prospective bridegroom had suddenly fled across the Channel, as much as anything to escape from Mme Dunoyer. In her eyes it was one thing to have the young and penniless François as an amusing guest, but it was quite another matter when he fell wildly in love with Olympe, or Pimpette as he called her. To make bad worse the girl seemed to return his feelings with equal ardour.

The letters François wrote were long and passionate, and seven years later, after the young man had become famous under the name of Voltaire, Mme Dunoyer published fourteen of them in a volume entitled *Lettres Historiques et Galantes*. But at the time she might justifiably have been alarmed, had she known about it, by François's wild scheme to spirit Pimpette back to Paris and the Jesuit Fathers at Saint Louis-le-Grand. There she was to be converted from the error of her Huguenot ways back to the Catholic church.

For two months the love affair continued under the Dunoyer roof, with Pimpette's mother apparently unaware of what was going on. But when she did discover the facts, she went immediately to the ambassador to complain. François, blithely returning to the embassy after a pleasant evening in the company of Pimpette, found himself summoned to the presence of a very angry ambassador. It was like one of the scenes with his father all over again, but there was an extra urgency about the Marquis de Châteauneuf's remonstrations: Mme Dunoyer had threatened to write about *him* in her scandal sheet. As a result it was only after much pleading that François was allowed to remain even forty-eight hours longer in The Hague before being sent back to Paris, and that only on condition that he did not leave the embassy.

But since there was no one suitable to act as escort for the journey back to Paris, considerably more than forty-eight hours were to elapse before François really was on his way. During that time the comedy reached its climax. Through his valet he wrote to Pimpette that he must have three letters from her: one for her father (a Catholic); another for her uncle; and a third for her married sister. And while she was about it, he added, she might as well send him her portrait. All these could be brought by her shoemaker, who would arrive at the embassy with his last, saying that he had come to mend M. Arouet's shoes. Letters from him to Pimpette would travel via his valet, who would claim to be a Norman manufacturer of tobacco-cases.

One after another the letters poured from his pen: loving, frantic, and full of advice, including the request that they should be burnt (which they were not, to Mme Dunoyer's later financial gain). Finally Pimpette suggested that, as he was so closely watched and could not leave the embassy, she might come to him in disguise. François was delighted with the idea and instructed her to send Lisette, the shoemaker's wife, to collect a bundle of male clothing. The trick worked, and they spent a blissful few hours together in private in the embassy. Afterwards he wrote:

> I don't know whether to call you Monsieur or Mademoiselle; you are charming in women's attire, but you are also a most delightful cavalier . . . you achieved the fiercest as well as the most graceful aspect of the cavalier, and I almost fear that you drew your sword upon the street to make the young man complete.

For one who only a few months before had been quite at home in the corrupt, dissolute and cynical atmosphere of the Temple it was all refreshingly innocent.

The next night he broke his word not to leave the embassy, and slipped out of a window to join Pimpette at the shoemaker's house, after receiving the only letter from her which has survived. It was on him when he was taken to the Bastille a few years later.

Do what you can so I can see you tonight. Just go down to the shoemaker's kitchen, and I guarantee you will have nothing to fear; for our quintessence manufacturess [Mme Dunoyer] thinks you are half-way between here and Paris. So, if you want, I'll have the pleasure of seeing you here tonight; and if this can't be done, let me go to Mass in the Embassy. [Pimpette, two years older than François, had an almost maternal attitude towards him.] Farewell! Sweet child! I adore you and I swear to you that my love will last as long as my life. Dunoyer.

News of the clandestine meetings reached the ears of the Marquis de Châteauneuf, and in a fury he ordered the immediate return of François to Paris. Although the young couple exchanged several more passionate letters, it was the end of the affair.

"Goodbye, my adorable Olympe, goodbye, my dear," François wrote. "If one could write kisses, I would send you an infinity of them, by the courier. I kiss, instead of you, your precious letters, in which I read my happiness."

On 18 December 1713 François left The Hague, reaching Paris on Christmas Eve. It might be the season of good-will but he did not risk going home, and went instead to see Father Tournemine at Saint Louis-le-Grand. He really had gone too far this time, and his father had taken the extreme course of procuring a *lettre de cachet*. This was a document by which a person could be committed to prison for an indefinite period without any form of trial or even a hearing. It was not only the prerogative of the king, but could be obtained by people of influence for use against troublesome or inconvenient members of their own families, and inevitably it was open to abuse.

François was disconcerted by his father's course of action, but not defeated. He wrote post-haste to Pimpette asking her uncle, who was a bishop, to intervene on his behalf. Also, he enlisted the aid of the fathers at Saint Louis-le-Grand, among them Father Tellier, the king's confessor. Whether this counter-attack was the cause of Maître Arouet withdrawing the *lettre* is uncertain, but he did so, and instead insisted that his troublesome son should go and seek his fortune in the West Indies. All his life Voltaire was to moderate valour with discretion, and now he wrote to his father begging just to be allowed to kneel humbly in front of him. Of course, he never left, but in January 1714 he was sent to work in the office of one Maître Alain.

The work could have been no more congenial than it had been when he was studying law before his brief visit to Caen. What was more, he was now under fire not only from his father, who had intercepted Pimpette's letters, but also from Mme Dunoyer, who was equally angry to discover he was still corresponding with her daughter. Mme Dunoyer set about making what she considered a much more suitable match for Pimpette, who was soon un-happily married to a Count Winterfield. The union was of short duration before the girl returned home. After her mother's death Olympe made her way back to France, where she eventually inherited a considerable fortune from an uncle. It does not seem that Voltaire met her again, but he retained an affection for his first and perhaps most sincere love. On one occasion he helped her financially, and on another defended her reputation against imputations made in a printed libel.

Life for François was made tolerable in Maître Alain's office by the friendship he struck up with a colleague, Nicolas Thieriot, who became a lifelong, though far from loyal, friend. Thieriot, who died in 1772, was at times unscrupulous and dishonest and something of a parasite to Voltaire after he became famous and rich.

François' position in Maître Alain's office lasted only about six months before the lawyer informed his father that the young man was wasting his time. This was not strictly true. What François learnt about the law and how to circumvent it would come in useful in his highly successful business transactions later in life. But the fact that François had entered a competition sponsored by the Académie Française, and was considered likely to win, could have been of little or no consolation. Much to his surprise the Académie did not award him the prize. It went to a certain Abbé Jarry, who declared in flatulent verses that the fame of Louis XIV had spread "from the burning Pole to the icy Pole". The poor fool reasoned that if the North Pole were cold the South must be blazing hot. Someone pointed out the error to one of the academicians, who complacently replied that it was really a matter which concerned the Académie des Sciences and not the Académie

Française. He added that perhaps there was a burning Pole, and anyway the Abbé was a personal friend.

François was not prepared to take quietly what he considered was a slight on his prowess as a poet, and he penned the first of many satirical verses. It was aimed at the blind Antoine de la Motte-Houdard of the Académie, who had voted for Jarry's poem. But the eminent academician had a forgiving nature (he was later to become one of Voltaire's warmest admirers) and soon François came to regret having written *Le Bourbier* (The Mud Puddle). But he continued to write polemical verse. His next target was the Marquis de Courcillon, a homosexual whom he attacked in *L'Anti-Giton*. This was followed by a piece entitled *Le Cadenas*, in this context meaning "The Chastity Belt". He was only just twenty, and perhaps the adulation of the elderly libertines at the Temple had turned his head.

Already Pimpette belonged to the past. Now François tried his luck in the more worldly arena of the theatre. He was himself becoming worldly, not to say calculating, and his affairs at that time with two celebrated actresses were practical rather than romantic. It was his ambition to have his tragedy *Oedipe* performed at the Comédie Française, and if it had the backing of a leading actress its chances would be greatly increased. His first liaison was with Mlle Duclos, but to his annoyance she preferred the Comte d'Uzès to the youthful genius. With the wit that was fast becoming customary he complained to one of his distinguished friends, the Marquise de Mimeure, that every morning Mlle Duclos took a few pinches of senna and cloves, and in the evening several helpings of the Comte d'Uzès. But soon she was eclipsed by another young actress, the celebrated Adrienne Lecouvreur. For a while both she and the Marquise de Mimeure were his lovers simultaneously. No doubt François felt that he had conquered both stage and salon, but *Oedipe* remained unacted.

At this time Caumartin, feeling perhaps that the young man was heading for trouble, suggested to Maître Arouet that his son should go to stay with his—Caumartin's—uncle near Fontainebleau, and there continue his studies. The uncle was the Marquis de Saint-Ange, and very much of the old school. The old man was an individual of rare integrity who had held office under

Louis XIV, and had much to say about life at Court when he had been a young man. Maître Arouet was thankful to accept the offer and get his son away from Paris, at least for a while.

In its way this semi-exile at the Château de Saint-Ange was as important an influence in the development of François as the Jesuit Fathers at Saint Louis-le-Grand, or the circle at the Temple. And undoubtedly it was the last experience that sowed the seeds of his subsequent anti-clericalism. Whether he learnt much law in the country is doubtful, but the château possessed a very fine library, particularly rich in historical works; and the elderly marquis, besides being a steadying influence on the excitable and spoilt young man, was a mine of information about life at Court.

The library and the nobleman's stories fired François with a consuming interest in history, which was to remain with him to the end of his life. Not only did Saint-Ange tell him numerous anecdotes about life at Court when the Sun King had been at his zenith, but the library opened to him the world of the Valois kings—especially Francis I and Henri IV. In addition to the inevitable flippant verses he was still producing there was one which suggested in mordant tones that Francis I's only crown was the pox.

> *Et de vérole quelques grains*
> *Composaient tout sa couronne.*

More elegant was a charming tribute he wrote to his host, declaring that he carried all the living history of his time in his brain, and all that was done and said by great men and wits was to be found in his head. By the time he left the château in August 1715 François had in his possession not only a mass of notes which one day would become the foundation of his *Siècle de Louis XIV*, but also the first draft of an epic poem, the *Henriade* (or *La Ligue*, as it was at first called). This work, though containing many striking episodes and well-turned phrases, is in great part almost unreadable today because of the convoluted allegories which interrupt the story of Henri IV, and in particular the Massacre of St Bartholomew. But it made Voltaire's name as a poet, and the epic became as widely read in France as Byron's *Childe Harold* or *Don Juan* a century later in England. Indeed,

Voltaire helped establish Henri IV in popular imagination as France's most dashing sovereign.

At Saint-Ange François was steeped in history, and in August 1715 he was aware that he was living through a time of importance for his country. Louis XIV's life and reign were drawing to a close. He had outlived both his son and grandson, and would be succeeded by a five-year-old boy. The Regent would be an illegitimate son of the old king, the Duc du Maine, whose mother was Mme de Montespan. Now there would be great changes in Paris, and François wanted to see the start of this new era for himself.

After Louis XIV died on 1 September 1715 the public celebrations would have been more suitable for a coronation than a funeral. The mean old man who, in the eyes of his subjects, had in the latter years of his reign divided the country with religious controversy and bled it white with taxes was dead at last, and all knew that everything would be very different. During his declining years Louis XIV had been under the influence of Mme de Maintenon and his confessor, and it was the latter who had been responsible for stirring up controversy involving the Jansenists. In particular they were detested by the Jesuits, who wanted the movement declared heretical, and in this they had the backing of the Papacy. Pope Clement XI promulgated the Bull *Unigenitus* which condemned the doctrines of the Jansenist Quesnel. The climax came in 1704 when the Papacy denounced five propositions of Bishop Jansen which were declared heretical, and this led to what became known as the *cas de conscience*. Communicants suspected of having Jansenist sympathies were forced by their bishops to sign a form condemning Jansen's propositions. Right to the end of the reign the bitter and vindictive controversy dragged on, souring the spiritual life of the whole nation. That, coupled with the heavy taxation to pay for the War of the Spanish Succession, made people feel that any change could only be for the better.

"France forgave Louis for his mistresses, but not for his confessor," wrote François. Already he had something of a reputation, and when mock invitations were went out to attend another funeral, that of the Bull *Unigenitus*, there were many who assumed that he must be responsible.

Almost at once after returning to Paris François rejoined the circle at the Temple, who felt they could now throw off what little restraint they had shown during the last few years. Once again Philippe de Vendôme was back in the capital from his exile. There had been a sensational change in the governing of the country. The wishes of Louis XIV had been disregarded, and the Regent was not the Duc du Maine, but the late king's nephew, the cynical, scandalous and luxury-loving Philippe d'Orléans.

In fairness to the Regent, he was also a man of some humanity and, as Saint-Simon noted in his memoirs, one of his first acts was to send for lists of all the *lettres de cachet* made in the previous reign. "The Regent restored everybody to liberty, exiles and prisoners, except those he knew to have been arrested for grave crimes, or affairs of state; and brought down infinite benedictions upon himself by this act of justice and humanity."

At the beginning of the eighteenth century the Bastille was far more dreaded than it was to be by the outbreak of the Revolution. In fact when it was stormed it contained only seven prisoners of no importance to the state. But it was a very different story at the start of the Regency. Saint-Simon recorded that one prisoner had been there for thirty-five years. He was an Italian who had been arrested on the day he arrived in Paris, and had never even known what the charge was against him. When he was offered his liberty he said that he had not a farthing, that he knew no one in France and that without doubt his relatives in Italy were all dead and his property divided. It was a pathetic story. "He asked to be allowed to remain in the Bastille for the rest of his days, with food and lodgings. This was granted, with as much liberty as he wished."

This was the place towards which François Arouet was heading because of his conduct and the satirical verses he was writing. But for the time being he was something of a literary lion in the salons of Paris. He read *Oedipe* to the circle at the Temple, and received advice for its improvement. Later he wrote to the Abbé Chaulieu: "This dinner was of great help to my tragedy, and I believe that all I need to ensure the success of anything I am writing is to drink with you four or five times." It was the slightly impudent comment of a young man riding for a fall.

François also diverted fashionable audiences with readings from the early drafts of the *Henriade*. It was not a particularly good day for him when he was invited to entertain the Duchesse du Maine, whose husband had been displaced as Regent. As a result, the couple were totally disloyal to Philippe d'Orléans and had gathered about them a group of equally disaffected friends and acquaintances. Their country residence at Sceaux, within a few miles of Versailles, was like a small rival Court to that of the Regent at the Palais Royal. And now that little rhymester, Arouet, had flown into their company. The Duchesse calculated that he might be made to use his pen at the expense of the Regent and his private life. After all, he wasn't "one of them" socially, and if there were trouble he could take the blame. What did a notary's son matter?

There was much talk concerning the Regent. His daughter, the Duchesse de Berry, descended on her mother's side from the royal house of Wittelsbach, sometimes revealed a streak of insanity which was to reach its tragic climax a century and a half later in Ludwig II of Bavaria. For the Duchesse de Berry's haughtiness bordered on the insane. According to Saint-Simon she was preceded through Paris by beating drums, a privilege normally reserved for the sovereign; while at the theatre she had her chair set on a dais in her box. But that was not what all Europe was whispering about. It was common knowledge that she had an incestuous relationship with her father.

The Duchesse du Maine and her friends were not slow to see parallels in the tragedy François had written, *Oedipe*, and the life of the Regent. They applauded his readings vigorously. In return he gratified his new patron with verses which were both elegant and offensive, and as a result anything that circulated anonymously in Paris was at once attributed to him.

Certainly there was nothing about the Regent that commanded respect: at least not after the business of the day had ended.

His supper parties were always a very strange company. His mistresses, sometimes an opera girl, often Madame la Duchesse de Berry, and a dozen men whom he called his *roués*, formed the party. The gallantries past and present of the Court and town, all old stories, disputes, jokes, absurdities were raked up; nobody was spared. Monsieur le Duc d'Orléans had his say like the rest. The company drank as much as they could, inflamed themselves, said the filthiest things without stint, uttered impieties with emulation, and when they had made a good deal of noise and were very drunk, they went to bed to recommence the same game the next day. (Saint-Simon.)

But even so there was some sense of propriety in the Regent's household, and the Duchesse de Berry, who was as promiscuous as her father, took an official lover for the sake of appearances. He was the Captain of her Guard. Not that anyone was deceived for a moment.

For his part François had now become the mouthpiece of the Duchesse du Maine, and he even made an oblique reference to the Regent's poor sight. He was blind in one eye and short-sighted in the other, and it was an illusion no one familiar with the Oedipus legend would miss. That was followed by an epigram addressed to the Duchesse de Berry which ended with a biblical reference.

> *Un nouveau Lot vous sert d'époux,*
> *Mère des Moabites:*
> *Puisse bientôt naître de vous*
> *Un peuple d'Ammonites!*

> A new Lot serves as your husband,
> Mother of the Moabites:
> Give birth soon
> To a new Ammonite people!

Next came a witticism that by comparison was completely innocuous. It was reported that the Regent had sold half the horses in the late king's stables. François commented that it would have been better if he had dismissed half the two-legged asses. Life taught Voltaire many useful lessons, but one he never learned was not to go too far. Out of the blue came an order exiling him to the little city of Tulle far to the south-west of Paris. His own and other anonymous epigrams had reached the ears of the Regent and, what was more important, the ears of the police. The latter were more concerned about the ruler's reputation than he was himself, and they felt that someone should be made into a public example. Who better, they decided, than this impudent young fellow called Arouet?

It may have been due to the example set by many of those he called his friends, or simply due to the prevailing atmosphere of the time, but the character of François was not improving. He promptly denied being the author of the epigram about the Duchesse de Berry.

Though relations between them were strained, Maître Arouet had never gone so far as to disown his son. When the order for exile to Tulle was made it was he who asked the Duc de Sully to intercede and have it changed to somewhere nearer Paris. Instead of being banished to a small provincial city François found himself a favoured guest at Sully-sur-Loire, the duke's own château not far from Orléans. The following five months were a holiday such as few have the good fortune to enjoy, but since his stay was compulsory François was soon pining for his old life in Paris. In a company which included the Duc de la Vallière, the Comtesse de Toulouse, and the beautiful Mme de Vrillière, life was one long *fête champêtre* by day, and by night one long party either in the château or its lamp-lit gardens. It was as though a painting by Watteau had come to life, but instead of a sad Gilles-like figure the scene was enlivened by this brilliant little poet who produced such exquisite verses for his companions, extolling the joys of Sully. What was more, the Duc de Sully possessed a library almost rivalling that of the Marquis de Saint-Ange, which served to rekindle François's enthusiasm for history. By a strange coincidence it was his idol Henri IV who had given the château to the ancestor of his host.

If it had been a voluntary visit to Sully-sur-Loire François might have wished to stay for ever, but since it was an order imposed from above he found it intolerable. Again he denied being the "infamous and vile author of those couplets" (about the Duchesse de Berry), and appealed to the Regent not for clemency but for justice. The indulgent Regent rescinded the order and in October 1716 François was back again in Paris, to the annoyance of his father. Maître Arouet had found the exile easier to bear than what he considered an over-hasty recall. Success and flattery had turned the young man's head, and in the notary's opinion his aristocratic friends and acquaintances were "sheer poisoners" for him.

At least for several months François kept out of trouble, spending much of his time at Saint-Ange, since he did not care to stay at his father's house. But in the spring of 1717 two curious sets of verses circulated in Paris which could not be ignored by the Regent or the police since they were a direct criticism of France and her rulers. One poem was known as the *J'ai vu*, and the other (in Latin) as the *Regnante Puero*. *J'ai vu* consisted of a condensed catalogue of all the author considered wrong with his country during the previous reign, and was in fact the work of Antoine Lebrun.

> I have seen the Bastille, and a thousand other prisons,
> filled with brave citizens, faithful subjects. . . .

> I have seen the devil in the guise of a woman [Mme de
> Maintenon] ruling the kingdom, sacrificing her God,
> her faith, her soul, to seduce the spirit of a too
> credulous King.

> I have seen the altar polluted,
> I have seen Port-Royal demolished. . . .

> I have seen the blackest deed
> which all the water in the ocean cannot wash away. . . .

The poem ends: "I have seen all these things and I am not yet twenty years old."

At that time Lebrun was thirty-six and François only twenty-two. Any anonymous verse was likely to be attributed to François, and a reference to the writer's supposed youth would only serve to confirm people's suspicions. Obviously it was a deliberate attempt by the older man to draw attention away from himself. But if that were Lebrun's object it was a mistake to have added the line "*J'ai vu Port-Royal démoli*", because François actively disliked the Jansenists whose headquarters the convent had been. His brother Armand had been a member of the sect, and François had suffered too much from his killjoy and humourless approach to life to have shed any tears over its fate. But of the two poems it was the *Regnante Puero* which was the more damaging. In form it was more like a series of brief reminders of what the poet wished to expand at a later date than a finished work.

> *Regnante puero*
> *Veneno et incestis famoso*
> *Administrante. . . .*

> A boy reigning
> A man notorious for poisoning and incests
> Administering
> Ignorant and unstable Councils.
> More unstable religion
> An exhausted Treasury
> Public faith violated. . . .

It was to be vanity which brought about François' downfall. In the past twelve months he had got away with so much that he must have been lulled into a sense of false security. Also, he could not resist boasting to a stranger who started a conversation with him at the Green Basket, the inn on the Ile de la Cité where he preferred to lodge rather than live at home. Not only did he boast about the epigrams and satirical verses that he had actually written, but also claimed the anonymous ones then in circulation were also from his pen. The stranger was interested, and asked what in particular he had against the Regent.

"What? Don't you know what that bugger did to me?" he exclaimed rashly. "He exiled me because I showed everyone that his Messalina of a daughter is a whore." Later the stranger, who was a police spy named Beauregard, recorded the conversation word for word in his official report, which is still extant. That much is fact. Whether the following story is true is less certain. Shortly after his conversation with the police spy François was sauntering in the gardens of the Palais Royal, where he was recognised by the Regent (who it will be remembered had very poor sight).

"Monsieur Arouet, I wager that I can show you something you haven't seen before." François asked what it was. "The inside of the Bastille," came the reply. "I'd rather take that as seen," retorted François impertinently.

The Regent was as good as his word. The next day he signed a *lettre de cachet*. "It is the order of His Royal Highness that Sieur Arouet *fils* be arrested and taken to the Bastille. This 16th Day of May 1717. Philippe d'Orléans."

François was asleep when the police burst into the Green Basket at one o'clock in the morning. Later he declared in a lighthearted verse that there had been twenty of them searching his room and reading his papers. He was told to get up, get dressed and come with them to the Bastille. No specific charge had been brought against him and there was nothing to indicate how long he might be held a prisoner: nor, under the terms of a *lettre de cachet*, was there any need for the Regent to do so.

That first stay in the Bastille was to form a most important episode in the future philosopher's life. Its most immediate effect was to cut him off from an existence in which nothing worthwhile was being achieved. Apart from working intermittently on *Oedipe*, life after his return from Saint-Ange was little more than a social round punctuated by epigrams and verses which served no useful purpose and would have been better left unwritten. Although he joked about it afterwards, it must have been a chilling experience to be driven off to the Bastille in the middle of the night. Not that he was to find himself flung into the deepest dungeon. On the contrary, he was the Regent's guest, and treated like one. The room he occupied was reasonably light and airy. He could use the bowling green, the billiard room, and from time to time he was invited to dine at the Governor's table. What was more he was allowed nearly all the visitors he wanted. Within a week he asked the Governor for a few possessions: two linen handkerchiefs, a bonnet, a night-cap, a bottle of essence of cloves, and a two-volume Latin edition of Homer. Cut off from a round of pleasures and distractions, he once again started to use his brain seriously. Before long he was immersed in the *Henriade*, and later he declared that the whole episode dealing with the Massacre of St Bartholomew came to him in a dream.

At home his father declared: "I told you so! I knew his laziness would lead to disgrace. Why didn't he take up a profession?"

But in the Bastille François underwent a transformation. Till then he had thrived on the insincere flattery of the fashionable world which was only interested in his latest witticism or salacious verses, and cared nothing for himself as a human being (not that he was particularly likeable at this period of his life). He even changed his name. Arouet lacked gravity, also the verb *rouer* meant "to break on the wheel". As a child at home he had been known as "*le petit volontaire*": the little wilful one. Volontaire became Voltaire perhaps. To this day the derivation of his name is not absolutely certain, but this contraction of *volontaire* seems at least as likely as the other theory of its origin: that it is an anagram on Arouet L.J. (*Le Jeune*).

François, whom the police took to the Bastille in May 1717, was the talented and spoilt son of Maître Arouet. The individual who left it on 11 April 1718, after Lebrun had confessed his authorship of the *J'ai vu* poem, was Monsieur Voltaire, aged twenty-four, a far more sensible and worldly-wise young man.

Chapter 4

FAME OVERNIGHT

Perhaps the only surprising thing about the French Revolution was that it did not occur before the end of the eighteenth century. Life was far worse for the ordinary people during the last years of Louis XIV's reign, and during the Regency which followed. If Louis XVI's ministers were inept at all levels of administration, their predecessors in office were unbelievably corrupt, while the Church in France was not an institution which could inspire the respect of sincere Christians. Obviously the nobles and clergy would have been those best able to bear taxation, yet it was they who were exempt. But such was the outlook of the French nation that when it had been mooted that they should be taxed even the man in the street spoke out against the idea, and it was abandoned.

After the Peace of Utrecht in 1713 France was in such a parlous financial state that something had to be done to prevent complete bankruptcy. A first step would have been to invite all the Huguenot craftsmen and merchants to return, bringing with them their skills and business expertise. But the Regent, though personally indifferent to religion, dare not do so for fear of being attacked by the Church as a supporter of heretics.

The Prime Minister, the Duc de Noailles, set up a *Chambre de Justice* to inquire into the worst abuses. Among the disclosures was one of gross dishonesty by the treasurer of the military police. He was sentenced to death, but his son-in-law the Marquis de la Fare appealed successfully to the Regent for his life, and even induced him to make over to him the whole of the treasurer's ill-gotten fortune. After that he left the destitute old man to fend for himself. But the most blatant misuse of public funds to come to light involved tax officials who failed to pass on part of the

34

revenues, claiming the money as expenses, and then using it to gamble on the Stock Exchange. It also emerged that money had been lent to the late king at rates of up to 400 per cent. Prominent people were involved, but they now had sufficient influence to stifle reforms by the Prime Minister or the Regent himself.

Some reform was achieved by the four Pâris-Duverney brothers, the financially gifted sons of an innkeeper. In 1722 the eldest became the Treasurer, while the youngest made a niche for himself as Court Banker. Between them the brothers had a virtual stranglehold on the financial administration of the nation for several decades.

A skilled though unofficial diplomat at this time was the dissolute Abbé Dubois, and it was he who was responsible for France's abandonment of the cause of the Old Pretender, thus making an alliance possible between France and England. As reward he was made a Cardinal, and Archbishop of Cambrai. Later his path would cross that of Voltaire, but now he was in the act of introducing the young Scotsman, John Law, into the tangled web of French finances. First of all he restored public faith in paper money (*billets d'état*), issued by the government. This he did by founding a bank of his own, accepting three-quarters of the sums in paper money and the remainder in gold. It was the custom for banks to issue their own notes, and John Law's were worth their face value, which was more than could be said for the paper money issued by his long-established rivals.

In the summer of 1717 his success attracted the Regent's attention. To stave off a take-over by the State he founded the Western Company to exploit the natural resources of Canada and Louisiana. But twice in quick succession he was nearly ruined. First, in 1718, the Condé family suddenly withdrew their capital from his bank. Then it was the father of Voltaire's school-friends, the Marquis and Comte d'Argenson, who nearly succeeded in breaking the power of the outsider. Since he was a minister he could not appear openly in the transaction, so huge sums, which included the salt tax, were transferred in the name of his valet from Law's bank to a rival business in which d'Argenson *père* had an interest. This time Law's bank did become state property, and in place of his own bank notes far less reliable ones were issued in the name of the young king.

By then the tax system had been overhauled, and it was said

that at least 40,000 tax officials had become redundant as a result, and the worst of the abuses and misuses of the system were checked.

It seemed that John Law could weather any financial crisis, and now he offered to take over the national debt itself, and lend the government fifteen hundred million *livres* to pay off its creditors. It was a breath-taking scheme, and one which would have given the Treasury a credit balance within a year or two. But then he made the suggestion which was to bring his financial empire down in ruin. As Controller-General he had reached the supreme power, and he suggested that the Council of State should require the Church to sell all that it had acquired over the last one hundred and twenty years. The reaction was inevitable. The Church and its allies counter-attacked by starting a run on his bank. The queue stretched the whole length of the Rue de Richelieu, and among those demanding their money was the Duc de Bourbon, who wished to draw out twenty million *livres* on behalf of his mistress, Mme de Prie. Somehow, even now, John Law was not yet completely broken, and he managed to have the tariffs abolished which existed between the *départements* which made up France. But his many enemies were closing in for the kill. Ministers hated him for opposing the sale of government positions, while in the eyes of the clergy the fires of hell were too good for someone who had suggested the confiscation of part of the wealth of the Church.

The inevitable happened, and the bottom fell out of the market. Law's life was in danger, and in 1720 he fled abroad, to die in poverty in Venice six years later. After a lapse of nearly seventy years history was to repeat itself when the Swiss financier Necker was forced to resign by the machinations of those who surrounded Louis XVI. Had he been allowed to carry through his reforms he might have saved France from bankruptcy, and perhaps even have prevented—or at least staved off—the Revolution of 1789. It has been said of the Bourbons that they forgot nothing and learnt nothing. The same could be said of the Establishment all through the eighteenth century in France, and whereas John Law had suggested the confiscation of only a small part of the wealth of the Church, when the storm finally broke the Revolutionaries ordered its confiscation *in toto*.

After his eleven-month incarceration in the Bastille Voltaire regarded any man acting in the interests of the Regent as almost a personal enemy, and he disapproved most strongly of Law— "the accursed Scotsman"—and his system. For Voltaire imprisonment had ended on 11 April 1718, but he was now ordered by the police to remain at his father's country house at Chatenay, which was no great distance from that hotbed of intrigue and discontent, the Duc and Duchesse du Maine's château at Sceaux.

For once Voltaire was not guilty of writings that had given offence, and he pleaded to be allowed to return to Paris to declare to the Regent that he was not the author of the *Regnante Puero*. Permission was granted, and at the interview Philippe d'Orleans was in an indulgent mood. "Be careful," he said, "and I will provide for you." But even in such a situation Voltaire could not resist an unwise answer. "I will be delighted if Your Highness will give me my board, but I beg you not to trouble yourself about my lodging."

The Regent, who shared with Charles II a tolerance of impudent young wits, even gave him an annuity, and in October the order for Voltaire's exile from the capital was rescinded.

In the autumn of 1718, at a time when the attention of most French people was concentrated on John Law's attempts to save the economy, Voltaire had something much more personal with which to occupy his mind. His tragedy *Oedipe* was to be produced by the Comédie Française. The play was a great success, running for forty-five nights—an unheard of triumph. But much of that success was due to the public's belief that it must be an indirect attack on the Regent's private life. The plot was a variation on the Oedipus legend, in which the appalling prophecy comes true that the son of King Laius of Thebes will eventually kill his father and marry his mother. The tragedy of Sophocles, *Oedipus Tyrannus*, has a searing inevitability quite missing in the straitjacket of Alexandrine verse used by Voltaire, which was then the accepted form for tragedy. It is difficult to say if *Oedipe* was just a conventional retelling of an ancient legend or whether it was something deeper: a comment on much that Voltaire felt was wrong with France and her rulers.

When the Earl of Essex was planning his rebellion against Elizabeth I he sent the players at the Globe Theatre money and asked them to stage *Richard II*, which showed the deposition of a monarch. In the Paris of 1718 it was common knowledge that the young Duchesse de Berry was pregnant, though apparently by her official lover, the Captain of the Guard. But everyone named a different father, and even the most innocent-minded member of that first night audience could not fail to be aware of the parallels with *Oedipe*.

With all the perversity of a moth flying straight at the flame Voltaire requested permission to dedicate the play to the Regent. However, he had to be satisfied with offering it to his mother (herself an illegitimate daughter of Louis XIV). What is interesting about that dedication is that it ends with the first recorded appearance of his *nom de plume*: "*Madame, de votre altesse royale le très humble et très obéissant serviteur Arouet de Voltaire.*"

Before the curtain went up on 18 November 1718 Voltaire was assured of a *succès de scandale*, if nothing more. In the theatre was the Duchesse du Maine with all her circle of partisan friends, relations and acquaintances. Also present was the Regent, sitting right at the front because of his poor sight. His infamous daughter, by then well advanced in her pregnancy, entered in royal style, accompanied by thirty ladies-in-waiting and surrounded by her own guards, and took her place beneath a canopy of state. By now her delusions of grandeur were such that her household numbered eight hundred persons, while in the Palace de Luxembourg a throne had been placed at the top of three steps from which she could receive the homage of ambassadors.

Those in the audience who hoped for an outright attack on the Regent were disappointed. Oedipus was shown as a sympathetic character, who really could be called a plaything of the gods. And what of the attack on the Church which many were expecting? Certainly there were criticisms of the priesthood, and individual lines were applauded—out of context—by an audience which interpreted the drama as it wished. But there was nothing that could be taken as deliberately insulting to the Church in France, and many knowing smirks must have faded into disappointment at the realisation that *Oedipe* was no crude onslaught against the established order. It was the tragedy itself that finally moved the audience. Some wept openly at the scene between Oedipus and Jocasta when their true relationship was revealed.

But that fashionable audience of 1718 read whatever it wanted into the play, and applauded wildly. Among them was Maître Arouet and, much as he disapproved of his son's conduct and choice of career, he could not help being carried away by the occasion. Every time there was a burst of applause he exclaimed: "The rascal! The rascal!"

For the present Voltaire was an extremely excited twenty-four-year-old playwright with a success on his hands. His interest in *Oedipe* was not only that of the author, but rumour declared that the pretty young actress who played Jocasta was his mistress. Suzanne de Livry had been among the band of amateur actors and actresses who took part in the theatrical performances given at Sully-sur-Loire, and it was there that Voltaire met her while staying as a guest of the Duc and Duchesse. This was before his imprisonment in the Bastille. He fell in love, and they continued to see each other after his return to Paris, and it was at that time that he commissioned Largillière to paint his portrait, which he presented to Suzanne. But during his eleven months in the Bastille she did not remain true to him, and what made it worse was the fact that he was supplanted by his closest friend, Lefevre de Génonville. In despair Voltaire later wrote that in the Bastille he had had to endure sleeplessness, cold food, warm drink, and betrayal by all, including his mistress. But he found it understandable that someone who possessed such a tender heart, such a fickle mind and a bosom like alabaster should go astray, and he forgave her. He could be forgiving in matters of the heart, but he could and did pursue personal and literary vendettas for decades with a single-mindedness which was nothing short of malevolent. In fact he forgave Génonville as well, and when the latter died, soon after, he was so grief-stricken that the latest of his friends, the Maréchale de Villars (whose acquaintance he was about to make at that memorable first night), was moved to invite him to stay with her at Vaux-Villars.

The triumph of *Oedipe* did not bring personal success to Suzanne de Livry, who by all accounts was not sufficiently talented for a major role such as Jocasta. But Voltaire remained on amiable terms with her, and there is a charming sequel to their friendship. After her failure at the Comédie Française Suzanne joined a company of actors who came to England. There the venture failed, and she was left penniless. She took a job in a London café run by a Frenchman, where one of the patrons, the Marquis de la Tour du Pin, fell in love with her, and offered to marry her.

Suzanne did not conform to the usual conception of the eighteenth- or nineteenth-century actress: painted, promiscuous and scheming. She came from a family which had been of some consequence in Sully-sur-Loire, and seems to have been a beautiful, perhaps rather reserved young woman. Because she was now penniless she refused the Marquis, lest he should later regret having made a misalliance. In fact she declined to accept any presents from him except a few lottery tickets. After a lapse of a few weeks the Marquis had a fake list of names printed which showed her as the winner of a large sum. After that she had no more scruples about marrying the Marquis, who of course had put up the money himself. It was a happy union. Fifty-seven years were to elapse before Voltaire saw her again, on his last and fatal visit to Paris in 1778. Both were eighty-four, and for them it was an occasion filled with nostalgia and emotion. When the world-famous philosopher was ushered into the salon he found the Marquise de Gouvernet seated beneath the portrait by Largillière which he had given her some sixty years before.

In *Mémoires*, his brief, semi-serious autobiography written in the third person (which he himself translated into English under the title of *Autobiography*), Voltaire recounted his own part in that first performance at the Comédie Française. After writing quite candidly that at that time he was "excessively dissipated and immersed in all the pleasures common at his time of life", he goes on to say that he "indulged in a thousand sallies on the stage, and at last wantonly laid hold of the train of the chief priest, in a scene where that pontiff was producing a very tragical effect". All his life there was a wicked little schoolboy lurking just below the surface in Voltaire, and like as not he would appear at the most serious moments. Among the audience was the Duchesse de Villars, who inquired who the young man was capering about on the stage, and was surprised to learn that it was the author. She had to meet such an unconventional individual and invited him to her box. There he was seated between her and her husband, the Maréchal-Duc de Villars. The audience craned their necks, and called out to him: "Why don't you kiss her?" He did, to everyone's delight.

There had perhaps never been such a first night in the history of the French theatre, and all the forty-five performances were equally well received. *Oedipe* was printed at top speed, and read in all the fashionable salons. Whatever the Regent may have thought of its possible allusions he never gave anyone the slightest indication that he was aware of them. In fact he joined the chorus of adulation and presented Voltaire with a gold medal and an annuity of 1200 *livres*, which was in addition to the pension granted after his release from the Bastille. His fame even spread across the Channel after the British Ambassador reported that he was perhaps the best poet France had ever produced. Flushed with success Voltaire sent George I a copy of *Oedipe*, and in return received a gold medal and a watch. Opportunistic as ever, he even saw a chance of improving his standing with his father. He wrote to the English Ambassador in Paris: "I beg you, my lord, to add to all your favours by sending to my father's house the beautiful watch which you showed me. A letter will charm him, and he will be delighted if the presents which the King of England deigns to make me pass through his hands."

It was obvious that the Regent bore him no ill-will, otherwise he would not have given him a gold medal and, what was of more practical use, an annuity. Voltaire felt it was a good moment to enlist his support over the printing of the *Henriade*, which, like everything else published in France, had to have the approval of the censor. He read extracts to the Regent, who at once foresaw trouble—for himself—if he gave the work his blessing. In the poem Voltaire had condemned the Massacre of St Bartholomew, and written favourably about Admiral Coligny and Queen Elizabeth, both of whom had been Protestants. Quite correctly, the Regent foresaw bitter resentment from the Catholic church if he allowed the work to be published. Voltaire knew what he was up against, and commented in the *Autobiography* that he lacked the art of combating his enemies with their own weapons, which was absolutely necessary in Paris, if a man wished to make a success of his career.

Much of the *Henriade* had been written at Saint-Ange, inspired by the books and conversation of the old marquis. Among its critics, one who may have gone a little too far was the Marquis des Maisons, who so stung the author that in a fit of exasperation he threw the *Henriade* into the fire. The marquis promptly retrieved it, and at a later date reminded Voltaire: "Remember, it was I that saved the *Henriade*, and that it cost me a handsome pair of ruffles." But knowing Voltaire one cannot help feeling that somewhere there was another copy of the poem.

Fame could have its disadvantages, as Voltaire soon found. Not only did it fix him prominently in the public gaze but also it increased the danger of anonymous attacks on the Regent being attributed to him. Now it was the Duc and Duchesse du Maine and their scheming friends who were shut up in the Bastille, and the charge against them was serious. They had been planning nothing less than a *coup d'état* to overthrow the Regent. Aiding and abetting them was the Spanish Ambassador, Cardinal Alberoni and Baron Görtz. Through the Duchesse Voltaire became acquainted with the baron, whose reminiscences of his one-time master Charles XII of Sweden were later to inspire the Frenchman to write the biography *Charles XII*.

At that time a major scandal was caused by the sudden appearance of three sets of verses. They formed a virulent attack on the Regent and his daughter and, since they were well-written, they were at once attributed to Voltaire. In fact the real author was a hanger-on of the Duchesse du Maine, one Le Grange-Chancel, who had been a page to the Prince de Conti. News of these verses, soon to be referred to as the *Philippiques*, reached the ears of the Regent, who asked Saint-Simon to procure a copy. Unwillingly the author of the *Mémoires* did so, but refused point-blank to read them out loud. In the poem the Regent was accused, amid much else, of planning to poison the young king.

I wished to profit by the dejected silence into which the reading of this poem had thrown M. le Duc d'Orléans, to take the execrable paper from him, but I could not succeed; he broke out into just complaints against such horrible wickedness, and into tenderness for the King. . . . I never saw a man so penetrated, so deeply touched, so overwhelmed with injustice so enormous and sustained.

Two previous poems had been laid at Voltaire's door, and now the authorities attributed the *Philippiques* to him as well. He was requested to leave Paris. But for him it was to be a very pleasant summer progress from château to château, staying with illustrious friends and acquaintances. Among them were the Duc de Sully, the Duc de Richelieu (Voltaire's old schoolfriend Louis du Plessis, who had succeeded to the title), and the Maréchal-Duc de Villars and his charming wife. This delightful existence only ended when Le Grange-Chancel could not resist claiming that he was the author of the *Philippiques*. He was arrested and sent to the penal colony of Iles de Sainte Marguerite, though he was allowed to return before the end of the Regency.

Both during his spell in the Bastille and during his latest exile (the fourth already, if his time at Caen on his father's orders is included) Voltaire's mind was far from inactive. Now he continued to work on the *Henriade*, and wrote his second play, *Artémire*. At Vaux-Villars he fell in love with his hostess, but at thirty-four she was sufficiently experienced to be able to keep his passions at boiling point without actually capitulating. Regrettably, the Duchesse rejected Voltaire not because she reciprocated her husband's single-minded devotion, which in itself was an object of cynical amusement in the circles in which they moved, but because she preferred the charms of a certain Abbé de Vauréal. However the gossips thought they knew best, and declared that Voltaire was her lover, when in fact the poet was literally making himself ill with unrequited love.

In an attempt to make the heartless Maréchale thoroughly ashamed of herself Voltaire gave out from Sully-sur-Loire that he was gravely ill. Much of his life would be spent *in extremis*, the crisis lasting either until he had his way or until he realised he was wasting his time, whereupon the recovery would be rapid and complete. But it was not his indifferent beloved who came hastening to his bedside. Instead he received a paternal letter from her good-natured husband.

Come to us and eat good soup at regular times, don't take more than four meals a day, and go to bed early! Keep away from paper, ink, dice and Lansquenet [a game of chance]! I allow you to play draughts! Two months of such a diet are far better than Vinache [Voltaire's doctor].

The letter from the sixty-four-year-old Maréchal ends on a note typical of the affection Voltaire inspired among those who knew his good qualities at first hand.

Here, my dear poet, you have all I can give you in bad prose in return for your verses. A thousand regards to the Duc and Duchesse de Sully, both of whom I wish good health so that you may undertake the journey to us. Right now we have good and numerous company; we are twenty-two at the table, but most of them will leave tomorrow.

After visits to Richelieu and the Marquis des Maisons Voltaire did return to Vaux-Villars. Some of the charm which endeared him to his friends lay in his ability to throw off elegant verses on the lightest of subjects, such as the current craze for amateur astronomy.

> We are muddling up the whole heavenly order,
> and take Venus for Mercury:
> But you ought to know that
> We have only opera glasses
> to observe the planets
> instead of your long telescopes.

Fame had come overnight to Voltaire with the sensational success of *Oedipe*, and in February 1720 he hoped to repeat that triumph with *Artémire*, which like its predecessor had a plot drawn from classical Greece. The first night was a failure, and after only eight performances it was withdrawn from the stage of the Comédie Française. Part of the failure of *Artémire* could be attributed to the fact that John Law and his "system" had just suffered one of its disastrous crashes, and the public was in no mood for theatre-going, which inspired Voltaire to comment: "Paper is now reduced to its intrinsic worth." *Artémire* was revised, but never published, and only fragments have survived. But its two opening lines were destined to pass into French literature and common currency.

> *Oui, tous ces conquérants rassemblés sur ce bord,*
> *Soldats sous Alexandre, et rois après sa mort.*

Chapter 5

"FOR AND AGAINST"

After all the years of doubt and disappointment Maître Arouet lived just long enough to see his son started on his career as a playwright and poet. Then, on 1 January 1722, he died, and was buried the following day. He left a considerable sum to be divided among his three children, but about 150,000 *livres* which were due to Voltaire were not immediately available: also it would have to remain in trust until he was thirty-five. Armand had inherited his father's office and, presumably because he had to take over the bond of 240,000 *livres* originally made by the Maître on first taking up his position, he was unable to pay his brother the full amount. The result was bad feeling. Voltaire, though generous on occasions, was undeniably sharp in matters of business. In addition to his gifts as a poet and philosopher, he also possessed to an unusual degree a businessman's ability to increase his capital.

Besides what he received from his father, Voltaire had the two annuities from the Regent, which brought in 4,250 *livres*, as well as a sum from *Oedipe* which was not to be despised. One of his financial ventures was to invest in the *Companie des Indes*, but soon he was writing to Mme de Bernières, the wife of the President of the Rouen *Parlement* (Law Court): "I, Madame, prefer your company, which is the most pleasant I have known, to the *Companie des Indes* in which I have invested a good deal of my fortune. Let me assure you I am thinking of the pleasure of visiting you at your country estate, rather than for the business we are going to transact."

By then Voltaire was a frequent visitor to the President and his wife, either in the country or at their town house in Paris.

He knew well enough that there were those who would say he sponged on his distinguished friends, and some years later Mme de Bernières refuted such an allegation by disclosing that on one visit Voltaire had paid 1,800 francs towards his expenses.

The fancy now took Voltaire to try his luck as a diplomat. It was a curious notion for a young man who already had been exiled officially from Paris on three occasions, and sent to the Bastille for eleven months. Nonetheless, he wrote an obsequious letter to the First Minister, Cardinal Dubois, offering his services. But that was as far as his present diplomatic career was to go, though some years later he was to contribute to the success of an alliance between France and Prussia.

At about that time an episode from his past caught up with him. One day in June 1722 he was invited to dinner by Le Blanc, the Minister of War. To his surprise and understandable fury he found that a fellow guest was none other than Beauregard, the police spy whose evidence had brought him to the Bastille four years earlier. He could not control his temper or his tongue. "I knew that spies were paid, but I did not know that they were rewarded with the privilege of dining at a minister's table."

Beauregard said nothing at the time, but later asked the minister's permission to give Voltaire a thrashing. Permission was granted and late one evening the police spy stopped the poet's sedan chair on the Pont de Sèvres, hauled him out and thrashed him with a cane. Voltaire could not, or did not, attempt to defend himself, to the joy of his enemies who accused him of cowardice. They even coined a verb: *Voltariser*—to beat with a cane. Voltaire applied to a magistrate for a warrant, and even took the case to the Châtelet in an attempt to obtain justice. But Beauregard was as elusive as an eel, and also had the protection of the Minister of War. But then Le Blanc was dismissed after shady dealings on the Stock Exchange came to light, and his successor ordered Beauregard's arrest. Fifteen months after the attack Voltaire had the satisfaction of seeing his enemy sent to prison, where he remained for a considerable time.

Shortly after the attack by Beauregard, Voltaire paid a visit to Brussels and The Hague. His intention, as he explained to Cardinal Dubois in a long letter, was to bribe one Solomon Levi to betray secrets involving the Austrian Empire. Nothing transpired from that side of the journey, which became more of a holiday in the company of the Marquise de Rupelmonde: "A young, rich and agreeable" lady who took him as her guest to entertain her on the journey, and perhaps find the answers to the questions and doubts about religion which were troubling her. The doubts of the fashionable Mme de Rupelmonde were to have far-reaching effects, for Voltaire attempted to answer them in a poem which set forth his own attitude to religion, and was to become the first real shot in the war between the philosophers and the Church.

Voltaire was likely to fall in love with any woman, especially if she were charming and well educated. It had been so with the Maréchale de Villars and Mme de Bernières, and while he was genuinely in love with both these women, in not all cases was it a physical relationship. He could love someone wholeheartedly for her attributes of mind rather than her physical charms, and this was certainly true as he grew older. But now he was still only twenty-eight, while the Marquise was a morally frail widow of thirty-seven.

At Cambrai the travellers found preparations under way for a peace congress, and the little city was filled with Austrians and Spaniards. At the prospect of meeting so many distinguished personages Voltaire and Mme de Rupelmonde decided to stop a while and enjoy the social life: in fact they stayed for four or five weeks. When it was discovered who the young man was there was a general demand that *Oedipe* should be performed at the local theatre. Not only was *Oedipe* given but it was followed by a burlesque, *Oedipe Traversi*. That in itself was something of a compliment, since it implied a general familiarity with Voltaire's work.

The couple stayed in Cambrai until September, and Voltaire devoted much of his time to the composition of light verses extolling the charms of his companion. Then they moved on to Brussels, where Voltaire was anxious to renew his acquaintance with Jean-Baptiste Rousseau, who was living there after being instrumental in causing the wrongful imprisonment of a one-time friend. He claimed that Saurin, a mathematician, was the author of libellous verses about mutual friends, which led to a court case, but when the truth was discovered—that he, Rousseau, was the real author—he fled to Brussels. Now he was living in permanent exile, and apparently a reformed character of almost excessive piety. Over the years he and Voltaire had exchanged letters, and now the younger man had come to pay his respects in person. The meeting was friendly enough on the surface. The fatal rupture was to come later. But even then Voltaire wrote: "He despises me because I neglect rhyme, and I despise him because he can do nothing but rhyme."

Voltaire read the fifty-one-year-old poet sections of the *Henriade*, which met with Rousseau's approval, apart from the sections which he feared might give offence to the Church. It seemed that after years spent attacking that institution with innuendoes and salacious verses—his favourite targets were monks and nuns—he was now most anxious for its reputation. But Voltaire accepted the criticisms, and when he and Mme de Rupelmonde left Brussels for The Hague the two men were still friends.

Holland had a fine reputation for toleration, perhaps the result of her appalling sufferings under the Spanish, and in particular at the hands of the notorious Duke of Alva. Voltaire hoped that he would be able to print the *Henriade* in The Hague without trouble from censors. But he was to be disappointed. He was told that it could only be printed in Holland if it also came out at the same time in an edition produced in France. Thus the project of a Dutch *Henriade* died stillborn. However, though nothing came of it, Voltaire's visit to The Hague and Amsterdam remained a delightful holiday, still in the company of Mme de Rupelmonde. Then it was time to return to Brussels, where he again called on Rousseau.

The poet had put all his resentment against the *Parlement de Paris*, which had exiled him, into a long poem. Voltaire listened to this rhymed catalogue of woe, and then commented that he thought it unworthy of the great and good Rousseau. Later they went for a drive in a carriage, and at that point Voltaire produced a poem he had written which was meant primarily for Mme de Rupelmonde, and as a means of assisting her during the period of doubts and uncertainties through which she was passing. This poem, called *L'Epître à Uranie* (Epistle to Uranie), and also known as *Epître à Julie* and *Le Pour et le Contre*, consisted of a codification of his own thoughts and opinions. It amounted to severe questioning rather than an outright rejection of Christianity, and in it he was nailing his intellectual colours to the mast. It cannot shock today as it did when first published clandestinely in 1732, and in recent years many of the statements in *Le Pour et le Contre* have been echoed by progressive clergymen. Indeed some have gone further than Voltaire ever did.

Le Pour et le Contre was not written to deride religion, but was the work of someone who genuinely regretted that he could not share the orthodox beliefs of the faith in which he had been instructed. He yearned for a God, but for him it could not be the God of the Old and the New Testaments, but a Supreme Being, such as the Deists believed in. Why, he wanted to know, did a God who had created human beings in His own image then make them sin so that they could be punished? Why did he give them a capacity for pleasure and then damn them for using that capacity? Why did He create man and then because of his sins drown him in the Flood, only later to die Himself for the redemption of man?

Voltaire also attacked the doctrine of original sin. Why should He remorselessly pursue the children for the sins of a first father, and why should punishment be meted out to a distant people whose only crime was that they had never even heard of Him?

It was *Le Pour et Le Contre* which more than anything was to give Voltaire the reputation which he still retains in the eyes of some: as a malicious, malevolent, destructive anti-Christian, whose chief aim in life was to help bring about the overthrow of established religion. The poem consisted of three parts: *Le Contre*, which was really an outpouring of Voltaire's own doubts and questionings; *Le Pour*, which set forth the orthodox view of Christianity; and at the end a request to the Uranie of the poem (in reality Mme de Rupelmonde) to make up her own mind what to believe, and at the same time a summary of the poet's own opinion: a belief in a natural religion, to use his own definition.

Belief that a modest bonze, a charitable dervish, can find grace in His eyes rather than a pitiless Jansenist or an ambitious pontiff. Ah, what does it matter by what name He is invoked? All homage is received, but none honours Him. A God does not need our assiduous attentions: if it is possible to offend Him, it is by injustice: He judges us by our virtues and not by our sacrifices.

Little wonder the Church would come to hate and fear him. For one thing, at the end of *Le Pour et Le Contre* he had denied the necessity of a priest to act as an intermediary between a man and his God. The cynical wit, scoffing and unbelief of such as the Abbé de Châteauneuf and the circle at the Temple, had borne fruit.

Voltaire was only half-way through reading *Le Pour et Le Contre* to Jean-Baptiste Rousseau before the latter interrupted, calling it a horrible profanity, forgetting that he himself had probably written more pointless and spiteful anti-clerical verses than any man, dead or alive. Voltaire did not react against Rousseau's self-righteous indignation, and they went off to the theatre together. After the performance Rousseau read aloud his *Ode to Posterity*, and as they parted Voltaire said: "You know, Master, that is an ode which will never reach its address." He had had the last word, but Rousseau's undying hatred would pursue him across twenty-five years.

October saw Voltaire once again in Cambrai. He had made the journey on horseback across Flanders, and alone, as Mme de Rupelmonde preferred to stay on in The Hague. His thoughts were entirely taken up with the *Henriade*, and he took it with him to read to Henry St John, Lord Bolingbroke, at *La Source*, his beautiful home in exile near Orléans. Until forced to leave England he had occupied a prominent position on the political scene, becoming Minister of War in his twenty-fourth year in a Tory administration. According to Voltaire, when the news of his appointment reached the ears of the London prostitutes they exclaimed: "Bolingbroke gets £5,000 a year, and all for us!" Later it was he who framed the terms of the Peace of Utrecht which enabled France to end the War of the Spanish Succession with a peace that was neither crippling nor humiliating. But after the death of Queen Anne in 1714 Bolingbroke was suspected of engaging in a treasonable correspondence with the Old Pretender, and he went into voluntary exile in France. At *La Source* he lived the life of a country gentleman, enjoying the pleasures of a simple existence, and embellishing his house and gardens. For him the exile was to last until 1723.

Voltaire first became acquainted with Bolingbroke through the mother of his old school friends, the Marquis and the Comte d'Argental, after which he was invited to stay at *La Source*. Usually it was Voltaire who captivated his host. But this time the attraction was mutual. Lord Bolingbroke and his mistress, soon to become his wife, were as captivated by the wit and charm of the poet as he was by them. He found the statesman a most complete English gentleman, and also something of a philosopher, whose thoughts were tinged with Deism. He was indeed a brilliant and cultured man, though there was something slightly *maudit* about his character, but now he and the Marquise de Villette were the perfect host and hostess to Voltaire, who was bubbling over with enthusiasm for the epic poem he was still polishing so lovingly. In a letter to Thieriot he described Lord Bolingbroke:

> This illustrious Englishman has all the erudition of his own country and all the polish of ours. This man, who has passed his whole life in pleasure and affairs of state, has nevertheless found a way of learning everything and remembering everything. He knows the history of the ancient Egyptians like that of England. He knows his Virgil as well as his Milton. He loves English, French and Italian poetry.

Now, on a second visit to *La Source*, after his return from The Hague and Brussels, he read the *Henriade* aloud. He must publish it, he was told. But how could he do so without the permission of the censor?

The year 1722 passed, and while the *Henriade* remained unpublished Voltaire was at work on *Mariamne*, a tragedy involving King Herod. It was Mme de Bernières who provided the solution. The poet had rented part of the de Bernières' town house in Paris, which he generously shared with the sponging Thieriot. Now she suggested that if it were not possible to have the *Henriade* printed in Paris perhaps it could be done in secret in Rouen, with her help.

Meanwhile, *Mariamne* was finished, and the President de Maisons had invited a house party to the Château des Maisons, to hear the author's own reading of the work. Among the thirty guests was the actress Adrienne Lecouvreur, who hoped to play the name part. Then Voltaire fell ill with smallpox. The diagnosis was made late at night. The other guests were roused, and departed in great haste. M. de Maisons sent for the best doctor in Paris, Gervasi, who came at once. Voltaire, fearing the worst, saw the local *curé*, confessed, and made his will. But Gervasi rallied the patient, carefully explaining his treatment and the reasons behind it. It worked, and Voltaire (who was up and about again within a month) afterwards declared that his life had been saved by being made to drink two hundred pints of lemonade.

During this time the printing of the *Henriade* had been going on in secret in Rouen. At the beginning of the eighteenth century Paris was still a compact city, more or less contained within the compass of its medieval walls, and complete with customs posts at the gates. But early in 1724 a wagon supposedly full of Mme de Bernières' furniture passed through without trouble. The *Henriade* had reached the capital.

The bindings were soon added, and before long the book was enjoying a success due less to its panoramic display of French history in epic verse than to the ideas and statements it contained which had been considered dangerous enough by the authorities to necessitate the banning of the book. Naturally, it became the success of the season. Did it not speak in praise of Elizabeth of England and Admiral Coligny? Had not Voltaire written: "I have seen favour and fury on both sides" and declared that he did not decide between Rome and Geneva? For a Frenchman to write about religion at that time without openly condemning Protestantism was not only novel, it was courting trouble. And what else could he be referring to but the late king's attempt to unite in himself temporal and spiritual powers when he wrote: "The throne is the altar, and absolute power places in the same hands the sceptre and the censer." Nor did he spare his readers any details of the Massacre of St Bartholomew: an incident which many still looked on as justified by the need to defend true religion from heresy.

There was no denying that the *Henriade* had increased Voltaire's fame, though not for purely literary reasons. *Oedipe* had enjoyed a *succès de scandale* because people chose to see parallels in it with the life of the Regent, and now here was the same little bantam-cock flying up at the all-powerful Church. But there were also those who, judging the work in literary terms, thought that Voltaire had at last given France an epic poem. Mathieu Marcius wrote: "The poem, *La Ligue*, by Arouet, which has been so much talked about, is being sold in secret. I have read it. It is a marvellous work, a masterpiece of the mind, as beautiful as Virgil. At last we have an epic in our own language."

It is a curious fact but there was no epic poem in the French language comparable with anything produced on the other side of the Channel. England had a tradition of epic verse stretching back to Saxon times, with poems such as *Beowulf* and the *Battle of Maldon*, but Norman France produced no epic to tell of the Conquest. In later times England could claim Milton and Dryden, but until 1724 France had nothing comparable. Ironically enough when it did appear it was by stealth and in secret: "a bastard," in Voltaire's own words. The author had let off a firework, as he recalled in the *Autobiography*.

All the poets in Paris, and even many of the learned, fell foul of him. Twenty pamphlets were let off against him. The *Henriade* was play'd at the fair [i.e., burlesqued].

The young author was filled with surprise and resentment at the reaction. It is curious that one so logical, who knew perfectly well what he was doing, never failed to be surprised at the uproar he caused. But so it was all his life.

"His dissipation," he continued, "had prevented him from making friends among the literati, and he had not the art of combating his enemies with their own weapons, which is said to be absolutely necessary in Paris, if a man wishes to succeed in any kind of pursuit."

Once again the atmosphere at Court had changed, but not for the better. In May 1719 the Duchesse de Berry had died quite suddenly, and inevitably it was whispered that she had been poisoned. Then in December 1723 it was the Regent himself who died without warning, and in his place the fourteen-year-old king was ruled by the Duc de Bourbon and his mistress Mme de Prie.

First there had been the dull Court of Louis XIV in his declining years, with its tone set by the devout Mme de Maintenon. Then had come the regency of Philippe d'Orléans; brilliant, corrupt and amoral. His successor, the Duc de Bourbon, was a man of moderate excesses, who was quite under the thumb of Mme de Prie. As for Louis XV, he appeared cold and aloof, but already he had the face of a sensual adult. He was in fact dominated by a homosexual clique headed by Cardinal Fleury and the First Minister Maurepas. Already he had been seduced by the young Duc de Tremouille, First Gentleman of the Bedchamber, who had thwarted an attempted liaison which Mlle de Charolais was trying to establish with her king. In a fit of jealousy another young duke, de Gesvres, told the new Regent the truth of the situation. Frenchmen may have sneered at the Court of George I for being dull and uncouth, but that of the juvenile Louis XV reflected a great civilisation turning to corruption. And now Mme de Prie had offered Voltaire an apartment of his own at Fontainebleau. He accepted with alacrity.

The consensus of opinion was that the sooner the king was married the better. A list of possible brides was drawn up which contained seventeen names, including royal families ranging from Russia to Modena in Italy. But others, including those most concerned, considered that such a list was a waste of time. What better bride could the king have than the Duc de Bourbon's sister, the twenty-one-year-old Princesse de Vermandois? But the Regent was reckoning without the redoubtable Mme de Prie. Would the Princesse be a puppet in her hands, and what did the girl think of her? The prospective bride lived in a convent, and Mme de Prie paid a visit under an assumed name. What, she asked the naïve girl, did she think of Mme de Prie? The Princesse opened her mouth and lost a throne. Mme de Prie was malicious and the most detested woman in France, she declared with more frankness than discretion.

Mme de Prie could play at politics with all the foresight of a chess player, and she set about destroying the girl's chances of being chosen as queen, but did it in such a way that the Duc de Bourbon never suspected what she was about. It was known that Louis XV could hardly live without Cardinal Fleury, his tutor, and Mme de Prie suggested to him that he was opposed to such a union, and that if he—the Duc de Bourbon—went ahead with the marriage, it would antagonise the Cardinal, who in his turn would set Louis XV against the Duc de Bourbon. So while appearing to have her protector's best interests at heart Mme de Prie had very neatly disposed of a dangerous rival to her own power at Court without appearing to have done anything.

Someone must be found who was of royal birth but of no political significance whatsoever. There was an excellent candidate in Maria Leszczynska, the twenty-one-year-old daughter of Stanislas, ex-King of Poland. The father and daughter lived in near-penury in Alsace, and could hardly believe the contents of the letter Stanislas received in the spring of 1725. It was a fairy tale come true, but it was not one that in the long run would have a happy ending. Mme de Prie was satisfied she would have no difficulty in moulding this Polish girl to suit her own purposes, and on 5 September 1726 the royal couple were married at Versailles. To the surprise of all and the chagrin of some Louis XV was by then genuinely in love with his bride.

The King bestowed Lorraine on Stanislas, who was now able to establish his own Court at Nancy and Lunéville. In the years ahead Voltaire would come to know Stanislas, who would treat him with fatherly indulgence, and invite him to be his guest at Lunéville.

Shortly before the marriage took place the Court was at Fontainebleau, and Voltaire wrote to Thieriot: "My address is care of Mme de Prie." He had been drawn right into the heart of that scheming woman's web, and without actually singing for his supper he was expected to provide entertainment for his patrons. Voltaire obliged with a trifle, written the year before while taking the waters at Forges, entitled *L'Indiscret*, in which he himself appeared as a far from perfect village priest. By then *Mariamne* had been performed in Paris (March 1724), but only for one night. The play failed because it contravened the hidebound theatrical traditions which decreed what could and could not be portrayed on the stage. Voltaire recorded the disaster in the *Autobiography*.

In 1722 [wrong date], he gave the tragedy of *Mariamne*. That princess was poisoned by Herod. When she drank the cup, the faction cried out, *the Queen drinks*, and the piece was damned.

The failure could have been due to a hostile claque provided by a rival author who had written a play on the same subject, but, whatever the reason, Voltaire revised *Mariamne*, and when it was given again in May it was a resounding success. "He is our greatest poet," wrote Marcius, who had praised the *Henriade* so warmly. In fact such was the success of *Mariamne* that not long after her marriage, Maria Leszczynska accepted the dedication of both *Oedipe* and *Herode et Mariamne* as Voltaire now called the piece. What was more, the queen granted him an annuity from her own resources.

Lord Bolingbroke sent a copy of the *Henriade* to Alexander Pope at Twickenham, who despite his limited knowledge of French gleaned enough to sum up the author with remarkable accuracy:

> I conclude him at once a Free thinker and lover of Quiet, no Bigot, but yet no Heretic: one who honours Authority and National sanctions without prejudice to Truth or Charity; one who has Study'd Controversy less than Reason, and the Fathers less than Mankind.

Confirmation of Voltaire's high intellectual ability spurred on Bolingbroke to write advising him to use that brain to the limit; to couple his great powers of imagination with reason. In other words, to make a serious study of philosophy. Bolingbroke recommended him to profit from the *Essay concerning Human Understanding* by Locke, whom he rated higher as a philosopher than Descartes.

Another copy of the *Henriade* had also found its way to England, sent by Voltaire himself to George I, with a flattering letter inspired perhaps by self-interest. "I dare to flatter myself that you will accord me your royal protection to print in your realms a work which must interest you since it is the eulogy of virtue."

Of course at this date there was no such thing as copyright, and there were others anxious to share in the financial success of the *Henriade*. One was the Abbé Desfontaines, an ex-Jesuit, a self-styled literary critic and notorious pederast, who had in fact been banned from visiting the theatres of Paris by the police. What he lacked in creative literary talent he made up for in verbose criticism, and by pirating the works of others more talented. Before long Desfontaines brought out his own edition of the *Henriade*, to which he made some inflammatory additions of his own. Voltaire tried to have the edition suppressed, but showed surprisingly little hostility against Desfontaines, later even proposing one of the Abbé's nominees to act as secretary to the Duc de Richelieu, the newly appointed Ambassador in Vienna, after the lazy Thieriot had turned down the offer. While he could be waspish in his feuds, Voltaire could also be quixotic to the point of irrationality, and this was the case with Desfontaines.

At about the time that Desfontaines made Voltaire's acquaintance he found himself in very serious trouble with the law. He was charged with sodomy, which carried the penalty of being burnt alive at the stake, though few people of consequence ever suffered if convicted. The charge against Desfontaines was dropped, but only a few months later, in April 1725, he was again arrested and charged on the evidence of two chimney-sweeps. Frantically the ex-Jesuit sought help, but the only one to offer assistance was Voltaire. The latter's humanitarian instincts were to be aroused to aid more estimable individuals, but apparently on this occasion he rose from his sick-bed to ride to Fontainebleau to ask Cardinal Fleury and Mme de Prie to intercede on behalf of the Abbé. Desfontaines could count himself lucky that the man whose epic he had pirated had such a generous nature. Again he was released, only to spend the next twenty years vilifying the philosopher, because he could not bear to be grateful to a man who had saved his life. And there would be occasions when Voltaire would be justified in wishing that he had left the odious man to his fate.

At Court there had been yet another shift in the power struggle between supporters of the Duc de Bourbon and Mme de Prie on the one hand and those in the circle of the Comte de Maurepas and Cardinal Fleury on the other. The latter were doing their utmost to regain control over the king. Fortune was on their side now, because Louis XV was already losing interest in Maria Leszczynska, the temperamental and immature queen. Fleury was not slow to exploit the rift to gain control over his pupil, and when the Duc de Bourbon arranged a private interview behind locked doors with the king he asked outright whether only

Fleury had His Majesty's confidence. Yes, answered Louis XV, and ended the interview in a temper. The Duc de Bourbon was ordered to send for Fleury, who had literally been locked out of the royal apartments. It was obvious that if the Duc and Mme de Prie wanted to retain their power they must counter-attack and break Cardinal Fleury and his followers once and for all. On such a struggle they were prepared to use any weapon, preferably character assassination. Two scandals broke simultaneously; the first engineered by the Duc de Bourbon to expose prominent homosexuals in Paris, among them Fleury and Maurepas, the second—which was none of his making—involving the notorious Mme de Tensin, the totally promiscuous sister and mistress of Archbishop Tensin. Another of her lovers objected to his rivals, and shot himself in her presence. Mme de Tensin did not report the suicide to the police, but contacted friends in the legal world, the President and the Procurator of the Grand Tribunal. They ordered the body to be buried at once in quicklime, and then gave out that the senator had died of apoplexy. But others had their doubts, and Mme de Tensin was arrested and taken to the Châtelet Prison. Soon however she was transferred to more comfortable quarters in the Bastille, thanks to the influence of Fleury and Maurepas. Although shaken by the revelations made about his private life, Fleury was still all-powerful. The Duc de Bourbon and Mme de Prie therefore decided to attack openly. René Hénault, the Commissioner of Police, who owed his position to Mme de Prie, ordered the arrest of Des Chaufours, the least influential and least important member of Fleury's circle. He was accused of sodomy, tried, found guilty, and actually burnt at the stake on the same day. Mme de Prie had succeeded in involving her enemies in a public scandal, at the price of a hideous death. Whether she was intending to use Voltaire in a campaign of malicious verses against her enemies is a matter of conjecture. But before that could happen he had landed himself in trouble over quite another matter, and had been consigned to the Bastille on the orders of Hénault. This was followed by three years of exile in England, which under the circumstances was the best thing that could have happened to him. The climate might have been damp, but in all other respects it was infinitely healthier.

When Voltaire returned to France it was as a philosopher who had been cured of much of his desire to receive social favours at the French Court. The events which he had undergone, or had witnessed during the years spanned by the regency, made him an enemy of the authority of the state, and in particular he was disgusted at the way the law could be manipulated by the most influential for their own ends. Then, after his return to France in 1729, the vindictive conduct of the Church first towards the helpless body of Adrienne Lecouvreur and then towards himself would make him its lifelong enemy.

At the same time that Voltaire was forcibly removed from a stage that was as sordid as it was dangerous Mme de Prie (who was after all his patroness at Court) herself fell from power, together with the Duc de Bourbon. The still undefeated Cardinal Fleury "suggested" to the Duc de Bourbon that if Mme de Prie and Pâris-Duverney, the Royal Treasurer, went to the country it would be easier to set matters right at Court. Mme de Prie chose to ignore the hint, and before long the king signed a *lettre de cachet* which not only exiled the Duc to Chantilly but specifically forbade him to hunt, his favourite recreation. As for Mme de Prie, she was exiled to Normandy. The fall was more than she could bear, and she committed suicide. Pâris-Duverney was imprisoned in the Bastille for eighteen months.

The incident which brought Voltaire to the Bastille for a second time sprang from an offensive remark made by the Chevalier de Rohan-Chabot. The Chevalier was a member of the family whose motto was *Roi ne puys, Duc ne daygne, Rohan suys*: (I cannot be King, I disdain to be a Duke, I am a Rohan), and he possessed all the pride which would help bring about the downfall of the more celebrated Cardinal Prince Louis de Rohan, when he became involved in the diamond necklace affair shortly before the Revolution. What made the Chevalier de Rohan-Chabot's conduct all the more deplorable was the fact that he had been acquainted with Voltaire for some time, and apparently they were on quite friendly terms. It all started one evening in December 1725, when the Chevalier was at the Opera. Quite gratuitously he sneered: "Monsieur de Voltaire, Monsieur Arouet, whatever your name is . . . "

Voltaire was never at a loss for words, however unwise they might be, and there are two versions of his answer to the supercilious nobleman. One: "I do not drag a great name after me, but I do know how to bring honour to the one I have." The other: "My name begins with me; yours ends with you." But whatever he said, he had made a mortal enemy. A few days later they again met, apparently in the box of Adrienne Lecouvreur. The Chevalier repeated the jibe, and Voltaire repeated his reply. At this de Rohan-Chabot raised his cane, and Voltaire's hand flew to the hilt of his sword, whereupon Adrienne Lecouvreur did the only thing a resourceful woman could do in the circumstances, and fainted. Again the incident closed without satisfaction to either party.

Not long after, on 4 February 1726, Voltaire was dining with his old friend the Duc de Sully at his town house in the Rue Saint-Antoine. A message was brought to him at the table that he was wanted by someone at the gate. Apparently his help was needed in an act of charity. Unsuspectingly, Voltaire went downstairs and out to the coach. He climbed onto the step and put his head in at the open window. Then he was seized from within and held while two men beat his shoulders savagely. They were lackeys in the service of the Chevalier de Rohan-Chabot, who was sitting in a coach nearby, watching the scene. This was his revenge on Voltaire: a public beating in broad daylight. "Don't hurt his head!" he is reputed to have called out, "something good may come out of that!" And the crowd of onlookers exclaimed at this example of patrician consideration: "Ah, the good seigneur!"

The beating over, Voltaire flew upstairs to the Duc de Sully, asking—almost demanding—that he should obtain justice for him. But Sully shrugged his shoulders. He himself was a duke, and the Chevalier was the younger son of a duke, as well as a kinsman. Voltaire was the son of a notary, a clever little nobody. It was the end of a ten-year friendship. No more would he visit Sully-sur-Loire, write charming light verses for his host, or have anything to do with the family. When the English edition of the *Henriade* came out references to the heroic exploits of Sully's ancestors had been deleted.

Once before Voltaire had been caned, by the police spy Beauregard, and now the fickle *beau monde* of Paris was laughing at him again, and it may have been the Prince de Conti who remarked: "What should become of the rest of us if poets had no backs?" Now Voltaire was dangerously angry, and he took fencing lessons, practising from morning to night. Hénault, who had him under observation, wrote to the chief of criminal police that Voltaire wanted watching, for his own safety, as well as that of the Chevalier de Rohan-Chabot. A *lettre de cachet* was prepared for use in an emergency.

The police were convinced that Voltaire would attack the Chevalier, and the Police Commissioner noted:

> Within the last six weeks he has repeatedly changed his residence, even his district, and it is known that at present he is staying with a certain Leynault, a fencing-master in the Rue Saint-Martin, where he keeps very bad company. It is said that he is friendly with soldiers of the Guard and that various bullies visit him. . . . All these reports make it seem advisable, perhaps this very night, to carry out the King's order concerning the Sieur de Voltaire.

The climax of the affair came a few evenings later, on 7 April, when the protagonists met again. "If money-making hasn't made you forget your insult to me, I hope that you will give me satisfaction," exclaimed Voltaire, with a barbed reference to the Chevalier's activities as a money-lender. The Chevalier agreed, and a duel was arranged for the following day, to take place at the Porte Saint-Martin. The De Rohan family was unwilling to let matters take their course, and one of their number—also a Cardinal de Rohan—went to the Duc de Bourbon asking him to act. For a second time Voltaire found himself being conveyed to the Bastille in the middle of the night. That it was a monstrous injustice was evident to at least one of Voltaire's illustrious friends. The Maréchal-Duc de Villars wrote: "The public, always ready to criticise, in this instance rightly found that both parties were at fault: Voltaire in insulting the Chevalier de Rohan; the latter in committing a crime which warranted the death penalty—he had a citizen beaten. The Government was at fault in failing to punish a criminal act, and for sending the aggrieved party to the Bastille to pacify the aggressor."

The confinement was not rigorous, and so many visitors came to wish Voltaire well that their numbers had to be limited to six a day. As for the Chevalier, he had been saved from the dreadful and ignoble fate of having to fight a duel with a member of the bourgeoisie. Sarcasm was the only weapon left to Voltaire, and he used it in a letter to the Minister of Justice:

The Sieur de Voltaire most respectfully brings to your knowledge that he was murderously assaulted by the brave Chevalier de Rohan with the assistance of six bandits behind whom he himself very courageously took his stand. The Sieur de Voltaire has since continuously sought an opportunity to reestablish, not his own, but the Chevalier's honour, which proved to be too difficult.... He requests the privilege of dining with the Governor and of receiving visitors. Still more urgently he asks permission for immediate departure for England. Should anybody question his departure an officer could escort him to Calais.

Even Hénault, who had limited the number of visitors he could receive each day, was not spared Voltaire's tongue. "What," he asked, "is done with people who forge *lettres de cachet*?" "They are hanged," replied the police officer. "Good, in anticipation of the day when those who sign genuine ones shall also be hanged!"

Nor had his wit deserted him. The next room was occupied by the infamous Mme de Tensin, and in a letter to her sister Voltaire wrote: "We are like Pyramus and Thisbe. It was only a wall that divided us, but we did not kiss, as they did, through a chink in the wall."

His request to be allowed to go to England was granted, and on 29 April 1726 the order was given for his release, though he did not actually leave until 3 May.

The Sieur de Voltaire is to be released from the Bastille. The intention of the King is that he shall be conducted to England. The Sieur Condé shall accompany him as far as Calais and shall see him embark and set out from that port. I beg you to obtain from the Sieur de Voltaire his consent in writing to conform to these orders.

Soon he was on his way to Calais in a carriage borrowed from

Mme de Bernières, under the watchful eye of Condé, the governor, who had been instructed to see the young man safely aboard the ship.

At least for three years he was leaving behind him a society which was in a state of almost unparalleled corruption, and perhaps the visit saved him from the fate of becoming an ageing socialite, living in an endless world of petty versifying and boudoir intrigue. That much he had at least to be grateful to the Chevalier for, though unwittingly the nobleman had done untold damage to the *ancien régime*, which would go echoing down the years to 1789. But of more immediate consequence to Voltaire was the fact that it had brought his youth and a whole chapter of his life to a close.

Chapter 6

THE ENGLISH INTERLUDE

On the 3rd instant M. de Voltaire was released from the Bastile [*sic*], and conducted as far as Calais, being allowed to go over into England, and forbid to come within fifty leagues of the Court. 'Tis said he will publish at London a large edition of his famous Poem of the *League*, whereof we have only an imperfect copy.

Thus in a brief paragraph *The British Journal* of 14 May 1726 recorded Voltaire's arrival in England. The piece was clearly the work of someone who wished him well, and wanted to obtain advance publicity for the *Henriade*. He did not leave France simply to find refuge on an alien shore where he was a stranger amid strangers. Apart from the ignominious circumstances leading to his exile there was nothing unpleasant about his residence of nearly three years. At *La Source* Voltaire had stayed with the exiled Bolingbroke, but now it was the exiled poet who visited the Tory minister, for since his return in 1723 Bolingbroke was once again a man of consequence in his own country.

Nor was he the only one to give Voltaire introductions. A recommendation was sent to the French Ambassador in London, the Comte de Broglie, from the Foreign Minister in Paris, while Horatio Walpole, the British Ambassador in that city, wrote commending him to the Duke of Newcastle, at that time Foreign Secretary.

Even the weather conspired to give Voltaire a favourable first impression of England when he landed at Greenwich. His description of that beautiful May morning is somewhat rose-tinted, suggesting perhaps that, despite his sophistication, he was permitting himself to see only what he wanted to see. After the in-justice of all he had undergone in the previous few weeks Voltaire was now in the land of the free, where all men had equal rights, and even the climate was perfect.

I landed at Greenwich, on the banks of the Thames. This beautiful river, which never overflows, and whose banks are adorned with greenness all the year, was covered for the space of six miles with two rows of merchant-vessels. Their sails were all spread in honour of the King and Queen [in fact there was no Queen in England at this time], who were rowed up the river in a gilded barge, preceded by a boat full of musicians, and followed by a thousand little rowing-boats. Each of these had two oarsmen, and all the rowers were dressed as our pages were in old times, with trunk hose, and little doublets ornamen-ted with a large silver badge on the shoulders. Everyone of these watermen showed by his looks, his dress, and his plump con-dition that he lived in freedom in the midst of plenty.

There was a race-course nearby, and at least in his narrative Voltaire was caught up in the throng of good-natured holiday-makers—going so far as to imagine himself transported to the Olympic Games. But before long the voice of the sharp-eyed realist and observer of the social scene breaks in on the torrent of excessive enthusiasm and hyperbole. He probably spent his first night in England at Bolingbroke's house in Pall Mall, where his introduction to ladies of fashion was something of a disappointment.

I was a little surprised to see that they had nothing whatever of the vivacity commonly shown by persons who have success-fully amused themselves. They were stiff and cold; they took tea and made a great deal of noise with their fans; they either said not a word or cried out all at once in slander of their neighbours.

Voltaire soon discovered the English preoccupation with the weather, and his account of being cold-shouldered by a number of hitherto friendly City merchants in a coffee house is a good example of his bantering style:

I ventured to ask them why they were all so miserable. One of them sulkily replied that the wind was in the East. At this moment one of their friends came in and said quite indifferently: "Molly cut her throat this morning; her lover found her dead in her room with a bloodstained razor beside her." This Molly was a young, beautiful, and very rich girl, about to be married to the very man who had found her dead. These gentlemen, who were all her friends, received the news without wincing. One of them merely asked what had become of the razor. He had bought the razor, was the cold reply. I was aghast at so strange a death and appalled by these Englishmen's indifference. I could not refrain from asking what had driven a young lady, seemingly so happy, to tear herself so cruelly from life. I got no other answer than that the wind was in the East. I could not at first understand what the East wind had to do with the melancholy mood of these gentlemen and with the death of Molly. I abruptly left the coffee house and went to the Court, pleasantly assuming, in my natural French way, that a Court was always gay. But gloom and wretchedness possessed everything there, even the very maids of honour themselves. They said in a melancholy manner that the wind was in the East. . . . A famous Court doctor, to whom I mentioned my surprise, told me that I ought not to be astonished yet; that I would see a very different state of things in November and March, when the people hanged themselves by the dozen; that almost everyone was really ill during those two seasons, and that a cloud of melancholy hung over the nation. "For," said he, "those are the months when the East wind blows most obstinately. That wind is the ruin of our island. The very animals suffer from it and have a woebegone look. The men who are strong enough to keep their health in this cursed wind at least lose their good humour. Everyone looks stern and cross and is disposed to form desperate resolutions. It was precisely in an East wind that Charles I was beheaded and James II dethroned. If you have any favour to ask at Court," he added in my ear, "never ask it unless the wind is in the West or South."

The wind may have been in the east, but at least Voltaire had found something healthier to laugh at than the corruption of the French Court. Not that he had decided to forget the episode involving the Chevalier de Rohan-Chabot. In fact he did a very foolish thing, and secretly went back to France on a flying visit. With a stature about equal to that of a fourteen-year-old school-boy, physical courage was not the strongest element in his character, but when he was consumed with anger, either personal (as in this case) or at some terrible act of injustice to an innocent or defenceless person, he was almost unaware of danger to his own person. Few details have survived concerning his clandestine return to France under an assumed name in search of the Chevalier.

Apparently he attended a performance of Racine's *Britannicus* in the hope of finding his enemy, but failed. In despair he wrote from his hiding place in the environs of Paris to Thieriot. It was a desolate letter. Voltaire could not make up his mind whether to live permanently in London, and he felt that all the world had rejected him. His volatile nature could touch the heights of elation, but it could also plumb the depths.

"If I still have some friends who mention my name when you are with them, speak soberly about me to them, and do not let them lose their remembrance of me."

The letter was dated 12 August 1726. Shortly afterwards he was back in England, but it was not Bolingbroke he sought out in his misery. At some time in the past he had become acquainted in Paris with an English merchant who invited him to stay if ever he came to England.

Everard Falkener was a prosperous, educated and cultured merchant whose business interests lay in the silk and cloth trade with the Levant. By inclination he was a classical scholar, a collector of antiquities, and interested in literature. A genuine, lifelong friendship developed between him and Voltaire, ending only with Falkener's death in 1758. When Voltaire went to stay at his large house in Wandsworth, then a village some distance from London, he was still a merchant. In 1735 he was appointed British Ambassador at Constantinople, and in 1745 he became private and confidential secretary to the Duke of Cumberland: first accompanying him to Flanders during the inglorious cam-

paign which included defeat at Fontenoy. A year later the duke
would earn the nickname of Butcher Cumberland, for his part in
the Jacobite defeat at Culloden. But now Falkener was acting as
host to the emotionally bruised and disillusioned Voltaire, who
was to pass several months in the quiet, civilised atmosphere of
his house.

But the autumn and winter of 1726 were not spent in idleness.
With all the enthusiasm Voltaire showed for any new project he
set about learning English, for when he arrived at Greenwich his
knowledge of the language must have been extremely sketchy.
While he was quick to master written English he had difficulty
with pronunciation, and for some time he could not have been
easy to understand. But before long he was showing off his new
knowledge, by writing in English to Thieriot. The letter is interesting. After his experience with the Duc de Sully, who had
refused to back him in his quarrel with the Chevalier, he no
longer quite trusted any of his more illustrious friends. He
described his poor health at some length, his lack of money and
his miserable spirits. He continued:

Another London citizen that I have seen but once in Paris
carried me to his country house, wherein I lead an obscure and
charming life since that time, without going to London, and
quite given over to the pleasures of indolence and friendship. . . . I have seen often my Lord and Lady Bolingbroke;
I have found their affection still the same, even increased in
proportion to my unhappiness; they offered me all, their
money, their house; but I have refused all, because they are
lords, and I have accepted all from Mr Faulknear because he is a
single gentleman.

Later, when the creative urge had returned, Voltaire set to
work on his notebooks and what became the *Letters on the English
Nation*, and in the French version the *Lettres Philosophiques*, in
which he made pertinent and almost revolutionary comments on
the differences between life in France and England. In fact his
statements led to the books being banned. And what were these
seditious and inflammatory observations? "An English merchant
presumes to compare himself to a Roman citizen, and indeed a

Peer's brother does not think traffic beneath him. . . ." A beating by the Chevalier's lackeys, followed by Sully's refusal to help, had left its mark. "In France the title of Marquis is given gratis to anyone who will accept it; and whosoever arrives at Paris from the most remote provinces with money in his purse, and a name ending in *ac* or *ille*, may strut about and cry *such a man as I! A man of my rank and figure!*"

Apart from the attacks on their social structure, the French must have detested being compared unfavourably with their uncouth Anglo-Saxon neighbours in Voltaire's essay on epic poetry.

> It is a great misfortune that there are so few French imitators of our neighbours, the English. We have been obliged to adopt their physical science, to imitate their financial system, to build our ships to their plan; when shall we imitate them in the noble liberty of allowing the mind to take all the flight of which it is capable?

After his return to France in 1729 Voltaire remained a champion of middle class merit as opposed to blind worship of hereditary position regardless of a person's ability or moral worth. When he dedicated his play *Zaïre* to Falkener it was regarded in Paris as an affront to the aristocracy. Surely this scribbler knew his place, and that he was dependent for his very existence on the goodwill of the aristocracy? A vicious burlesque of *Zaïre* and Falkener was staged, and when the second edition of the play was printed Voltaire did not hesitate to comment on the episode in the preface:

> Certain persons, corrupted by the unworthy custom of rendering homage only to grandeur, have tried to ridicule the novelty of a dedication made to a man who, at that time, had nothing but merit.

Later, after Falkener had been appointed Ambassador at Constantinople, Voltaire hammered home his opinion when he re-dedicated the play to his friend:

Your new dignity does not prevent me from making use of a title more sacred than minister. The name of friend is far higher than Excellency. To the ambassador of a great king and a free nation I dedicate the same work which I formerly dedicated to a plain citizen.

Less than sixty years later the word Citizen would be on everyone's lips.

So often Voltaire expressed his most serious thoughts in a witty epigram, and so it was when he summed up the English as he saw them in one of his best known quotations:

The English nation is like a hogshead of their own ripe ale— the froth at the top, the dregs at the bottom, but good in the middle.

Soon after his arrival in England Voltaire suffered a double misfortune, the first financial and the second personal. He had a letter of credit on a banker named Medina, but he delayed presenting it, and when he finally did so it was to discover that the man had become bankrupt the day before; which resulted in a loss of about 20,000 francs. At the time he described Medina as a damned Jew in a letter to Thieriot, but later recorded, "He had the generosity to give me a few guineas which he was able to spare me." In October he belatedly learnt of the death of his sister Marguerite-Catherine, and a letter to a friend shows how depressed he still was at the course his life had taken.

You were very wrong—allow me to say so with affection and sorrow—you were very wrong to suspect that I had forgotten you. I have committed many faults in the course of my life. The bitterness and the sufferings which have marked almost all its days have often been of my making. I feel how little I am worth; I pity my own weaknesses and I am horrified at my own faults. But God is my witness that I love virtue, and that therefore I shall be tenderly attached to you for the whole of my life.

At this time, perhaps more than any other, Voltaire needed his friends, and it could not have failed to hurt when he learned that the night after he was committed to the Bastille Mme de Bernières went to the opera with the Chevalier himself. After rapping her knuckles in passing, Voltaire then wrote of more personal matters.

I pardon your having been at the opera with the Chevalier de Rohan, on condition that you felt yourself a little confused.

My sister should have lived and I should have died; the mistake was fate's; I am sadly affected by her loss; you know my heart, you know what affection I had for her. I really believed it would be she who would wear mourning for me. Alas! Madame, I am even more dead than she to the world, and perhaps to you. Remember at least that I have had a share in your life. Forget everything about me except those moments when you told me that you would always be my friend. Count among my misfortunes the occasions when I may perhaps have displeased you, and love me out of generosity if you can no longer love me out of inclination.

But Voltaire's fortunes were turning. Everard Falkener had proved an ideal host to see him through a time of great depression and ill health. From January 1727 onwards Voltaire started to re-emerge into the world. After the success of *Oedipe* in 1718 he had sent George I a copy of the play (and since the sovereign could only converse with his English courtiers in French he might even have read it), and received in return a watch and a gold medal. Now he was to make the king's personal acquaintance at an interview which was recorded in the *Daily Journal* of 27 January 1727.

Last week M. Voltaire, the famous French poet, who was banished from France, was introduced to his majesty, who received him very graciously. They say he has received notice from France not to print his Poems of the League; a prosecution still depending against him, by the Cardinal de Bissy, on account of the praises bestowed in that Book on Queen Elizabeth's behaviour in matters of religion, and a great many strokes against the abuse of popery and against persecution in matters of faith.

Detestation of their fathers by their sons was almost hereditary with the early Georges, and the Prince and Princess of Wales had their own quite separate Court, and thanks to Lord and Lady Bolingbroke Voltaire found himself accepted there as well. In his depressed state he might feel that almost everyone he had known had deserted him, but that would have been less than just. Horatio Walpole (Sir Robert's brother) wrote to the Duke of Newcastle enlisting his aid on Voltaire's behalf. In his letter of recommendation he wrote:

> He has been indeed in the Bastele [*sic*] but not upon the account of any state affair; but for a particular quarrel with a private gentleman, and therefore I hope your Grace will readily give him your favour and protection in promoting the subscription.

The subscription was the list of prospective purchasers of the English edition of the *Henriade*.

A month after Horatio Walpole wrote the letter George I died, and George II and Queen Caroline came to the throne. Obviously there was now a younger element at Court, and a number of those about the new king and queen were already known to Voltaire; among them Lady Sundon, at that time George II's mistress. Others he came to know included clever, painted, waspish Lord Hervey and his beautiful wife, Molly Lepell. She could claim the distinction of being the only Englishwoman to have her looks extolled in English by Voltaire.

> Hervey, would you know the passion
>   You have kindled in my breast?
> Trifling is the inclination
>   That by words can be express'd.
>
> In my silence see the lover;
>   True love is by silence known;
> In my eyes you'll best discover
>   All the powers you own.

For months Voltaire had been improving his English, in particular at the theatre. Among his acquaintances was the celebrated poet Colly Cibber (later the Poet Laureate) and through this contact the prompter at Drury Lane Theatre always lent him his copy of the play being given on that particular night, so Voltaire could follow the piece from his seat. One day his knowledge of English had a very practical use. England might not be at war with France, but the average Londoner had very little use for Frenchmen. While out for a walk Voltaire found himself surrounded by a hostile group which seemed about to stone him. Quick-witted as ever, Voltaire jumped up on to some steps or a mounting-block and exclaimed: "Brave Englishmen! Am I not unfortunate enough in not having been born among you?" To the crowd's astonishment this little frog not only spoke English but was aware how unfortunate he was not to share the good fortune of their birthright. Instead of being stoned he was cheered and very nearly carried home.

Voltaire's acquaintances in England were not confined to Everard Falkener and the aristocratic circle into which he was introduced by Lord and Lady Bolingbroke and Horatio Walpole. It was widened to include most of the literary figures of the day. Among them were Pope, Swift, Thomson (author of *The Seasons*), Young (future author of *Night Thoughts*) and the playwright Congreve.

Some four years previously Pope had written to Bolingbroke at *La Source* warmly praising the *Henriade*, and as a result a correspondence started between the two poets. Personal meetings followed, and when Voltaire heard that Pope's carriage had overturned while fording a stream, and that he had cut his hand on broken glass, he wrote him a letter of extravagant but not necessarily insincere concern. The almost effusive praise, thanks or concern for another need not be regarded as false, since it was the expression of a particularly highly-strung creative individual. In the same way all his life Voltaire was excessively sensitive to criticism, and the less important the critic the more he seems to have been stung by it. It was one thing to expose the shortcomings of others, but quite another matter to have his own paraded in public. Occasions when insincerity patently dripped from his pen are to be found in many of the dedications of his works to royalty, or when he sent illustrious people copies in the hope of increasing the sales.

The English literary scene was no more free from malice and denigration than its counterpart in France, and several pointless and spiteful stories circulated about Voltaire and his friendship with Pope, which were later perpetuated by Dr Johnson, who regarded the Frenchman as an atheist and therefore an abhorrent being. According to one story, the first time Voltaire was invited to dine at Twickenham he so shocked Pope and his mother with an account of an internal disorder contracted in Italy (a country he never visited), that the old lady had to leave the room. According to another version it was his blasphemous speech which caused her departure, after which Pope ceased to have any social contact with him. It will be remembered that at the time of their first meeting Voltaire still spoke little English, and Pope even less French. Another story had it that Voltaire was a spy, sent to worm secrets out of Lord Bolingbroke on behalf of the Court and his political rival Sir Robert Walpole, and that he was exposed by Pope. In fact Voltaire had no interest in English politics, and was friendly with both Walpole and Bolingbroke. Pope could never have held public office because it was no secret that he was a Catholic—which spoils yet another story that Voltaire was "base enough to denounce Pope as a papist". After his return to France Voltaire inquired about Pope through friends, referring banteringly to him as a glutton. Later his blue-stocking friend the Marquise du Châtelet started a correspondence of her own with Pope, telling him: "He [Voltaire] has always spoken to me about you with an infinite esteem."

Another introduction from Horace Walpole in Paris was to Bubb Doddington (Lord Melcombe), a would-be politician whose corrupt practices brought him surprisingly little success in an age of political corruption. Politics apart, he was educated and witty, and something of a patron of writers. For three months Voltaire was his guest in Dorset, and it was through him that he met Edward Young. One day talk turned to Milton and *Paradise Lost*, which Voltaire was later to discuss at some length in his *English Essay on Epic Poetry*. He found much to admire in the poem, going so far as to describe it as "the noblest work which human imagination hath ever attempted". But also there were episodes that he disliked intensely, including the one on Sin and Death. "That compilation of horrors, that mixture of incest, that heap of monsters, that loathsomeness so far-fetched, cannot but shock a reader of delicate taste." Young defended Milton in their argument, ending with the epigram:

> You are so witty, profligate and thin,
> At once we think thee Milton, Death and Sin.

Voltaire's acquaintanceship with Congreve was limited to only one or two meetings. It was not a wholly successful relationship:

> He was infirm and almost dying when I knew him. He had one defect: he did not sufficiently esteem his first profession of authorship, which has made his fortune and his reputation. He spoke to me of his works as trifles which were beneath his notice, and in our first conversation he told me to look upon him merely as a gentleman who lived a very simple life. I replied that if he had had the misfortune of being only a gentleman, like any other, I would never have come to see him. I was shocked at vanity so out of place.

There was yet another famous writer whom Voltaire would meet, Jonathan Swift. That came about in the spring of 1727 when the Dean of St Patrick's, Dublin, was in England for a stay of six months. As the future author of such fantastic tales as *Zadig* and *Candide* Voltaire was attracted to *The Tale of a Tub* and *Gulliver's Travels*. In particular *The Tale of a Tub* appealed, as any work was bound to do in which Rome and Geneva had their heads banged together with cheerful impartiality:

> It is a treasure-house of pleasantry which one gets no idea of in any other writer. Pascal is only amusing at the expense of the Jesuits; Swift diverts and instructs at the expense of the human race. How I love the English daring! How I love people who say what they think! We only half live if we dare only half think!

While praising the first half of *Gulliver's Travels* Voltaire had reservations about the second part, in which the author perhaps

76

seemed to be repeating a successful formula when wit and originality had started to flag.

The reader's imagination is pleased and charmingly entertained by the new prospect of the lands which Gulliver discovers to him; but that continued series of new fangles, follies and fairy tales, of wild inventions, palls at last upon my taste.

The two men got on well together, and in Voltaire's opinion Swift was superior to Rabelais.

He has, like Rabelais, the honour of being a clergyman and of jesting at everything; but Rabelais was not above his age, and Swift is far above Rabelais. Our Meudon curé, in his extravagant and unintelligible book, is of abundant gaiety and of still more abundant impropriety: he is lavish of erudition, of dirt and of dullness. A good story of a couple of pages is paid for by volumes of stupidities.

When Voltaire learned that Swift was thinking of visiting France in the summer of 1727, he at once sent him two letters of introduction, one to the Comte de Morville, the Foreign Secretary, and the other to M. de Maisons. Also he promised that if Swift travelled by way of Rouen he would give him an introduction to Mme de Bernières.

Voltaire met many other well-known figures of the time, including Sarah, Duchess of Marlborough. The famous friendship between her and Queen Anne had ended in a quarrel. On a visit to Blenheim Palace Voltaire asked the redoubtable Duchess if he could glance at her unfinished memoirs. "Wait a little," he was told. "I am at present altering my account of Queen Anne's character; I have begun to like her again since the present lot have become our governors."

John Gay became another of the exile's friends, and read *The Beggar's Opera* to him shortly before its first performance in 1728. Only the intervention of death stopped Voltaire from meeting Sir Isaac Newton, but at least he saw the philosopher-scientist's funeral procession entering Westminster Abbey, and he marvelled that in England the greatest names did not disdain to come and pay their last respects. Such a thing could never happen in France, he thought regretfully. He did however meet the great man's niece, and it was from her that he heard the story of the apple, which he passed on to the world, recounting it on two separate occasions in his writings.

Another who must have been of great interest to Voltaire was Samuel Clarke, a close friend of Newton: and it was he who first aroused the Frenchman's interest in metaphysics. But the subject was too abstract to appeal for long to a mind in which the power of reason was paramount. "One day," he wrote later, "full of these great investigations which delight the mind by their immensity, I said to a very enlightened man in the company: Clarke is a far greater metaphysician than Newton. Very likely, he coldly replied. In other words you only say that one blows better bubbles than the other. This reply made me retreat into myself. Since that time I too have ventured to prick some of those bubbles of metaphysics, and I have noticed that nothing came out of them but wind."

The first fruits of Voltaire's stay in England came from the presses towards the end of 1727. It was entitled *An Essay upon the Civil Wars in France*. 'Extracted from curious *Manuscripts*. And also upon the Epik Poetry of the European Nations from Homer to Milton. By M. de Voltaire.' In a sense the essay on the civil wars was a foretaste of the *Henriade*. Voltaire always had a keen eye for business, and he did not miss the opportunity of advertising his forthcoming epic in the preface. "As to the present Essay it is intended as a kind of Preface or Introduction to the *Henriade*, which is almost entirely printed, nothing being wanting but the printing of the Cuts, which I must recommend here as particular Masterpieces of Art in their kind: 'tis the only Beauty in the Book, that I can answer for."

More important were the *Letters on the English Nation*, which however would not be published until several years after his return to Paris. Based on letters to Thieriot, they covered a diversity of subjects, among them being religion, class, government, philosophy, trade and writers, including Shakespeare.

It is perhaps no exaggeration to describe the *Letters on the English Nation* and their French counterpart, *Lettres Philosophiques*, as one of the most important books written in the eighteenth century. Bayle's *Dictionnaire Historique et Critique* had set men thinking along scientific lines, and its enemies claimed it was the start of scepticism and disbelief. And as Bayle (1646—1706) directed men's minds towards a rational as opposed to a divine origin for the terrestial world, so Voltaire's *Letters on the English Nation* questioned the social order, and also the integrity of the Church in France. In his excellent book on Voltaire Gustave Lanson called it "The First Bomb thrown at the *ancien régime*". Today historical hindsight has to be used to appreciate its explosive effect in the Paris of the 1730s, where it was not only proscribed, but even publicly burnt by the executioner.

In the writings of Descartes the philosopher separated science and faith, and affirmed the existence of God both by intuition and by deduction, which—inevitably—brought down the wrath of the Church on his head. Voltaire wrote: "Des Cartes [*sic*] was injuriously accused of being an atheist, the last Refuge of religious scandal; And he who had employed all the sagacity and penetration of his genius, in searching for new proofs of a God, was suspected to believe there was no such Being."

Voltaire had seen too much to have any illusion about most of the Abbés in France:

That indefinable being, neither ecclesiastic nor secular, in a word, the man whom we call an Abbé, is an unknown species in England. When an Englishman is told that in France young men who are notorious for their debaucheries, and who have been raised to the prelacy by women's intrigues, openly make love, divert themselves by composing amorous songs, give dainty and prolonged suppers every night, and then go to implore the illumination of the Holy Spirit, and boldly call themselves the successors of the Apostles, he thanks God that he is a Protestant.

If there was only one religion in England, it would be a despotism and dangerous; if there were only two, they would cut each other's throat; but there are thirty, and they live in peace and happiness.

Variations on that sentiment included the well-known quip that England has thirty religions but only one sauce; while in another aphorism he declared: "An Englishman, like a free man, goes to Heaven by the road he likes best." But even he could find nothing to say in praise of the English Sunday.

To Voltaire the Royal Exchange served as an example of how men of many differing faiths could meet together and transact business in amity.

> ... and gives the name of infidel to none but bankrupts. There the Presbyterian confides in the Anabaptist, and the Churchman depends on the Quaker's word. At the breaking up of this pacific and free assembly, some withdraw to the synagogue and others to take a glass. . . . Others retire to their churches, and there wait for the inspiration of Heaven with their hats on, and all are satisfied.

Voltaire showed little interest in English party politics, and to all intents and purposes there were none in France. But he liked English liberty and toleration, though he was not all that enamoured of the ordinary people. For although he was to become one of the greatest champions of the oppressed and the wronged it is highly unlikely that he *loved* ordinary people for their own sake, whatever their nationality. And he certainly had his own prejudices, which included a streak of anti-semitism. It is unlikely that he would have agreed with Schiller: "*Seid umschlungen, Millionen! Diesen Kuss der ganzen Welt!*" (Oh, ye millions, I embrace ye! Here's a loving kiss for all the world!)

As a son of the *bourgeoisie* who had been first applauded and then beaten and even repudiated by members of the aristocracy, he had a somewhat ambivalent attitude towards class. In particular he was filled with wonder at the way men of letters were rewarded in England.

> In France Addison would have been a member of some Academy, and might have got, through some lady's influence, a pension of twelve hundred *livres*. . . . In England, he was Secretary of State. Newton was Master of the Mint; Congreve held an important appointment; Prior was a plenipotentiary; Dr Swift is an Irish Dean, and is made much more of in Ireland than the Primate himself. . . . Nothing so much encourages

English men of letters as the consideration which is shown them. The Prime Minister's portrait is on the wall of his own study; but in twenty houses I have seen the portrait of Pope.

In comparing the role of the aristocrat in France and in England Voltaire drew the reader's attention to the fact that Lord Townshend had a brother who was a City merchant, while an Earl of Oxford had a younger brother acting as an agent in Aleppo.

In France the merchant hears his profession so disdainfully spoken of that he is foolish enough to blush for it. Yet I do not know which is the more useful to the State, a well powdered Lord who knows to the moment the hour at which the King rises and at which he goes to bed, and who gives himself grand airs while he is really playing the part of a slave in a minister's ante-chamber, or a merchant who is enriching his country, who gives from his office orders for Surat or Cairo, and who contributes to the happiness of the world.

Such sentiments were tantamount to treason in the Paris of the 1730s.

Though possibly of little importance today, Voltaire's criticisms of Shakespeare in the *Letters on the English Nation* are entertaining, if to modern eyes wildly inaccurate. For while the observations on religion and the social structure show Voltaire at his crusading best, much of the part dealing with Shakespeare shows him at his journalistic worst. But it was not only Voltaire who regarded Shakespeare as belonging to some cultural pre-history, while anyone writing earlier than Elizabethan times hardly existed. Even Swift thought the Wife of Bath was a Shakespearian character. In regarding Shakespeare as at best a barbarous genius who had the misfortune not to be born a century later so that he could have profited from a study of the dramatic construction of a Racine or a Corneille, or even of Addison, Voltaire was merely reflecting the attitudes of his day.

In his opinion Addison's frigid tragedy *Cato* was a masterpiece which others could imitate with advantage. Dryden met with his approval, especially *Alexander's Feast*, an epic poem he particularly appreciated. Another poet he considered seriously underrated by his English contemporaries was the Earl of Rochester, whose merits are to this day still eclipsed by his no doubt justified reputation as a libertine and wit. Frequently Voltaire complains that Shakespeare was coarse and barbarous, and yet almost in the same breath he bestows his approval on Wycherley's *Country Wife* and *The Plain Dealer*. But even he had to write of *The Plain Dealer*: "The English play is an interesting one, and its intrigue is ingenious, but it is too daring for the French taste." Years later he was to make what amounted to a reworking of it, in French, under the title of *La Prude*.

At that time the English novel was still in its infancy, and he considered Richardson's *Clarissa* overwritten and long drawn out. His opinion of *Tom Jones* was little better, though he found more to approve of in *Tristram Shandy*: "A very unaccountable and original book, a mixture of buffoonery and philosophy." And that could quite well have been his verdict on Shakespeare.

Though he was an innovator, visionary and genius when it came to the theatre Voltaire was completely of his time, and accepted the strict conventions of the theatre which were only surpassed by those of the contemporary Italian *Opera Seria*.

With what pleasure I saw in London the tragedy of *Julius Caesar*, which has been the delight of your nation for a hundred and fifty years! [Voltaire was addressing Bolingbroke.] I certainly do not pretend to approve of the barbarous irregularities with which it abounds, the only astonishing thing is that there are not more of them in a work which was composed in an ignorant age, by a man who did not even know Latin, and whose only master was his genius. The French, perhaps, would not endure the appearance on their stage of a band of Roman artisans and plebeians, they would not permit Caesar's bleeding body should be exposed to the gaze of the people, and that the populace should be excited to vengeance from the public Rostrum. It is for custom, the queen of the world, to change the tastes of nations, and to turn into pleasure the objects we view with aversion.

Voltaire as a young man
after Largillière

Louis XV
after Rigaud

Time and again Voltaire would praise and damn Shakespeare in the same paragraph:

Shakespeare is a man of genius. The Italians, the French, and the men of letters of all countries who have not passed some time in England, take him for a mere mountebank of the fair, a droll far below harlequin, the sorriest buffoon who ever amused the mob. And yet in this same man there are passages which exalt the imagination and penetrate the heart. Truth and Nature themselves speak their own language without any mixture of art. He reaches sublimity without having searched for it.

What are we to conclude from this contrast of grandeur and coarseness, of sublime reason and gross foolery, and, in short, from all the contrasts that we find in Shakespeare? That he would have been a perfect poet if he had lived in the time of Addison.

The last sentiment is like wishing that Beethoven had modelled himself on Cherubini.

During the course of his long life Voltaire wrote some fifteen million words, and needless to say not all of them are pearls of great price. He could at times make comments that have all the smart superficiality of a journalist writing in a popular journal.

I am certainly very far from justifying the tragedy of *Hamlet* as a whole; it is a coarse and barbarous piece which would not be endured by the lowest of the populace of France or Italy. *Hamlet* becomes mad in the second act, and his mistress becomes mad in the third; the Prince, pretending to kill a rat, kills the father of his mistress, and the heroine throws herself into the river. Her grave is dug on the stage; gravediggers make puns worthy of them holding deaths-heads in their hands, and Prince Hamlet replies to their abominable coarseness by no less disgusting extravagances. Meanwhile one of the actors conquers Poland. Hamlet, his mother, and his step-father drink together on the stage; at table there is singing and quarrelling, fighting and killing. It would seem that such a work is the fruit of the imagination of a drunken savage. But, amid these gross irregularities, which even to the present day make the English stage absurd and barbarous, this play of *Hamlet*, by a still greater whimsicality, has sublime touches, worthy of the greatest genius. It seems that nature took pleasure in bringing together in Shakespeare's head the strongest and grandest imagination with the lowest and most detestable of dull grossness.

Yet it was Voltaire who aroused the interest of the French nation in Shakespeare and other English writers, starting what amounted to a fashion for things English. Indeed, towards the end of his life he came to regret having made Shakespeare known in France, with the result that his own gods, Racine and Corneille, were almost eclipsed. In 1768 he wrote somewhat peevishly to Horace Walpole:

> You have almost made your nation believe that I despise Shakespeare. I was the first to make Shakespeare known to the French; I translated passages from him forty years ago, as well as from Milton, Waller, Rochester, Dryden and Pope. I can assure you that before I did so no one in France knew anything about English poetry. . . .
>
> Destiny also decreed that I should be the first to explain to my fellow-countrymen the discoveries of the great Newton. I have been your apostle and your martyr, and it is really unjust that the English should complain about me. A very long time ago I said that if Shakespeare had appeared in the age of Addison he would have joined to his native genius the elegance and purity for which Addison is to be commended. I said that his genius was his own, and that his faults were the faults of his age.

The interest in Shakespeare and the English drama had an immediate effect on Voltaire. While he was still staying with Everard Falkener at Wandsworth he began a full-length tragedy, in English, about the early Roman consul Lucius Brutus, who lived at the time of Tarquin. *Brutus* had strong republican overtones, and included the downright revolutionary sentiment that the Senate's glory was to represent the people. One of the more obvious features of the Revolution of 1789 was the desire among some of its leaders for the trappings of republican Rome, and its ideas of democracy "for the people," which coloured the speeches and writings of many of the protagonists. Besides this work Voltaire set about translating the first two acts of *Julius Caesar* into French towards the end of his stay in England.

Discovery of the English writers occupied only part of his time in England. In addition to the notebooks kept in English of everything he saw and heard which stimulated his imagination he worked on his history of Charles XII of Sweden. Here he was fortunate. Not only did the Duchess of Marlborough give him an account of a meeting between her husband and the warrior-king, but also Bolingbroke introduced him to a minister who had known him during his exile in Turkey. Baron Fabrice had shared his master's misfortunes, and later he came to England as Chamberlain to George I. Now he was a mine of information for Voltaire. Most of the book was written in 1728, though not published (and, as was almost inevitable, banned) until 1731.

Charles XII was not only a most elegantly written biography, it was also important as a history by a European writer not written from a specifically Christian standpoint. In it nothing was considered to have been preordained by a Divine Providence, and in 1728 that in itself was revolutionary. Here for the first time was an objective essay in historical writing, and its most celebrated offshoot would be Gibbon's *Decline and Fall of the Roman Empire*.

All that would have been enough to occupy most men's time, but Voltaire was also fussing over the *Henriade*. In January 1728 the subscription list was opened, and in March it at last appeared, complete with the inevitable fulsome dedication, to Queen Caroline:

Madame, it is the fate of Henry the Fourth to be protected by the Queens of England. He was assisted by that famous Elizabeth, who was in her Age the Glory of her Sex, and the Pattern of Sovereigns. By whom can his Memory be so well protected, as by her in whom Elizabeth revives.

Businesslike as ever, Voltaire enlisted the aid of Swift to help promote the *Henriade* in Ireland. He assured the Dean: "The subscription will be but one guinea in hand." And two more guineas to be paid on publication. Even the Queen of Prussia sent Voltaire a medallion containing the portrait of her friend, the Queen of England; while George II gave him a sum reputed to be as much as 500 guineas. The English edition of the *Henriade* was to form the foundation of Voltaire's very considerable fortune, despite a brisk skirmish with a bookseller whom he considered was trying to cheat him. The first edition was lavish and, at three guineas, expensive, limited to 344 subscribers. But according to the author three less expensive editions were printed in as many weeks.

Much of the success of the *Henriade* was undoubtedly due to the fact that the original French edition had been denounced and banned by the Establishment, on the grounds that it was anti-Catholic. But a French Protestant refugee raised a discordant voice in the chorus of praise, claiming that the book must be anti-Protestant because nowhere did Voltaire condemn the Catholic religion outright.

"M. de Voltaire arrives in our island with a book against our religion," he fulminated. "He is received with open arms; the King and Queen send him presents; the nobility eagerly assist the publication of his book; from the highest to the lowest, all is rivalry to receive him well!"

Then, quite abruptly, the English interlude was over. In 1727 Voltaire had applied for permission to return to France for a limited period, but never followed it up. Then, in March 1729, he was back once again in his own country, with permission to live in Paris, though advised to keep away from the Court. He had been in exile for nearly three years, during which time he had taken stock of himself, and was able to see his country as others saw it—dispassionately and from without. He himself had changed. Now he was a mature adult with mental reserves in plenty for the many battles that lay ahead.

Chapter 7

LETTRES PHILOSOPHIQUES AND A
LETTRE DE CACHET

Voltaire was once again in Paris, but on the advice of Hénault he did not make himself conspicuous. The exile had left its mark. Not only was he enthusiastically in favour of the freedom of mind and body which he believed was to be found in England but he was still resentful of the injustice he had suffered at the hands of society in his own country. His true feelings were only revealed by the pen-name Voltaire chose for himself: Sanson, the family name for the *hommes rouges* who for generations had been the hereditary executioners of Paris. Some fifteen years after his own death the Sansons would come into their own in the Place de la Révolution as the *ancien régime* that he so despised was swept away in a sea of blood.

Although they were not without influence on his future life, and though the three years spent in England receive hardly a mention in the *Autobiography*, there is a reference to the fact that he had had the *Henriade*, banned in France, printed in England with the aid of an "immense subscription" raised by the then Princess of Wales:

Their liberality laid the foundation of his fortune: for on his return to France in 1728 he put money into a lottery established by Mr Desforts, Comptroller General of the Finances. The adventurers received a rent charge on the Hôtel-de-Ville for their tickets; the prizes were paid in ready-money; so that if a society had taken all the tickets, it would have gained a million of livres. He joined with a numerous company of adventurers, and was fortunate.

Voltaire's shrewd business instinct was never put to use more wittily than in the episode of the fund-raising lottery staged by the City of Paris. There was nothing particularly immoral in the fact that the poet-philosopher made a fortune after noticing that the Comptroller-General had miscalculated in the terms of the monthly draw. If Desforts could not get his sums right why should Voltaire and his acquaintances (including the Pâris-Duverney brothers) be considered to have acted dubiously in forming a company and buying up all the bonds on offer for that particular month? But they did, and made what can only be described as a killing. The Comptroller-General tried to induce the authorities to withhold the prize-money, but the members of the syndicate were declared the winners. Voltaire's share alone came to about a million francs. Everyone knew that he was the originator of the scheme, and in view of his unpopularity in official circles he decided to go and stay in the country with the Duc de Richelieu. Soon afterwards Desforts lost his job, and Voltaire felt it was safe to return.

Now, for the first time in his life, he was a man of some substance and no longer an impecunious poet dependent on the bounty of others for his survival. The change began to affect his whole outlook. Now Voltaire could afford to say what he really thought (not that he ever guarded his tongue), and make a stand on what he considered were matters of principle. In short, he could afford to have a social conscience. First there was the money from the English edition of the *Henriade*, and to that he now added his share of the Lottery. Only a few months later he repeated the whole episode—again very profitably too—with an issue of bonds in Lorraine. Nor was that all: under the terms of his father's will he was entitled at thirty-five to his share of the money.

When Voltaire went into exile in England he lost his pensions from the king and queen. But now he wrote to Cardinal Fleury, asking if they could be restored. The Cardinal refused to consider the suggestion, so he enlisted the help of a friend, who approached Maria Leszczynska. The initiative proved successful, and his pension was restored.

For the moment Voltaire could not claim that he was neglected or penniless, and considering the disfavour in which he was held in many quarters he was prospering to a remarkable degree. But the lull was not to last. His play *Brutus* was performed in December 1730, and thanks to friends and admirers the first night was a great success, but it only survived for fifteen performances before being withdrawn. The failure was due partly to the lack of human interest in the plot, and partly to its republican sympathies.

Next, the English edition of the *Henriade* was not allowed to be imported into France. Only a few copies reached Paris, the unbound sheets having been used as wrappings for other books. And after 2,600 copies of *Charles XII* had been printed it too was banned, the official reason being that it contained statements which if true would be displeasing to Augustus II, King of Poland. Voltaire was even taken to task for stating that Stanislas (Maria Leszczynska's father) dealt more leniently with prisoners of war than Augustus II. These criticisms provoked the author into one of his most celebrated retorts: "As if this true account contained anything injurious, and as if one owed to Kings who are dead anything but the truth."

In this case the fact was that the authorities were deliberately making trouble, and had Voltaire put it in writing that Paris was the capital of France the statement would probably have been suppressed as subversive. But official disapproval had the inevitable effect on a man of Voltaire's temperament. His reaction was to go to Rouen in order to induce the printer Jore to bring out an edition of *Charles XII*. He knew, too, that in that city he would be assured the protection of his old school friend Cideville, the President of the Rouen *Parlement*. Providing it did not last too long, excitement was a stimulus to Voltaire, and if he could add his own touch of theatricality, so much the better.

After giving out that he was going to England (to Canterbury in fact) Voltaire slipped away to Rouen, staying at L'Hôtel de Mantes, an inn hard by the cathedral. There he told anyone who might be interested that he was an English milord, who preferred to leave his own country for a while to escape from some unspecified persecution. Soon the proof-sheets of *Charles XII* were arriving regularly to be corrected.

The spring of 1730 was passed at a pleasant farmhouse outside the city. There, in a pastoral setting of apple-blossom and farmyard animals, the highly sophisticated Parisian worked away happily. Now he was correcting the proofs of the *Henriade*, as well as working on two more plays: *La Mort de César* and *Eriphyle*. *César* was heavily influenced by Shakespeare, though inevitably Voltaire made his tragedy conform to the unities of time and place, as well as casting it in Alexandrine couplets.

Even Thieriot was under the impression that he was in England, and in June Voltaire wrote to him: "I could not have done as much work in Paris in three years. But you know what a prodigious difference there is between a collected mind in a peaceful retreat, and a mind dissipated in the world." By September *Charles XII* was circulating privately in Paris, largely thanks to the assistance of the Duc de Richelieu.

Voltaire had seriously antagonised the authorities by introducing the banned *Henriade* into France, and then having *Charles XII* printed clandestinely after official permission had been withdrawn. But that was nothing to the hatred of the Church which he incurred in the matter of Adrienne Lecouvreur, the greatest actress of her age. In the eyes of the Church in France (but not in Italy) all actors, actresses and even playwrights were considered beyond respectable society, and were automatically denied Christian burial. Even Molière had to be interred at night and in haste, as though he had been an executed criminal.

Adrienne Lecouvreur's life had been unconventional, though no more so than that of many contemporary women of fashion. Her greatest love was the celebrated Maurice de Saxe, who came within grasping distance of the throne of Russia, and whose son she bore. In March 1730 Adrienne played Jocaste in *Oedipe*, and on the 15th of that month gave what was to be her last performance in any play. Towards the end she was taken ill with stomach pains, and returned to her home in the Rue de Marais, where once Racine had lived. There she was visited by Voltaire and the Comte d'Argental. The latter she renounced as a lover for his own good and for the honour of his family, expressing her feelings to his mother in a letter of great dignity and pathos (which foreshadowed a celebrated episode a century later first in the writings of Alexandre Dumas *fils* in *La Dame aux Camélias*, and later in Verdi's *La Traviata*).

Now Adrienne Lecouvreur was literally dying in Voltaire's

arms. Her stomach pains may have been made worse by the medicine which she had been taking, but later it was said she had been poisoned by a Polish rival for the love of Maurice de Saxe.

The Church only allowed confession to actors and actresses who believed themselves to be dying on condition that they signed a document promising to renounce the theatre as a profession should they recover. The priest from Saint-Sulpice came to the house, and not without a trace of bitterness Adrienne Lecouvreur assured him that she had not forgotten the poor of her parish in her will. Then she indicated a portrait of Maurice de Saxe, and quoted a line of verse: "*Voilà mon univers, mon espoir, et mes dieux.*" Soon afterwards she died, deserted by all her so-called friends other than Voltaire and d'Argental.

The two men then left the house, intending to return the following day. But not long after their departure it was visited by a police officer sent to make sure the body was not spirited away and given decent burial, contrary to the demands of the Church. At midnight the deceased actress was carried downstairs by two street porters and placed in a hired carriage which was driven to waste land near the Seine. There it was put in a hastily dug grave, covered with quick-lime, and buried by the light of lanterns. Then the earth was stamped down and so the thirty-seven-year-old actress was consigned to physical oblivion.

Voltaire was profoundly outraged. It was bad enough to persecute the living, but to exhibit such petty self-righteousness on the dead was obscene. By that one act the Church did more than anything to ensure his lifelong enmity. From that time onwards opposition to its oppressive power and intolerance would be a prime factor in his life. The authorities had stamped down the earth over her lifeless body, and his reply would be; "*Ecrasez l'Infame!*"

Fresh in his mind was the treatment accorded to actors and actresses in England, there the actress Anne Oldfield had actually been buried in Westminster Abbey. The whole episode was like a challenge to battle, and his first shot in the campaign was the poem *La Mort de Mlle Lecouvreur*, which included the following lines:

Que direz-vous, race future,
Lorsque vous apprenez la flétrissante injure
Qu'a ces arts désolés font des prêtes cruels?
Un objet digne des autels
Est privé de la sépulture!

What will you say, future race,
When you hear of the degrading injury
Done by cruel priests to the arts in mourning?
One worthy of altars is deprived of burial!

Then comes the inevitable comparison with England:

What, is it only in England that mortals dare to think?
O rival of Athens, London, happy land! No art despised there!
Lecouvreur in London would have been buried among kings
   and heroes and men of genius.
There the spirit of Greece lives on.
But the laurels of Apollo wither in the sterile fields of France.

Her epitaph could well have been the telling lines:

Elle a charmé le monde et vous l'en punisses.

She charmed the world and you punished her for it.

Angry and distressed though he was, Voltaire had no intention of
publishing the poem or even of letting it circulate in manuscript
form. But Thieriot not only read it aloud wherever he was
invited but allowed others to make copies. Voltaire was at Rouen,
still supervising the printing of the *Henriade* and *Charles XII*, when
he heard that the poem had reached the wrong ears. He knew
whom he had to thank:

I am told that you were in touch with people who have betrayed you with the aid of their good memory; the strongest
parts especially were remembered; these have been distorted;
they have reached the ears of the ministry and it is not safe for

me to return to France whither my work calls me. . . . Tell me whether you advise me to write or to speak, or to lie low and wait for better times.

Thieriot was still under the impression that Voltaire was really in England.

But Voltaire was not prepared to remain in obscurity for long. The next twelve months were to be a restless time, even by his standards. For a while he lived as the guest of the Comtesse de Fontaine-Martel, an intelligent but unattractive woman who maintained a literary salon in the grand tradition. It was in her private theatre that *Eriphyle* was given for the first time by actors from the Comédie Française. However, the venture failed, largely because of the number of privileged spectators who were allowed to seat themselves on chairs set on the stage itself. Later the custom was finally discontinued, through the efforts of Voltaire, to the relief of the actors. As it was, what should have been a highly dramatic appearance of a ghost in *Eriphyle* went for nothing, or at least nothing serious. But any setback inevitably spurred on Voltaire to further effort, and he set to work on *Zaïre*. Written at white-heat in twenty-two days, it was destined to become his greatest theatrical success.

The direct stimulus to write *Zaïre* came from complaints by the ladies among his play-going admirers that his stage works lacked a good love story. He set out to please them by writing a real tear-jerker—though one cast in Alexandrine couplets to conform with tradition. But even so Voltaire was not content merely to provide emotional satisfaction for the female half of his audience, and *Zaïre* became an impassioned plea for toleration for a couple united by love but divided by religion. And for Voltaire love was greater than the barrier that divided Christian from Moslem.

Zaïre is a beautiful girl who since infancy had been a captive in Jerusalem, unaware of her Christian origins. The Sultan of Jerusalem, Orosmane, loves her, and she returns his love in full measure. But, discovering her real identity from her brother, Néristan, who tells her that their father (also a captive) is dying, Zaïre promises to renounce Orosmane and to be baptised as a Christian. The effect of this is to make her love for the Sultan even greater than it was before. Orosmane becomes suspicious, and when she meets Néristan at a secret rendezvous he stabs her. Néristan then admits that although his sister wished to be baptised she none the less loved the Sultan more than anyone in the world. Filled with remorse Orosmane stabs himself and dies, much as "the noble Moor" had done in *Othello*.

The success of *Zaïre* eclipsed even that of *Oedipe*, and it was quickly translated into German, English and Italian (the last by Gozzi). With great pleasure Voltaire dedicated it to Everard Falkener, only to give offence to Parisian society, who felt that a poet and playwright should know his place, and dedicate his works to members of the aristocracy, not to unheard-of English merchants. The authorities even went so far as to express their disapproval by suppressing the dedication. The attitude of Parisians must more than ever have made Voltaire feel that he was justified in all that he had written in the *Letters on the English Nation*, soon to be published in French under the title *Lettres Philosophiques*.

Works which followed in quick succession at this time, 1732–3, included the charming *Les Vous et les Tu*, in which he gently chided the one-time Mlle de Livry for not wishing to know him socially after becoming the Comtesse de Gouvernet. The sting in the tail of the poem was the use of the informal *tu* in place of the formal *vous*. If anyone crossed his path professionally Voltaire could display the ferocity of a tiger, but in personal relationships he often revealed a forgiving and even gently humorous side.

Zaïre was followed by *Adélaide du Guesclin*, a romantic drama based on an episode in French history. And for private amusement Voltaire started *La Pucelle*, a bawdy and irreverent parody of a then celebrated poem about Joan of Arc by Chapelain. For years to come its recitation ensured his success at any houseparty. Such was the diversity of his talent that almost at the same time that he was writing this masterpiece of bad taste he was also working on *Le Temple du Goût* (The Temple of Taste).

While *Le Temple du Goût* has inevitably lost its impact, except as a survey of Voltaire's personal likes and dislikes, it none the less displays genuine feeling as well as satire. The piece is quaint, rather charming—and short. There is a musical quality about the structure, with prose and verse alternating like recitative and aria. The journey to the Temple of Taste is undertaken by the author in

94

the company of a cardinal and an abbé. The temple in question has been salvaged from the Classical world, and brought to France by Francis I. There it had been repaired by Cardinal Richelieu and later decorated by Louis XIV. Even before Voltaire reaches its hallowed walls he has sharpened his quill at the expense of scholarship for its own sake. Indignantly the pedants assure him they are not going to the Temple of Taste:

> Thank God, we have nothing to do with that. Taste is nothing; we are accustomed to record at length and in detail what was thought, but we ourselves do not think.

Next, the travellers meet a rich patron, fat and fast asleep. Between snores he informs the group of painters, sculptors, gilders, pseudo-connoisseurs and flatterers who surround him that he learns nothing and knows everything. The painter begs him to wake up and admire his genius, modestly declaring that Raphael never understood the art of decorating a palace. When the patron does wake up, a little bystander (*un petit curieux*) complete with lorgnette is at hand to advise him:

> "Glance at this, look here. It's for your chapel! On my word you must buy this picture. It's God the Father in His eternal glory, very courtly, and painted in the manner of Watteau!"

The visitors pass on, and there must have been a bird-like glitter in Voltaire's eye at the coming encounter with Jean Baptiste Rousseau, and with the Critic who acted as guardian of the Temple door. The Critic "with her severe and just eye" bars the way to the ceaselessly advancing Goths and Vandals. Here many are in for an unpleasant surprise:

> How many men of consequence, how many fashionable people who preside so imperiously at our little societies, are not received into the Temple, despite all the dinners they have given to the wits, and in spite of all the praise they had received in the press.

Voltaire dips his quill in vitriol and observes that the Critic also roughly repels "these obscure enemies of all outstanding merit, these insects of society, only noticeable because they sting."

Those refused admittance to the Temple include the Reverend Father Albert Garassus:

"I preached better than Bourdaloue, he claimed, for Bourdaloue never made people burn books; whereas I declaimed with such eloquence against Pierre Bayle, in a provincial district which though small was full of intelligence, that six of my hearers burnt his book."

But the Critic does not react as he expects:

"Go away, Brother Garassus, go, barbarian; leave the Temple of Taste; get out of my presence, you modern Visigoth, you have insulted the man who inspired me."

At this moment another versifier arrives, supported by two little satyrs, and crowned with laurels and thistles. Jean Baptiste Rousseau has also reached the Temple of Taste.

"I have come from Germany to see you," he informs the Critic, "I have come in the spring time." And he promptly breaks into bad verse which ends with "Brekek-kek-kek, koax, koax, koax." For his spitefulness the Muses have changed his voice into that of an Aristophanic frog. But the Critic allows him to enter the Temple, where he is enraged to find his arch-enemy Fontenelle installed in a place of honour. Of his own accord Rousseau leaves, bent on shaping a spiteful epigram, while Fontenelle watches his departure "with philosophic compassion," thus making the whole episode more telling than if Rousseau had never even crossed the threshold of the Temple. Evidently Rousseau tried his hand at writing operas, but they have vanished and only the name of one is known, *Adonis*. In the name of good taste Voltaire exhorts him to burn them along with his comedies, allegories, odes, German epigrams, ballads and sonnets.

Having vented his spleen, Voltaire then takes a kindlier look at the arts and personages gathered within the Temple of Taste. There the travellers encountered Mme de Sévigné: "Loved by all those who inhabit the Temple," and today best remembered for her letters to her daughter and that timeless line: "The more I see of men, the more I admire dogs."

Nearby is Ninon de Lenclos, who delivers a short discourse on the subject of sensuality, and Adrienne Lecouvreur. Even the Jesuits are included, their contribution to good taste lying in the fact that in Voltaire's opinion they wrote the best *belles lettres*. Here all the arts are reviewed, giving us an insight into Voltaire's own remarkably sound tastes. For most of his judgements in the arts have been endorsed by posterity.

All Lully's operas are offered to the God of Taste, as well as several by Destouches and Campra; though the God is made to wish that Lully's airs were a little less frigid. In the Library the travellers notice that all the books are new editions.

"The works of Marot and Rabelais are reduced to five or six pages. Saint-Everemont [*sic*], to a very small volume. Bayle, by a single volume."

Among the great writers also present is Corneille, whom Voltaire is glad to note has at last "joined a spirit of discontent to his vast genius"; while the elegant, tender and ingenious Racine holds up portraits of the principal characters he has depicted in his plays, including Bajazet, Britannicus and Titus.

Then there is La Fontaine with his fables, but the Master of Parnassus is none other than Voltaire's old friend Boileau. Molière is there of course, and even the great Colbert, for as much as anything *Le Temple du Goût* is Voltaire's own panegyric to *Le Grand Siècle*. How he wishes that Louis XIV had directed his energies towards embellishing Paris rather than waging war, as then it would have surpassed Rome in its taste and magnificence. In addition, his aversion to the art of the Middle Ages is aired. "*Un jour, vous n'aurez plus de Temples Gothiques.*" A statement which happily has not come true.

Architecture comes in for considerable attention. Laid on the altar of the Temple of Taste is the plan of the façade of the Louvre: "which was constructed by Louis le Vau, an admirable man, and too little known." Voltaire goes on to praise the Porte Saint-Denis; the statues on the Fontaine des Innocents, and the portal of Saint-Gervais. The plan of Versailles is also laid on the altar, though the God of Taste has put an interdiction on it, or at least on the side fronting the *Cour d'Honneur*: "*Un chef-d'oeuvre de mauvais goût et de magnificence.*"

There is even a model of the Château des Maisons, whose exterior is coupled with the interior of the Hôtel Lassay, making in the eyes of the God of Taste a perfect whole. René de Maisons, whose Château Voltaire has just immortalised, died in 1731 in Paris, at the age of thirty, having been President of the *Parlement* for more than ten years. As a tribute to his friend—whose untimely death from smallpox has deeply distressed Voltaire—he includes him among those admitted to a place in the Temple. There they meet, and the reunion brings tears to the eyes of Voltaire, who wishes that it had been he, and not René de Maisons, who had died. Of all the assembled personages it is he who receives the most open-hearted tribute from the traveller to the Temple of Taste.

Obviously *Le Temple du Goût* was written in a hurry, and consequently Voltaire revised it more than once. The first edition included a chapter from the *Letters on the English Nation* which, together with references to Ninon de Lenclos (and a few other brief passages), were omitted from the later editions, including the one published at Amsterdam later the same year, and again in 1738–9. But in the latter edition there was no attempt to placate either Church or State. By then the mutual hatred, in particular with the Church, had made any moderation on his part inconceivable.

Voltaire had discovered that the most deadly and effective weapon with which to fight tyranny, in any form, was ridicule. The more it was allied to moderation, the more effective it would be. Both Church and State hated *Le Temple du Goût* (the former because of a very mild reference to the Papacy, and its infallibility). He had also dared to mock the arbiters of fashion in all the arts who had the approval of the Establishment; but he had done so without himself overstepping the bounds of taste. The fact he could now do so (when he wished) is indicative of the maturity he had achieved during his three years in England. Thus, although he was quite capable of producing a smutty epic such as *La Pucelle* for private circulation, he was also now able to join his wit with seriousness of purpose, as in *Le Temple du Goût*. Some twenty years later this union would culminate in *Candide*. Also, though it would be a considerable while before they formed part of a book, the ideas and opinions which he would express in the *Dictionnaire Philosophique* were already forming in his mind, and the passing of time would only make them more sharply defined.

Voltaire, the thinking, suffering man, was fully fledged by 1734, his fortieth year. He would still be capable of much that was reprehensible, but from now on his escapades, serious or otherwise, call for no harsher criticism. Now he was a man with a conscience, although it would still be many years before it really showed itself in his championing of the greatly wronged. What he did to rehabilitate Calas, Sevrien, La Barre and General Lally seems at this distance of time worth nearly all his philosophical and scientific writing put together. Capable of the most profound flights of reasoning, he was also capable of sharing almost physically the torture inflicted on such as Calas or La Barre. The result was that he would pursue what he saw to be justice and truth without regard for open hostility and the very real danger of physical harm.

The *Dictionnaire Philosophique*, with its separate entries for nearly everything that he considered of interest, was to be a summing-up of what he had learnt and thought out for himself during the first half of his life. And, what was more, it would be written in elegant and lucid prose, for, unlike so many philosophers, Voltaire was capable of expressing himself clearly and in language which can be easily understood. But then he himself declared he was no metaphysician. Not only did he make people examine their beliefs, but also their consciences.

If the *Dictionnaire Philosophique* was the fruit of his intellect, the *Lettres Philosophiques* were to be the fruit of his powers of observation. Their publication would result in a fifteen-year retirement from the literary and social battlefields of Paris to the idyllic delights of the Château de Cirey. But now, for all his badinage, Voltaire had come to take the world seriously, and the authorities were well aware of it, especially after the publication of the *Lettres Philosophiques*. From now on the savage laws against dissidents and those who spoke out against the abuses of Church and State would make it necessary for him to lie on frequent occasions, disowning the authorship of numerous books and pamphlets.

Voltaire's cynicism was born of necessity, and the extent to which his writings upset the Establishment can be gathered from an interchange between the Chancellor, d'Aguesseau, and his secretary on the occasion of the publication of *Epître à Uranie*. There were few pieces Voltaire had written which were more likely to give offence to the authorities, and a copy was handed to d'Aguesseau. He asked his secretary what should be done with such a man as Voltaire. "Monseigneur," the man replied, "Voltaire should be locked up somewhere out of reach of pen, ink and paper. He is capable of destroying a state."

Voltaire knew that by bringing out the *Lettres Philosophiques* he was asking for trouble, but even so he went ahead. He was not acting as one who wished to cause a sensation for its own sake, but as a writer who had something serious to say which he felt should reach the ears of all. The publisher would again be Jore of Rouen. He and his father before him had a reputation as men who did not fear the restrictions of the censor, and in fact the father had been imprisoned three times in the Bastille. It was thanks to the intervention of Voltaire himself that the son was saved from also going there in 1731, for publishing an account of an ecclesiastical trial, with a preface by the Abbé Desfontaines. Now, in 1733, it was Jore who was publishing the *Lettres Philosophiques*.

Copies of the original version, the *Letters on the English Nation*, had circulated in Paris, and news of the activities at Rouen had reached the ears of the authorities. Hastily Voltaire wrote to Jore to hide the edition at the house of a friend, and when a detective arrived he found nothing. But both author and printer narrowly escaped being sent to the Bastille.

"It seems that Jore has a fixed vocation for that delightful abode," wrote Voltaire. "I shall try to evade the honour of accompanying him."

The publication of the *Lettres* was not the only undertaking that Voltaire had in hand. He was trying his luck as a match-maker with his old schoolfriend the Duc de Richelieu. In a letter to Cideville he wrote:

I am on my way to a wedding that I have brought about. It has long been in my mind to make the Duc de Richelieu marry

Mademoiselle Guise. I have worked it out, like a comedy plot, the *dénouement* is to take place at Montjeu, near Autun.

Meanwhile one or two copies of the *Lettres* were sent to Paris by Jore to be specially bound for Voltaire's own use. But the bookbinder seized the chance to bring out a pirated edition for his own profit. Now there were two versions being produced illegally. While Voltaire and Jore were still waiting for what they considered would be the most auspicious moment to release their copies, the unscrupulous bookbinder launched his edition in Paris.

But for the time being perhaps even the *Lettres Philosophiques* took second place in Voltaire's thoughts. He had just remade the acquaintance of the woman he was to call "the divine Emilie."

When she was a child, Gabrielle Emilie Le Tonnelier de Breteuil had met Voltaire at his father's house, though the meeting had made so little impression on her that she remembered nothing of it. In the spring of 1733 their paths crossed again, when she came as a visitor to the poet's house in the Rue du Long-Pont. The child he had known had grown into a charming and extremely intelligent woman of twenty-seven. Since the age of nineteen she had been the wife of the Marquis du Châtelet, and was the mother of three children, two boys and a girl.

The marriage was typical of its class and time. The couple were fond of each other, but not to the extent that it would expose them to the ridicule of their acquaintances, as was the case with the Maréchal-Duc de Villars. They appeared together in public, but in most other respects they went their own ways. The inclinations of the Marquis took him to Court and to the field of battle, while Emilie du Châtelet preferred the quiet of the study, where she sought out the best scientific and philosophical brains of the day.

This was not to say that her life was that of a celibate: far from it. She showed a sturdy appetite for love, and, ever-practical, she combined it with the pursuit of knowledge by becoming the reputed mistress of the scientist Maupertuis. In fact she integrated her social and intellectual life in a manner worthy of a philosopher, which was what she most wished to be considered. In an age in which elegance was less artificial than it would become with the full flowering of the Rococo it was possible for society ladies to become the pupils of philosophers or scientists without being thought *poseurs* or eccentrics.

In Nattier's portrait "the divine Emilie" appears as a woman with large, kindly features, not strikingly beautiful, but with an air of confidence and determination. She was the sort of person who could be relied upon to remain calm and sensible in a time of crisis, and of whom people would say: "Emilie will know. Ask Emilie." From her appearance one would never have guessed her to be the translator of Newton's *Principia* from Latin into French.

That the Marquise had a mind of her own is shown by the fact that she was a supporter of the philosophy of Newton, and not that of Descartes. As Voltaire was the apostle of Newtonian philosophy in France it was inevitable that she should gravitate towards him. Like most women she fell under his charm, and before long intellectual attraction had turned to a love, which was warmly returned by Voltaire.

Their relationship was to prove the most satisfactory episode of its kind in his life, for its basis was not simply sexual but also expressed the common interests of two highly intelligent beings. In later years it was a matter of relief for Voltaire when Emilie looked elsewhere for physical satisfaction. But neither could foresee that the taking of another lover would result in the birth of a child that would kill her, to Voltaire's profound grief; a grief quite without rancour towards the father.

All that lay in the future, and for the present Voltaire had gone off into the country south of Paris to attend the Duc de Richelieu's wedding. With him was Mme du Châtelet. She knew all about the *Letters on the English Nation*, and was well aware of the existence of the French edition about to be distributed in Paris. Evidently she expected trouble, for she instructed a servant to take horse and warn Voltaire as soon as he heard that the authorities were planning action against him.

Her fears were justified. In June 1733 the pirated edition appeared in Paris, and to make bad worse it included *Remarks* on the thoughts of M. Pascal, a chapter which was bound to give offence to the Church. And there on the title page for all to see was his name. In the discourse on Pascal the author agreed that he was one of the greatest Christian thinkers of the seventeenth century, but he expressed reservations about the overall merits of his celebrated *Pensées*. The book, he claimed, was not a finished work, but consisted of ideas and first drafts which would have required considerable revision had Pascal lived. Not only was he incapable of sympathising with his religious beliefs but Voltaire considered his style deliberately obscure. When Pascal wrote " . . . let the truth of religion be recognised in its very obscurity, in the little understanding of it that we have, and in our indifference about knowing it," Voltaire was stung to retort: "What strange marks of truth Pascal advances! What other marks does falsehood possess? What! In order to be believed it would be enough to say: *I am obscure*; *I am unintelligible*." For Voltaire, Pascal took a too despairing view of man's lot in this world, and on another occasion he was to comment:

He taught men to hate themselves.
I should like, despite him, to teach them to love each other.

Now such sentiments, as well as his views on class, religious toleration and government in England, were being read avidly all over Paris. The authorities took immediate action. Assuming that it must be an edition brought out by Jore, the printer was ordered to the Bastille. There he disclosed that in fact his edition was stacked away in the house of Voltaire's friend de Formont in Rouen. An immediate search was ordered of Voltaire's house in Paris, and a cupboard containing papers and money was taken to the Lieutenant of Police.

That was the least that Voltaire had to worry about. A *lettre de cachet* had been issued for his arrest, and a messenger dispatched by Mme du Châtelet's servant was galloping towards Montjeu to warn him to flee. In Paris the *Lettres Philosophiques* were condemned by the authorities as being "scandalous and offensive to religion, good morals and respect owed to the State, [and it] should be burnt by the executioner, at the foot of the great stairway." The great stairway was in the Cour de Mai of the Palais de Justice, and there the public hangman first tore up and then burnt the book on 10 June 1733.

Voltaire's courage lay in having said what needed saying in the *Lettres*, and there was nothing to be gained by offering himself for martyrdom, and he left Montjeu with all speed. He turned eastward, entering the independent Duchy of Lorraine, where he would be safe from French jurisdiction. The Marquis du Châtelet owned a château at Cirey. It was neglected, in a state of disrepair, and miles from anywhere—except the frontier between France and Lorraine. What better place could there be for Voltaire? Not only would Emilie have him all to herself, but at the first whisper of danger he could take horse and be over the frontier and into safety.

The poet-philosopher might have felt pleased with the marriage he had arranged between the Duc de Richelieu and Marie de Guise, but the bride's family were not altogether happy about the alliance. Once the Guise had been one of the most important and influential families in France, even rivalling the ruling house of Valois. The conduct of the present Duc and Duchesse de Guise was a matter of gossip and scandal, but the fact they added nothing to the lustre of the family name did not stop them or their relations from criticising others. The Duc de Richelieu was the great-nephew of the celebrated Cardinal, but even so the Guise did not consider his family the equal of theirs, overlooking the fact that Marie de Guise brought no dowry with her, because her parents were unable to provide one. To their way of thinking Marie de Guise was marrying beneath herself. The Richelieu title only dated from the fifteenth century, and in a society where only the "old nobility," whose titles were created before 1400, had the right of entry to the private apartments of the sovereign and his consort, such a detail was of vital importance. So strongly did some members of the Guise family feel about the match that two of the bride's cousins, the Prince de Lexin and the Prince de Pons, refused to sign the contract. For Lexin his attitude was to have tragic consequences.

Meanwhile, Voltaire was not yet free from his own worries. At the beginning of May the authorities had decided to act, and sent the order for his arrest to Dijon, which precipitated his flight into Lorraine. It was there that he heard that Richelieu, who was in the Army, had challenged the Prince de Lexin to a duel after being insulted. Off he went to join his old schoolfriend, perhaps feeling in some part responsible for the present situation.

There was nothing Voltaire could do to stop the duel, which

ended with the death of Lexin and the wounding of Richelieu. But as a philosopher who hated war the visit to the battle front must have given him much food for thought. The cause of the war, which had taken the French well into Germany, was Stanislas Leszczynsky. Polish kings were not hereditary rulers, but were elected by the nobles, and for a second time the already exiled Stanislas had been chosen. But the throne was occupied by Augustus II, placed there by Charles VII, acting in collusion with Russia. Louis XV backed his father-in-law, and so France was now at war with the Empire.

What Voltaire saw was the siege of Philippsburg, near Karlsruhe, which was being defended by Prince Eugene. All his life the onlooker had a horror of suffering and the futility of such wars, and in a letter to the Marquise du Châtelet he commented: "*Voila, Madame, la folie humaine dans toute sa gloire et dans toute son horreur.*" But by and large he did not take the campaign much more seriously than those officers engaged in its execution. They welcomed his presence as a diversion from more serious matters. Everyone knew why he was there, to avoid a *lettre de cachet* ordering him to be detained in the fortress of Auxonne, and all regarded that as a great joke.

Voltaire went wherever he chose in and about the French camp, and on one occasion he was arrested as a spy. Later he remarked to Frederick the Great, "Actually, I was always afraid that the powers-that-be would have me hanged instead of drinking with me."

His friend, the Comtesse de Neuville owned a country house not far from Cirey, and for a while he stayed there. For Voltaire the *vie vagabonde*, which had lasted since his return from England, was nearly over, at least for the next sixteen years. In August 1734 he left the Comtesse to move into the empty Château de Cirey, where he had been offered a home by the Marquis and Marquise du Châtelet. In addition he was given *carte blanche* to make such improvements and additions as he chose, which he paid for out of his own pocket, and eventually he added a whole new and elegant wing.

Chapter 8

"THEY RETIRED TO CIREY"

He was intimately acquainted with the illustrious Marchioness of Châtelet, with whom he studied the principles of Newton, and the systems of Leibniz. They retired to Cirey, in Champagne, for several years, two of which Mr Kaenig, an eminent mathematician, passed with them. Mr Voltaire caused a gallery to be erected, where they performed all the experiments on light and electricity.

Thus Voltaire described the beginning of the longest single episode in his life, until his final retirement to Ferney. The brief autobiography written in the third person, is yet another important piece of Voltaire's writings which Theodore Besterman has rescued from oblivion. It appears as an appendix to his *Voltaire* published in 1969. Originally published in French and English in 1776 under the title of *Commentaire*, it is not to be confused with the *Mèmoires* written in 1759.

Although he was retiring to the depths of the country (the nearest town of any size was Nancy, some fifty miles away), a peaceful existence devoted to writing and to carrying out scientific experiments with Mme du Châtelet was not what lay ahead. Voltaire could not for long remain out of trouble with the authorities, just as a child who has been warned not to touch a hot stove frequently does just that, and then is loudly and tearfully astonished when it gets hurt. So Voltaire courted trouble with at least two poems, *La Pucelle* (The Virgin) and *Le Mondain* (The Worldly One), the second of which was completed at Cirey. He even managed to be surprised that the resulting furore forced him to seek temporary safety in the Netherlands. Not unnaturally he could not resist showing what he had written to his friends, and they in their turn made copies for their own use, despite promises not to do so.

Another lesson he never learnt was that because something seemed a self-evident truth to him, particularly in matters of belief (or what he regarded as superstition), everyone else would also share his point of view, or even be grateful for having their ideas jolted. But for the present there was nothing more vexatious on his horizon than the petty frustrations and delays attendant on building work at the château. For three months Voltaire exercised his taste and judgement at Cirey, and day by day the old place came alive again.

In Paris Mme du Châtelet pursued her studies with Maupertuis, but in September her third and youngest child died, a boy little more than a year old. As a result it was October before she appeared at Cirey, worn out by a particularly uncomfortable journey, and surrounded by no less than two hundred parcels and packets. By nature Voltaire was gregarious, and within days of his own arrival at Cirey he was enjoying the company of two new acquaintances, M. and Mme Champbonin, as well as the Comtesse de Neuville, who was already known to him. He might be the most celebrated man of letters in Europe, but it was as a charming and friendly neighbour that they and others in the district were to come to know and love him; and love is not too strong a word. His language, both written and spoken, was at times so gushing that it might seem to smack of insincerity, but for all that he had a kind heart and the gift of making people feel they mattered to him and that he was glad of their friendship. It is something that comes out time and again in his letters, and forms a side to his nature which provides a pleasant contrast to his literary quarrels.

Professional criticism of his writings was his blind spot. Voltaire never failed to take offence, whether or not there were grounds for doing so, and he pursued his enemies down the years with relentless ill-will worthy of a better cause. But such was the affection in which he was held that when he and his host and hostess all went off to Brussels together in 1739 their neighbours at Cirey were left desolate. His absence was only temporary, but even so they missed his clarity and, what was more important in day-to-day relationships, his warmth. Indeed, M. Champbonin wrote to his son, "There never has been a friend with a kinder heart or more worthy of respect. He leaves adored by the whole countryside, and we all lament his absence."

Although most of Voltaire's friends possessed titles his social life was not a conscious upwards ascent like that of Proust. He and many of the aristocracy accepted each other in a way far removed from the days when as a precocious young man he had exclaimed at the Prince de Conti's: "Here we are all princes or poets!" He had matured from being a fashionable young wit, poet and darling of the salons into something far deeper, justifying the affection of those who really knew the man and not merely his reputation.

Among Voltaire's gifts was the ability to sustain a friendship over many years without frequent meetings. Such a case was that of Everard Falkener. Apart from their unrecorded first meeting in Paris, and the occasions when Voltaire was his guest at Wandsworth, he never met him again after returning from England. But till the time of Falkener's death in 1758 they corresponded regularly, and a number of Voltaire's letters have survived.

About a year after taking up residence at Cirey he heard that his English friend had been knighted and appointed Ambassador to the Porte at Constantinople. At once he wrote to him in English.

18 September 1735

My dear friend! Your new title will not change my sentiments nor my expressions. My dear Falkener! friendship is full of talk, but it must be discreet. In the hurry of business you are in, remember only I talk'd to you, about seven years ago, of that very same embassy. Remember I am the first man who did foretell the honour you enjoy. Believe, then, no man is more pleased with it than I am, I have my share in your happiness.

If you pass through France in your way to Constantinople, I advise you I am but twenty leagues from [the road from] Calais, almost in the road to Paris. The Castle is called Cirey, four miles from Vassy la Champagne, on Saint-Dizier's road, and eight miles from Saint-Dizier. The post goes thither. There lives a young lady called the Marquise Du Châtelet, whom I have taught English to, and who longs to see you. You will lie here, if you remember your friend.

But Falkener took a different route to the Mediterranean, and for a while Voltaire toyed with the idea of visiting him on the shores of the Sea of Marmara, and in those days it would have been not so much a journey as an adventure, for the cultural and religious gulf between Turkey and Europe was infinitely greater than the mere geographical distance.

Cirey 22 February 1736
But I must bid adieu! to the great town of Constantin, and stay in my little corner of the world, in that very same castle where you were invited to come in your way to Paris, in case you should have taken the road of Calais to Marseille. Your taking an other way, was certainly a sad disappointment for me, and especially to that lady who makes use of your Locke and of more of your other books. Upon my word! a French lady who reads Newton, Locke, Addison and Pope, and who retires from the bubbles and the stunning noise of Paris, to cultivate in the country the great and amiable genius she is born with, is more valuable than your Constantinople, and all the Turkish Empire.

Most of Voltaire's letters to Everard Falkener after this date contain offhandedly affectionate references to Mme du Châtelet.

Bruxelles 2 March 1740
Dear Sir, I take the liberty to send you my old follies, having no new things to present you with. I am now at Bruxelles with the same lady Madame du Châtelet, who hindered me some years ago from paying you a visit at Constantinople, and whom I shall live with in all probablity the greatest part of my life, since for these ten years I have not departed from her. She is now at the trouble of a damn'd suit in law, that she pursues in Bruxelles. We have abandoned the most agreeable retirement in the country, to bawl here in the grotto of the Flemish chicane. . . . I hope I shall return to Paris with Mme du Châtelet in two years' time. If, about that season, you return to dear England by the way of Paris, I hope I shall have the pleasure of seeing your dear Excellency at her house, which is without doubt one of the finest in Paris, and situated

in a position worthy of Constantinople; for it looks upon the river and a long tract of land interspers'd with pretty houses, is to be seen from every window. Upon my word, I would with all that, prefer the vista of the Sea of Marmara before that of the Seine, if I could live without the lady, whom I look upon as a great man, and as a most solid and respectable friend. She understands Newton; she despises superstition, and in short, she makes me happy.

Two years later Voltaire was still regretting—and at the same time revelling in—his bondage.

If I have forgot the scraps of English I once had gathered, I'll never forget my dear ambassador. I am now at Paris, with the same she-philosopher I have lived with there these twelve years past. Was I not so constant in my bargains for life, I would certainly come and see you in your kiosk, in your quiet and your glory.

Emilie du Châtelet must indeed have been a remarkable woman. Without reservation Voltaire had accepted her as his equal, and that estimation of her abilities remained even after his infatuation had given way to an almost platonic relationship. Obviously she was a very intelligent woman, but with such men as Maupertius, Voltaire and Koenig at her elbow to direct her thoughts, how much of her thinking or philosophical writing was original? There were those who declared very little. But for the most part her critics were either consciously or unconsciously jealous of her hold over Voltaire, and the fact that she kept him all to herself at some godforsaken place no one had ever heard of. She had in fact carried off the biggest literary prize in Europe, to the intense annoyance of a large number of people.

The beginning of their life together at Cirey was curious. No sooner had Mme du Châtelet arrived from Paris with all her parcels than Voltaire immediately departed for Brussels. Whether she had brought news that he was in danger is a matter for conjecture, but it was not until the following year that they were both established at the Château de Cirey, leading the life that she had originally envisaged.

The Marquise might have had a formidable intellect, but she was woman enough (as Voltaire confided to Mme Champbonin) to want to change all the alterations he had planned at the château, and put doors where he wanted windows, and chimneys where he had wanted staircases. Now it was she who left Cirey, to spend Christmas in Paris, while Voltaire remained alone in the country. After the excitements and upheavals of the previous twelve months he was now quite isolated, apart from such neighbours as M. and Mme Champbonin. The desire and the opportunity to work without interruption was his, and he settled down to writing the play *Alzire*, as well as adding more cantos to *La Pucelle*. It was a striking example of a creative talent producing two violently contrasted works at the same time. The former was as high-minded as the latter was bawdy.

Alzire was to mark another step forward in Voltaire's development as a playwright. In *Zaïre* he had fashioned a romantic tragedy out of two lovers divided by religion. Now he took a more profound look at Christian morality, and in particular whether the coming of Christianity was an unmixed blessing, at least so far as the races of America were concerned. The preface itself drove yet another wedge between himself and the Church, containing as it did the following outspoken sentiments:

The religion of a barbarian is to offer to his gods the blood of his enemies. An ignorant Christian is often no better. To be assiduous in certain useless practices, and to ignore the true duty of man; to pray, but to keep one's vices; to fast, but to hate; to conspire, to persecute, such is his religion. That of the true Christian is to consider all men as his brothers, to do good and to forgive evil.

The complicated plot describes the love of Alzire, daughter of the Inca King Montèze, for Gusman, who has recently succeeded his father as Governor of Peru. His father has been in favour of leniency towards the Incas, but Gusman wants to take a harsher line. At the end of the play Alzire's former love, Zamore, whom she had believed dead, returns and fatally wounds Gusman in a battle against the Spanish conquerors. Zamore is offered his life by the dying Governor provided he becomes a

Christian (Alzire is already converted). He refuses. The dying Gusman still forgives him and Alzire, who has helped in the rebellion.

By modern standards *Alzire* was a farrago of dramatic conventions, but it had the distinction of being the first play by a Frenchman to be set in America, and its exotic costumes must in themselves have been something of a sensation. Also, in *Alzire* Voltaire did not assume that the Spanish must be all good because they were Christians (a verdict which history has since endorsed in the light of their activities as colonists in Central and South America), and that all the Indians must be bad because they were not. That in itself was radical thinking in 1735, well before Jean-Jacques Rousseau made the cult of the "noble savage" fashionable in the drawing-rooms of Europe.

As it was, the thinking playgoer was left with the inescapable feeling that Gusman's magnanimous gesture was motivated less by a sense of Christian forgiveness than by political expediency. Certain lines, taken out of context, were bound to give offence to Voltaire's opponents. For instance;

> The pitiless rage of your countrymen
> Has made them as hateful as their God.

But *Alzire* is not as simple as that. Voltaire was not merely using the wronged Incas as a mouthpiece for his own sentiments. His argument has much in common with the celebrated observation attributed to him (and later quoted by Bismarck among others): "God is on the side of the big battalions"; or its equally cynical variant, "God is on the side of those who shoot best."

To most of his contemporaries Voltaire's play was a beautiful tragedy in which non-Christians of noble character embraced the spirit of Christianity. Gusman's harsh treatment of the Incas is atoned for, at least in his own eyes, by his forgiveness of Zamore and Alzire, when he declared almost with his dying breath:

> Montèze, Americans, who were my victims,
> Consider that my clemency has surpassed my crimes.

Alzire was a play in which different people could find different meanings, but there was nothing ambiguous about its success when it was given in January 1736. If not quite the long-running success that *Oedipe* had been, it ran for twenty performances, and was given twice in the presence of the Court. According to the journal *Mercure de France* it netted Voltaire 53,000 *livres*, all of which he gave to the actors and actresses; a generous custom he was to maintain to the end of his life. The only factor to spoil Voltaire's triumph was that he could not be present. To the authorities he was still *persona non grata* in Paris, so he remained in the remoteness and safety of Cirey. When he heard of the play's success he commented sourly that as far as the Parisians were concerned his absence seemed to make their hearts grow fonder.

Voltaire had an undoubted talent for friendship, though its recipients were not always worthy of the affection he lavished on them, or the trouble he took on their behalf. One such was Thieriot, and another was the Abbé Linant. The latter was a plump, shortsighted young man with a stammer, who had poetic aspirations which aroused Voltaire's interest. He recommended his new friend to Cideville, the President of the Rouen *Parlement*. In the days when large households were the rule rather than the exception among the well-to-do his position was that of an undefined hanger-on. Like Thieriot he was extremely lazy, and apparently under the impression that the world owed him a living.

"What shall I do with him? "asked Voltaire on one occasion, for he was well aware that he was befriending a very lame duck. "He can't become a secretary, as he cannot write legibly, and I very much fear that he has the amiable quality of laziness, which is no small vice in a man who has to make his career." Couldn't Cideville secure a position for him with the Archbishop of Rouen? For years Voltaire concerned himself about the bumptious young man's future: even giving him an outline based on the life of Rameses to turn into a play, which needless to say was never written.

In Paris Linant did nothing to justify Voltaire's hopes that one day he would become a successful poet. Against Mme du Châtelet's wishes he invited the Abbé to come to Cirey as tutor to her son. Her objections were fully justified, since she first had to teach the new tutor enough Latin to pass on to her son. The boy was to grow up to become an Ambassador to the Court of St James's, only to perish during the Revolution.

Linant, however, was not only very lazy but also extremely tactless. He actually wrote to Mme du Châtelet, while staying away from the château though still in the neighbourhood, that "the tediousness of Cirey is of all tediousnesses the greatest." Emilie was all for dismissing him, but Voltaire interceded on his behalf. In fact, not only was he forgiven but his demand—it was no less—that his sister should join the establishment as a governess was accepted. Finally, however, both brother and sister proved so insufferable that they were dismissed. Michel Linant died in 1750 "of poverty brought on by his own laziness." Voltaire's friendship with Everard Falkener showed the poet at his most open-hearted and good-natured, while his quarrels with the Abbé Desfontaines and J. B. Rousseau revealed him at his most waspish. Both aspects of his character were in evidence during his life in the heart of the Champagne countryside.

Ever since he had saved Desfontaines from the stake the Abbé had nursed an irrational grudge against him, though to his face he assured him of his eternal gratitude and good wishes. But he wrote a most spiteful review attacking *Le Temple du Goût*.

The feud between them continued to develop. One of the most important books Voltaire wrote on scientific matters was *Eléments de la philosophie de Newton* (published in 1738) in which he made Newton's ideas comprehensible to educated Frenchmen. Since nearly everything Newton had written contradicted the theories of the revered Descartes, some savants attacked Voltaire and his *Eléments*. He replied: "Apparently a poor Frenchman is not allowed to express his belief in the proven existence of a general gravitational force, or of a vacuum in space, or that the earth is flat at the poles, and that Descartes' theory is absurd".

Voltaire delayed publication of the book in France, hoping vainly for official approval from the minister whose secretary had once remarked that he was capable of destroying a state, but an unscrupulous printer went ahead with a pirated edition: even getting a mathematician to provide the last chapter, which Voltaire had cannily withheld in an attempt to stop just such a thing happening. On its title page the work was inscribed as *mis à la portée de tout le monde*: made comprehensible for everybody. When Desfontaines reviewed it the sentence came out as *mis à la porte de tout le monde*; shown the door by everybody.

Voltaire reading to Frederick the Great, contemporary engraving

Sans Souci, Potsdam, the summer residence of Frederick the Great

Catherine the Great, Empress of Russia,
drawing by *Staal*, engraved by *W. H. Mote*

It was one thing for Voltaire to mock other writers, as when he said that J. B. Rousseau's *Ode to Posterity* would never reach its address, but it was quite another when someone was funny at *his* expense. Nor did Desfontaines leave the matter there, but published *Voltairomanie*, a muck-raking pamphlet which included material derogatory and defamatory to the poet. Moreover, it was probably Desfontaines who eventually put the authorities on to a copy of *Le Mondain*, which Voltaire had not allowed to be published, and which he did not know had been surreptitiously copied and circulated in Paris.

Written just after *Alzire* in 1736, *Le Mondain* today seems quite innocuous; the sort of thing Hilaire Belloc might have written in one of his lighter moments. It was no more than a send-up of that never-never time, the Golden Age, when men and women (who were all perfect physical specimens) lived in some Arcadian land blessed with the most temperate of climates, where there was no such thing as discord or disease. In the poem Voltaire candidly admitted that he preferred the comforts of his own day. Already the delights of Cirey were casting their spell over him as he helped to bring the old château back to life with elegant furniture, porcelain, paintings, tapestries and *objets de vertu*. And at that time he was even considering commissioning Boucher to design cartoons for tapestries based on scenes from the *Henriade*. He was surrounded by beautiful objects, paid for out of his own pocket, and in *Le Mondain* he was cheerfully celebrating the pleasures of such an existence.

The poem included the line, "*Le superflu, chose très nécessaire,*" and for Voltaire luxury justified itself as the cradle of the arts. But it was not this Epicurean reasoning which gave offence. Voltaire was also flippant about Adam and Eve, suggesting that these God-created beings had long hair and dirty nails, and— an unforgivable fault to his fastidious nature—they never washed.

> *Sans propreté l'amour le plus hereux*
> *N'est plus amour, c'est un besoin honteux.*

> Without washing the happiest love
> Is not love, it is but a shameful need.

Nor was he concerned with the precise site of the Garden of Eden, as discussed by scholars. For him *"Le paradis terrestre est où je suis."*

About this time Voltaire's other long-standing quarrel with J. B. Rousseau came to the boil again. Not unnaturally the exile resented the pen-portrait of himself in *Le Temple du Goût*. Now a pen-portrait of Voltaire started to circulate which was probably the work of Rousseau, and although it would probably be grounds for libel today, much of it is as unflatteringly recognisable as a drawing by Rowlandson or Gillray.

He is thin, has a parched constitution, a jaundiced air, sparkling and malicious eyes. . . . Gay by nature, serious on principle, open without frankness, politic without subtlety, sociable without friends. He loves grandeur and despises the great. He is at ease with them, and stiff with his equals. . . . His mind is just, his heart unjust, he thinks all things and mocks everything. A libertine without lust, he also moralises without having any morals. Vain to excess, but even more avid he works less for fame than for money.

And that was how not only unsympathetic contemporaries saw him, but also the nineteenth century, with of course the exception of such scholars as Desnoirterres.

Voltaire revelled in publicity, except when it blew back in his face after some literary indiscretion such as *La Pucelle* or *Le Mondain*, but he never went out of his way to create a public image. Perhaps he was too honest to do so, or too indifferent to public opinion, though he loved being the hero of the hour, as he was after the success of such plays as *Oedipe*, *Zaïre* and *Alzire*. Two statements at least in the pen-portrait are blatantly untrue, for he was the most loyal of friends, and not all of them came from an aristocratic background. To despise him for making money sounds suspiciously like sour grapes, especially when it came from a penniless exile.

J. B. Rousseau was a permanent exile from France, but thanks to the influence of the young Duchesse de Richelieu and Mme du Châtelet the order banning Voltaire from the capital was now withdrawn, though the head of police said he hoped that in future Voltaire would behave like a responsible adult. Accordingly, he went to Paris on a short and not particularly rewarding visit. During his absence an interest in science had become fashionable, occupying the place of theological studies among earlier generations of educated people. And Maupertuis had become the idol of this world. Furthermore, Maupertuis was now the apostle of Newton. Voltaire, who had introduced Newton to France when all self-respecting savants were good Cartesians, returned to Cirey with his nose somewhat out of joint.

His time there was as productive as ever, and it included the most intellectual writing he had produced to date. In addition to *Alzire*, something of a problem play, there were the *Eléments de la philosophie de Newton* (banned from publication in France and pirated in Amsterdam with an ending that was not his own); *La Mort de César*, another republican tragedy; *L'Enfant Prodigue*, a comedy; two more *Epîtres à Uranie*; and the seven sections on equality, free will, envy, moderation, pleasure, happiness and virtue, which made up the *Discours en Vers sur L'Homme* (1734–7). To all this could be added the inevitable squib, in this case *Le Mondain*, as well as his intermittent work on *La Pucelle*.

At that date Joan of Arc was still thought of as a peasant girl who won the confidence of her king, gave the English a sound drubbing, and was then betrayed to her death. To the eighteenth century she was more of a folk heroine than a saviour inspired by God, and her canonisation would not take place until 1920. In *La Pucelle* Voltaire was not so much making fun of the girl herself as debunking the tangled web of legend and credulous beliefs that had grown up about her, especially the issue of her virginity. It was almost believed that the fortunes of France stood or fell by that, and her protagonists had set out to equate her with the Virgin Mary in people's minds, claiming that it was her purity which had given her the supernatural power to drive out the English. Such reasoning was likely to bring out the worst in Voltaire, and the Maid's first meeting with Charles VI is described in remarkable terms.

> *Donc, se tournant vers la fière beauté,*
> *Le roi lui dit, d'un ton de majesté,*
> *Qui confondrait tout autre fille qu'elle;*
> *"Jeanne, écoutez: Jeanne, êtes-vous pucelle?"*

Thus, turning towards the proud beauty,
The King asked her in a majestic voice,
Which would have confounded any other girl than she;
"Jeanne, listen; Jeanne, are you a virgin?"

To this Jeanne replies that she has nothing to fear from doctors with spectacles on their noses, nor matrons, clerks, pedants and apothecaries, who are all welcome to investigate such feminine mysteries. Voltaire saw her as a down-to-earth peasant girl, who did a good job in ridding her country of the English; but he did not see her as having a divine mission. The weak-minded king was convinced of her supernatural powers on the flimsiest evidence.

" . . . dites moi dans l'instant
Ce qui j'ai fait cette nuit à ma belle?
Mais parlez net!" "Rien de tout," dit-elle,
Le roi surpris soudain s'agenouilla,
Cria tout haut, "Miracle!" et se signa.

" . . . tell me quickly
What did I do last night to my fair one?
But keep it clean!" "Nothing at all," says she,
Surprised, the King suddenly kneels,
Crying aloud, "Miracle!" and he crosses himself.

There were more serious sections in which Voltaire attacked his favourite target, superstition and religious persecution. These included an allegory in which Stupidity presides. Among the objects to be found in her domain is the pyre on which Urbain Grandier of Loudun had been burnt, and an edict of Louis XIII ordering to the galleys those who taught any philosophy except that of Aristotle. Among those consigned to hell were the Emperor Constantine; Saint Louis, for his wanton killing of Saracens in the Holy Land; and Calvin, for his harsh, uncompromising self-righteousness. All in all, it was something that Voltaire could well have left unwritten. The fact that he kept it under lock and key, and only read fragments of it to a chosen few, lent added glamour to the work, with the result that it soon acquired a reputation for being even more daring than it was. *La Pucelle* remained unpublished until 1755, and the result was that when it started to circulate in manuscript in Paris, parts which Voltaire had withheld were filled in by others with material far grosser than anything he had written.

In August 1736 Voltaire received a long letter in French signed "Fédéric, P.R. de Prusse." It marked the start of his long and not always smooth relationship with the future Frederick the Great. In a Court ruled by a father he regarded as little less than hateful, the Crown Prince had turned his thoughts towards France—a land of true culture—and the man he looked on as the apostle of free thought and humanism. Already he was possessed by the thought that when he succeeded to the throne of Prussia he might lure Voltaire to Berlin, where art and intellect were at present chiefly noticeable by their absence.

"Sir," he wrote, "Although I do not have the satisfaction of knowing you personally, you are nonetheless known to me through your works. These are treasures of the intellect . . . and elaborated to so fine a taste, such delicacy and art, that they acquire new beauties whenever we read them. I think I have recognised in them the character of their gifted author, who does honour to our own century and to the human mind. The great men of modern times will one day be indebted to you, and to you only, if ever the dispute about the relative values of the ancients and the moderns arises again, for you will weigh the balance in their favour."

The Crown Prince then went on to praise Voltaire's abilities as a poet and philosopher. He continued:

The kindness and support which you show to all those who devote themselves to the arts and sciences make me hope that you will not exclude me from the number of those you find worthy of your instruction. By this I mean your correspondence, which cannot but be profitable to every thinking being.

It would seem that even in Prussia Frederick had heard of *La Pucelle*.

It is this that makes me desire so ardently to possess all your works. I beg you, Monsieur, to send them to me, and to communicate them to me without reserve. If among your manuscripts there happens to be one that you think it prudent to conceal from the public eye, I promise you to keep it a close secret, and to content myself with applauding it in private.

I know, unfortunately, that the faith of princes has lost credit in these days, but I hope nevertheless that you will not be governed by general prejudices, and that you will make an exception in my favour.

Nature is pleased to create men with power to advance the arts and sciences, and it is for princes to reward their labours. I could wish no higher glory than to crown your successes. . . . If my destiny does not favour me so far as to secure you for myself, I hope at least that I may one day see the man whom I have so long admired from afar, and that I may assure you by word of mouth that with all the esteem and consideration due to those who follow the torch of truth and consecrate their works to the public good, I am,

> Monsieur,
> Your affectionate friend,
> Fédéric, P.R. de Prusse.

Voltaire was flattered by the letter, the first of nearly a thousand, but, as he made clear in his reply, he was not prepared to leave Cirey and the woman he described as his she-philosopher. His reply began with something of a Court bow.

Monseigneur, one would have to be insensitive indeed, not to be infinitely touched by the letter with which your Royal Highness has deigned to honour me. . . .

At the end he expressed his feelings quite plainly:

I should regard it as a great happiness to come and pay my respects to your Royal Highness. One goes to Rome to see the churches, pictures, ruins and bas-reliefs. A prince like yourself is a more wonderful rarity, and far better worthy a journey. But friendship, which brought me to my present retreat, does not allow me to leave it. Doubtless you are of the same mind as

Julian the Apostate, that great and calumniated man, who said that friends ought always to be preferred to Kings.

In whatever corner of the world I end my life, be sure, Monseigneur, that I shall continue to pray for your welfare; that is to say, for the happiness of a whole people. My heart will be numbered among your subjects; your glory will always be dear to me.

Any satisfaction which might have been gained from this correspondence, which was followed by more letters and presents from Frederick, must have been dimmed by the news that *Le Mondain* had fallen into the wrong hands in Paris, and that there was now a threat of prosecution. Years later Voltaire blandly referred to the episode in his *Autobiography*.

Although this poem was only comic, yet there was found to be much more fancy in it than in the *Henriade*; but it was so vilely disgraced by some shameless scoundrels, who printed it with horrid lewdness.

Much as she hated the thought of losing him, even for a short while, Emilie du Châtelet advised Voltaire to flee the country.

Chapter 9

THE PASTORAL YEARS

The Marquis du Châtelet may have been aware of his wife's former liaisons with the Duc de Richelieu and, reputedly, with Maupertuis, but his relatives were not prepared to accept his complaisant attitude towards his wife's present attachment. If only she had chosen someone from their own circle, then the affair would have been of little interest to anyone outside. But as it was she had selected someone whose every word and every action was of interest across the whole of Europe.

By threatening to write to M. du Châtelet, Emilie's relatives intended to put him in an awkward position by publicly drawing attention to what everyone knew was going on at Cirey. For if the Breteuils wrote that letter, and he chose to ignore it, he would be branded in the eyes of all who knew him as a complaisant husband. The fact that most upper-class husbands were in the same situation was beside the point. That alone would have been enough to make Voltaire's absence from Cirey advisable. But he had trouble from another quarter too.

One of Voltaire's old acquaintances at the Temple, the Abbé de Bussy, later became Bishop of Luçon. This man had been a recipient of a copy of *Le Mondain*, and on his recent death the verses had been discovered among his papers. The poem was passed on to the authorities, and a prosecution was imminent.

Emilie du Châtelet found herself pulled in two directions. More than anything she wanted to keep Voltaire at Cirey, but at the same time she was anxious for his safety. Eventually she decided that he must go.

But Voltaire was determined to derive what advantage he could from his enforced departure from Cirey, so he made his way via Brussels and Antwerp to Amsterdam, where he could supervise the printing of his *Eléments de la Philosophie de Newton*. During his progress towards that city he was generally welcomed as an honoured guest.

However, in Brussels his old enemy J. B. Rousseau did his utmost to poison the atmosphere by putting it about that he had only come there to preach atheism. Consequently he only stayed one night, but even so a special performance of *Alzire* was staged in his honour. At Leyden crowds gathered just to catch sight of him, while in Amsterdam he was lavishly welcomed. Reports of his arrival reached London, and twenty young admirers crossed the North Sea to pay their respects in person. Moreover, a certain Mr Bond went so far as to mount a production of *Zaïre* at his own expense, and took a leading role. But so great was his excitement that he died immediately after the first performance.

At Cirey the Marquise fretted over Voltaire's health and welfare. But he for his part almost forgot to write to her in the midst of so much kindness and attention. Her chief fear was that he might fall for the blandishments of the Crown Prince of Prussia, and be lured to Berlin. And this fear was not without foundation. An item in the *Gazette* of Utrecht announced:

The Prince Royal of Prussia, who has a great appreciation of belles-lettres, and who honours with a special esteem those who cultivate them and are distinguished in them, has written to M. de Voltaire a letter as courteous as it is eloquent inviting him to visit His Royal Highness at Berlin. M. de Voltaire, who is as sensible of the honour which the Prince has done him, as he is grateful for his goodwill, has gone forthwith to Champagne, on the way to Berlin. He expects to remain there some time, and then go to the English Court.

Mme du Châtelet poured out her heart in a letter to their mutual friend, the Comte d'Argental. It looked as though the one thing she had feared all along was coming to pass, and that Voltaire was being lured to Prussia by the Crown Prince. What worried her most of all was what the king would do. The old man was not on the best of terms with his son, and would disapprove of Voltaire and all he thought he stood for. Indeed, in Emilie's opinion he was capable of having Voltaire arrested and handed over to the French authorities.

That was not all that was worrying her, as Emilie confided in another letter to d'Argental. If Voltaire went ahead and printed his *Eléments de la Philosophie de Newton* it would give offence in France, because in it he contradicted almost every theory expressed by Descartes on metaphysics and science.

"At the moment I have to save him from himself and I use more diplomacy in guarding him than the Vatican does to keep Christianity in chains."

Ironically, it was Emilie's health which suffered as a result of Voltaire's visit to Holland. He seems to have quite forgotten about it, as people are prone to do when something all-absorbing comes along. Now she was begging d'Argental to write to him saying how ill she was, and that he ought to return to Cirey at once. As much as anything she was annoyed that preoccupation with the forthcoming publication of the *Eléments* had—at least for the time being—displaced her as the centre of his existence. Angrily she wrote to d'Argental:

> He sends me the first proofs of this miserable book *Eléments de la Philosophie*. I tell you that it is all he thinks about. But he will be ruined if it is published in Holland. If he must ruin himself, he should at least know what danger he is running. I beg you, on my knees, write emphasising that if he will not give in and return he is lost.

But Voltaire really was quite taken up with preparing his *Eléments* for the presses, and even if he had no intention at this point of following up the invitation, it was very flattering to have the Crown Prince of Prussia practically begging him to come.

After the quiet of Cirey it must have been pleasant for Voltaire, who relished being a celebrity, to receive such an enthusiastic welcome in Holland. It was not all adulation, though, for he talked with the savants, and at Leyden attended the lectures by 's-Gravesande. He even found time to write a defence of that troublesome child, *Le Mondain*. But *Le Défense du Mondain* did not attempt to justify what he had written. On the contrary, he stoked the fire with more verses in which he made fun of a self-righteous, self-mortifying Jansenist priest. In one episode the priest (Monsieur Saint) inveighed against luxury while drinking a cup of coffee. With apparent innocence Voltaire described the cup and its contents, as well as the five-course dinner which had preceded it. The coffee came from Arabia; the beautiful porcelain cup from China: "Made for you by a thousand hands"; and the vessels of silver from mines in the New World. His little paean of praise for the delights of the modern world ended with this insult:

> *Tout l'univers a travaillé pour vous,*
> *Afin qu'en paix, dans votre hereux courroux,*
> *Vous insultiez, pieux atribilaine,*
> *Au monde entier, epuisé pour vous plaire.*

All the universe has worked for you,
So that you, in your smug rage,
Can insult it with pious acrimony,
The whole world, exhausted for your pleasure.

It would be hard to say which gave the greater offence in certain fanatical quarters: *Le Mondain*, or its defence.

Meanwhile, the letters continued to arrive in Paris for d'Argental from Emilie du Châtelet, imploring him to get Voltaire away from danger, real or imaginary. Now she had heard that he had even lent the Crown Prince of Prussia a manuscript copy of the *Eléments*, which to her seemed the height of folly. But to her intense relief Voltaire was back once again at Cirey in March 1737, after giving it out that he was going to stay in England. It was his feelings for Emilie which had drawn him back, but he was not so blinded by love that he did not appreciate the advantages of living in a country like Holland. Be that as it may, for the present, life at Cirey resumed the course it had taken before his hurried departure.

Opinions of Emilie du Châtelet vary from witness to witness, but on the whole accounts written by men are more favourable than those by women. A number of the latter seem to have been jealous of her intellect, which made them deride her as a bluestocking philosopher and scientist. Or possibly they were jealous of her hold over Voltaire, formerly the darling of the salons in Paris.

Maupertuis, who should have known her intellect and nature better than most, declared that it was marvellous to find "sublime knowledge" allied to such lovable qualities in a woman. Although witty, he declared, she did not indulge in spitefulness. Maupertuis, d'Argental and Cideville all considered her attractive, even beautiful in some degree, but her own sex was not inclined to be so generous. Her cousin declared: "We would never hear of Mme du Châtelet without bursting out laughing." But the most destructive portrait was that of Mme du Deffand, who maintained a life-long correspondence with Voltaire, while at the same time writing extremely spitefully about him in letters to her other friends. She and Emilie had moved in the same circles in Paris, and it was as a hostess to the young Voltaire that she had first come to know the Marquise. In her eyes Emilie was little more than an intellectual *poseur* who sought the company of such men as Maupertuis, Clairaut, Algarotti and Voltaire to feed her vanity, rather than to further her knowledge.

"She worked so hard to appear what she is not," Mme du Deffand wrote, "that she no longer knows what she really is."

Mme du Deffand's description of Emilie's appearance made her sound more like a reject from the King of Prussia's regiment of giant guardsmen: huge arms and legs, huge feet, flat chest, tiny head, bad teeth and a weather-beaten skin. In addition, she claimed that Emilie had tiny eyes (not borne out by her portraits); wore cheap underwear; had no dress sense, and decked herself out with too much jewellery.

Emilie might have Voltaire all to herself once again at Cirey, where she could keep some check on his indiscretions, but even so he was not out of reach of the importunate Prince Frederick, whose subject, Count Kaiserlinck, Voltaire called "an ambassador plenipotentiary to the Court of Cirey". But Kaiserlinck, though in a sense a spy, seems to have been an amusing and amiable character.

It was his task to study the two philosophers in their own setting, and at the same time he amused his hostess and Voltaire with his wit and pleasant personality. For their part they entertained him royally. There was even a firework display with a portrait of his master as the centrepiece, with the words: "To the hope of the Human Race."

There was one thing that Frederick wanted almost more than Voltaire himself at his little court at Rheinsburg: a copy of *La Pucelle*. He was consumed with a devouring curiosity to see the poem (which Voltaire would continue to add to for the next twenty years), but it was Emilie who kept it under lock and key. So Kaiserlinck returned to Rheinsburg without the poem. Instead, he was allowed to take with him part of the *Siècle de Louis XIV*, which was still in the process of being written.

Voltaire's secluded life in the country did not mean that he had cut himself off from the luxuries of Paris which were so dear to him. When he wrote in *Le Mondain*, "*Le superflu, chose très nécessaire*," and had been attacked for it by his equally comfort-loving enemies, he was speaking from the heart. At this time he was busy buying pictures by leading artists, as well as having his portrait copied by La Tour. He had a shrewd eye for investment, and among the paintings he acquired were canvases by Lancret, Albani, Boucher, Teniers, Tiepolo and Watteau.

At that time science was for the most part still a matter for the amateur, who acquired his knowledge as best he could. Such a man was Algarotti, a young Venetian, who stayed as a welcome guest at Cirey while on his way to England, which for him meant the homeland of Newton. Just as Voltaire was making the theories of Newton comprehensible to the French in his *Eléments*, Algarotti was doing the same for the ladies of Italy with his *Newtonianismo per le dame*.

Voltaire might be an amateur in matters of science, but his approach was not that of a dilettante. Both he and Emilie du Châtelet were interested to learn in the spring of 1738 that the Académie des Sciences proposed to have a competition for the best essay on *The Nature and Diffusion of Fire*.

At once Voltaire set to work with experiments, and a scientific theory that he proved to be correct was that certain substances actually increase on calcination, resulting from the absorption of matter in the atmosphere. Quite independently Emilie also entered the competition. Their papers received honourable mention, but the prize was awarded jointly to three other entrants. Since the judges were supporters of the theories of Descartes, while the two scientists at Cirey were Newtonians, they considered themselves the victims of prejudice: "The heretics of philosophy."

Once before Voltaire had played the matchmaker, on behalf of the Duc de Richelieu, and now he thought he would do the same for one of his nieces. His sister, Marguerite-Catherine Mignot, died while he was in England, leaving two daughters and a son (the Abbé Mignot). Now her husband had also died, and at the age of twenty-six the elder daughter was well on the way to becoming an old maid by the standards of the age. Voltaire decided to take a hand.

M. and Mme Champbonin were now close friends. In fact Mme Champbonin had a room always at her disposal at Cirey, and she became something of a confidante of Voltaire's. In the philosopher's opinion their son would make an excellent husband for his niece, Marie-Louise. When the two young women visited the château early in 1738 he tried to bring about the marriage. But Marie-Louise thought differently. In fact she showed no interest in young Champbonin, a shadowy figure at the best of times. What was more she had no intention of living at Cirey.

Marie-Louise must have possessed some degree of musical talent, for she had been a pupil of the great Rameau. More importantly, in the present situation, she loved the life in Paris and was appalled at the prospect of spending the rest of her days in the country. Also, she felt some ill-will towards Emilie du Châtelet for having carried off her uncle. So, despite the promise of a dowry from Voltaire if she married as he wished, she made her own choice. Her husband was to be Nicolas Denis, a man of about her own age, who was connected with the legal side of supplying provisions to the Army.

They were married in February 1738, and in April they visited Cirey together, to receive a warm welcome from Voltaire, who was apparently quite unruffled by his niece's rejections of his choice. In a letter Marie-Louise revealed her feelings:

I am desperate. I think him lost to all his friends; he has fettered himself so that, it seems to me, he can never break his chains. They live in an awful, inhuman solitude. . . . That is the life which the greatest genius of the century is leading—true, it is with a highly talented and very pretty woman, and one who employs every imaginable trick to hold on to him.

There are no ornaments she does not wear, and no passage from any of the great philosophers she cannot quote, to please him. Everything will be lost. He seems more bewitched than ever before.

That summer the younger of Voltaire's nieces, Marie-Elizabeth, married Nicolas Joseph de Fontaine. But he refused to attend the ceremony, declaring weddings to be:

A gathering of the relations, unfunny quips about marriage, dirty jokes which make the bride blush and the prudes purse their lips, a lot of noise, interrupted conversation, indifferent food, false bonhomie, dutiful kisses and little girls taking it all in out of the corners of their eyes.

While Voltaire was not prepared to dissemble to the point of attending either wedding, he did give both his nieces handsome dowries. So did his unloving and unlovable brother, Armand.

Voltaire had been living in peace now for about two years, working on his *Siècle de Louis XIV*; conducting scientific experiments; reading widely, entertaining visitors, and dining and conversing with his she-philosopher. Even in the château, if they were apart for more than a few hours Emilie was in the habit of writing notes to Voltaire. For his part he played the role of Seigneur during the frequent absences of the Marquis du Châtelet. Emilie occupied rooms in the main part of the building, while he lived in the wing which he had had built, and where he carried out his scientific experiments. To attend him he had a valet and two footmen. The latter waited at table during dinner, at which Emilie, her two children, and a guest such as Mme Champbonin would be present. And until his dismissal the boy's tutor, Michel Linant, would also take his meals with them.

Eventually Emilie's relations gave up trying to make Voltaire a cause of contention between her and her husband. The Marquis was no intellectual, and knew it. He could not enter into his wife's world of mathematics, science and philosophy any more than Voltaire could enter into his life as a soldier. When he was not on active service or at Court the Marquis led the life of a country gentleman at Cirey, and was fond of both his wife and her companion, in a kindly, detached manner. Unconsciously he was subscribing to one of Voltaire's dictums: "To constrain the freedom of a fellow-creature is to me a crime against humanity." No one could accuse him of constraining his wife.

The first intimations of another stormy period in Voltaire's life came in the form of a squabble with Jore, his publisher in Rouen. In itself it was of no consequence. But his enemies in the literary world were always looking for an excuse to attack and denigrate him. Chief among them were Fréron, Nonotte, La Beaumelle, Clément, Saint-Hyacinthe, and of course J. B. Rousseau and Desfontaines. It was Desfontaines who was now preparing the most intensive attack Voltaire had yet had to endure. Already he had caused a great deal of trouble by revealing Voltaire as the author of *Le Mondain*, a copy of which had been found among the late Bishop of Luçon's papers, and handed to the authorities.

Now Voltaire still hoped to obtain permission to publish the *Eléments* in France, and had therefore not allowed the Dutch printer to go ahead with publication in Holland. But a definite answer was not coming from the Chancellor d'Agesseau, and while the author delayed, a pirated edition full of mistakes did come out in Holland. This was the edition which Desfontaines reviewed with the sneer that it had been "shown the door by everyone".

Instead of pointing out that Desfontaines had been reviewing a pirated edition full of errors, Voltaire put down his head and charged. First, he made sure that a short poem drawing attention to Desfontaines' crimes against Newton and morality (". . . *ses erreurs sont toujours des péchés contre nature*") was circulated round Paris by Thieriot. Of course Desfontaines heard about it, and replied through the pages of his journal, *Observations*. In it he referred to the foolishness of an elderly poet turning to philosophy, and especially that of Newton, whom no real philosopher considered seriously.

In fury Voltaire dashed off an anonymous pamphlet entitled *Le Préservatif contre les Observations*, in which he evidently went through every back number of *Observations* that he could lay his hands on, and pointed out all the mistakes made by Desfontaines, and even catalogued the printer's errors. He also reminded his readers how he had saved the Abbé from being burnt at the stake, and how immediately afterwards the ungrateful man had written an offensive pamphlet about Voltaire, which he had shown to Thieriot, who was supposed to have burnt it. Voltaire pretended that this understandable, if unworthy, effort had been written by a certain Chevalier de Mouhy, a second-rate literary hack he had helped in the past.

Within a month of the pamphlet's publication in November 1738 Desfontaines retaliated with *La Voltairomanie, or the Letter of a Young Lawyer*. It too was supposed to be the work of someone else, in this case a young lawyer who had sprung to the defence of Desfontaines. It began with a destructive catalogue of Voltaire's books and plays. The author declared that the former only succeeded because they were blasphemous, while of the latter *Charles XII* was nothing more than a rag-bag of old stories. As for the *Lettres Philosophiques*, they were so shocking that their author was shunned by decent society, and forced to live in the country. Then Desfontaines absolved himself of the criminal charges which had brought him to the Bicêtre Prison, and denied that a pamphlet attacking Voltaire had ever existed.

Two copies of *Voltairomanie*, which became a best-seller over-night in Paris, were sent to Cirey. They arrived on Christmas Day. Emilie was not above reading the incoming and outgoing post, whether it was for her or not, and she found one copy of the pamphlet, which she kept from Voltaire. He for his part had found the other, and both spent a miserable few days thinking that each was hiding the wretched thing from the other, to spare unnecessary suffering and distress. In the end it was the she-philosopher who took it upon herself to uphold Voltaire's reputation. If he attacked Desfontaines with a rapier, she now picked up a cudgel. One by one she dealt with the Abbé's statements about Voltaire, ending by blaming the Almighty for having created such a detestable man. More important, she wanted Thieriot to speak up and confirm that there really had been a pamphlet written by Desfontaines against Voltaire after he had been released from the Bicêtre.

Thieriot behaved most oddly. When pressed about the pamphlet he would not give a straight answer, and even pretended that he did not know who was the author of *Voltairomanie*. Emilie was furious, the more so because she and Voltaire had in their possession a number of letters from Thieriot in which he referred to the pamphlet. When pressed, all Thieriot could remember was that at some time Desfontaines had shown him a polemic which he, Thieriot, had asked him to burn.

At Cirey, Emilie eventually plucked up courage to tell Voltaire about *Voltairomanie*, only to discover, of course, that he had known about it all along, and had been under the impression that it was he who had been hiding it from her. Now he wrote to Thieriot, not in a rage, but in an unexpectedly mild and coaxing tone. He ended:

> Friends who have known me for two days are burning to defend me, and you leave me in the lurch, you, a friend whom I have cherished for twenty-five years! But, my friend, does one live for oneself alone? Is it not a fine thing, to vindicate one's taste and the choice of one's heart by standing up for a friend?

In the past Thieriot had received financial help from Voltaire, including the royalties on the *Letters on the English Nation*, and the subscription for the *Henriade*, which he pocketed without permission, and which Voltaire had to refund when the epic was banned in France.

Wearily Voltaire commented in a letter to Cideville: "I regret having freed him from the Bicêtre and the Place de la Grève. In the end it is better to burn a priest than leave him to bore the public."

In the *Autobiography*, Voltaire made quite sure that his readers remembered what Desfontaines' offence had been, and how magnanimous he had been to him in his time of trouble:

> His character was well known. He had been taken in the fact with some Savoyard boys, and imprisoned in the Bissetre [*sic*]. His indictment was begun to be drawn up, and it was intended to burn him alive, as it was said Paris was in need of an example. Mr de Voltaire prevailed upon the Marchioness de Prie to use her interest in the criminal's favour. There is still extant one

of the letters written by Desfontaines. . . . "I shall never forget the obligations I lie under to you: the goodness of your heart is still superior to your genius. I ought to employ my life in giving you proofs of my gratitude. I conjure you likewise to obtain for me a revocation of the *lettre de cachet*, by which I am delivered from the Bissetre, and banished thirty leagues from Paris." A fortnight later, this same man wrote a defamatory libel against the person in whose service he ought to have employed his life. . . . This Abbé Desfontaines is the person who, in a conversation with the Count d'Argenson, attempted to vindicate himself by saying, *I must live*, to which the Count replied, *I see no necessity for it*. . . . Such were the people with whom Mr de Voltaire had to do, and he whom he called *the rascality of literature*: *they live*, said he, *upon pamphlets and foul deeds*.

After that, in January 1739, Voltaire decided against writing any more pamphlets on the subject, and said he would bring a lawsuit against Desfontaines. Friends rallied round, either enlisting the aid of influential people, or writing what amounted to testimonials. Even the Marquis du Châtelet waded in. On 10 January 1739 he wrote to Thieriot urging him to give evidence on Voltaire's behalf; that Desfontaines had calumniated him in a pamphlet, immediately after the philosopher had been instrumental in saving him from execution on a charge which had been proved. He ended by threatening the luxurious, double-dealing Thieriot as follows:

Regarding the lapse of memory which you claim to suffer in this affair, that can be shown to be a sham by printing the letters which are in the possession of Monsieur de Voltaire. These are to be worked up into a clear memorandum which all his friends, among whom I have the honour to count myself, have advised him to send to the Chancellor and to publish. In addition to the respect which you will earn by playing the part of a man and a true friend in this matter, you will win the full esteem of the one who calls himself,

Monsieur,
Your devoted and obedient servant,
Châtelet.

Now the Chevalier de Mouhy, whose name had been used on the title page of *Le Préservatif*, started blackmailing Voltaire by threatening to reveal him as its true author. As if that were not enough, Thieriot, who was supposed to send anything concerning Voltaire to Prince Frederick, saw fit to include a copy of *Voltairomanie*. The only thing that was consistent about Thieriot was his refusal to give evidence against Desfontaines, in spite of the pressure being put on him by so many people.

The affair dragged on into the spring of 1739. The police commissioner, who could have had little love for Voltaire, refused to take action. He suggested that the two men should apologise for their respective pamphlets, but without success. Obsessed by the affair, Voltaire was in danger of committing what he himself regarded as a deadly sin: that of becoming a bore.

Finally the Marquis du Châtelet went to Paris, and forced Desfontaines to sign a statement.

I herewith make it known that I am not the author of the pamphlet entitled *La Voltairomanie*, that I absolutely disapprove of it, that I regard everything said in it about M. de Voltaire as slanderous, and that I should consider myself dishonoured had I even the least part in writing it, as I entertain for Monsieur de Voltaire the feelings of respect that his talents deserve and which the public brings him with such good reason.

It was a peace without honour, and the only people to emerge with any credit from the whole affair were those who helped bring an end. But the Abbé's reputation as a literary critic was broken. The authorities scanned all the new issues of *Observations*, and since few people read it for its literary merits anyway its readership dwindled. In 1743 Desfontaines started a quarrel with the publisher of a journal entitled *Géographie*. He practically black-mailed the editor, declaring: "I live by my pen and as a critic I am the scourge of authors. Woe to him who does not write as I please!" But the editor refused to accept these terms for a good review, and Desfontaines set about ruining the sale of *Géographie* by encouraging booksellers to tell their customers that it was not selling. Before a legal action could be brought, in 1743, the authorities intervened, and took away his permit to publish *Observations*. Two years later he was dead from dropsy, and Voltaire and the whole literary scene in Paris were rid of a most dangerous enemy.

Chapter 10

THE ONLOOKER

While Voltaire and Emilie du Châtelet were hiding their feelings from one another after the discovery of *Voltairomanie* in the post, a certain Mme de Graffigny had arrived at Cirey with every intention of staying at least six months. Born Françoise d'Issembourg d'Happencourt, she was descended on her mother's side from Jacques Callot, the celebrated engraver. At an early age she was married to Huget de Graffigny, Chamberlain to the Duke of Lorraine. But de Graffigny became insane, beating her on several occasions, and in the end he had to be kept under restraint. Mme de Graffigny obtained a separation, but she was left penniless, and had to live on the kindness of friends and acquaintances who passed her from one to another.

It was the Duchesse de Richelieu who asked Emilie du Châtelet to give her a home until she herself returned from Toulouse. So, in December 1738, she arrived at Cirey; but she came with the attitude of a privileged guest. Behind her were a number of half-hearted love affairs, usually with men younger than herself, and she came to the Château with the intention of passing on everything she saw and heard, however trivial, about her hostess and Voltaire.

Mme de Graffigny possessed a large circle of acquaintances at Lunéville, where Stanislas had his Court. Among them was François Devaux, Mme de Graffigny's current lover, who was employed as reader to the ex-king. The position was almost a sinecure at a Court where the only occupation anyone took seriously was the pursuit of amusement. "What in the world do I want with a reader?" asked Stanislas truthfully. "I have about as much use for one as my son-in-law has for a confessor."

Pan-Pan, as Mme de Graffigny called him, was to be the recipient of almost daily letters, giving an hour-by-hour account of life at Cirey. She seemed absurdly confident of her ability to understand everything and everybody, given to making sweeping and inaccurate statements which were soon forgotten by herself, but continued to be repeated by others until they were accepted as gospel truth. With her arrival at Cirey she had established a pipeline for gossip, pumping information to her dear Pan-Pan to pass on to the whole Court at Lunéville. She was extremely badly off, and wrote with such clockwork regularity that one cannot help wondering if she were not being paid for all her gossip.

Mme de Graffigny arrived with her maid, from a friend whom she charmingly described as living in the *Château de l'ennui*. She reached Cirey, as she hastened to tell Pan-Pan, after a simply terrible journey, when they were set down miles from anywhere, and had to feel their way up a mountain to reach the château, and it was two in the morning before they arrived. Of course Mme du Châtelet was waiting to welcome them with open arms—though she did want to tell her at once all about a lawsuit in which her husband's family was involved. Mme du Châtelet was wearing a cotton dress, with a long black apron, and her hair was piled up on the back of her head like that of a little child. And it suited her so well. In fact she started her letter by saying that she knew her Pan-Pan would jump for joy when he saw where she was writing from. Then at last she was allowed to go to her room.

One moment later there appeared—guess who? Your idol, a little candle in his hand, like a monk. He said a thousand courteous things to me; he seemed so glad to see me that he kissed my hand ten times and showed a touching concern for my health. As for your idol, I don't know whether he had powdered himself in my honour, but all that I can tell you is that he was arrayed as he would have been in Paris.

At once Mme de Graffigny decided that she had found her true setting, in a well-ordered household where the conversation was intelligent and stimulating. Within hours she came to the conclusion that the Marquis was not even in the running, conversationally speaking, and anyway he was leaving for Brussels that very day. Already in her letters she had nicknamed him *le bonhomme*, while Emilie became *la nymphe*. According to her, both *la nymphe* and Voltaire had taken her into their confidence. "Here we are a threesome! And nobody will weep on that account. We have already confided as much to one another." And, at least according to her, the threesome joined hands and danced round in a circle at the prospect of the Marquis du Châtelet's departure.

Be that as it may, Mme de Graffigny's account of the daily routine is undoubtedly more accurate. Evidently no one got up particularly early at Cirey, and since Emilie was in the habit of working until 5.00 am that was hardly surprising. Coffee was served at 11.30 until 12.30 in one of Voltaire's rooms. That was only for the *élite*. The others, including the Marquis, Mme Champbonin and her son, had their "coachman's dinner" at twelve, while Voltaire, Emilie and Mme de Graffigny continued to make intelligent conversation until about one. Then Voltaire would rise, bow, and the two ladies would retire to their own rooms. They dined at 9.00 p.m., and retired either to bed or to continue their studies, at about midnight.

Although the Marquis was expected to leave any day for Brussels, he was still boring Mme de Graffigny by sitting next to her at dinner every evening—despite having had his "coachman's dinner" at twelve. Although she and her hostess had apparently become bosom friends on sight, for her part Emilie never even mentioned her guest's arrival in her own correspondence.

Inaccurate too was Mme de Graffigny's account of Cirey itself. According to her the château was dominated by a slagheap of a mountain, when in fact there were no real mountains for miles. This imaginary mountain was so close to Mme de Graffigny's window that she claimed she could touch it with her hand. Then she promptly contradicted herself by saying that at the foot of the mountain there was a little meadow, "perhaps fifty feet wide, on which one sees a little river [la Blaise] winding and making a thousand detours."

Although she was a guest, and therefore did not pay a penny for her keep, Mme de Graffigny was not deterred from complaining that her room was not properly warmed, despite the fact that half a cord of wood (about sixty-three cubic feet) was burnt in her fireplace every day. "You would think you were watching the burning of Troy," the ungrateful woman merrily informed Pan-Pan.

Mme de Graffigny was on safer ground when she described the interior of Voltaire's wing. This was entered through a little ante-chamber, which in turn gave way to his bedroom. It too was small and low-ceilinged, with crimson velvet hangings and gilded panels, and contained paintings, looking-glasses, lacquer corner-cabinets, chinoiserie, furniture, china and a clock. In addition, Mme de Graffigny wrote, it was all so clean you could kiss the parquet flooring. She even counted the contents of Voltaire's jewel box: twelve rings set with cameos, and two set with diamonds. After this she was ushered into the gallery by her host. He had a simply dreadful cold, and only that morning she had had to chase him out of her own room because it was so chilly. So this was where he did his writing and carried out his experiments. The gallery was thirty to forty feet long, with three windows on one side and between them two statues: one of Hercules, and the other of the Farnese Venus. Opposite were two cupboards to hold his scientific instruments, while the walls were panelled in yellow lacquer. But, oh dear, exclaimed Mme de Graffigny, there were no arm-chairs, and the only sofa wasn't very comfortable. That might well have been a deliberate attempt on Voltaire's part to discourage just such as she from making herself too much at home.

The next day *la nymphe* took Mme de Graffigny to see her own rooms. The whole colour scheme was light yellow and blue silk, and the bed was set in an alcove covered with India paper. Even the dog basket matched its surroundings. On the panelled walls were paintings by Watteau, with frames of gilt filigree, and look-ing glasses with well-cleaned silver frames. Then there was an amber desk, a present to Emilie from Prince Frederick; a big arm-chair and two stools, covered in white taffeta. In Mme de Graffigny's opinion even the lavatory was divine, being decorated with pretty engravings. Emilie's jewel box surpassed even that of the Duchesse de Richelieu, according to her inquisitive guest. It was crammed with valuable jewellery and trinkets, and Mme du Châtelet possessed at least twenty valuable snuff-boxes. That *was* strange, mused Mme de Graffigny in her letter to Pan-Pan, because when the Marquise had stayed at Craon all she had owned was one snuff-box of tortoiseshell. With malicious innocence she left Pan-Pan and his circle at Lunéville to work out the rest for themselves.

Next, Mme de Graffigny described her own room. It was huge and dark, she claimed, because of the mountain outside, and its one small window didn't fit properly. The bed upholstery didn't match, which jarred on her very delicate aesthetic susceptibilities, and despite the half cord of wood burnt daily the fireplace was not adequate to warm the room. All the furniture was old. Even that in her maid's room was better. In her opinion there was only one word for it: squalid.

Before long Mme de Graffigny came to the inevitable conclusion that Mme du Châtelet didn't really understand Voltaire; whereas she did, of course. He lent her his manuscripts, and even a copy of *Newton*, which she dutifully read so that she could discuss his interests. According to her, the domineering Emilie wanted Voltaire to forget all about history and concentrate on her own subjects—science and philosophy. In fact she had even gone so far as to lock up his manuscript of *Le Siècle de Louis XIV*, so that he could not get on with it. For her part, Mme de Graffigny had read it, and found parts quite divine.

Mme de Graffigny even had the conceit to tell Pan-Pan: "It is lamentable when people who have such intelligence can bring themselves to talk such follies [about Newton's theories]. However, as you may well believe, I do not argue such a matter."

The guest was convinced that she had made a conquest of Voltaire, and even offered unsolicited literary criticism about a scene in his play *Mérope* of which she did not quite approve. "I am glad you speak to me so frankly," she declared that Voltaire had said. "There is something uncommonly observant in your criticism."

A little theatre had been fitted up in the attic, where performances were given by visiting troupes of itinerant actors, as well as by Voltaire and his friends for their own amusement. Mme de Graffigny's claim that on one occasion twenty-one acts of plays and two and a half operas were given one after another between noon and seven o'clock the following morning may be discounted as a typical exaggeration.

Other visitors came and went, including Mme du Châtelet's brother, an Abbé, whom they all found most entertaining. Mme de Graffigny also obtained an invitation for another of her lovers, Leopold Desmarets, to stay at Cirey. Desmarets, like Pan-Pan, was a hanger-on at Lunéville. He came shortly before her premature departure from the château, and with ungallant speed informed her that he no longer loved her. But he remained to become—at least in Mme de Graffigny's eyes—the best actor of them all. According to her, Voltaire suggested that Pan-Pan should also come and join them, at which she declared that he would be much too shy to open his mouth in front of such a beautiful lady as Mme du Châtelet. In the end he never did come to Cirey. Even kindly Mme Champbonin was the victim of her spitefulness, for Mme de Graffigny likened her to a character in a Marivaux play, *The Upstart Peasant*.

At any time her chattering would have made her a trying guest, and by Christmas she evidently proved too much for Voltaire, who had received the bombshell of *La Voltairomanie*, which he thought he was keeping to himself. He took to his bed with a temperature, and it was through the open door of his room that he heard midnight mass celebrated in the private chapel of the château.

Not long after her arrival at Cirey mention was made to Mme de Graffigny of Desfontaines' attack on Voltaire in his journal *Observations*, and she was given his retort, *Le Préservatif*, to read. But neither he nor Emilie mentioned *Voltairomanie*, preferring to nurse it in private, like a bad tooth.

As the weeks went by not even Mme de Graffigny could convince herself that she was the centre of attraction. Emilie was deep in her wretched Newton, and Voltaire was either conducting experiments or else dictating to his secretary, leaving the guest to her own devices. Now her letters to Pan-Pan took on a complaining note. For one thing her room was so draughty it nearly blew out the candle. Emilie, she decided, was not nearly as nice as she had thought at first, being hard and cold, while Voltaire seemed a bit cracked on the subject of Desfontaines and J. B. Rousseau. But Pan-Pan must be careful what he wrote to her.

One evening Voltaire burst into her room in a state of extreme agitation, exclaiming that he was lost and that his fate was in her hands. Copies of *La Pucelle* were circulating in Lunéville, he claimed. The situation was serious enough for him to consider fleeing to Holland. Mme de Graffigny was the obvious suspect, and he begged her to write to Pan-Pan and get the copies back, adding that the Marquis du Châtelet was waiting to take the letter to Lunéville. Vainly she denied having taken a part of the work from a locked drawer and copied it out. Harshly Voltaire exclaimed: "Don't wriggle, Madame, you sent it yourself." Apparently Pan-Pan had been reading it aloud at Lunéville, and saying that it was she who had sent it.

The storm continued for an hour, and then Emilie entered. Her rage was worse than Voltaire's. "You miserable creature, you beast. I've been sheltering you for weeks, not from friendship, God knows, but because you've nowhere to go, and now you've betrayed me—murdered me—stolen a paper from my desk and copied it!"

Mme de Graffigny could make no defence except that she was a poor little thing, and that Emilie had no right to speak to her so. When she asked what proof there was against her Emilie said that she had been told what was being repeated in Lunéville, and had opened Pan-Pan's next letter. In it was the sentence: "The stanza from *Jeanne* is charming." Mme de Graffigny declared that this merely referred to an account she had given Pan-Pan of a reading by Voltaire from *La Pucelle*. At long last Voltaire said that he believed her story, and apologised. Emilie followed suit, but with a very bad grace.

Although Mme de Graffigny was no longer welcome, she did not leave for five or six weeks, because she was penniless and had nowhere to go. Even if she had not taken part of *La Pucelle* from a locked drawer and made a copy, she had abused the hospitality shown her by sending back to Lunéville an endless stream of petty-minded and spiteful gossip. And now everything had caught up with her. The last straw must have been when she discovered that her pet dog had come into season, and been seduced by one of the local mongrels.

No longer did she join Voltaire and Emilie for coffee in the morning, but stayed in her room. Now she referred to her hostess as the Shrew, and described the books she was offered to read as deadly dull. In the middle of February Desmarets arrived for a week, and when he departed for Paris Mme de Graffigny left with him.

As soon as she was away from the château Mme de Graffigny wrote Pan-Pan a spiteful account of the inhabitants of the château, saying that Voltaire was eaten up with jealousy of other writers, while Emilie was jealous of him.

Voltaire's fears that copies of *La Pucelle* would reach the authorities were groundless, and calm returned to Cirey. Four years had gone by since Voltaire had withdrawn into the country, and the only interruption had been his flight to Brussels for a few weeks in 1735. Meanwhile the lawsuit involving the du Châtelet family, which had been going on for years, now became of more than academic interest to the Marquis when his cousin, the Marquis de Trichâteau, made a will in his favour, and showed signs that he had not much longer to live. At the same time Emilie was negotiating the purchase of a house on the Ile Saint Louis in Paris, which Voltaire shrewdly noted was a district which was ceasing to be a fashionable residential area.

The purchase was negotiated without Emilie's presence, and on 8 May 1739 the household set out on a slow progress towards Brussels, with Mme du Châtelet travelling with her husband, her lover and her mathematician. They were accompanied by Koenig. It was indeed a progress, for at Valenciennes they were the guests of the officers of the garrison, while there were more functions to attend at Louvain.

From Brussels the party moved on to Paris, reaching it in high summer. There the capital was *en fête* for the betrothal of the King's sister, Elizabeth, to Philip, son of Philip V of Spain. But Voltaire considered the illuminations second-rate, and commented dryly that the stands for the festivities were set up in the Place de la Grève where the day before two thieves had been broken on the wheel.

Paris in August was less than charming, and before long the travellers were glad to escape back to Cirey, where soon after they were visited by the Duchesse de Richelieu. And it was at this time that Voltaire added a new name to his list of friends. For two years he had corresponded with Claude Helvétius, who like himself had been a pupil at Saint-Louis le Grand. Helvétius was then a *fermier général* (responsible for the collection of taxes in a particular district), and it was not for some years yet before he would become known as a leading *philosophe* and freethinker, who would have his book *De l'esprit* burnt by the hangman. But now he had just made the personal acquaintance of Voltaire, and found in him a kindred spirit.

Voltaire now produced two minor works: *Pandore*, an opera libretto, which to his disappointment never reached the stage; and *La Prude*, the reworking of Wycherley's *The Plain Dealer*. Besides acting as host to the Duc and Duchesse de Richelieu, he was also revising *Zulime*, and the quite recently completed *Mahomet*. In addition, he was now starting to correct Prince Frederick's verses written in French.

It was Frederick's ambition to be everything his hateful old father was not: enlightened, civilised and a patron of the arts with a Court at Potsdam adorned with the finest talents of the day. In accordance with these ideas he was working on the *Anti-Machiavel*, a book refuting the theories of government put forward by Machiavelli. At this time military conquest and the glorification of war were very far from his thoughts. Then, on 30 May 1740, Frederick Wilhelm I of Prussia died, and the Francophile who signed himself Fédéric because it sounded more euphonious, ascended the throne of Prussia. Now he would stop at nothing to lure the incomparable Voltaire to his Court.

Chapter 11

KING FREDERICK

Hardly had Frederick become King of Prussia than he began to have second thoughts about the *Anti-Machiavel*. He wrote to Voltaire asking if he would have the edition stopped which was actually being printed at The Hague by Van Duren. If the whole book could not be suppressed, at least certain sections must be altered. If power corrupts, in Frederick's case it could be said to have started with his attempts to suppress his own book. Before long it would become obvious that he had assimilated many of the Italian's precepts, and in the years ahead would apply them ruthlessly in politics, and also in his campaign to separate Voltaire from Emilie, by making his name so odious in France that he would be glad to seek refuge at Potsdam.

However, at this date (July 1740) Voltaire was acting as the new King's unofficial agent. Going to The Hague, he tried to stop the printing of the *Anti-Machiavel*, and promptly fell out with Van Duren. "All publishers are fools and knaves," he wrote. "They misunderstand their own interests as much as they cling to them."

He tried to outwit the Dutchman, who was unwilling to give up the edition, and would only agree to Voltaire correcting the proofs in his office where someone could always watch what he was doing. At first Voltaire was very modest in his alterations, with the result that he was allowed to work on his own when he returned the next day. Now he covered the sheets with almost indecipherable corrections, making them virtually unreadable, and then left at once for Brussels.

But Voltaire had underestimated the Dutchman, who called in another writer to make what he could of the pages, which he then printed without further reference to Frederick or Voltaire. The king was annoyed that everyone could now see the difference between his high-minded theories on the nature of kingship, written when he was Crown Prince, and his actual conduct once he became ruler. In self-defence he had to allow the original version, as amended by Voltaire, to appear. But after that he preferred to disclaim paternity of this troublesome child altogether.

At Cirey Emilie was also experiencing the tribulations of authorship. While Voltaire was an out and out Newtonian, she still subscribed in some degree to the theories of the German Leibniz, whose writing had been introduced to the French by Christian Wolff. Although he tolerated this rival to his own god, Newton, Voltaire suffered from slight feelings of jealousy at Emilie's book, *Institutions de Physique*, in which she wished to do for Leibniz what he had done for Newton in the *Eléments*. He could not resist commenting: "It is deplorable that a Frenchwoman such as Mme du Châtelet should use her intelligence to embroider such spiders' webs and make these heresies attractive."

Voltaire was not the only one to criticise her *Institutions de Physique*. Her mathematics teacher, Koenig, had left in something of a huff after a quarrel over a nice point in metaphysics. Maupertuis sided with him, thus bringing to an end his own relationship with Emilie. Now Koenig claimed that the book was nothing more than a reworking of lessons that he had given her, and an unedifying quarrel followed. Emilie maintained, apparently with justification, that she had first propounded her views on Leibniz a whole year before Koenig came to Cirey. If that were so it strengthens her claim to be taken seriously as an independent writer and thinker, and not, as some have implied, one who had her writings "improved" out of all recognition. *Institutions de Physique* was written with uncommon clarity, and since Voltaire could not tolerate Leibniz at any price it is unlikely to have been his work.

With the accession of Frederick there began a strange episode in literary history: the struggle for control of Voltaire. The philosopher found himself like a rag doll in a tug of war between Emilie and the King of Prussia. But it was not till her death nine years later that the victory went to Frederick.

A few days after his accession, Frederick informed Voltaire that he wished only to be addressed as an ordinary man, and that he shared his contempt for titles, names and outward show. For his part Voltaire playfully addressed him as *Votre Humanité*, and hoped that before the year was out they would meet. He also pointed out that the Queen of Sheba longed to see Solomon in all his glory. But Solomon had not the slightest desire to meet the Sheba from Cirey, and with fatuous persiflage advised Voltaire that the brilliance of two such divinities at the same time would blind him. Already the would-be philosopher and patron of the Enlightenment and the arts was planning his first military campaign, and a much publicised meeting with Voltaire on his frontier could form a useful blind to his real activities.

Voltaire and Emilie went to Brussels while Solomon in all his glory approached from Berlin, accompanied by Count von Kaiserlinck, and the nucleus of his *élite*, Algarotti and Maupertuis. The two philosophers moved to Antwerp, where it was planned that Frederick should stay with them, incognito, for a few days, before they all went on to Brussels. But when he had almost reached the frontier the king fell ill. In fact he was too ill to travel further, but even so he wished Voltaire to come to him where he was staying at a dilapidated castle outside Wesel, itself not far from Cleves. He made it clear that, though he would be just well enough to receive Voltaire, despite his fever, he was too ill to receive Emilie. In the circumstances there was nothing she could do, except watch Voltaire depart, and suspect that in the King of Prussia she had met her match. The first round had certainly gone to Frederick, and for a while her letters to him were brusque to the point of rudeness.

Voltaire reached Moyland on the evening of 11 September 1740. That same day Frederick sent an ultimatum to the Prince Bishop of Liège, who held sovereignty over the district adjoining the Prussian frontier. The first meeting between two of the most famous figures of the eighteenth century was hardly a distinguished occasion:

> I was led into His Majesty's apartment. There was no furniture but the four walls. By the light of a candle I saw, in a dressing-room, a small truckle-bed, two and a half feet wide, on which

there was a little man muffled up in a dressing-gown of coarse blue cloth. It was the King, sweating and trembling under a wretched quilt, in a fit of violent fever. I made my bow, and began my acquaintance by feeling his pulse, as if I had been his chief physician.

Voltaire was playing the part of a bogus doctor to Frederick's equally bogus patient. For having established the fiction, largely for the benefit of Emilie, he promptly got up:

He dressed himself and took his place at table. Algarotti, Kaiserlinck, Maupertuis and the King's minister to the States-General [the Netherlands] were at this supper with us, at which we talked profoundly about the Immortality of the Soul, Liberty, and the androgynes [bisexual beings] of Plato.

Voltaire was completely unaware that King Frederick was on a secret military campaign, and really believed that *Votre Humanité* had come to pay his homage to France's greatest poet, philosopher and playwright. And, what was more, he had left the majesty of kings behind in Berlin. A day or two later he wrote to Cideville:

He chooses not to remember that he is a king when he is with his friends, and forgetting it so completely that he almost made me forget it, too, and I had to make an effort to remember that I saw, sitting at the foot of my bed, a sovereign, who commanded an army of a hundred thousand men.

The good opinion was mutual, and Voltaire basked in the king's good will.

I naturally felt myself attached to him; for he had wit, graces; and, moreover, he was a King, which always forms a potent seduction, so weak is human nature. Usually it is we of the writing sort who flatter kings, but this king praised me from head to foot, while the Abbé Desfontaines and other scoundrels were busy defaming me at least once a week in Paris.

Frederick was equally enthusiastic about Voltaire. In a letter not intended to be seen by him he wrote:

He has the eloquence of Cicero, the elegance of Pliny, and the wisdom of Agrippa. In a word, he unites all the virtues and talents of the three men of antiquity, and his mind works without ceasing; every drop of ink is a gleam of wit from his pen. . . . The du Châtelet is very fortunate to have him; for of the good things he throws out at random, a person who has no gift but memory might make a brilliant book.

In his enthusiasm Voltaire even helped to write a manifesto against the Bishop of Liège, so sure was he that the author of the *Anti-Machiavel* must be right in his claims against the prelate. Within a few months, though, Voltaire was having second thoughts about Frederick's integrity, and after that time he believed as much as he wished to believe, and saw as much as he wished to see.

On 14 September Voltaire set out on his return journey. But first he went to The Hague, on the troublesome business of the *Anti-Machiavel*. There he had the satisfaction of staying in the old and extremely decrepit palace which served as the Prussian Embassy. He was moved to comment on the rotting floorboards, windowless windows, rat-gnawed books and the thickest cobwebs in Europe. Still, the address had a fine sound to it: *Le Palais du Roi de Prusse*.

Emilie returned to France with her husband, staying at Fontainebleau while the final touches were being added to her new house in Paris, the Hôtel Lambert. In The Hague Voltaire was busy supervising the printing of the revised *Anti-Machiavel*, and trying to get together a company of actors to be sent to Berlin. Both he and Emilie must have been saddened at this time to hear of the death in childbirth of the vivacious and charming Duchesse de Richelieu. It was he who had brought the marriage about.

Death was in the air among the royal houses of Europe. First Frederick-Wilhelm of Prussia had died, then in October it was the turn of the Emperor Charles VII in Vienna, and soon after he was followed by the Empress Anne of Russia. For ruler Austria now had the twenty-three-year-old Maria Theresa, who would find herself at the mercy of the King of Prussia. Already Frederick had increased his army by sixteen battalions, and was planning the invasion of the Austrian province of Silesia.

Voltaire knew something of what was afoot, and got in touch with the now very elderly Cardinal Fleury, who forgot his enmity towards the philosopher, and decided to make use of him on the visit he was about to pay Frederick. Fleury wrote a long and friendly letter, full of praise for the *Anti-Machiavel*, and he also asserted that he wished to be a friend of the King of Prussia. Voltaire understood perfectly well that he was meant to show this private letter—in the strictest confidence—to Frederick himself.

He also had some business of his own, namely, to present Frederick with a bill for expenses incurred while seeing the *Anti-Machiavel* through the press. Also, he felt it was about time the king paid for all the publications which Thieriot had sent over the last four years. He set out for Prussia. But not far from Herford the coach broke down, and Voltaire decided to continue on horseback. When he reached the town gate he was challenged by a sentry. "Who goes there?" the man demanded. "Don Quixote," he replied. "And under that name I entered the city."

When Voltaire encountered Frederick on this second occasion, the king was indulging in one of his more pacific pursuits; playing a flute concerto of his own composition. Both men kept a careful watch on their purses, and Frederick was annoyed to find that Voltaire had even included the cost of his present trip to Berlin among his expenses in connection with the *Anti-Machiavel*. He commented: "as court jesters go, this one is expensive."

Financially, the visit was not as rewarding as it should have been, since Frederick forgot to pay up for the publications sent by Thieriot. Before he left, after a stay of six days, Voltaire wrote to Maupertuis, for whom he had secured the post of President of the Berlin Academy, describing the King of Prussia as "*La respectable, singulière et amiable putain.*" Twelve years later, after he had quarrelled with Maupertuis, the latter undoubtedly showed it to Frederick.

Even making allowances for the overblown, not to say gushing, language of the period in which letters were frequently written, the verses exchanged between Voltaire and the man he had just described behind his back as "an amiable whore" are astonishing.

Voltaire appeared to be doing in jest what Wagner did in calculated seriousness when he encouraged Ludwig II's infatuation for him. Voltaire might have his tongue in his cheek, but Frederick's replies, also in verse, were genuine.

First Voltaire wrote:

> *Non, malgré vos vertus, non, malgré vos appas,*
> *Mon âme n'est point satisfaite ;*
> *Non, vous n'êtes qu'un coquette*
> *Qui subjuge les coeurs et ne vous donnez pas.*

> No, spite of your virtues, no, in spite of your charm,
> My soul is unsatisfied;
> No, you are only a coquette
> Who subjugates all hearts but never gives herself.

Frederick replied in a similar vein, blaming his rival, Emilie:

> *Mon âme le prix de vos divins appas ;*
> *Mais ne présumez pas qu'elle soit satisfait.*
> *Traître, vous me quittez pour suivre une coquette :*
> *Moi, je ne vous quitterais pas.*

> My soul feels the worth of your divine charm,
> But do not presume that it is satisfied.
> Traitor, you leave me to follow a coquette:
> I, I would never leave you.

Voltaire had the last word on the subject:

> *Je vous quitte, il est vrai, mais mon coeur déchiré*
> *Vers vous revolera sans cesse :*
> *Depuis quatre ans vous êtes ma maîtresse,*
> *Un amour de dix ans doit être préféré.*

> I leave you, 'tis true, but my sundered heart
> Will fly back towards you unceasingly:
> For the last four years you have been my mistress,
> But a love of ten years is to be preferred.

But Voltaire did not fly as straight as an arrow from a bow, or in any other poetic manner, back to the fretful and displeased Emilie. Instead he went to visit other members of Frederick's family, including his wife, his mother and sisters.

In what must have been a fit of pique Emilie attempted to revive the old love between herself and the recently bereaved Duc de Richelieu, but without success. She left Fontainebleau to await Voltaire's return to Brussels. But she was in for a second shock. First Richelieu had declined her overtures, and now Voltaire declared he was too old for a physical relationship.

Certainly Emilie was a woman with a healthy sexual appetite, while Voltaire's constitution was somewhat puny. But that was not the reason. For him the wind had started to blow in a different direction. All Emilie was to know, however, was that her lover had told her that for the good of his health there must be an end to their relationship as lovers. Hypochondria could be carried too far, she would have been justified in thinking.

In addition, she depended on Voltaire for the furtherance of her scientific studies. While her paper on the nature of fire was her own work, in which she suggested that the colours of the spectrum were related to their heat (violet being the coldest and red the hottest), much of her glory was a reflection of Voltaire's. If she were to be recognised as France's leading female savante, it would be largely thanks to him. Now everything was going wrong, and it was all the fault of that siren at Potsdam. To d'Argental she wrote:

> Would you believe that the idea that occupies me most in these fatal moments is the frightful grief which M. de Voltaire will feel when his infatuation with the Prussian Court has faded? I cannot bear the thought that one day my memory will be a torment to him. Those who have loved me must never reproach him.

In her eyes, whoever might be in the wrong it could not possibly be herself. The couple met again in Brussels, and at least on the surface everything was as before.

In April 1741 they started the journey back to France, travelling by way of Lille, where Voltaire's nephew by marriage, Nicolas Denis, was living with his wife, Marie-Louise. Once again Voltaire found himself the centre of an enthusiastic and admiring public. The company of actors he had originally gathered for Berlin, but who had never gone because Frederick was preoccupied with plans for war with Austria, were performing in Lille. It was decided to put on *Mahomet* in his honour, and the performance took place on 10 April.

Not all the drama was on the stage. The inhabitants of Lille disliked the Austrians (who ruled over the adjoining part of the Netherlands) and consequently were favourably disposed towards Frederick. During one of the intervals a note was handed to Voltaire. It came from the King of Prussia. The playwright stood up in his box and read it out to the audience. "It is said that the Austrians are in retreat, and I believe it is true."

The audience was delighted at the news of the Battle of Moll-witz. In fact, however, at the outset the Austrians seemed likely to be the victors, and Frederick rode off the battlefield rather prematurely. Maupertuis, who was with him, had climbed a tree to watch the conflict, and found himself surrounded by enemy soldiers. He was stripped of all his fine clothes, and eventually sent back to Vienna, where he was unusually well treated. Years later, after Voltaire had quarrelled with Frederick, he remarked that the only living creature for whom the King had any gratitude was the horse that had carried him away from the field of battle at Moll-witz. But for the present both Voltaire and Frederick were the heroes of the hour in Lille.

However, Voltaire was rapidly becoming disillusioned with Frederick. He was particularly upset by the invasion of Silesia. So much for Voltaire's hopes of finding a refuge with someone who shared his own views on the composition of the perfect state. From now on the situation between the two men was not unlike some fable by La Fontaine: a verbose and apparently high-minded cat trying to lure a wary little bantam-cock into his domain.

As a result of the lawsuit involving members of the du Châtelet family, Emilie and Voltaire now led a somewhat nomadic life. From Brussels they returned to Cirey, where the Marquis de Trichâteau had died, having made du Châtelet his heir. From there the couple travelled on to Paris, and for only a week they stayed in Emilie's new house on the Ile Saint Louis. Then it was sold back to its original owner at a profit, and Emilie bought a smaller residence in the Faubourg Saint-Honoré.

Encouraged by the success of *Mahomet* when it was produced in Lille, Voltaire now approached Cardinal Fleury, who liked it sufficiently to make some amendments to its style. It was then passed over to the censor, Crébillon the Younger, who disliked the work, but reluctantly gave his approval for its performance. This was delayed, however, because it was felt that it might offend the susceptibilities of the Turkish Ambassador who was then in Paris. Today it would be impossible to revive *Mahomet* without giving unparalleled offence to the whole Islamic world.

Eventually the play received its first performance at the Comédie Française on 29 August 1742, when it was most enthusiastically received. In fact, the first night of *Mahomet* was one of Voltaire's greatest triumphs. But as well as his friends and admirers the audience included his critics and enemies, among them Desfontaines and Nicolas Piron. If Piron is remembered at all, other than as a literary enemy of Voltaire, it is as the author of an exceedingly coarse *Ode to Priapus*. Now he and Desfontaines drew the attention of the clergy to certain features in *Mahomet*.

Although the play purported to be about the founder of Islam, they claimed that it was in fact a veiled attack on Christianity, and that Mahomet, depicted as a ruthless, tyrannical and totally unscrupulous character, was really meant to be Jesus Christ. It was a ridiculous suggestion, but Voltaire's enemies were sufficiently powerful to force the play off the stage. Desfontaines denounced the piece to the Advocate-General, an ardent Jansenist. The chief of police sent for the author, who went accompanied by Emilie. And after a difficult interview Voltaire agreed to *Mahomet* being taken off after only three nights. Ironically he declared afterwards that he would dedicate the offending play to the Pope, and two years later he did just that.

Among those who attacked the play was a worthy doctor at the Sorbonne who worked himself up into a state of hysteria, running through the streets crying out that it was a bloody satire against the Christian religion. He claimed that it was no coincidence that the names Mahomet and Jesus Christ had the same number of syllables, and for him that was sufficient proof of Voltaire's wicked intention to equate the founder of Islam with the founder of Christianity.

The subtitle of the play was *Le Fanatisme*, and its real subject was fanaticism and superstition. It was the first time such a subject had been attempted on the stage in France, and the French church was hypersensitive to criticism, and ready to take offence at anything which came from the pen of that scoffer and freethinker, Voltaire.

Mahomet's plot is complicated, even by the standards of the day. Mahomet wishes to seize Mecca from its ruler, the elderly Sheik Zophire. Years before, Zophire's son and daughter were thought to have been killed in a fight with Mahomet, but they were in fact now among his slaves. Séide and Palmine, not aware that they are brother and sister, are in love with each other. At the same time Mahomet (who knows their origins and relationship) plans to make Palmine one of his concubines. She repulses him, and in a fit of thwarted passion Mahomet arranges that Séide—on condition that he murders Zophire—should be allowed to marry Palmine. Diabolically, Mahomet gives the youth a slow-acting poison. Séide stabs Zophire, who as he dies seems to recognise the assassin as his own son. Mahomet denies that he ever gave Séide orders to kill Zophire, and again tries to win Palmine's affection. Séide, temporarily saved from Mahomet's clutches, leads an insurrection against him, but as he raises his dagger to kill him he falls dying from the effects of the poison. Mahomet's claim that this is an act of God is believed by the populace, who are convinced that he must have supernatural powers. At this Palmine kills herself. Mahomet shows signs of remorse, but the play ends with him asking his lieutenant never to speak of this show of human feeling on his part.

Voltaire summed up all he was trying to say in *Mahomet* in a letter to Frederick. He explained that Mahomet was originally virtuous, but had become fanatical, and thinking that he is carrying out God's will by murdering an old man who loves him (Zophire). "It concerns an impostor [Mahomet] who orders this murder, and promises the murderer an incest as a reward." Highly cynical words are put into the mouth of Mahomet, to the effect that he must found a new religion to hold the people in bondage, and his authority is based on the assumption that might is right.

As if the hornets' nest stirred up by *Mahomet* were not enough, Voltaire now found himself in trouble on a political level, thanks to Frederick, who was doing his best to make life impossible for Voltaire in his own country. In a typically indiscreet letter to the King, Voltaire had spoken of Paris as being his capital, and that wherever he went he was mobbed by people who wanted to know if he had really met the King of Prussia. Soon copies of the letter were circulating among ministers in Paris, and a copy even reached Mme de Mailly, at that time the king's mistress. Everyone, from President Hénault downwards, was furious with Voltaire, who had been made to look thoroughly unpatriotic.

Voltaire issued denials, calling on the French Ambassador in Berlin to obtain the offending letter, so that everyone could see he had never written the comments attributed to him. Fleury chose to believe Voltaire, because he was the only man in a position to find out what Frederick really had in mind. Before long he and Emilie were back in Brussels. From there Voltaire set out on a kind of diplomatic mission to Frederick, who was taking the water at Aix-la-Chapelle: "the capital of Charlemagne and of hypochondriacs."

Frederick was forthcoming on every subject, except what he had in mind for future military campaigns, and Voltaire left after five days, having obtained neither information nor payment for all the publications sent to Potsdam by Thieriot. Nor for that matter was he paid for the paintings by Lancret which he had acquired.

At the end of January 1743 Cardinal Fleury died at the age of eighty-nine. Politically it was a loss to France, for while Louis XV had proved adept at boudoir intrigue he was showing himself rather less interested in statecraft and diplomacy.

Fleury had been numbered among the Immortals, and that meant that there was now a vacant seat in the Académie Française, and for all his feud with the established order Voltaire was sufficiently human to want to belong to the chosen forty. On his side was the king's new mistress, the Duchesse de Châteauroux (sister of the now deposed Mme de Mailly), while ranged against him were the secretary of state, Maurepas, and the Bishop of

Mirepoix, who was scandalised at the idea of a cardinal being succeeded by Voltaire. The bishop was tutor to the Dauphin (himself the father of the future Louis XVI), and his see was designated as the Ancient Bishopric of Mirepoix. The bishop, who was no scholar, abbreviated the word *ancien* to *anc*, and Voltaire put it round that what the old man was really writing was not *l'anc de Mirepoix*, but *l'âne de Mirepoix*: the ass of Mirepoix. Naturally Bishop Boyer was not in a mood to support Voltaire's nomination to Fleury's seat.

While this lobbying was going on Voltaire's latest play, *Mèrope*, had taken Paris by storm. Set in Classical Messina, it was a tragedy in the manner of Sophocles or Aeschylus, and as such succeeded admirably. For more than six years Voltaire had worked at it, on and off, continually rewriting, and he was rewarded with a play that made theatrical history. For the first time in the French theatre the author was called on to the stage on the first night to receive the applause of the enthusiastic audience.

In its way *Mèrope* was just as much a play against fanaticism and unscrupulous conduct for personal gain as *Mahomet*. But this time no one saw any parallels with Christianity, and Voltaire found himself a hero, at least with the theatre-going public. Immediately after the performance he left the Comédie Française, but was sought out and brought back to satisfy the demands of the audience. First he went to the box of the Duchesse de Bouffleurs and the Duchesse de Luxembourg, and kissed their hands. Then he hurried to the one occupied by the Maréchale de Villars and her young daughter-in-law. Nearly a quarter of a century before, the Maréchale had welcomed him to her box during another tumultuous first night, that of *Oedipe*, when the audience had called to her to kiss Voltaire. "Madame la Duchesse!" they shouted, and history was repeated.

That formed a pleasant interlude in the protracted episode surrounding Voltaire's attempt to become an Immortal. How much his pride had been hurt by his exclusion till that time can be judged from a letter which he had circulated both in Paris and at Court. In it, he declared that Newton, whose disciple he was, firmly believed in the existence of God. For his own part, he adored religion, which had been his support during thirty difficult years. He even went so far as to declare that he particularly desired to succeed to the chair of Cardinal Fleury so that he could praise him, his religion and his pupil the king, in his first address to the Académie.

But it was all in vain. Four intellectual nonentities were elected to vacant seats during the next few years, but at last, in April 1746, Voltaire was elected. But in 1743 at least one honour did come his way. He was made a member of the Royal Society of London. *"Dr Franciscus Arouet de Voltaire, Parisiensis."*

The rejection by the Academie in 1743 hurt Voltaire deeply, but beyond the Rhine the siren-king gloated over his humiliation: this was another reason why the philosopher should wish to leave France. Frederick went out of his way to rub salt in the wound, pointing out that if he came to Potsdam he would be assured of an appreciative welcome. Not all the manœuvring was on a personal level. Moreover, Voltaire's special relationship with the Prussian King was considered invaluable by the French government for finding out Frederick's plans. France had entered the war on the same side as Prussia, only to find its army left in the lurch. Now England was backing Austria with a large loan, and France wanted to discover exactly what Frederick had in mind for his next move.

An elaborate and devious plan was devised, worthy of Frederick himself, to give Voltaire a good reason for leaving France. The Comédie Française prepared to put on *Le Mort de César*, only to have it forbidden by the police the night before the first performance. That provided the reason for his departure, while money to cover his expenses would come from a year's advance on his pension, as well as the monopoly (which he shared with two cousins) from providing clothing for the Army, and hay for its horses. No doubt it was felt that he must be sweetened with a really large sum, to prevent him from selling out to the Prussians.

Before long everyone heard that Voltaire had had enough of his cavalier treatment in France, and was going to Potsdam. Frederick was triumphant, believing that at long last he really had defeated Emilie du Châtelet, and succeeded in wresting Voltaire away from her. But Emilie was not prepared to see him depart without a fight, and in the end he had to pacify her by explaining that the whole adventure was being undertaken on behalf of king and country. As a guarantee of good faith he promised that all his confidential despatches should pass through her hands on their way to the ministers and even to the king himself. Even so, she was in floods of tears for days afterwards. About the only consolation Emilie could draw from the impending visit was the fact that where Voltaire was going he was hardly likely to be ensnared by a female rival.

Chapter 12

ROYAL FAVOUR

In this journey he performed a singular service to the King his master, as we see in the letters which passed between him and Mr Amelot [de Chaillon], the Minister of State.

Perhaps Voltaire was overestimating the importance of his mission in the *Autobiography*, for the stream of letters he sent back contained very little that was likely to be of use to Louis XV's ministers. But by then Frederick had become adept at the art of saying nothing at considerable length.

First Voltaire went to The Hague, to stay in the dilapidated palace which served as the Prussian Embassy. There he remained for nearly three months, enjoying the company of the ambassador, Count von Podeswils, and his Dutch mistress. At the end of August he and the Ambassador set out for Prussia. The king was in residence at Charlottenburg, and there the travellers were received. Voltaire was welcomed like an old friend. It was an entirely male Court, and the queen lived elsewhere with her own household, and the only female Voltaire encountered was an Italian dancer. But, he commented, even she had a figure like an athletic young man.

The king rose at five in summer and six in winter. There was none of the formality which marked off the hours of Louis XV's day with unaltering and unalterable regularity. Frederick possessed a beautiful bedroom, with a silver rail around the alcove, but behind the curtains was not a bed but a bookcase. He preferred to sleep on a mattress hidden behind a screen. The day began with coffee, shared with several of the younger members of his household. Then came affairs of state, which in their turn were followed by a military review. After dinner—for the main meal came in the middle of the day—the king would shut himself away to write poetry in French, and in the early evening there would be a concert, at which he played the flute. The evening would end with a supper party and conversation which may have begun on a high plane, but soon descended to denigration of all and sundry, and bawdy talk.

Although both men were courteous to each other, with Frederick playing the host to Voltaire's model guest, they were both thoroughly disingenuous. Voltaire might consider Frederick the hope of intellectual Europe, and imply that his was the only Court worth living in, but at the same time he was employed as an agent for his sovereign, Louis XV. For his part Frederick showed Voltaire his most charming face, and behind his back set about making it impossible for him ever to return to France. But he lacked sufficient finesse to bring off this particular piece of scheming.

Frederick knew what had brought Voltaire to Berlin, and Voltaire knew that he knew, but they kept up the charade according to the rules of the Rococo. To make it easier for both, Voltaire even drew up a questionnaire for Frederick to answer, and the King obligingly filled it in for him.

Q. Is it not clear that the peace party will without fail be the victors in Holland? Is it not clear that France shows strength and prudence?

A. I admire France's prudence; but may God save me from imitating it!

Q. Wouldn't you bring immortal glory on yourself simply by proclaiming yourself the protector of the Empire? Isn't it in Your Highness's interests to prevent the English from setting up your enemy, the Grand-Duke, as head of the Holy Roman Empire?

A. France is more interested in preventing that than Prussia; and, my dear Voltaire, your information is faulty on that point. The Emperor cannot be elected without the unanimous vote of the princes, and so, you see, the election still depends on me.

Q. Anyone who has talked for as much as a quarter of an hour with the Duke of Aremburg, to Count von Harrach, Lord Stair, with anyone from Austria, has heard them say that they are burning to invade Silesia. Have you, another ally than France?

A. Let them come; they shall have a warm reception.

> *On les y recevra, biribi*
> *A la façon de Barbari*
> *Mon ami* [a nonsense song]

Q. Whichever part your Majesty may take, will you honour me with your confidence as one who desires to spend his days at your Court? May I have the distinction of accompanying you to Bayreuth? I must know in time, however, in order to prepare myself for the journey.

A. If you wish to come to Bayreuth, I shall be glad to see you there, provided that the journey will not injure your health. It is, therefore, up to you to make what preparations you think best.

Q. If your Majesty will make me the bearer of some pleasant information to my Court, I implore you to give me this order.

A. I am not in communication with France; I have nothing to hope nor to fear from it. If you wish I will write a compliment to Louis XV which will not contain one true word. But politically we have nothing in common, and it is not for me to speak first.

Q. Do what you will, I love your Majesty with all my heart.

A. I love you with my whole heart; I respect you; I shall do everything to get possession of you, barring actions which would make me look ridiculous and be harmful to my interests and honour. The French monarchy is a strong body without a soul or nerve.

In due course Voltaire sent this extraordinary document back to France, to M. d'Amelot. Meanwhile Frederick stealthily set about ruining Voltaire's reputation at the French Court. He wrote verses which included the sentiment that Louis XV was the stupidest of kings, which he then stitched on to some authentic prose by the philosopher. But since he could hardly ask Voltaire to correct them, their inferiority stood out. He told the Prussian

Ambassador in France: "I want to embroil him for ever with France, so that I can get him to Berlin." A copy reached the Ass of Mirepoix, but almost at once Voltaire was warned, and he spiked Frederick's guns by informing d'Amelot what was going on:

> Not being able to win me over in any other way he thought he could do it by disgracing me in France, but I swear I would rather live in a Swiss village than enjoy at such a price the dangerous favours of a king capable of planting treachery into friendship itself.

In the questionnaire Frederick had said that he would do anything short of compromising his honour to possess Voltaire. But he had just done that. He was so confident of having his own way that he had even furnished a house in Berlin, ready for Voltaire:

> Choose an apartment or house; arrange for yourself all that you need for the comfort and luxury of your life; let your circumstances be such as you need to make you happy. I will see to the rest. You will always be free and entirely the master of your fate. I desire to hold you only by friendship and an agreeable life.

Voltaire was not prepared to be lured by honeyed words, and in the end Frederick asked him not to disclose that he had turned down the offer of a house in Berlin. Quite unperturbed at what was going on around him, Voltaire prepared to accompany the King to Bayreuth, where his sister Frederica Wilhelmina was the Margravine. Voltaire had met the king's three sisters, Ulrika, Amalia and Wilhelmina, on an earlier visit, when he and Ulrika had struck up a genuine friendship. Later, she would become Queen of Sweden, and mother of the future Gustav III Vasa, who one day would be assassinated at a masked ball in the opera house in Stockholm.

Among the most charming of his lighter verses are those he wrote for the three sisters. The first is to Ulrika alone; the second to Ulrika and Amalia; and the third to all three of them. Aptly Carlyle described them as "three consummate madrigals":

A Princesse Ulrique

Souvent un peu de vérité
Se mêle au plus grossier mensonge :
Cette nuit dans l'erreur d'un songe,
Au rang des rois j'étais monté
Je vous amais, Princesse, et j'osais vous le dire !
Les dieux à mon réveil ne m'ont pas tout ôté,
Je n'ai perdu que mon empire.

Aux Princesses Ulrique et Amélie

Si Paris venait sur la terre
Pour juger entre vos beaux yeux,
Il couperait la pomme en deux,
Et ne produirait pas de guerre.

Aux Princesses Ulrique, Amélie et Wilhelmina

Pardon, charmante Ulrique ; pardon, belle Amélie ;
J'ai cru n'aimer que vous le reste de ma vie,
Et ne servir que sous vos lois ;
Mais enfin j'entends et je vois
Cette adorable Soeur dont l'Amour suit les traces,
Ah, ce n'est pas outrager les Trois Grâces
Que de les aimer toutes trois.

Often a little truth mingles with the crudest falsehood.
Last night in the error of a dream,
I mounted to the rank of Kings.
I loved you, Princess, and I dared to tell you so!
The gods, at my awakening, took not everything away.
I have only lost my kingdom.

If Paris came on earth anew
To judge between your lovely eyes,
He'd cut the golden fruit in two,
And rouse no war about the prize.

Forgive me, charming Ulrique; forgive me, beautiful Amélie;
I thought that I should love only you for the rest of my life,
And serve under your laws only. But at last I hear and see
This adorable sister, whose footsteps are followed by love,
Ah, it wrongs not the three Graces, to love them all three.

(*Trans:* Alfred Noyes)

Voltaire had been accepted as one of the family, and Ulrika
requested her brother to write her a reply in the same vein, in
verse.

Back in Berlin, Frederick did all he could to please his guest,
even staging an opera Voltaire was particularly anxious to hear,
and doing everything in his power to delay his departure. But on
13 October Voltaire left, staying with another of Frederick's
sisters at Brunswick.

At Brussels he found Emilie was more reproachful than loving.
Voltaire had been a less than adequate correspondent, allowing as
much as three weeks to pass without a word from him. She also
had a lengthy catalogue of aches and pains to relate, and this was
hardly likely to rekindle a flame that had burnt low, at least on
Voltaire's side. Emilie confided in d'Argental, much as she had
done when the affair with Desfontaines was at its height, and he
mildly reproved their mutual friend.

The journey back to Paris was by way of Lille, where Voltaire
again visited Mme Denis. For most of that winter, which was
spent in Paris, he was unwell. When first in love with Emilie,
Voltaire had literally made himself ill. He was still living with her,
but the truth was that he was hotly in love with his niece, herself
a married woman with an agreeable husband. Life in the household in the Rue Saint-Honoré could hardly have been idyllic.
Emilie spent much of her time playing cards, while Voltaire did
no creative work, but made himself disgreeable and complained
about his health. At Cirey the Marquis was growing bored with
living alone, and wanted Emilie to return. By the spring Voltaire's
thoughts had returned to writing, and since he now needed quiet
he agreed to go back to the countryside. There the clouds
disappeared, and he became his old self again.

Within a short while of their return to Cirey, Voltaire received word that M. Denis was seriously ill. A few days later the news came that he was dead.

After the unpleasant atmosphere which marred their stay in Paris—Voltaire's temper and Emilie's moodiness—the summer of 1744 at Cirey was one of the happiest they had ever known. It was peaceful, and Emilie spent much of her time sharing in his scientific experiments. By then she had abandoned what was to him the heretical study of Leibniz, and she was in fact planning to translate Newton's *Principia* from Latin into French. What more could he ask of her?

Voltaire had agreed to return to Cirey so that he could settle down to serious work, but events conspired against him. A marriage had been arranged, between the Dauphin and the Infanta Maria Theresa of Spain, to take place early in 1745, and his friend the Duc de Richelieu was in charge of the ceremonies. He now requested Voltaire to write a suitable entertainment, for which Rameau would provide the music. It was to be called *La Princesse de Navarre*, an opera-ballet, with a great deal of spectacle. Half a century before, Lully had been the musical dictator at Versailles, and in Rameau he had a worthy successor. As far as he was concerned, Voltaire was just another librettist to be browbeaten into dutiful submission, and one who would produce exactly what he wanted and not a line more or less. The surprise was that Voltaire could not have been more co-operative, although Rameau's whole attitude was enough to have antagonised a lesser man of letters. President Hénault wrote to the Comte d'Argenson: "What do you say about Rameau who is beginning to correct verses by Voltaire! *I've* written to Richelieu about it." Again and again revised verses for *La Princesse de Navarre* were sent to Richelieu, who to Voltaire's annoyance passed them around among his friends at Versailles.

During the summer of 1744 it seemed very likely at one time that entertainments for a coronation would be needed, as well as for a wedding. In August, Louis XV, accompanied by his mistress the Duchesse de Châteauroux and her sister, set out on a visit to the fortress-city of Metz, which at that time was threatened by the Austrians who were advancing into Alsace. Suddenly he fell seriously ill, but such was the hold the two sisters had over him that they would not allow the princes of the blood or any of the ministers to enter his room. On 12 August the royal physician believed that his death was only a matter of time. A courtier forced his way into the king's presence, but the clergy and the ministers found themselves in the humiliating position of having to negotiate with the sisters. But now the smell of hellfire was in Louis's nostrils, and the Church refused to allow extreme unction unless he gave up Mme de Châteauroux. Not only did he have to renounce his mistress but both she and her sister had to be clear of Metz itself before he could receive the Sacrament. Then he rallied, and made a rapid recovery. But at least the hold over him by Mme de Châteauroux had been broken.

Such a miraculous recovery could not pass uncelebrated, and all Paris was *en fête* in September 1744. A benign Providence had restored the king to his people, and henceforth he would be known as *Louis le bien-aimé*. By the end of the reign, thirty years hence, the nickname would be entirely ironical. Seldom can a monarch have earned more adulation for less reason than Louis XV did in the late summer of 1744. That December Mme de Châteauroux died in mysterious circumstances, and exactly a year after his recovery the daughter of M. Poisson became the Marquise de Pompadour. In her Voltaire would find that he had a sympathetic champion at Court.

Voltaire and Emilie arrived in Paris just as the festivities for the recovery of the king were getting under way. Another who returned to the capital about this time was Mme Denis. Since her husband had died there was nothing to keep her in Lille. Before long she had formed her own little salon, which was visited frequently by her uncle. With a show of frankness that concealed the truth, Voltaire had informed Emilie after his third visit to Berlin that he no longer considered himself her lover, in the accepted sense of the word. She took that statement at its face value, and never suspected the real reason: his passion for Mme Denis.

For Voltaire, the relationship was to remain a secret for nearly two hundred years, eventually coming to light in a correspondence which had hitherto remained unpublished. The letters which give the clue to the relationship were not disposed of after Voltaire's death by Mme Denis, when she sold most of his papers to Catherine the Great. These were located by Theodore

Besterman, who published 142 of them in French and English editions: *Lettres d'amour de Voltaire à sa nièce*, 1957; and *Voltaire's love letters to his niece*, 1959.

All through the winter of 1744–5 Voltaire wrote and rewrote the libretto for *La Princesse de Navarre*, taking more than usual care to ensure perfection. *La Princesse* could be the stepping-stone which would bring him back to favour at Court, and he was leaving nothing to chance. That, together with a full social life, occupied his time. For a she-philosopher Emilie had a remarkable addiction to gambling, and spent much of her time in Paris in that way, despite the fact she seldom won. There was one occasion when she had to borrow from Helvétius to settle a debt.

The unpromising month of February 1745 saw the great names of France converging on Versailles for the wedding of the Dauphin. Five days before the performance of *La Princesse*, Voltaire's brother Armand died, leaving him a half-share in his estate. Since there had been little real affection between the two, Voltaire did not let the event mar the royal celebrations for him. As he commented to Cideville in a letter, he had in the entertainment "to praise the King most extravagantly, to extol the Dauphin superlatively, to handle the royal family with kid gloves, to satisfy the Court and not to displease Paris."

The piece was given in a specially constructed theatre in the grounds of the palace to an audience who, in Voltaire's opinion, outshone the spectacle on the stage with the magnificence of their dress. Following the king's example, they chattered through the whole performance, which became little more than background music. What was worse, afterwards some complained that they had been bored by the whole entertainment. But at least Louis XV declared himself satisfied, and that was what mattered. Soon afterwards Voltaire was appointed Royal Historian, and promised the position of *gentilhomme ordinaire de Sa Majesté*. So at last M. Arouet, the notary's son, had been accepted at Court, and offered an official position. But even a salary of 2,000 *livres* per annum did not dilute a sense of bitterness. Voltaire had no illusions about the position of intellect at Court. To Thieriot he likened himself to an atheist in church; while to Cideville he wrote that he was "a poor devil who at the age of fifty had become a king's buffoon."

He had produced a tailor-made libretto for a royal entertainment, not one word of which was listened to, and it was for this that his talents had been rewarded.

In considering the awards by which His Majesty contributes to the advancement of literature, the King has this day [1 April] found no one more worthy to receive proof of His favour and to be distinguished by a title of honour, than the Sieur de Voltaire, who has made the most rapid progress in every science he has undertaken, the fruits of which are his writings, which have found well deserved approval.

The last sentence must have caused Voltaire to smile. Denounced; confiscated; suppressed; impounded, and burnt by the hangman would have been a more accurate description of the fate of his works in France.

> *Mon Henri quatre et ma Zaïre,*
> *Et mon Americaine Alzire,*
> *Ne m'ont valu jamais un seul regard du roi;*
> *J'avais mille ennemis avec très peu du gloire;*
> *Les honneurs et les biens pleuvent enfin pour moi*
> *Pour une farce de la foire.*

> My *Henry IV* and my *Zaïre*,
> And my American *Alzire*,
> Never won me a single glance from the king;
> I had a thousand enemies and very little glory;
> Honours and benefits at last rain down on me
> for a fair-ground farce.
> (Quoted in French and English in the *Autobiography*)

The belated taste of success was indeed bitter in Voltaire's mouth. With the appointment as Royal Historian went the use of an apartment at Versailles, though the address was better on paper than in reality. The rooms were situated above the public privies, and the kitchens allocated to the Prince de Condé. But at least he did not have to wait too long before his services were called upon in his official capacity. The French had scored a major victory over the English at the Battle of Fontenoy, at which several of his friends, including Richelieu and the Marquis d'Argenson had acquitted themselves well, and now he was called upon to write the official account. As well, he wrote the *Poème de Fontenoy*, which was a popular success, and even received the accolade of royal approval by being printed on the royal press in the Louvre. He was later surprised and interested to learn that a Falkener had taken part in the campaign, as confidential secretary to the Duke of Cumberland. He wrote asking if by any chance he was related to his friend Everard Falkener.

> Though our nations are enemies at present, yet for ever they ought to entertain a mutual esteem for one another. My intention is to relate what the Duke of Cumberland has done worthy of himself and his name, and to enregister the most particular and noble actions of your chiefs and officers, which deserve to be recorded, and what passed most worthy of praise at Dettenghen and Fontenoy. . . .
>
> I dare or presume to apply to you, sir, on that purpose; if you are so kind as to send me some memoirs, I'll make use of them. If not, I'll content myself with relating what has been acted noble and glorious on our side, and I will mourn and leave in silence many actions done by your nation, which it would be glorious to relate.

That was written in October 1745. It was his old friend, and the following June he again wrote to Falkener, requesting him to enquire into the well-being of a prisoner named the Marquis d'Egnilles.

Such a victory could not pass without due celebration at Versailles, and Rameau and Voltaire were to concoct another entertainment. Either Voltaire had finally got the measure of the composer, or else the latter was becoming less exacting in his old age, but *Le Temple de la Gloire* was produced with less friction than its predecessor. The central character was Trajan, or rather Louis XV in a toga, and the whole piece was an exercise in flattery. Inevitably it brought out the cynical side of Voltaire, which was never very far beneath the surface, where important personages or institutions were concerned. For his part, Rameau provided some of his most elegantly charming music.

Although he was intensely sensual, Louis XV was a curiously unloving individual, and except for a few intimates he almost seemed to repel friendship when it was offered, however tentatively. Voltaire was an ornament to his court, because he was esteemed all over Europe, but the king could not find it in his heart to like him, and the celebrated man of letters did not go out of his way to make himself endearing. Perhaps he was over-anxious not to be impressed by the monarch who reigned over the most magnificent Court in Europe; or perhaps he lacked a suitable degree of *gravitas*. At any rate during the performance he said to Richelieu within earshot of the king: "Is Trajan pleased?" Louis XV was offended at this familiarity, and Voltaire was left under no doubt that he had committed a gaffe. But, even so, more honours came his way. In December 1746 he was made a Gentleman of the Bedchamber, which caused bad feelings among those courtiers who were jealous of their privileges and resented the intrusion into their ranks of someone who was not of noble ancestry.

Then, three years after being snubbed by the Académie Française, Voltaire realised his dearest wish. He was elected to the seat made vacant by the death of Bouhier, a magistrate. Since he was officially in favour at Court, the Académie could hardly pretend he did not exist. On 9 May he was installed, and promptly broke with tradition in his address. For instead of paying a lengthy tribute to Cardinal Richelieu as the founder, and also eulogising his predecessor Bouhier, Voltaire dealt briefly with them, and then went on to examine the French language in detail, mentioning those who were models for all time, including Racine, Corneille, Montaigne and Boileau.

Next, he named three foreigners who all spoke French perfectly: Frederick, his sister Ulrika, the Empress Catherine of Russia, and Pope Benedict XIV. In conclusion Voltaire praised the elegance with which certain of his contemporaries used the language. Among them were Richelieu, President Hénault, Montesquieu, Fontenelle, Crébillon Senior, and his old Jesuit teacher Father Olivet.

Voltaire's speech divided literary society into two factions.

Those who had been mentioned by name thought it excellent; those who had not considered it a monstrous and tasteless diversion from tradition. A stream of spiteful pamphlets was turned out, complaining about his election, and any word or action on his part which could be turned to his disadvantage was carefully waited for. But at least two voices were missing from the shrill chorus: J. B. Rousseau had died in 1741, and the Abbé Desfontaines in 1745.

The strangest fruit of Voltaire's appointment as Royal Historian was the *Manifesto of the King in favour of Prince Charles Edward*. Written in 1746, it was intended to precede the landing of an army on British soil led by the Duc de Richelieu in support of the Young Pretender. But before that could happen all Jacobite hopes were extinguished in the slaughter of Culloden, and after that the idea of restoring the Stuarts was nothing more than a romantic dream. Voltaire had been instructed to write a manifesto, but it turned out to be no clarion call to arms, nor even an indictment of the House of Hanover. His hostility may have been inhibited by the reasonably happy years and much kindness he had received in England, but a cynic might have thought that he was hedging his bets against the failure of the Jacobite Rebellion.

His Majesty [Louis XV], in affording this just assistance to his relation, the descendant of so many Kings, and a Prince worthy of a Throne, takes this step for the people of Europe, fully persuaded that the most Serene Prince Edward depends upon the good will of the people, and looks upon the support of their liberties, laws, and happiness, as the purpose of all his undertakings; and lastly, because the greatest Kings of England have been those, who, like him, being bred in adversity, have deserved the love of the nation.

It is in these sentiments that the King assists the Prince, the son of him who was born the lawful heir of three kingdoms, a warrior, who comes to throw himself into their arms, and, notwithstanding his valour, expects nothing from them and their laws, but a confirmation of his most sacred rights: who never can have a separate interest from theirs, and whose virtues have at length softened the souls that were most prejudiced against his case.

A year before, in 1745, Voltaire set about redeeming the reputation of his play *Mahomet*, which had been so savagely denounced as anti-Christian. He dedicated it to the Pope. This gesture was neither mischievous nor insolent, though undeniably full of self-interest. Benedict XIV was probably the most enlightened, widely educated and humane Pontiff to occupy the Throne of St Peter during the eighteenth century. What was more he was a man of humour. When there was a deadlock during the election he told his fellow Cardinals: "If you want to elect a saint, choose Gotti; if you want a statesman, choose Aldobrandi; if you want a good fellow, elect me."

In a way he had more in common with Voltaire and his scientific consideration of the whole field of human endeavour than with the dogmatic fanatics of the Church in France who considered themselves its spiritual guardians, and persecuted Voltaire so relentlessly. Not only did Benedict XIV disapprove of the way they pursued the heretical Jansenists, but he even attempted to ameliorate the lot of the American Indians by issuing a Bull intended to ensure better treatment for them at the hands of their rapacious conquerors.

Through a friend of a relation of Emilie, *Mahomet* was offered to the Pope, complete with the dedication and the hope that in return His Holiness might be so gracious as to give him his portrait.

The Abbé de Tolignan, who acted as intermediary in Rome, was given two medallions of the Pope to pass on to Voltaire. "Holy Father," wrote Voltaire in Italian, "Your Holiness will excuse the liberty taken by one of the most insignificant yet most devoted admirers of spiritual nobility, in dedicating to the Overlord of the True Religion a work written against the founder of a false and barbaric creed.

"To whom could I better dedicate this satire on the cruelty and the errors of a false prophet, than to the representative and successor of a God of Peace and Truth.

"With the permission of Your Holiness I lay at your feet the work and the author. I make bold to ask your protection for the work. Your blessing for its creator. With this feeling of deep devotion I kiss Your Holy foot. Paris August 17, 1745."

There is a saying which was current in Tudor England: when

there is a search the safest place is under the candle. The Pope received *Mahomet* and Voltaire's letter with graciousness tinged with circumspection. He was not committing himself on paper to anything the Frenchman could turn to his own advantage.

Pope Benedict XIV to his beloved son.
Greetings and Apostolic blessing.
Several weeks ago we were brought your most beautiful tragedy [*bellissima tragedia*] *Mahomet*, which we read with great pleasure. After that the Cardinal Passionei delivered to Us in your name the splendid ode on Fontenoy. Signor Leprotti conveyed to Us your letter of August 17. Each of these proofs of good-will deserves a special acknowledgement. But We combine them all and send you the thanks due to so many proofs of unusual friendship for Us, with the assurance of Our respect for merits which are so outstanding as yours.

The letter went on to defend Voltaire's use of the Latin *hic* as a short word, which had been criticised by a Frenchman in Rome as incorrect. The Pope cited Virgil as a precedent for using either a long or a short form, and ended with his Apostolic blessing. Nowhere was there any mention of the contents of *Mahomet* or the supposed grounds for its censure in France. But what mattered to Voltaire was the fact that its author had received a gracious acknowledgement from the Supreme Head of the Catholic Church. Surely, even Louis XV must be impressed by that.

For years Voltaire had minded deeply that he had been excluded from the Académie Française, and whilst welcome at nearly every foreign court in Europe he had not been recognised at that of his own king. But now both those coveted doors had been opened to him, though acceptance at the highest level did not make him particularly agreeable to others: rather the reverse. At the same time he was embarking on a clandestine love affair with his niece, and the intensity of his passion was affecting his health. For much of 1746 he appears to have been in a highly nervous state, which manifested itself in attacks on others.

Years before, Voltaire had jibed that he had changed his name from Arouet to avoid being confused with the poet Roy. There had been mutual dislike between the two men, and now it flared into open hostility. Roy was older than Voltaire, and in literary circles he was considered a poet of some repute. Now he had been passed over for election to the Académie Française in favour of his rival, and Roy retaliated by writing a parody of the Fontenoy poem, and reissued a poem of his own setting forth all the discreditable or humiliating episodes in Voltaire's life.

Another clash was with a violinist at the Opera, who was supposed to have circulated pamphlets which were discreditable to Voltaire. In the old days it had been others who had applied for *lettres de cachet* for use against Voltaire. Now he enjoyed the bitter satisfaction of using such weapons on his enemies, whether their conduct merited it or not. By mistake the police arrested the violinist's elderly father, a man of blameless reputation. Although he was released at once, the episode lost Voltaire a great deal of goodwill. With tact Cideville urged Voltaire to behave less arrogantly, but a number of friends were becoming exasperated with his off-hand manners, and also those of Emilie du Châtelet. When these two were invited as guests they showed little interest in anyone else, being deep in their own private conversation. Voltaire was riding for a fall.

In the autumn of 1746 Emilie and Voltaire followed the Court to Fontainebleau. Emilie was a remarkable mathematician who, it was said, could divide nine figures by nine figures in her head, but she was no card player. At Fontainebleau luck was against her, and before long she had squandered all her own money and was borrowing from Voltaire. One evening when playing at the Queen's table Emilie lost 84,000 *livres*. Voltaire, who was watching from behind her chair, at last could bear it no longer. He whispered in English that Emilie was playing with cheats. Horrified that others must have heard and understood the comment she rose and left the room. Such was her fear that Voltaire might be killed by some outraged courtier that she sent for her coach and horses and, although it was well after midnight, they left at once with only the minimum of luggage.

This was something that not even Voltaire could shrug off. His previous gaffes were trivial compared with this episode. Believing that it would not be safe to go to Paris, in haste he wrote in great agitation to his old friend the Duchesse du Maine, whose salon he had enlivened as a young man. Years before she and her husband had been actively hostile to the Regent, and now she was sympathetic to Voltaire in his dread at the wrath which, he was convinced, was about to break over his head.

Any writer who fell foul of Louis XV was sure of the friendship, or at least the goodwill, of the Duchesse, and here was France's leading literary figure pleading for her protection. But there was a slightly theatrical atmosphere about the whole affair. By day Voltaire remained hidden in a room in an unused part of the château. Then, after everyone else had gone to bed, he crept down to the Duchesse's room, where a table was laid by the side of her bed. There they dined and talked all through the night.

Good came of the episode, for Voltaire passed the days shut up in his room by writing the first of his *Contes Philosophiques*. These tales, which held the mirror of truth up to contemporary Paris in a series of fantastic stories, were gently satirical in character. They marked a new departure for their author. In tales such as *Zadig*, *La Princesse de Babylone*, *Micromegas*, *Memnon* and *Babouc*, Voltaire gave the world light-hearted trifles which can still be read with pleasure, and which contain observations that are still relevant.

Babouc tells of a Scythian sent by the genie Ithuriel to investigate whether Persepolis (Paris) deserves to be destroyed. After hearing Babouc's account the genie decides that there is something to be said in its favour. "For if all is not well, all is passable." Thus already Voltaire was gently attacking the theory of optimism as set forth by Leibniz. In *Candide* he would give it its death blow.

Voltaire's footman, Longchamps, has left an account of these midnight meetings with the seventy-year-old Duchesse du Maine.

It was from the depths of this retreat that he descended every night to the room of the Duchesse du Maine, after she had gone to bed, and all her servants had retired. One footman only, who was in her confidence, would then set a little table at the side of her bed, and bring in supper for M. de Voltaire. The Princesse took great pleasure in seeing him and talking to him. He amused her by the liveliness of his conversation, and she added to his information many old anecdotes of the Court which he did not know. Sometimes after supper, he read a tale or a little romance which he had written during the day for the purpose of amusing her. It was in this way that he composed *Babouc*, *Memnon*, *Scarmentado*, *Micromegas*, and *Zadig*, of which he wrote several chapters every day.

Perhaps the only people to know Voltaire's exact whereabouts were Emilie and the Comte d'Argental. Even Mme Denis may have been under the impression that he had fled abroad. For her part Emilie was back in Paris, trying to settle her gambling debts. Voltaire had lavished a great deal of money on the additions made at Cirey, but he did not seem inclined to help Emilie out of her present difficulty. When he laid out money he wanted to be sure of a good return, and he held that speculating was one thing but that gambling was for fools, besides being an inexcusable waste of time, and if the experience had taught her a salutary lesson so much the better.

When all debts had been settled, Voltaire returned to Paris, without fuss and almost unnoticed. He soon realised that he was not really welcome at Court, and made the mistake of paying too much attention to Mme de Pompadour. Everyone knew what she was, but propriety demanded that the fiction be maintained. The period of royal favour was over, and there was nothing to be gained by his presence at Versailles, so in the summer of 1746 Voltaire and Emilie went to stay with the Duchesse du Maine at her country house at Anet in Normandy.

In the recent past the couple had made themselves unpopular as guests because of their absorption in each other, and their mutual interests, and it was the same at Anet.

The winter of 1747 found both Voltaire and Emilie at Sceaux, where he committed an extraordinary *faux pas*, arranging for an evening of amateur theatricals without even asking permission from the Duchesse du Maine. He informed his friends and acquaintances that on 15 December a new comedy (*La Prude*, after Wycherley) would be given in the theatre at Sceaux. "All are welcome, without ceremony, at 6 o'clock precisely." Without warning, the Duchesse found herself overrun by five hundred strangers pushing into her house, where they were received almost regally by Voltaire, while she herself was quite ignored. It was a remarkably ill-bred action on his part, which led to his and Emilie's departure from Sceaux.

According to Longchamps there were quarrels between Voltaire and Emilie after their return to Paris. Although their relationship was no longer physical, Voltaire could have been jealous of Clairaut, who was helping Emilie with her translation of Newton. On one occasion when she was late for supper Voltaire rushed upstairs to her study and kicked in the locked door. Whatever he found on the other side was enough to set him screaming. Recently Emilie had become indifferent to the feelings of others, but after that episode she went out of her way to humour Voltaire. For his part, he was still writing inflamed love letters to Mme Denis. "How is my beloved? I have not seen her, but I am afire to see her every day, every hour."

Early in the New Year 1748 the couple returned to Cirey, for the last time. They travelled by night, following a whim of Emilie's. She considered that by so doing she saved valuable time, quite forgetting the hours she frequently spent at the gambling tables. All went well until the back axle of the overloaded coach broke. It fell on its side, injuring one of the footmen. Voltaire was buried under Emilie, her maid and numerous parcels. Eventually he was dragged out feet first through the door which now faced the sky. He was screaming like an enraged parrot. Help would have to be brought from the nearest village, which was several miles away, so there was nothing to do but wait. The ground was covered with snow, though the sky was clear and brilliant with stars. Like true philosophers the couple made the most of their situation, settled down on cushions by the roadside and contemplated the heavens. The pleasures of astronomy were interrupted by the arrival of some peasants, who righted the coach and mended the axle to the best of their ability. But trouble followed over the meanness of their reward, and they had the satisfaction of seeing the coach break down again after it had gone only a few yards. If the travellers still wanted their assistance they could pay for it, generously. It was broad daylight before they reached the house owned by an acquaintance, M. de Chauvelin.

At Cirey the château came alive again, and rehearsals were started for a comedy to be given in Voltaire's little theatre in the attic. It was almost as though they had never been away.

Chapter 13

THE END OF AN ERA

Now little more than a year of life together remained for Voltaire and Emilie. After their precipitate flight from Fontainebleau Emilie was sensitive to the suggestion that she was probably no longer welcome at Court. So, when the Jesuit Father Menou suddenly appeared at Cirey with the news that the presence of Madame la Marquise and her friend Voltaire was required at the Court of ex-King Stanislas she was delighted to accept. Was he not the father of Maria Leszczynska, and therefore the father-in-law of Louis XV?

The exile from Poland of Stanislas had been softened by the gift of the Duchy of Lorraine, and its independence from France had been one of the reasons which had brought Voltaire to Cirey in the first place. If he heard of any danger, the police or a *lettre de cachet*, he could be over the frontier after only a short ride. The ex-king's capital was at Nancy, which he transformed into the handsomest town in France, a title it still claims over two centuries later. But he too must have his Versailles, and another palace was built in the small garrison town of Lunéville. His residence would not have disgraced Warsaw itself. As a retreat for a king in exile, it was truly magnificent.

The reason for Father Menou's visit was not simply because Stanislas wished for the company of two of the most remarkable brains in Europe. It was also motivated by a desire on the part of the Jesuit to disrupt the relationship between ex-king Stanislas and his mistress, the Marquise de Bouffleurs, who was known to both Emilie and Voltaire. For his own ends he decided to introduce a rival at the little Court. But unfortunately for him, and tragically for Voltaire, Emilie was to take the wrong bait.

From the start the plan miscarried. Emilie and the Marquise became the dearest friends instead of the deadliest enemies. There was worse to come: Emilie regarded Stanislas almost as a favourite uncle, and the Jesuit had achieved nothing.

Voltaire soon tired of Court life at Lunéville, but Emilie revelled in it. Mme de Bouffleurs was recognised as the ex-king's official mistress, but she did not let it interfere with her private life. Until recently the younger of her lovers had been the Marquis de Saint-Lambert, an army officer, poet and courtier at Lunéville. But when he returned from a spell of active service it was to discover that he had been replaced by the Vicomte d'Adhémar. Consequently, when Emilie arrived he was quite ready for a new adventure. Of course Mme de Bouffleurs soon heard what had happened, and did all she could to smooth the path of true love, by making sure that Voltaire did not find out what was going on.

The first visit to Lunéville ended when Stanislas went to stay with his daughter at Versailles, and Emilie and Voltaire returned to Cirey. There Emilie spent her time thinking about Saint-Lambert, who was with his regiment at Nancy. Before long she became thoroughly jealous, imagining that already he was unfaithful to her. By then they had returned to Paris, so that Voltaire could supervise the rehearsals of *Sémiramis*. Soon Emilie insisted that they must go back to Lorraine, where the little Court-in-exile was now at Commercy. She thought Mme de Bouffleurs might try to snare Saint-Lambert again, and she hoped that her husband might receive a Court appointment, which would give them a valid reason for living at Lunéville.

It was at Commercy that Voltaire was left in no doubt about what was going on. One evening he walked into Emilie's apartment without formality, and was coldly informed by Saint-Lambert that if anything was annoying him he could leave the room, implying that no gentleman would interrupt another at such a time. Saint-Lambert even added that he was prepared to challenge him to a duel. But Voltaire's duelling days, such as they were, were long past, and he returned to his own suite of rooms. There he sent for Longchamps and instructed him to go into Commercy and obtain a carriage, so they could return to Paris at once.

Instead, Longchamps went straight to Emilie and told her of Voltaire's orders. She knew his temperament. Give him a few hours and he would calm down, and even be laughing at his discovery. But at all costs he must be prevented from leaving Commerçy. That would set all tongues wagging, and since Emilie wanted Stanislas to give her husband a position at Court, that might be awkward. She told Longchamps to return to his master and say no carriage was available. This he did, but Voltaire was still angry, and he told Longchamps to go to Nancy first thing in the morning and find a carriage there. Back he went to Emilie, who decided it was time to intervene personally.

The meeting was stormy. Voltaire reproached her infidelity, and she basely retaliated with comments on his lack of virility. The circumstances being what they were, it was a charge he could not deny, even when she spitefully added that she had every consideration for his health and did not wish to kill him. So, she reasoned, he could hardly object if she turned to one of *his* friends to act as a deputy. The argument had a certain logic, and before long he was laughing at the ridiculous side of the affair. Perhaps he was also laughing up his sleeve over himself and Mme Denis.

Emilie had won half the battle, and the next day she talked Saint-Lambert out of any idea of challenging Voltaire to a duel. Voltaire even told Saint-Lambert that he was still at the happy age when love was a reality. "Make the most of it," he advised the thirty-three-year-old usurper, adding hypocritically that such pleasures were not for someone as old and sick as himself.

Stanislas, who must have known what was going on, suggested that Voltaire should accompany him on a return visit to Paris. There he could attend the first performance of *Sémiramis*, the kindly monarch pointed out. Mme de Bouffleurs had been advised by her doctors to take the waters at Plombières, a spa in the Vosges, and the ex-king suggested that Emilie should accompany her. Since Saint-Lambert had to remain at Lunéville, it was perhaps his punishment for the way she had hurt Voltaire. At any rate, Emilie gained little pleasure from the visit, and came near to quarrelling with Mme de Bouffleurs. Nor was Voltaire's expedition to Paris much more successful, since *Sémiramis* was not a triumph, giving neither offence nor great delight. At any time Voltaire was inclined to live on his nerves, and the strain of the rehearsals now made him physically ill. He even quarrelled with Mme Denis, and decided to return to Lunéville.

The journey was most unwise in his state of health, and it seemed more than likely that the life might suddenly go out of that frail body. He was forced to break his journey at Châlons-sur-Marne, and when he left the hotel he had to be carried down the stairs by Longchamps. The further he travelled from Paris, and the nearer he drew to Emilie, the more he recovered. Not only had Emilie regained her cavalier, now that she had returned from Plombières, but at last Stanislas had given her husband the appointment she had been seeking so assiduously for months. The Marquis du Châtelet became *Grand Maréchal des Logis de la Cour.*

There was one person who did not like the turn events had taken at Lunéville, and that was Father Menou. His plan had been to sow discord between the ex-king and his mistress (and eventually replace her either with a second wife, or at least with a mistress over whom he could exert his influence). But his plan has misfired completely, and, what was worse, Emilie du Châtelet was practically the uncrowned queen of Lunéville. She organised everyone to her heart's content, arranged plays, scientific experiments and the like. The Jesuit's schemes could not have gone more wrong if he had been up against the Evil One himself, and now when he complained of Voltaire's presence at Lunéville all he received from Stanislas was a snub.

By Christmas the two philosophers were back at Cirey, and Emilie had made up her mind to finish her translation of Newton, and write the commentary on it. For both of them the year had been diverting, but unsettling, with moves from Cirey to Lunéville, Commercy, Paris, Plombières, and back again.

Within a few days of her return to the Château Emilie discovered that she was pregnant. At once Voltaire showed the practical side of his nature by inviting Saint-Lambert to come to Cirey to discuss the matter. Emilie's husband was with his regiment, and they decided that she should write and ask him to come home on business connected with the estate. For years the marriage had to all intents and purposes been in a state of abeyance, but what Emilie now embarked on was little less than the seduction of her own husband, to cover up a most awkward situation. When she at last whispered her little secret, the poor man really believed that the child was his, and there were celebrations. Even Versailles heard what was going on at Cirey, and it was commented that to want her husband at such a time could only be the cravings of a pregnant woman.

Not only had Emilie two grown-up children but she was forty-four, and dangerously old for another child after so long an interval. Without reticence she asked Stanislas if she could have the use of the late queen's apartments for her lying-in, and as usual she had her own way. But for the moment she was in Paris, working on her beloved Newton. Voltaire was also in the city, consumed with nervousness as the first night of another play, *Nanine*, drew near. To Frederick's delight he had almost promised to go to Berlin after the birth of Emilie's baby. Half Europe seemed to know about the extraordinary triangle at Cirey, and all Frederick's jealousy of Emilie showed when he remarked to one of his sisters: "A certain Saint-Lambert enjoys the glory, her husband the shame and Voltaire the spectacle." Much as he wanted Voltaire back at Potsdam he was not above saying that the Frenchman had all the endearing qualities and also the malice of a monkey.

Unwittingly, Emilie nearly ended the longstanding friendship between Voltaire and Richelieu. Both men were to be present, along with other members of the Académie Française, at a sycophantic audience with Louis XV to congratulate him on the recently concluded Peace of Aix la Chapelle, though there was little enough in it for the French to rejoice about. Voltaire had written a panegyric for Richelieu to deliver, as President of the Académie, to Louis the well-beloved. But when he arrived at Versailles he was annoyed to overhear someone else reciting the speech. Afterwards there was a fearful row with Voltaire, who for once was innocent of any trickery. What had happened was that Emilie had shown the speech to Mme de Bouffleurs, who asked for copies for her own friends. Not for the first time did one of Emilie's indiscretions end in laughter all round, but it nearly cost Voltaire a long and valuable friendship.

The time was now approaching when Emilie must go to Lunéville for the birth of her baby. Before she left Cirey she had set everything in order: the management of the estate; her own personal affairs, and even her literary undertakings. It was as though she had some premonition of what would happen.

Typically, she was working at her desk when the birth took place. With very little warning a baby girl was delivered, into the apron of a startled maid. For about a week all went well for Emilie, but then her temperature started to rise, and quite suddenly she died. Voltaire was beside himself with grief, and he tumbled down a flight of stairs, to be picked up by Longchamps and the unwitting cause of the tragedy, Saint-Lambert. But there was no rage or bitterness in Voltaire's strange heart. All he said was: "*Ah! Mon ami! C'est vous qui me l'avez tuée.*"

Voltaire showed and felt grief to a degree that he had never experienced before, or would again. Emilie had had a very strong and dominating personality, but despite all their quarrels and upsets he in his own quirky way had loved her for nearly two decades.

Soon after her mother's death the baby girl also died, a matter of indifference to Voltaire. To the Court at Lunéville it was like a party game which had gone tragically wrong. The laughter was replaced by shocked silence, and all Voltaire wanted was to get away from Lorraine and Cirey, with all its memories. Now Paris was the immediate goal.

Frederick hid his undoubted satisfaction at Emilie's death under the mask of decorum, and began a letter to Voltaire: "I am the oldest of your friends." That was not strictly true, but at the age of fifty-five Voltaire suddenly found himself rootless and in need of friendship and security. If he went to Prussia he would be exchanging the possessiveness of one individual for that of another, but it was a condition that he was prepared to accept. Paris had been soured for him by the malice of his enemies, while at Potsdam he would have the favour of a sovereign who had shown himself to be one of the most powerful in Europe.

Chapter 14

POTSDAM

During the years at Cirey Voltaire had been widening his horizons until he must have known as much about this planet and man's life on it as the most erudite of his contemporaries. That knowledge would prove the basis of the wisdom of his old age, and be returned to mankind through his contributions to the *Encyclopédie*, and in his own *Dictionnaire Philosophique*. Both were the works of a man who could see beyond the horizon of his own culture, race and religious background (even if he did not subscribe to that religion), and today it is difficult to realise how uncommon that was in the eighteenth century.

In the *Lettres Philosophiques* Voltaire had used a comparative method to show his countrymen what he considered was wrong with France. *Charles XII* on the other hand was perhaps the first biography which read as grippingly as a novel. In it he contrasted the Swedish king's overweening desire for conquest and glory, while his contemporary, Peter the Great, set about building a new and westward-looking Russia out of a disunited and benighted medieval kingdom. Then in *Le Siècle de Louis XIV*, which would take twenty years to mature, he achieved a brilliant survey of all aspects of a country's development and achievements.

But now the poor man wandered disconsolately through the house in Paris, at night and in the dark, miserably calling Emilie's name. Until the final years at Ferney that liaison was to form the longest single episode in his life. Like an old married couple they had taken each other for granted, and it was only now that Voltaire realised just how much Emilie had meant to him. Yet, demanding as she was, it had been Emilie who had been terrified of losing Voltaire to Frederick. For his part Voltaire had loved her, been exasperated by her, taken her for granted, and admired her mind. In short, he had shared himself more completely with her than he was to do with any other person during his life. His relationship with his niece was in a completely different category. That was a passion for a plump, middle-aged woman, who was described as being more female than any woman had a right to be.

Severely practical in all matters except metaphysics, Emilie had satisfied her desires in much the same way that she might have eaten a good meal when hungry. At least until Saint-Lambert appeared there was nothing particularly romantic about her infidelities, as far as her husband and Voltaire were concerned. It was simply a case of a bout of love-making, and then back to Newton.

Together, Voltaire and the Marquis du Châtelet grieved for Emilie. The philosopher had spent 40,000 francs on enlarging the château, but since the Marquis could only repay 10,000 francs Voltaire accepted an I.O.U. for the remainder. To d'Argental he wrote:

I can no longer bear to see Lunéville where I lost her in the saddest way. But I like to see the place which she made beautiful. I have lost half of myself, a spirit for which mine was made, a friend for twenty years. The most adoring father loves his daughter no differently.

It took several weeks to pack up all his books and possessions; furniture, pictures, statuary and *objets d'art*. Then it was time to say goodbye to the Marquis and neighbours such as the kindly Mme Champbonin. They were never to meet again, though they kept up a correspondence.

In Paris Voltaire bought Emilie's half-share in the house they had occupied together. But few visitors were now welcome. Among the few who came to sympathise were Richelieu, d'Argental, and Voltaire's own nephew, the Abbé Mignot. In December 1749 Mme Denis came to keep house for him. Work, and the hostility he encountered in literary circles in Paris may have helped to distract Voltaire at this time. There were two more plays on themes drawn from the ancient world: *Catilina* and *Oreste*. The latter was on a subject already used by the much revered Crébillon, and on the first night his followers barracked for three hours. In the end the claque was defeated by the applause from Voltaire's admirers, urged on by the playwright himself. Voltaire lent out of his box shouting: "Applaud, applaud! brave Athenians! It is like Sophocles!"

In Berlin, Frederick was preparing to welcome Voltaire, while at the same time attempting to speed his departure from France by the most devious of tricks. In the end, however, it would be the writer's own pen which would make it wise for him to leave the country. The Church in France owned between a fifth and a quarter of the country's wealth, but it made no financial contribution to the State. In 1750 Louis XV planned to tax the clergy, but nothing came of the attempt. This provoked Voltaire to write the pamphlet *La Voix du sage et du peuple*, in which he exhorted the king to assert himself as the true ruler of France against the selfish and antisocial. Of course it was like thrusting a stick into a hornets' nest. The pamphlet was banned by the Vatican, as might be expected, and the following year it was even condemned by the very administration in whose support it had been written. After that Voltaire was in a receptive frame of mind and ready to listen to Frederick's blandishments. But at the same time the King of Prussia set about stinging Voltaire's self-esteem.

One of the most detested of his literary critics was Fréron (an ex-Abbé who incidentally married his own niece), and now Frederick let it be known that he was considering using him to keep him in touch with all that was going on in the literary world in Paris. It was the position which had been originally held by Thieriot. In Voltaire's elegant phrase Fréron was "the worm that had crawled out of the carcass of Desfontaines," and he rose like a fish to Frederick's bait:

I am informed that a certain Fréron has been proposed to Your Majesty. Permit me to inform you that for this position of literary correspondent you need a man who possesses the confidence of the public. Fréron has no such standing. His reputation is tarnished and he is generally despised, etc:

Next, the king further goaded Voltaire by praising the poet

D'Arnaud Baculard in verse, saying that France's Apollo (Voltaire) was in decline, while Baculard's sun was only just rising, to herald an even more glorious day. When Voltaire felt threatened by a rival, real or imaginary, he could show a jealousy worthy of an Italian *prima donna*. That, plus the odium incurred by the pamphlet *La Voix du sage et du peuple*, was sufficient. On 24 June he informed the Duchesse du Maine, after a performance of his *Rome Sauvée* at Sceaux, that he was leaving early the following morning for Prussia.

Voltaire had only reached Compiégne when he was writing to the Comte and Comtesse d'Argental: "Why am I here? Why am I going further? Why have I left you, my dear angels?"

Well might he ask. Unknown to him Frederick had instructed his Ambassador at Versailles to inform the French authorities that it was all Voltaire's idea to come to Berlin, and that if they wished, he (Frederick) would make him less than welcome. Voltaire knew that he was in bad odour at Court. He had been deprived of his official title of Historian to the King, though he was allowed to keep his pension of 2,000 francs, and his title of *Gentilhomme ordinaire de Sa Majesté*. An attempt to induce Mme Denis to accompany him had failed. In her eyes Berlin was a cultural desert, and she refused to leave Paris. Besides, she must have known that she would be no more welcome to Frederick than Emilie had been.

The journey continued, and Voltaire went by way of Fontenoy, so that he could see the site of the battle. Then on to Berlin, where he was warmly welcomed by Frederick on 10 July. It was a triumph for the king. First he had induced Maupertuis to take the chair as President of the Berlin Academy, and now he could tell Europe that Voltaire had come to be his guest. It was an honour which was recognised by the citizens, and recorded by Collini, Voltaire's secretary. Soon after arriving, Voltaire attended a Carousel, modelled on the military parades of Louis XIV at Versailles.

> All the Court had come from Potsdam to Berlin. A little while before the King himself made his appearance, there suddenly arose a murmur of admiration, and I heard everywhere around the name Voltaire! Voltaire! Looking down, I saw Voltaire

accordingly; among a group of great lords, who were walking over the arena towards one of the Court boxes. He wore a modest appearance, but joy was painted in his eyes: you cannot love glory, and not feel grateful for the prize attached to it.

For his part, Voltaire was more than willing to be dazzled, at least initially. In a letter to d'Argental he wrote of his new patron:

He carries the burden of kingship from five o'clock in the morning till dinner. He gives the whole of the rest of the day to *belles lettres*. He deigns to work with me for three hours on end. He submits his great genius to criticism; and at supper, he is the most amiable of men.

Later he was to describe his revision of Frederick's verses more succinctly, though far less flatteringly.

While Frederick might be happy to regard Voltaire as the sun in his sky, there were others who were less pleased to have their own radiance dimmed. The young scientist Algarotti, who had stayed at Cirey, was well disposed to Voltaire, which was more than could be said for most of Frederick's circle. Until his arrival, Maupertuis had been the uncrowned king of the intellectuals at Potsdam. But now that position had been usurped by the very man who had obtained the position of President of the Academy for him. Maupertuis was vain, and as fiery as his own red wig, and a clash with the newcomer was inevitable.

When Frederick had been wooing Voltaire he wrote: "You resemble the White Elephant, which causes the Shah of Persia and Mogul Emperor to fight each other, and which the victor uses to increase the number of his titles. Adieu, if you come here you will see my list of honours: Frederick, by the Grace of God King of Prussia, Elector of Brandenburg, Possessor of Voltaire etc."

Now he possessed Voltaire, but there was someone he definitely did not wish to acquire at the same time. For years Emilie had stopped him from coming to Berlin, and when he asked if Mme Denis could join him the king gave a flat refusal. Voltaire would occupy a pleasant room in Sans Souci, the king's summer residence at Potsdam, but Frederick was not having any woman intruding into his little kingdom within a kingdom; not even to please Voltaire.

Sans Souci (which survived the bombing of the Second World War) was a charming and intimate rococo villa occupying a position among the royal palaces in and around Berlin comparable to the Petit Trianon at Versailles. But there was one drawback. There were no fireplaces, and when autumn came Voltaire was accorded the privilege of moving into the City Palace in Potsdam, where he was allotted rooms below the apartments occupied by the king.

Flippantly Voltaire wrote to Mme Denis: "I have been handed in proper form to the King of Prussia. My marriage to him is therefore made, but will it be a happy one? After a flirtation lasting so many years this marriage was inevitable."

Frederick was most solicitous for his guest's welfare. At midday Frederick dined with his officers. The food was as abundant as it was heavy, and not at all to Voltaire's liking.

I have extricated myself from the midday meal; too many generals and too many Princes in attendance there. I could never become used to sitting opposite a King *en cérémonie*, and be obliged to talk with him in public. The evening meal is shorter, more cheerful, and more healthy. I should die in three months time if I were obliged to dine every noon with a King in public.

During that first summer at Potsdam he filled his days working on *Le Siècle de Louis XIV*, and correcting the king's verses. His was a privileged position, and he knew it.

He [Frederick] has never sent me to the stone-quarries for correcting his verse; he thanks me, changes his poetry, and always for the better. He writes admirable verse. His prose is as good as his poetry, but he writes it all in too much haste. His friends here are good courtiers who have told him that all he does is perfect; but what is really perfect is the fact that he trusts me more than he does those flatterers, and that he really loves me and senses the truth when he hears it.

After the treatment he had received from Louis XV it was indeed flattering to have a king who not only asked his advice, but even acted on it. But that did not stop him being witty about Frederick's homosexuality. The king himself was sensitive about the amusement it gave at other Courts, and had indulged in the ploy of trying to cause a scandal with a member of the opposite sex. From the outset of their marriage, the queen had lived apart with her own household, and in an attempt to redress the balance Frederick paid well-publicised attention to Barbarina, a popular Italian dancer at the Royal Theatre in Berlin. She was invited to visit the king in his box, and he visited her in her own apartment. Voltaire was thoroughly uncharitable, declaring that Barbarina only appealed to Frederick because she had legs like a man. The episode was largely staged for the benefit of Mme de Pompadour, his principal detractor at Versailles, but she remained unconvinced.

It was a curious situation in which Voltaire found himself at Potsdam. He was the greatest literary prize in Europe, standing head and shoulders above all others who surrounded the king. That in itself was enough to ensure their dislike. He had his own rooms, his secretary, and could speak to Frederick as an equal; but he was not part of the king's circle. During the day he kept to himself, occupying his time with writing, or improving the king's verses and prose. Frederick had wanted him to come to Berlin, and he had done so, but now his life was being lived on his own terms. Without realising it, he was storing up ill-will, and there were those who lost no time in making mischief.

Frederick was very anxious to be accepted as a serious man of letters, and not just as a dilettante, and unwittingly Voltaire was undermining his self-confidence. Before long he became disenchanted with his guest, and disenchantment led to spitefulness. Voltaire heard indirectly that Frederick had said of him: "We squeeze the orange, and then throw away the peel." Then Maupertuis passed on to the king an unwise remark made by his guest. General Manheim had apparently asked for help with his *Reminiscences of Russia*, when a messenger arrived with the king's latest verses, also in need of correction. Voltaire was said to have told the General: "Better come back some other time! Here the King has sent me his dirty linen to wash. Next time I'll wash yours."

When questioned, Voltaire denied ever having made the remark, but Frederick was not convinced that he was telling the truth, and the episode formed the first of two almost simultaneous cracks in their friendship.

Wherever he found himself, Voltaire never missed the chance of increasing his fortune, and not long after his arrival in Berlin such an opportunity came his way. In the War of Austrian Succession, which resulted in the annexation of Silesia, the King of Saxony had been forced to issue paper money to maintain his currency. After the Peace of Dresden in 1745 this paper money had a face value only half that of its equivalent in gold. In the treaty there was a clause which stated that Prussians who held Saxon paper money were to be paid at par. Therefore, Prussian speculators were buying all the paper money they could obtain by way of Holland, paying only half its face value. The money was then sold to the Saxon agent in Berlin, who had to redeem the notes at their face value. Eventually the Saxon Government complained to Frederick, who forbade the practice, but was unable to stop it. The transactions were merely carried on with greater secrecy.

Voltaire was to receive 20,000 francs a year from Frederick so long as he remained at his Court, and during his first winter in Berlin he instructed a Jewish dealer in furs and jewels named Hershel to go to Dresden and buy 40,000 francs' worth of paper money which he—Voltaire—would then sell in Berlin, making a one hundred per cent. profit. But something went wrong with the transaction, and Voltaire was more than anxious to have his bill of exchange back. Hershel, however, was only willing to return it after Voltaire had bought some of his jewels. Voltaire went to an independent jeweller to have them valued, and found that they had been absurdly over-priced. It was blackmail, and unwisely Voltaire brought a court case. Perhaps he thought that as the guest of the king this kind of conduct (which would be condoned or at least winked at among highly placed courtiers in France) would also be tolerated in Prussia. But he was mistaken. Frederick was angered by the whole episode, and forbade him to live at Sans Souci while the affair was before the court.

Voltaire claimed that at the time he had sent the entrepreneur to Dresden with the 40,000 francs to buy jewels and furs for his theatrical performances, and produced a list of the articles he had considered acquiring. This was in his own handwriting, and contained several amendments, as well as Hershel's signature. But Hershel declared that it was a forgery, which he had never signed. By law he was a Protected Jew—protected, that is, from the worst forms of anti-Semitic oppression, but hardly looked on as a true Prussian citizen.

The court found against him. But such a sordid episode reflected no credit to either party. It lowered Voltaire's standing in the eyes of the Berliners, and was a profound shock to Frederick. The man he had honoured with the Order of Merit and made his Chamberlain had been involved in a case which was as complicated as it was unedifying. His idol had turned out to have feet of clay: but Voltaire merely received a small fine for having indulged in illegal speculation.

Frederick was both lonely and possessive. Although always surrounded by people, for he could not bear to be alone, there were few he cared to call friends. He still wanted Voltaire at Sans Souci, and offered him the chance of returning in a letter which, though it contained a dignified rebuke, was far removed from the petulance which marked their previous differences.

If you want to come back here, you are at liberty to do so. I do not wish to hear any more about lawsuits, including your own. As you have won it, I congratulate you, but I am glad the whole affair is ended. I trust you will have no more lawsuits, whether with the Old or the New Testament. Such things leave scars, and even all the talents of the greatest French genius cannot hide the stains which such demeanour must leave on your good name and your reputation.

Ever since Maupertuis had repeated Voltaire's witticism about washing Frederick's dirty linen, the poet had nursed a grudge against the quick-tempered savant. Maupertuis' contribution to science included one important discovery which enhanced his prestige throughout Europe. He had undertaken an expedition to Lapland, where he made on-the-spot calculations which proved Newton's theory that the earth was slightly flattened at the poles. He was every bit as jealous of his scientific reputation as Voltaire was sensitive to literary criticism.

One evening the king chose as his guests leading members of

the French residents in Berlin. Among them were Maupertuis and Voltaire. The sharp-featured poet in his neat peruke greeted Maupertuis, whose round complacent face was framed by the firey aureole of his wig. Voltaire congratulated his fellow country-man on his latest book, *Letters on Happiness*. Then he qualified his approval: "Your book, President, has given me pleasure, apart from a few obscurities which we'll discuss together."

Touchy as ever, Maupertuis retorted: "Obscurities, Monsieur! It might very well have obscurities for you."

Voltaire went very quiet, and addressed the man who in the past he had called the pole-flattener: "You have my esteem, President. You are brave. You want war. You shall have it. In the meanwhile, let us eat *le rôti du roi* in peace."

It was to be the start of yet another quarrel; not the last, but certainly the most entertaining for the onlooker. Maupertuis showed the courage of a charging bull, while Voltaire was to prove a singularly agile matador.

Among those who came to Berlin hoping to make their fame and fortune under that patronage of Frederick was an obscure writer, Laurent de la Beaumelle, who brought with him a banal little book, *Mes Pensées*, published in Copenhagen in 1751. He wished to introduce himself and his masterpiece to Frederick, and approached Maupertuis to furnish the necessary introduction. Among the would-be epigrams it contained were the following:

Voltaire is not the greatest of poets: but he is the best paid.
The King of Prussia rewards men of letters on the same principle as the German princes lavish their favours on dwarfs and Court buffoons.

One can only think that Maupertuis read *Mes Pensées*, for he handed it on to Voltaire, requesting him to make the introduc-tion. Voltaire chose to treat the book as a joke, which he shared with Frederick at one of his convivial supper parties at Sans Souci. Maupertuis was among the guests, and later he solemnly told La Beaumelle that Voltaire had discussed the book with the king. After a lapse of a few days La Beaumelle called on Mauper-tuis, to inquire why he had not been summoned by the king. Now he was told Voltaire had been making fun of his pearls of wisdom, and that Frederick had said that for his part he would confer the office of bleating idiot on the young man. Not only did La Beaumelle retaliate by spreading calumny and malicious statements about Voltaire, but when the size of his debts made it necessary to leave Berlin in a hurry, he went to Frankfurt and there brought out a pirated edition of *Le Siècle de Louis XIV*. What was worse, he made inaccurate and offensive additions of his own, which devalued Voltaire's work among those who had no access to the authentic text.

Although *Louis XIV* was a panegyric in praise of seventeenth-century France, the authorities could still see no merit in it. If Voltaire heaped praise on Louis XIV, it could only be intended as an unspoken criticism of Louis XV. Moreover, La Beaumelle went on to attack Voltaire's *Supplément du Siècle de Louis XIV*, in which he disavowed the pirated edition. In an open letter he told Voltaire:

The whole world abandons you, Sir. Disgraced in Berlin, where it only rested with you to be happy, you have been rebuffed at Hanover, where you asked for all recompense only an annuity of a thousand pounds sterling, etc., etc.

One of the more unpleasant aspects of the eighteenth-century literary quarrels was the manner in which they were conducted in the full glare of publicity. Thus Voltaire had to endure the stings of the gadfly La Beaumelle as well as accept that *Louis XIV*, on which he had worked for years, had been banned in France.

There was one friend who remained constant, although they had not met for nearly a quarter of a century. He was Everard Falkener, and Voltaire always took a lively and warm-hearted interest in his affairs. In 1747 the ex-ambassador to Constantinople married a member of the Churchill family, and, shortly before the death of Emilie, Voltaire wrote to congratulate him:

You acquaint me you are a husband and a father, and I hope you are a happy one. It behoves a secretary to a great general, to marry a great officer's daughter, and really I am transported with joy to see the blood of a Marlborough, mixed with that of my dearest Falkener. I do present your lady with my most humble respects, and I kiss your child.

For his part Falkener kept Voltaire abreast of English publications, and advised him about his publishing interests in London. When *Louis XIV* caused trouble, it was in a letter to Falkener that Voltaire opened his heart. In the past the goodwill of George I and George II had helped ensure the success of the *Henriade* in England, and he hoped that Falkener would present a copy of *Louis XIV* to the Duke of Cumberland, and so stimulate interest in the work in English society.

Now the quarrel with Maupertuis was to come to a head, and Berlin proved to be as intrigue-ridden and disingenuous as any society Voltaire had encountered in Paris, even during the Regency of his youth.

Koenig, the Swiss mathematician, held the position of Court Librarian to the Princess of Orange at The Hague. Before taking up the appointment he had numbered himself among the intellectuals surrounding Frederick, and through Maupertuis had been elected to the Berlin Academy. A scientific quarrel grew up between the two men, concerning the principle of the earth's minimum resistance. Maupertuis claimed that he had made a discovery in this field, but Koenig politely suggested that it had already been investigated and commented on by Leibniz in letters to a certain Professor Hermann. Maupertuis flared up and insisted that Koenig should publish his theories, being convinced that the younger man would back down when confronted with the wrath of none other than the President of the Berlin Academy. But, far from backing down, Koenig published his theories, and clinched the argument by quoting from an unpublished letter by Leibniz.

Now it was Maupertuis who refused to modify his claims. For years he had fed on flattery and adulation, and could not believe that anyone would dare to question his capabilities for original research or thought. He said outright that the letter quoted by Koenig was a forgery. When it was proved to be perfectly genuine he set about publishing a pamphlet in his own defence entitled *Appeal to the Public*. But before it could be released from the printers there was another pamphlet circulating in Berlin,

entitled *Reply to an Academician*, which exposed the crude behaviour of Maupertuis towards an inoffensive scholar and
scientist. The President of the Berlin Academy had actually
written to the Princess of Orange asking her to advise Koenig to
keep quiet, or risk losing his job in her household.

The pamphlet was well written, reasoned, and moderate in
tone. Everyone knew who the author must be: Voltaire.

The Berlin Academy was Frederick's favourite intellectual
brain-child, and he was enraged that Voltaire, his guest, had seen
fit to join in the quarrel. To criticise Maupertuis was akin to
lèse-majesté, for Frederick himself had come to his defence with a
pamphlet which uncritically praised the scientist.

It was a quarrel which brought out the better side of Voltaire's
nature. He was not simply motivated by jealousy of Maupertuis,
as Frederick suggested. As he saw it, a powerful man was using
all his influence to crush a lesser one, simply because a scientific
statement had not proved to be as original as he had claimed.

The episode had become a question of intellectual integrity,
and Voltaire foresaw the inevitable outcome, and set about
transferring his funds from Prussia. He wrote to Mme Denis:
"Can you believe it, instead of being indignant the King has hotly
taken the side of the tyrannical philosopher. He won't even read
Koenig's reply. Nobody can open the eyes that he wants to keep
shut. Once a calumny has entered into the mind of a King it is like
gout in a prelate. It can never be driven out."

The king and Voltaire continued to behave as though nothing
out of the ordinary were happening, but it was only a matter of
time before there was a break between them. The form it would
take, however, was something which no one could have foreseen.

Apart from his intervention in the quarrel between Maupertuis
and Koenig, life for Voltaire had become less hectic. It seems
likely that, in the absence of Mme Denis, he was having an affair
with the thirty-seven-year-old Charlotte-Sophia, daughter of the
last Count of Oldenburg and wife of a younger son of the first
Earl of Portland. The marriage broke up in 1740, and the ensuing
lawsuit even had political overtones, because the future of several
north German principalities were involved. When Voltaire met
her she was living in Berlin. He found her charming, intelligent,
and entertaining: a rare quality in Frederick's city. In fact the

king became jealous to the point of having Voltaire's correspondence with the Countess intercepted.

Late in 1752 Voltaire conceived what was to become his most important literary work. Its shape was still vague and all he knew was that it was intended for the "advancement of human reason." Years later it would be published as the *Dictionnaire Philosophique*: one of the seminal works of the eighteenth century. But for the moment philosophy was put to one side as the comical literary quarrel between Voltaire and Maupertuis began to develop. It all began with a collection of short essays by Maupertuis, published under the title of *Lettres*. Voltaire described them in a letter to Mme Denis:

> In the midst of these quarrels, Maupertuis has gone quite mad. You may not know that he was shut up at Montpellier twenty years ago, during one of his fits. His malady has returned, violently. He has just published a book in which he contends that the existence of God can only be proved by an algebraic formula; that everyone can predict the future by exalting his soul; that, if one wishes to discover the nature of the human understanding, one must go to the South Seas and dissect giants, ten feet high. The whole book is in this style. He has read it to some of the Berliners who find it admirable.

Voltaire was not letting his imagination run away with him, and inventing a book such as Swift might have written about in one of his satirical tales, but accurately describing the President of the Berlin Academy's latest contribution to scientific thought. Among the suggestions were:

(1) That life should be prolonged to several hundred years by closing the pores of the skin with a form of varnish to prevent sweating.

(2) That a huge pit should be dug to the centre of the earth so that scientific measurements could be carried out there.

(3) That one of the Great Pyramids should be blown apart with gunpowder to discover just what was inside. (Maupertuis was convinced that the Sultan would be only too glad to satisfy the curiosity of the French King, and readily give permission.)

(4) That a Latin town should be built, in which everyone, however menial, spoke only Latin. Everything, including sermons, plays and lawsuits, would be conducted in Latin, and youths who flocked there from all over Europe would learn Latin far quicker than they could do at a University.

(5) That doctors should only be paid if their clients recovered.

(6) That criminals should be used for vivisection, and perhaps in this way the connection between the body and the soul might be discovered.

Cold-bloodedly Maupertuis wrote:

I would willingly see criminals used for these operations, however little hope of success there might be in them. Possibly one might make discoveries relating to the marvellous union of the soul and body, if one dared to search for the connection in the brain of a living man. One should not be affected by considerations of cruelty in this. One man is nothing compared with the human race. A criminal is less than nothing.

Since it might be easier to discover that connection in a brain which was larger than average, Maupertuis also suggested sending an expedition to the bottom of the world to dissect the brains of Patagonians, since they were reputed to be a race of giants ten feet tall.

Frederick read the book, and even wrote congratulating him, and telling him to ignore his critics:

set your mind at rest, my dear Maupertuis, and pay no attention to the buzzing of insects. Your reputation is too well established to be upset by the first puff of wind.

But even so he felt it was necessary to defend the reputation of the jewel in the crown of his Academy, and he did so in an anonymous pamphlet. Who the author was was made obvious by the presence of the Prussian royal arms at the top of the first page. "He enjoys among us," wrote Frederick, "during his life, the glory which Homer had long after his death. Berlin and Saint-Malo [the birthplace of Maupertuis] dispute which of the two is his true home. We look upon his merit as our own; his science as giving the greatest splendour to our academy; his works as conferring all their practical benefits upon us; his reputation as that of our institution, and his character as that of an honest man and a true philosopher."

The king went on to attack Voltaire openly because of his pamphlet in defence of Koenig, referring to him as a "*misérable*," and "a maker of libels without genius, and a contemptible enemy."

The phrase "we look upon his merit as our own," was a warning to all and sundry that any criticism of Maupertuis would be taken as a personal attack on the king. Voltaire noted the warning and declared: "I have no sceptre, but I have a pen."

He must have known that whatever he wrote would cause a break with Frederick, but he was entirely disillusioned with this would-be intellectual and patron of the arts, and all too successful man of steel, as he had now become. Since the Treaty of Dresden, by which Austria ceded Silesia to Prussia, he had been called "The Great".

Voltaire might have only a pen, but now he used it to write the funniest and most deflating ten or twelve pages in all his vast output. What was more, it was not a vicious personal attack on Maupertius, but—at least for Voltaire—a reasonably good-natured parody, somewhat in the style of *Le Temple du Goût*. In a tongue in the cheek move to disarm would-be critics, he presented his pamphlet (it is too short to be called a book) as a defence of Maupertuis' reputation, which he pretended to believe had been harmed by some young unknown author using the great man's name to put over a book full of his own ridiculous ideas. Called the *Diatribe of Dr Akakia*, it began with an obscure joke. In the early seventeenth century the doctor to Francis I called himself *sans-malice*, which he later changed to the Greek, *Akakia*. According to Voltaire, his Dr Akakia was physician to the Pope. The actual diatribe begins:

Nothing is more common today than for young authors who feel themselves overlooked to attribute well-known names to works that are unworthy of that claim. There are charlatans of all kinds. And there is one who has taken the name of a very illustrious academy to sell some very peculiar drugs. It is obvious that it is not the respected President who is the author of the books attributed to him; for this admirable philosopher who has discovered that Nature always operates according to the simplest laws, and added that she is always sparing in effort, would certainly have spared the small number of readers capable of reading his work the additional labour of reading the same thing twice over, first in the book entitled *Oeuvres*, and then in the one called *Lettres*.

One by one Voltaire demolished the admittedly very curious propositions made by Maupertuis in his *Lettres*, concluding with derision for his suggestion that life could be prolonged by stopping the pores with a form of varnish. He ends the *Diatribe*:

It can be seen from the account we have given that if these imaginary letters were written by a president, it could only be a president of Bedlam, and that they are incontestably, as we have said, the work of some young man who wanted to make use of the name of a sage, who, as we know, is respected throughout Europe, and has consented to be called *a great man*.

Everything considered, we submit to the Holy Inquisition this book imputed to the President, and we leave it to the infallible illumination of that learned tribunal, in which, as one knows, doctors have so much faith.

Next comes the Decree of the Inquisition of Rome:

We, Père Pancrace, etc., inquisitor for the faith, have read the *Diatribe* of Monsignor Akakia, doctor in ordinary to the Pope, without knowing what he means by *Diatribe*, and find nothing in it contrary to the faith, or to the decretals. The same cannot be said of the *Oeuvres* and *Lettres* of this young unknown author disguised under the name of a president.

We have, after invoking the Holy Spirit, found in these works many propositions that are temerarious, scandalous, or smelling of heresy.

We specially and particularly anathematise the *Essay on Cosmology*. . . . in the said Cosmology the author then makes out that there is no other proof to the existence of God than that Z equals BC divided by A plus B². Now these characters being drawn from Grimoire, and visibly diabolical, we declare them prejudicial to the authority of the Holy See.

And, according to custom, we have not understood a word clearly with matters which go by the name of *physics*, *mathematics*, *dynamics*, *metaphysics* etc., we have handed the unknown young man over to the reverend professors of philosophy at the College of Wisdom, to give us a faithful account. And God help them.

The Church's hatred of Voltaire was not altogether without justification. *Dr Akakia* illustrates his methods of using wit to attack a serious subject: in this case the ridiculous claims and suggestions of a pompous man who, because of his eminence, expected to be taken seriously. Also, he ridiculed the blind denunciations made by the Church concerning matters which it did not understand, of which the most celebrated example was its attack on Galileo nearly 120 years before.

Now that he had written the piece, Voltaire was anxious that it should reach as wide a public as soon as possible. But how could that be achieved? Before long Frederick heard of its existence, and filled with curiosity he sent for Voltaire, who came and read it to his host. Before long both of them were laughing together over the *Diatribe*. But the king still insisted that it could not be published. With a theatrical gesture Voltaire threw it into the fire. Frederick promptly retrieved it, but Voltaire threw it back. For a second time the king pulled it out, scorching his lace ruffles as he did so. Then, according to legend, Voltaire and Frederick linked hands and danced round the manuscript as it lay on the floor.

Shortly after completing *The Diatribe of Dr Akakia*, Voltaire applied to the king for permission to publish an essay on Lord Bolingbroke (not to be confused with his *Examen Important de Milord Bolingbroke*: Voltaire's most chilling attack on Christianity, which first appeared in 1767). On the last page of the manuscript the king wrote giving his approval for it to be printed on the royal press in Berlin. There was nothing to specify that permission was given only for the essay, and with it went the manuscript of *Dr Akakia*. Even before Voltaire had read the *Diatribe* to

Frederick it had been introduced like a Trojan horse into his own printing house. Already copies were circulating in Berlin, while others were being sent out of the country.

Of course when Frederick heard what Voltaire had done, despite the fact that in private he had been most amused at the mockery of Maupertuis, in public he was furious. "We look upon his merit as our own," he had written warningly. Now, by association, he had been ridiculed. There was nothing arch or affectionate about the letter sent to Voltaire:

> Your effrontery astonishes me after what you have just done, which is as clear as day. You persist, instead of admitting yourself guilty. Don't imagine that you will make me believe black is white ... if you push this affair to the end, I shall have everything printed, and people will see that if your works deserve statues, your conduct deserves chains.
> The publisher has been questioned, and has told all.

Now Voltaire found a sentry posted outside his door. At first he had denied all knowledge of the piece; but copies complete with the royal cypher were in Frederick's hands, and the tale of the joke which had misfired was common knowledge in Berlin, and soon it would be spread the length and breadth of Europe. On Christmas Eve 1752, the public hangman burnt copies of *Dr Akakia* at three places in Berlin. One of them was under Voltaire's own window, and some of the ashes were actually sent by Frederick to Maupertuis as a "cooling powder" for his outraged sensibilities.

Voltaire had gone too far with an injudicious remark at the Court of Louis XV, and now the same had happened with Frederick the Great. It would only be a matter of time before he once again packed his bags. In his annoyance Frederick wrote a curious document for Voltaire to sign:

> I promise His Majesty that, as long as he does me the favour of making me the guest in his palace, I will not write against any person or any government.

Voltaire refused to sign. To do so would have been to admit

that he had acted against the king's wishes. Instead he prepared for his departure. On New Year's Day 1753 he returned his Chamberlain's key and his order, *pour le mérite*. With them went a quatrain:

> *Je les reçus avec tendresse,*
> *Je vous les rends avec douleur,*
> *Tel qu'un amant dans sa jalouse ardeur,*
> *Rend le portrait de sa maîtresse.*

Voltaire himself translated the lines in his *Autobiography*:

> With rapture I those gifts received,
> Now to return them much I'm grieved;
> Such pangs the jealous swain attack,
> Who sends his mistress' picture back.

But Frederick would not accept their return, and sent them back to Voltaire. It was not going to be as easy to leave Berlin as it had been to arrive two and a half years before. He tried to excuse himself on the grounds of his health, always a source of interest and conversation. It was so bad, he claimed, that he must go to take the waters at Plombières. But Frederick was not impressed with this pretext, pointing out that the baths at Glatz were quite as good as those at Plombières. Eventually he gave way, but hoping that he could induce Voltaire to change his mind he invited him to supper on six evenings in succession. Voltaire, however, was determined to go.

One morning when Frederick was on the parade ground at Potsdam reviewing his troops, he was informed: "Monsieur de Voltaire awaits Your Majesty's orders."

Brusquely the king asked: "Well, Monsieur de Voltaire, you really want to go?"

"Sire, I am forced to go by matters which cannot be postponed, but especially by the state of my health."

"Monsieur, I wish you a good journey," answered the king, and turned back to his troops. They would never meet again, and although their relationship had still to reach its lowest ebb, their friendship would only be ended by Voltaire's death.

The little figure, only five foot three inches tall, who walked off the parade ground where once Frederick-Wilhelm's regiment of giants had drilled may have walked out of Frederick the Great's life in the literal sense, but their relationship was to continue in a curious and spasmodic fashion for the next twenty-five years.

There was nothing furtive or shamefaced about Voltaire's departure from the Prussian capital in his large coach and four, accompanied by his secretary Collini, two servants, and a mountain of luggage. As he sat inside he kept a watchful eye on a box full of gold coins.

Chapter 15

THE WANDERER

First Voltaire went to Leipzig, the centre of the printing and book trade, where he wrote what amounted to a sequel to *Dr Akakia*. The *Diatribe* had been mischievous enough, but its sequel must have completely deflated whatever remained of the reputation of the President of the Berlin Academy, The *Diatribe* had not exhausted the catalogue of the President's suggestions, and in its sequel Voltaire continued to write as the unknown young puppy who had been taking the name of the President in vain to air his own ludicrous ideas. If a hole were to be dug to the centre of the earth, would it not be wiser to wait awhile, and get in touch with the workmen who were responsible for the Tower of Babel? No doubt they would have something useful to say. Also, wrote Voltaire, Maupertius had ordered the building of a great ship to carry him to the South Seas so that he could dissect giants and men with long tails—and at the same time breathe his native air. Another of Maupertius' strange ideas, an abortive attempt to mate a mule with a turkey, was now recounted for the delight of those who would read the pamphlet.

Of course a copy soon reached Maupertius, who wrote a letter threatening Voltaire with physical violence. Voltaire retaliated by printing the letter—as though coming from Dr Akakia—omitting a reference to the caning he received from Rohan-Chabot's lackeys, and ending with a theatrical "tremble!" Now Dr Akakia appealed to the university of Leipzig to help protect him and his reputation, and save his life from a savage Laplander, who curiously enough was also a native of Saint-Malo. What purported to be a serious notice appeared in the *Leipziger-Zeitung*:

A certain man has written a letter to an inhabitant of Leipzig in which he threatens to murder him. As attempted murder is not in the spirit of the Leipzig Fair we request that everybody should inform us if this man appears within the walls of Leipzig. He is a philosopher of distracted appearance and rapid walk; his eyes are small and round, and so is his wig; he has a flat nose and a fat, moon face, with a repulsive smug expression. He always carries a dissecting knife to take great people apart. Whoever shall give any information about him shall receive a reward of a thousand ducats which can be claimed in the Latin city this gentleman is having built.

After a stay of about a month, Voltaire left Leipzig on 18 April for Gotha, where he became the guest of the Duke and Duchess of Saxe-Gotha. It was a happy time, free of writing or malice. But a letter was received from Countess Bentinck, asking in essence that he should let bygones be bygones, forget Maupertuis and the quarrel, and resume his old friendship with the king. It was obviously inspired by Frederick the Great himself, but Voltaire was unmoved by this plea, and on 25 May he left Gotha for Frankfurt.

Now the sentimental side of Frederick's nature gave way to a less friendly aspect. During those cheerful and irreverent evenings at Sans Souci, Frederick had written his share of lampooning verses, with Louis XV and his ministers among his targets. What if Voltaire had copies which in his present frame of mind he might make public? It was an alarming thought.

Scarcely had Voltaire, his secretary, servants and luggage, arrived in Frankfurt than the Prussian who represented the king in the Free City (though it was within the borders of the Holy Roman Empire) appeared, and ordered Voltaire's arrest. He insisted on the return of the order *pour le mérite*, and also of the keys which were the badge of his office as Chamberlain, which Frederick had previously refused to accept back from his guest. At that date Voltaire had not definitely left Prussia for good, having merely received permission to visit Plombières for the benefit of his health, on the understanding that one day he would return.

Obviously Voltaire had no intention of returning, so without even consulting the Council of Frankfurt the Prussian Resident ordered his arrest, and also that of his secretary Collini. Even Mme Denis was "placed under restraint" when she reached the city a few days after her uncle's arrival there on 29 May.

The period of arrest stretched on for five weeks, until 5 July, during which time Voltaire's feelings towards Frederick came close to hatred. The king was demanding the return of a book of his own verses, *Oeuvres de Pöesie*, which would be a source of great embarrassment if they were circulated or even published by Voltaire. His luggage was searched, but the all-important manuscript was not found, for the simple reason it was in a box being brought to Frankfurt by carrier. Only when it arrived, and the copy of *Oeuvres de Pöesie* was in the Resident's possession, were Voltaire, Mme Denis and Collini released from arrest. In the *Autobiography* Voltaire described the event as happening at the hands of an honest German who loved neither the French nor their verses, and who ". . . in bad French demanded the works of *Poeshy* of the King his master."

After their eventual release Mme Denis had had enough, and returned to Paris while her uncle set out for Mainz. Now Voltaire chose to stay within the confines of the Empire, going to enjoy the civilised pleasures of the Elector's Court at Mainz. There he was treated as an honoured guest; banquets were given on his behalf, and performances of four of his plays.

While staying at Saxe-Gotha, Louisa Dorothea had persuaded him to write a history of the Holy Roman Empire. But his heart was not in it, and he produced one of his few dull books: *Annals of the Empire of Charlemagne*. But when it was published in Colmar a few months later Louisa Dorothea was so impressed and delighted that she sent Voltaire a present of a thousand *écus*, though she was not a rich woman. With finesse, he declared that writing the book was in itself sufficient reward, and declined to accept the money.

Something that Voltaire did not know was that Louisa Dorothea and Wilhelmina, Margravine of Bayreuth, had been attempting to calm Frederick the Great, for he had worked himself into a condition bordering on the unbalanced when he realised that Voltaire had gone for good. One wild statement after another poured from his pen. First he declared that Voltaire was entering the service of the Queen of Hungary; then it was that of George II of England. To Wilhelmina he wrote that Voltaire was the greatest rascal in the universe, and that many had been broken on the wheel for less. Now he could say nothing bad enough about Voltaire, even claiming that the philosopher had defended Koenig against Maupertuis because he, Voltaire, wanted to become President of the Berlin Academy. He raged that even now Voltaire was "distilling new poisons," and he wrote to George Keith, a particular favourite of his at Sans Souci, who was now Ambassador in Paris, to spread that particular fiction round the capital. In fairness to Keith, while not actually siding with Voltaire he did his best to pacify the king.

The storm, while it lasted, was vicious, and then it blew itself out. Frederick was prepared to resume a correspondence which first began in 1736. The letter with which he broke the silence was remarkable:

> You wronged me, absolutely. I have forgiven everything, I even want to forget everything. Do you want compliments? I will tell you the truth; I esteem you the greatest genius that centuries have created; I admire your poems; I love your prose, in particular the frivolous parts of your miscellaneous writings. Never before has any writer had such perfect tact, such a certain and refined taste. You are charming in conversation; you know how to instruct and entertain at the same time. You are the most fascinating person I know, able to make yourself loved by anyone you wish. You have such charm in your wit that you can offend and be forgiven at the same time. In short, you would be perfect, if you were not human.

In its way Frederick's letter contains as accurate a summing up of Voltaire's better side as any made by a contemporary. But Voltaire had had enough of kings and royal patrons. He was in his sixtieth year, and, although he did not realise the fact, poised on the threshold of an old age which would see the literary and intellectual culmination of all the turbulent and often far from edifying years which had made up the greater part of his adult life. Years of scurrying between various châteaux, the Bastille, Courts great and small, contact with the famous and the obscure—

all would find their consummation in more of the *contes philo-sophiques*; those wise little tales of which *Candide* would be the supreme masterpiece. The long interlude with Emilie at Cirey would have its place too. As well as the scientific experiments, he had read and read, until his knowledge of almost everything under the sun could be described as encyclopedic, and would find its outlet in his contributions to the *Encyclopédie*.

But for the present (August 1753) he was staying at the White Bear Inn at Strasbourg. It was an indifferent establishment, but Voltaire chose it because it was run by the father of a waiter who had looked after him particularly well while he was in Mainz. But soon he moved to a rented house with a large garden, where he worked hard at the *Annals*.

In October that year Voltaire moved to Colmar: "half German and half French." and famous for its publishers and printing houses. There the *Annals* would be published. Together with Collini and Babet, a girl who acted as cook, he lived in a rented apartment until June the following year.

What should have been a period of calm in the charming old city was marred on two occasions. First Mme Denis declared that she was pregnant by Voltaire. Judging by some of the very intimate physical details mentioned in letters written by him a few years earlier, such an actuality was not beyond the bounds of possibility. But evidently there was nothing in the allegation. A second devastating piece of information was contained in a letter in January 1754, in which she advised him that Louis XV did not want him to return to Paris. In other words, he had been unofficially exiled from France.

There were two reasons for the ban. First Louis XV did not wish Frederick the Great to be angered by Voltaire possibly returning to his native country. Secondly, and more important, a publisher at The Hague had got hold of some of Voltaire's writings and printed them without permission. These included a history written in 1739, for the benefit of Frederick the Great, which, as Voltaire informed Mme de Pompadour in a frantic letter of 30 December 1753, was stolen from the King's personal baggage while he was on one of his campaigns during the War of Austrian Succession.

Certainly the text had been tampered with, to most damaging

The Château de Ferney, from the *Gentleman's Magazine*, 1789

effect for Voltaire. The manuscript, originally entitled *Histoire Universelle*, would one day become the *Essai sur les Moeurs*: to be numbered among his most influential writings and a work which would have a profound influence on liberal thought during the last quarter of the eighteenth century. But the pirated edition was truncated to the point of being a travesty of the original, and contained deliberate and damaging alterations. For instance, the word 'kings' had been substituted for 'historians' in the following passage:

> In this respect historians are like certain tyrants of whom they speak, who sacrifice the well-being of the whole human race to that of a single individual.

In another place Voltaire had written:

> The King of Persia had a son who, having turned Christian, proved unworthy to be one, and revolted against him.

That appeared as:

> The King of Persia had a son who, having turned Christian, revolted against him.

As if this bastard edition of the *Histoire Universelle* were not harmful enough, at the same time portions of *La Pucelle* were being printed at the other end of Europe, in Vienna.

This was not just another literary escapade which would blow over, like the publication of *Le Mondain* or even the *Diatribe of Dr Akakia*. *L'Histoire Universelle* (as printed at The Hague) had ensured the hatred of the king and of the Church. Even Voltaire's old friend ex-king Stanislas dare not let him visit Plombières in Lorraine, for fear of offending his father-in-law.

Suddenly, the world must have seemed a very bleak place, even to the irresistible and resourceful Voltaire. Colmar lost its charm as a refuge, after a Jesuit priest had preached a sermon to such effect that—as Voltaire told one of his friends at Sans Souci (the Marquis d'Argens)—seven persons brought their copies of the writings of Bayle to be burnt in the public square, along with a copy of the *Lettres Juives* by d'Argens himself.

It was time to move on. But where? Despite the ban on his entry into Lorraine, Voltaire did visit Plombières to take the waters, and enjoy the company of the Comte and Comtesse d'Argental. Not far away was the Benedictine Abbey of Senones, whose head was an old friend, Dom Calmet. The man who was to all intents and purposes a Deist, and whose battle cry would soon be *Ecrasez l'infâme* (crush infamy: i.e. superstition), now turned to him in his time of trouble. He spent one or two months late in 1754 at the Abbey, almost in retreat, in the modern sense of the word, finding consolation in the calm atmosphere of the abbey's great library.

Voltaire was now entering his late period, and for him it would be a time in which both profundity and humanity would be fused together to a rare degree. But the transition was not easy. The future author of *Candide* had endured one misfortune after another, culminating in Louis XV's order (which, however, was never committed to paper) banning him from France; while the Jesuits and Jansenists in Colmar came together in an unlikely alliance to bring about his expulsion from the whole of Alsace.

That Easter he chose to go with Collini, a staunch Catholic, to Communion. Voltaire was in a rare mood of defeat. He felt betrayed by his philosopher-king; France had barred him, and he was becoming increasingly aware of the power of a Church whose displeasure he had incurred. How sincere he was being when he presented himself at the altar rail is a matter of speculation. Collini has left an account which is still quoted as an example of Voltaire's deliberate mockery of the Church. But was it altogether that? No one looks their best with their tongue out, however devout their action, and Voltaire's face and reputation were against him.

I confess that I profited by so rare an occasion to examine Voltaire's expression during this act. God will pardon me for my curiosity and distraction; which did not lessen my fervour. At the moment when he was about to receive the Sacrament I raised my eyes to heaven as if in devotion, suddenly glanced at Voltaire's demeanour. He presented his tongue and fixed his wide open eyes on the priest's face. I knew those looks.

In his room in the Abbey of Senones Voltaire had a crucifix. When this was reported to Frederick the Great he circulated the fact among the fraternity of philosophers, hoping to give the impression that Voltaire had either lost his reason or was in his dotage. But there could have been another reason for Voltaire seeking Absolution and then receiving the Sacrament. For the first time since his exile in England, he no longer felt safe in the knowledge that he had a powerful patron, and all his life he was convinced he was at death's door. Now, in the spring of 1754, he of all people was haunted by the fear of burial in unconsecrated ground. The fate of Adrienne Lecouvreur came to mind, and in a letter to her one-time lover, d'Argental, he wrote:

I am in my bed, and I do not see how I can be buried in consecrated ground. I shall have the fate of your dear Adrienne, but you will not love me less.

While he mocked at much related to the Bible, and despised the corruption, arrogance, cynicism, immorality, and downright disbelief of many churchmen in France, yet for all that something within him craved a being or a power greater than himself. In short, he no longer felt self-sufficient. Seventeen-fifty-four was the black night of his soul.

It was a strange period, those months at Senones, where Voltaire lived almost as a monk, attended Mass, and worked in the library on his *Essai sur les Moeurs*, as his *Histoire Universelle* had now become. While the time spent high in the Vosges Mountains did not make a Christian of Voltaire, despite the Abbot's opinion that it had resulted in the conversion of "the greatest Deist the world has ever seen," the stay did mark the beginning of the final and greatest period of his life.

Although he could not know it at the time, the course of the last twenty-four years was set in April 1754, while still in Colmar, when he received a most polite letter from Gabriel and Philibert Cramer. These brothers were publishers in Geneva, and they offered to produce anything he cared to send, promising that only the best quality paper and typeface would be used, and that the greatest attention would be paid to proof-reading. The letter came at a time when Voltaire was even feeling disillusioned with the firm of publishers who had been the cause of his moving from Strasbourg to Colmar.

The Cramer brothers were courteous, businesslike and pleasant to correspond with. Only nine months after they first contacted him Voltaire was requesting permission to become a resident and property-owner in the Republic of Geneva. Before that had come the stay at Senones, and an unauthorised visit to France. His appearance in the theatre in Lyon was wildly applauded, but a visit to an acquaintance from the days of his youth was a warning of what he could expect if he remained on forbidden ground. He went to see Cardinal Tencin. Many years before he had occupied the room next to the churchman's sister and mistress, when they had both been imprisoned in the Bastille. The meeting with the Cardinal only lasted a minute, but it was long enough for him to inform Voltaire that since he was under the king's displeasure he could not be invited to dinner. France was not for him, that was obvious. Accompanied by Collini, Mme Denis and a valet, Voltaire set out for Switzerland.

Chapter 16

ARRIVAL IN SWITZERLAND

The Château de Prangins, near Nyon, was to be Voltaire's first home in Switzerland. But it proved impossibly large for him and his small household. On 20 January 1755 he and Mme Denis went to look over a charming villa built some fifteen years previously, which stood about four and a half miles outside Geneva. For Voltaire it was love at first sight. The villa was just what he had been seeking, and it had a large garden. "It is the palace of a philosopher with the garden of Epicurus: it is a delicious retreat."

After legal difficulties had been overcome, particularly the fact that as a Catholic he was not supposed to own property in the Republic of Geneva, Voltaire became the new owner, and promptly rechristened the villa *Les Délices*. He was in fact the first Catholic to hold property there since the time of Calvin. With the title deed went permission "to live in the republic of Geneva during the good pleasure of their lordships." If Voltaire had chosen to honour Geneva by wishing to live within sight and sound of the city, its rulers returned the compliment in their own way by showing him a rare distinction. Unfortunately, the relationship was soon to go sour.

But for the present Voltaire was filled with a happiness he had not known since the best days at Cirey, and he celebrated his moving into *Les Délices* in March 1755 in a lighthearted poem. Nothing, it seemed, could mar a serene old age at *Les Délices*, and all had been conducted under the beneficent gaze of the city fathers, who had waived the rules so that he could become a property-owner. But Voltaire was still Voltaire, and soon *La*

Pucelle cast her irreverent shadow across his path, and a Calvinist city such as Geneva was no place for one such as she.

One of the reasons given by Voltaire for wishing to settle permanently in the republic was to be near his physician, Dr Tronchin. In fact it was only after moving to *Les Délices* that he came to know Théodore, the doctor, and other members of his family. But it was a good enough reason, and flattering to the Genevese who felt that they had living among them a doctor into whose hands Europe's greatest hypochondriac was prepared to place himself.

Even if Dr Tronchin did not become a crutch for Voltaire's old age, at least he acted as a steadying influence on the wayward genius who at times could be as perverse as a strong-headed child. Voltaire was impressed by the doctor, describing him as "a man six feet tall, wise as Aesculapius, and handsome as Apollo."

The Calvinist doctor was certainly highly intelligent and perceptive. In a letter to that other celebrated philosopher in exile, Jean-Jacques Rousseau, he wrote:

> What can be expected of a man who is constantly at war with himself, whose heart is always disappointed by his head! His moral condition since his childhood has been so unnatural, that his nature has become an artificial entity that finds kinship in nothing. Of all his contemporaries, he himself is the one he knows least. All his relations with other people are in disorder. He wanted to attain more happiness than he was entitled to expect. . . . The fear of death (for he trembles before it) does not stop him from complaining about life, and, not knowing whom to blame, he rails at fate, while he should be dissatisfied with himself alone.

Much of what Dr Tronchin wrote was undoubtedly true, but what he saw and comprehended was the man, and not the troubled, contradictory and at times almost demonic spirit which had its being within his puny body. At sixty, Voltaire could not change (not that he had any desire to do so), only mellow. And his new-found pleasure in *Les Délices* struck a chord which had not sounded since he had busied himself with additions to the

Château de Cirey. Once again he became a lover of cultivated nature, and his new passion found expression in a poem cele-brating both the beauties of the villa and the tolerance which he imagined existed in Geneva.

> Oh house of Aristippus! Oh gardens of Epicurus!
> You who offer me in your varied parts,
> What my verse often lacks,
> The merit of art subjected to nature,
> Empire of Pomona and her sister Flora!
> Receive your new possessor!

For Voltaire there was the pleasure of creating a garden from nothing. In his own words, he was founding Carthage: requesting flower seeds, ordering some two hundred and fifty fruit trees, bordering the paths with lavender, setting onions, planting herbs, and of course furnishing the house itself. But Voltaire and happiness were not to remain companions for long.

First, a bookseller's assistant named Grasset attempted to blackmail him by threatening to publish some of the broader sections of *La Pucelle*, a work which the Calvinists would take exception to as readily as the Catholics, if for different reasons. Then Voltaire's decision to present his plays at *Les Délices* incurred official disapproval. Such a frivolous and ungodly activity had always been frowned on by the authorities in Geneva, which did not possess a single theatre. Consequently there was a ready audience to come to the theatre fitted up in a gallery in the villa. Among the pieces given was the recently completed *Orphelin de la Chine*, by no means one of his best works, but important because it marked a break with the tradition of serious dramas being written in Alexandrine verse. When given in August 1755 its success was out of proportion to its merit, and almost at once the citizens were banned from attending further theatrical performances at *Les Délices*.

That in itself must have hurt Voltaire, living under the im-pression that he had found a haven where the watchwords were liberty and tolerance. But Geneva was not Amsterdam, and he received a letter which included the ominous sentence: "It would be very agreeable to us to see you enter into our views, and to co-operate with all our men of letters, when occasion offers, to dissuade our youth from irreligion which always leads to libertinism."

A particularly sharp disappointment was the fate of the poem which he had written to express his pleasure at settling just outside Geneva. Now it was burnt in public. But these setbacks coincided with a period of almost unparalleled complexity, a time when much of importance would happen all at once.

Most important were his contributions to the *Encyclopédie*, presided over by d'Alembert, the illegitimate son of Mme de Tensin. D'Alembert shared with Diderot the task of overseeing the work, and canvassing articles from the leading philosophers of France, including those like Voltaire who were in exile.

From the outset the *Encyclopédie* earned the hostility of the Church, which interpreted its intention of ending superstition as an attack on itself. In 1752 Voltaire had written an encouraging letter to d'Alembert, a man twenty-three years his junior:

> You and Diderot are engaged upon a work which will be France's glory and the shame of those who have persecuted you: Paris is rich in penny-a-line-hacks, but of eloquent philosophers I know only you and him.

Three years later, when he had begun to feel the displeasure of the Genevese authorities, Voltaire again wrote to d'Alembert:

> As long as there is a breath of life in me I am at the disposal of the authors of the *Encyclopédie*. I shall always regard it as an honour to be permitted to contribute even only modestly, to this, the greatest project that the French people and French literature have set for themselves.

In France in the middle of the eighteenth century the Church owned between a quarter and a third of all the land, but many peasants literally starved. The philosophers felt that if they could undermine people's blind acceptance of everything in the Bible (or at least in the Old Testament) they were half-way to breaking the power of the Church in France. And since this was closely linked with the Crown, the authority of the latter would also be diminished, if not actually overthrown. The one could not survive without the other, and both knew it. That was the underlying fear of the authors of the *Encyclopédie*, which resulted in the continual harassing of such as d'Alembert and Diderot.

The aim of the Encyclopedists was to give the reader the facts, simply and succinctly. And if the truth gave him a jolt and set him thinking, so much the better. Had Voltaire died after his departure from Potsdam he would have left behind two or three really worthwhile pieces: the *Lettres Philosophiques*, *Charles XII*, and *Le Siècle de Louis XIV*; a reputation as a wit, and as the author of elegant verses, plus the scandalous and unfinished verse-epic, *La Pucelle*. But there would not have been very much else, apart from the *contes philosophiques*, that posterity would care to read. By the time he took his leave of Frederick the Great he had acquired a European reputation, and now during the considerable number of years which remained to him he would match that reputation with achievement. What would give him his rightful place in the history of the eighteenth century was the blending of learning and philosophy with humanity. The former would produce his contributions to the *Encyclopédie*, which were later expanded into his own *Dictionnaire Philosophique*, and the *Contes Philosophiques*. As for the latter, at an age when many would be content to sit back and let the world go by, for better or for worse, he stirred himself as no one else in Europe cared to do, to fight miscarriages of justice.

Eighteenth-century Court life, with its intrigue, flattery and false values, proved the worst possible setting for a man of his mercurial, not to say unstable, personality. For although Voltaire thrived on excitement it almost inevitably had the effect of making him over-reach himself, as happened in France, and later in Berlin. But the best thing that could happen for himself and for posterity was when he fell out with Frederick the Great over *Dr Akakia*, and he turned his back on Courts and kings for good.

But now, in 1755, at *Les Délices*, in the midst of serious and trivial vexations, he was hard at work. In addition to working on the *Encyclopédie*, and conducting a vast correspondence, he had been requested by the Empress Elizabeth of Russia to write a history of Peter the Great and his times.

The entries for the *Encyclopédie* came from a lifetime of hard thinking and bitter experience. His ideal among leaders of men was perhaps the benign autocrat, and he certainly admired the English Whigs of his day. But he was also too much of a realist to believe there could ever be a society that was completely just:

> On our unhappy globe it is impossible for men living in society not to be divided into two classes, one of oppressors, the other of the oppressed.

Liberty of thought and expression, toleration, the supremacy of reason over religious authority, and a fluid social system were all desirable goals. But Voltaire had a personal hatred of war, and he feared the destructive element in man's nature. It was his ambition that free government should contain no ecclesiastical law which was valid without the express approval of the government, because the clergy were subjects of the State like anyone else. He also wanted to see one standard weight, one measure and one tax: "only vice should be infamous; and all imposts should be proportional."

As he was to write, law was necessary to preserve family life, property, security, and to check abuses of power. A cynic would comment that as a wealthy man and property owner he was bound to hold such a belief. While his political creed was one of liberalism, while maintaining the *status quo*, the religious beliefs which he now started to expound were far from orthodox.

> God gave you understanding to do right, and not to penetrate to the essence of things which He created. Besides, what would immortality mean, and what could a soul be which felt with no body, heard without ears, smelled without a nose, and touched without hands?
>
> Belief in a God who rewards good deeds and punishes bad ones, is the belief most useful to mankind. It is the only curb on men who skilfully commit secret crimes.

Those sentences contain the quintessence of Voltaire's thinking on the question of religious belief. It is the Voice of Reason, as later generations would come to understand the term when applied to the second half of the eighteenth century. Analytical, logical and totally unsentimental. Elsewhere, he would write that he believed religion was necessary for the masses, but that educated upper-class individuals need not be expected to believe, and that was a state which certainly existed to a large degree in contemporary France, and also among many he had known in Prussia.

Among the innumerable quotable and quoted epigrams and sayings attributed to Voltaire there is one that seems to have applied to himself while contributing to the *Encyclopédie*: "If you want to bore the reader, tell him everything."

His entries certainly have an unmistakable pithiness and pungent wit that could only be described as Voltairian.

Envy. If you wish your children to hate one another, caress one more than the other; the prescription is infallible.

Emulation is nothing more than envy restricted within the bounds of decency.

Equality. What does a dog owe to a dog and a horse to a horse? Nothing. No animal depends on his equal. But man having received from God that which is called reason, what is the result? That almost everywhere on earth he is a slave.

It is impossible for men to be equal as for two preachers of divinity not to be jealous of each other.

On Miracles . . . when faith speaks, it is well known that reason ought to be silent.

Whence come so many martyrs escaped unhurt out of boiling oil, but were unable to resist the edge of the sword? It is answered, such was the will of God. But the philosophers would wish to see all this themselves, before they believe it.

Tolerance . . . The Christian Church divided in its cradle, and was divided even in the persecutions which, under the first emperors, it sometimes endured. This horrible discord, which has lasted for so many centuries, is a very striking lesson that we should pardon each other's errors: discord is the great ill of mankind; and tolerance is the only remedy for it.

On the soul. What becomes of this unknown entity, if the foetus it should animate dies in the belly of its mother? It seemed still more ridiculous to me that God should create a soul at the moment a man lies with a woman. It seemed blasphemous that God should await the consummation of an adultery, an incest, to reward their turpitudes by creating souls in their favour. It is still worse when I am told that God draws immortal souls from nothingness to make them suffer tortures for eternity.

The one-time courtier and versifier had made a long journey of the mind, even since the days at Cirey, and in the *Encyclopédie* and its offshoot the *Dictionnaire Philosophique* he was making some very disturbing statements, and posing some agonising questions. As long ago as 1736 he had written *Le Tombeau du Fanaticisme*, but this destructively anti-Christian piece was not published until 1767. It is a work which Voltaire's apologists tend to overlook, though it runs to some 108 pages. Starting with the Old Testament, this biting condemnation ends with Voltaire's own day, and contains a comment which might have been written during the Revolution itself:

> The more the laity is enlightened, the less harm can be done by the priests. Let us try to enlighten even them, to make them blush at their errors, and to cause them little by little to become citizens.

Le Tombeau, also called *L'Examen Important de Milord Bolingbroke*, was no piece of superficial journalism, for Voltaire had obviously read deeply about the history of the Church: Catholic, Protestant and Orthodox.

Despite his experience of absolute monarchs, he did not share the views of his contemporary Montesquieu (who died in that same year of 1755), who, while favouring a benign monarchy as the best form of government, made a celebrated comment that virtue was the active principle of republics, while honours were those of monarchies. It was a statement which was to have a profound influence on Robespierre, with his almost obsessive concern with virtue among national leaders and, for that matter, at all levels of society.

And yet, for all the plays he had written in his younger days with republicanism as their theme, Voltaire was not a true republican at heart. In his day there was no Parliament (Estates General) in France where the voice of the people could be heard, and in fact it would not be called until the eve of the Revolution, more than ten years after his death.

Voltaire had chosen to become an adopted son of Geneva, but there was another philosopher who could claim citizenship by right of birth: Jean-Jacques Rousseau. The two men could not have been more different in outlook and temperament. Voltaire was a lover of the good things in life. On the other hand Rousseau was something of a drifter, despising the comforts of civilisation, and almost a social misfit. As a young man he had been employed as a copyist of music, and had considerable knowledge of the subject, and to this day his little one-act pastoral opera *Le Devin du Village* receives an occasional performance. Born a Protestant, he became a Catholic, only to revert in later life to his original faith. He chose to form a lifelong relationship with a one-time servant girl, Thérèse Lavasseur, an illiterate of almost subnormal intelligence, whom he eventually married. He showed little or no concern for their children, all of whom were left on the doorstep of a foundling home.

Born in 1712, Rousseau belonged to a younger generation, which almost regarded Voltaire as the grand old man of free-thinking philosophers. In his youth Rousseau was an ardent admirer of all that Voltaire published, but by 1750 he had struck out on his own. He did not believe that all progress was for the best, or that European civilisation was necessarily the most desirable goal for mankind. For him there was no pleasure or stimulus to be found in the elegant salons of Europe, but only amid nature, and preferably in a landscape which had not been tampered with by man. He was in fact the forerunner of the whole Romantic movement which would span the turn of the eighteenth and nineteenth centuries and include such names as Goethe, Wordsworth, Byron, Turner, Berlioz, Ingres and Géricault.

Before long Rousseau's antagonism towards Voltaire became open:

Tell me, famous Arouet, how many works of virile beauty have you sacrificed to your finesse, how many great master-pieces has that spirit of gallantry cost you, who are so fertile in producing petty trifles?

Rousseau considered himself the apostle of man free in his natural state, and as such he regarded Voltaire as the symbol of all that was artificial or mannered. As a visible protest against what he considered was a materialist society he took to wearing the simplest clothes, and leading a life that today would probably earn him the label of drop-out.

He made his name with his two *Discours*, in which he preached that man was by nature free, virtuous and happy, but had been corrupted by society and the acquisitive desire for property and possessions, as well as falling victim to inequality and the despotism of his fellow men. The message he preached was that it was time to return to nature and the simple life. Among those the idea appealed to most strongly were the very sophisticated and well-to-do in the fashionable world. But whether their interpretation of his philosophy was what he really had in mind is another matter.

Now, at the age of forty-two, he renounced Catholicism, and returned as a welcome citizen to his birthplace, Geneva.

Voltaire loved the theatre, while Rousseau considered it a thoroughly bad influence, and that would cause their first quarrel. But the conflict did not begin immediately. In his own phrase Voltaire had settled at *Les Délices* to let his clothes dry after the thunderstorm, and the last thing he wanted was a quarrel with the City Fathers.

Before long Rousseau returned to Paris, despite the fact the city must have been the epitome of all he professed to despise as being corrupting to man. There he wrote *The Origin of the Inequalities of Man, and the Fundamental Reasons Therefore*. Not only did he dedicate the work to the Genevese Republic, but in his preface declared that it possessed a perfect constitution, the best authorities in the world, and pastors who were devoted protectors of the holy truth.

But although the preface might prove an acceptable dish of cream the contents of the book were less so. Geneva might be a republic, but as elsewhere some were more equal than others, and the ruling class thoroughly disapproved of Rousseau's statements that all men were equal in their natural state, and that society and civilisation were responsible for the inequalities in the world. To him instinct, or intuition, was higher than reason, which led to the extraordinary statement that the man who thinks is a degenerate animal.

The Genevese authorities were offended, while Voltaire, who had received a copy of the book at the same time, was greatly amused. But the only reason he did not exercise his destructive wit on it was because he feared that Rousseau might retaliate by making trouble for him with the Encyclopedists in Paris:

> I have received the book which you have written against mankind, and I thank you for it. It is impossible to paint in stronger colours the horrors of the civilisation upon which we in our weakness prided ourselves. On reading your book one feels tempted to go on all fours. As it is, however, sixty years since I gave up this habit, I am sorry to say that I am unable to take it up again, and I leave this natural position to people who are more worthy of it than you and I.

You can almost see Voltaire's tongue in his cheek, but Rousseau took the remarks at their face value:

> When I sent you my poor dreams, I did not stop to think that I was giving you something that was worthy of you; I only wanted to fulfil an obligation, and pay you the homage which we all owe to you as our leader.

But it was a great disappointment that Voltaire had chosen to settle in his own city. If he—Rousseau—returned, he would have to share the glory with Voltaire; so he chose to remain in France, in a house lent by Mme d'Epinay, a banker's wife.

Voltaire might enjoy making comparatively gentle fun of the earnest, self-contradictory Rousseau, but by that time he was himself in bad odour with the Genevese. Prominent citizens had disobeyed the ban on attending his theatre, especially when Voltaire invited Lekain, the leading actor of the day, to take part.

More important, though, was the indignation arising from the publication of the *Essai sur les Moeurs*, which included an article on Geneva. In this Voltaire praised the Genevese wholeheartedly and sincerely for their toleration, but also made certain criticisms of Calvin. In the ensuing correspondence he wrote what amounted to an open letter to Thieriot, knowing that it would be either published or at least widely circulated:

> It is not a trifling example of the progress of human reason that the essay on history has been printed at Geneva, with public approval, though it says that Calvin had an atrocious soul as well as an enlightened mind. Today the murder of Servetus appears abominable.

Servetus had been condemned to death for denying the divinity of Christ, and when actually bound to the stake Calvin gave him one last chance to recant, which he refused to do, and Calvin ordered the fire to be lit forthwith. Voltaire never realised that what he saw as obvious truths others frequently saw as offensive or defamatory comments. What had been meant as an example of Geneva's toleration was thought to be an attack on the city's father figure, and Voltaire found himself in real disgrace. He had come to the Republic in the hope of finding a place where he could live in an atmosphere of high-minded toleration, and, at a more personal level, of friendliness. But his poem expressing his delight at coming to live near Lake Geneva had been publicly burnt. The reason for this at first sight seemed obscure: in it he had mentioned a certain Duke of Savoy who in medieval times had lived a somewhat dissolute life on the shores of the lake. At the time the poem was published the Duke's descendants were attempting to have him canonised, making the reference doubly unwelcome.

But Voltaire could exhibit perfect manners when he chose. Now age was bestowing dignity, and at least he refrained from polemics or mischievous attacks on his critics of the article in the *Essai sur les Moeurs*. He saved his feelings for the privacy of a poem called *Les Torts*. An English translation is given in the *Autobiography*, which is almost like a parody of Dryden. It ends:

> Ye base unsightly crew avaunt,
> Silence your vile unmeaning cant,
> That cheats the gaping throng;
> Your stupid hymns, your sermons vile,
> I don't think them worth the while,
> And, am I in the wrong?

Even for Voltaire 1755 was a year of almost excessive mental activity. Contributions to the *Encyclopédie*; finishing the *Orphelin de la Chine* (which was given on 20 August at the Comédie Française, and for the first time privileged spectators were cleared from the stage itself, largely thanks to Voltaire's representations); work on the *Life of Peter the Great*; keeping up his huge correspondence, and playing host to a large number of visitors.

D'Alembert came in person to Geneva to collect material for his article on the city for the *Encyclopédie*, and he too fell foul of the hypersensitive citizens. For although he heartily praised their clergy, he wrote an article which practically rationalised their religion out of existence. It was said that Voltaire was the real author of the article, but for once he was not to blame. Such was the resentment caused by the piece that d'Alembert resigned from the editorship of the *Encyclopédie*.

Now Rousseau added to Voltaire's problems. He had finally understood the meaning of Voltaire's letter thanking him for a copy of *The Origin of the Inequalities in Man*. In revenge he added his voice to those attacking Voltaire's theatre, forgetting that in his younger days he had been an opera composer himself, and that *Le Devin du Village* had delighted Louis XV and the Court at Fontainebleau. Now he wrote his *Lettre sur les Spectacles*, which was aimed primarily at stirring up trouble for Voltaire with his theatre at *Les Délices*.

In the midst of all his work, worries and annoyances, Voltaire maintained an almost English passion for his garden. If anything could give him unalloyed pleasure it was the creation of the garden at *Les Délices*.

He was not above lying to save his skin, denying authorship of something everyone must have known could only have come from his pen. Yet, when it came to serious matters which did not concern him personally he could be uncompromisingly honest. It was flattering to be asked to write a life of Peter the Great. But he could, would and did write the unvarnished truth:

The Russians ought certainly to regard Peter as the greatest of men. From the Baltic Sea to the frontiers of China, he was a hero. But ought he to be a hero to ourselves? Was he comparable in valour to our Condés and Villars; and, in know-

ledge and intellect, morals, was he comparable with a crowd of
men among whom we live today? No. But he was a king, and a
badly instructed king; and he did what perhaps a thousand
sovereigns in his place would not have done.

In November an event occurred which was to affect Voltaire
powerfully for the rest of his life. It happened on one of the most
important days in the Christian calendar, All Souls Day—when
the churches were full. Lisbon was shattered by a great earthquake. The tremor only lasted a few seconds, but half the city
was left in ruins, and 20,000 lay dead. With bitter irony it indeed
became the Day of the Dead: *Le Jour des Morts*. Before and since
there have been worse natural disasters, but what shocked men
such as Voltaire was the pointlessness of it all.

For years educated people all over Europe had believed in the
theory of optimism as expounded by Leibniz. Since it was the
theory that "all happens for the best in the best of all possible
worlds" which Voltaire was to demolish so ironically in *Candide*
(written three years later), it should be made clear exactly what
was meant by "optimism" in the eighteenth century. Today
optimism is a matter of hoping that something will turn out
satisfactorily. To the followers of Leibniz it meant that everything *happened* for the best, no matter how awful or inexplicable
it might seem. For instance, if you fell and broke your leg a
follower of Leibniz might argue that, though this was an undoubted misfortune, you might have suffered worse—been run
over by a brewer's dray, for example—had you continued on your
way.

Now Voltaire's reaction was speedy. Before the month was out
he had written the *Poème sur le désastre de Lisbonne*, in which he
piled agonised question upon question. Here was a freethinker,
or Deist, searching for an answer to the unanswerable. Was there
a guiding hand in the universe; a force which controlled destiny?
Of all his poems *Le Désastre* is perhaps the most relevant today, in
a century which has seen not only such natural disasters as the
eruption of Mont Pelée or the Messina earthquake, but the man-
made horrors of Dresden and Hiroshima.

The six pages that make up the *Poème sur le désastre de Lisbonne*
contain some of the bleakest reasoning ever put into verse, and

are a cry from the heart of a humanitarian who has just witnessed the death of optimism. It holds the key to Voltaire's outlook on life for the remaining twenty-three years. From now on he clearly believed, not that this was the best of all possible worlds, but that one should do one's best to make it bearable for others. Rhetorically he addressed the philosophers of optimism and called on them to come and gaze upon the frightful ruins: women and children crushed and dismembered by falling marble, or dying without help beneath their collapsed roofs:

> Do you say, on seeing this pile of victims;
> God is avenged, their death is the price of their crimes?
> What crime, what fault have these children committed
> On their mothers' crushed and bloodstained breasts?
> Lisbon, which exists no more, had she more vices
> Than London, or Paris, plunged in pleasure?

Further on Voltaire writes:

> All is well, you say, and all is necessary.
> What! Would the whole universe have been worse without
> This hellish chasm, without engulfing Lisbon.
> Are you sure that the eternal cause, which makes all,
> Which knows all, which created all, could not have cast
> Us into this miserable world without setting fiery
> Volcanoes beneath our feet?

In one revelatory sentence he writes:

> I respect my God, but I love the universe.

Then he asks:

> In the best of all possible worlds,
> Leibniz does not tell me by what unseen knots,
> An eternal disorder, a chaos of misfortunes,
> Mixes our vain pleasures with real sorrow,
> Nor why the innocent suffer this inevitable evil
> Along with the guilty.

Un jour tout sera bien, voilà notre espérance;
Tout est bien aujourd'hui, voilà l'illusion.

One day all will be well, that is our hope;
All is well today, that is the illusion.

For Voltaire the destruction of Lisbon had meant the death of optimism, but in its place there was still the consolation of hope. In later editions, however, he qualified even that. It took an event which he never saw, which did not affect him personally, to make his heart beat in time with the pulse of humanity itself. From then on he would strive to help the oppressed and the wronged, and bring about a world in which there was greater equality; though he could never be described as an egalitarian, as the word came to be understood during the French Revolution. The mischievous joker of *Dr Akakia* was dead, and when Voltaire came to write *Candide* he was joking in deadly earnest.

Chapter 17

CANDIDE

In 1756 Voltaire was sixty-two, and he had changed more profoundly in the last few years than at any time since his visit to England. In addition to his advancing years and ill health he had also been exiled from France and, more especially, the king and his Court. Frederick the Great, he felt, had betrayed him over the matter of the *Diatribe of Dr Akakia*, and his attitude was incomprehensible to the philosopher. In Frankfurt he and Mme Denis had been arrested, and in Colmar his stay had ended after pressure had been exerted for his expulsion by the clergy. Even here at Geneva his attempts to get on good terms with the republic and its citizens had misfired.

Three other factors added their contribution to Voltaire's rejection of "optimism": the pointless horror of the Lisbon earthquake; the equally pointless bloodshed and wastage of the Seven Years War then in progress, and the execution of Admiral Byng in 1757.

Apparently Voltaire and the future Admiral met during the former's exile in England. Now in 1756 the Duc de Richelieu had scored a definite victory over the English in the Mediterranean, and hurt their pride. He had stormed Fort Mahon on the island of Minorca, and, considering his forces to be quite outnumbered, Byng had withdrawn with his fleet rather than risk what he felt would be a hopeless engagement. Public opinion in London was outraged. Prior to Richelieu's success the French fleet in the Mediterranean had been regarded as no more than a collection of Seine ferry boats. Now a scapegoat was demanded, and that would have to be Admiral Byng.

It was curious that Voltaire should have known Richelieu

while he was at school, and also met John Byng while in England. In the course of their correspondence the Duke mentioned that the Admiral had fought bravely, contrary to popular opinion. The philosopher's humanitarian instincts were aroused. He knew what it was like to be a victim of prejudice, and to be persecuted. Voltaire asked Richelieu to send him his own account of the engagement, which he could then forward to Admiral Byng for use in his defence. Richelieu, though not in some ways a sympathetic character, responded nobly:

I am deeply distressed to learn of the charges against Admiral Byng. I can give assurance that all I have seen or heard of him does great credit to his honour. As he did all that could reasonably be expected of him, he should not be criticised for having suffered a defeat. Every time that two rival commanders fight for victory, no matter how even their forces, one must be defeated. And this is all that can be said against Admiral Byng. His conduct was that of a capable seaman throughout the engagement, and I am amazed that he should have been brought to trial. The two fleets were evenly matched: the English had thirteen vessels, and we had twelve, but ours were better equipped and more manoeuvrable. The fortune of war, which determines the outcome of all battles, and naval battles in particular, was more in our favour than that of the enemy, since our fire did more damage than theirs. I am perfectly convinced, and so is everyone else who was present, that had the English stayed and fought it out their whole fleet would have been annihilated. Nothing could be more unjust than the action that is being taken against Admiral Byng. Every man of honour, every officer on either side, must follow this trial with the closest attention.

Voltaire forwarded the tribute with a covering letter:

Monsieur, although I am almost unknown to you, I consider it my duty to send you the copy of a letter which I have just received from the Maréchal de Richelieu. Honour, Humanity, and Justice compel me to place it in your hands. This noble and unsolicited testimony from me of the most upright and great-hearted of my countrymen makes me confident that your judges will be no less fair in dealing with you.

Many, including George II, wanted clemency for Byng, but at the court-martial the vote went against him, and he was sentenced to death. On 14 March 1757 he was shot on the quarter-deck of his own ship, the *Monarque*, as she lay in Portsmouth harbour, surrounded by scores of small boats carrying spectators. The brief for his defence was sent to Voltaire, along with a note:

The late Admiral Byng wished to assure you of his respect, his gratitude and his esteem; he fully appreciated what you did, and died consoled by the justice that was done him by a noble soldier.

Among Byng's last words were: "They make a precedent of me such as admirals hereafter may feel the effect of."

Two years later *Candide* appeared with a famous paraphrase of this ironic comment: "*En Angleterre on fusille un Admiral pour encourager les autres.*"

Voltaire's defence of Admiral Byng was the first of the disinterested acts of humanity which distinguished the later years of his life, and were perhaps the noblest achievements in a career that had more than its share of discreditable acts. Already the underlying theme of *Candide*, the demolition of the idea of blind optimism, was taking shape in his mind, and in a letter he could write, "happy is the man who can look with a tranquil eye on all the great events in this the best of all possible worlds."

While Rousseau preached an almost oriental fatalism, that it was man's lot to accept suffering, Voltaire was the exact opposite. This was not the best of all possible worlds, he maintained, and it was up to man to try to improve matters—to combat evil and oppression whenever and wherever he could. Soon there would be an open breach between the two philosophers, and in a different way the next few years would be as stormy for Rousseau as anything Voltaire had known in the recent past.

In October 1758 Rousseau wrote his *Lettre sur les spectacles*, attacking d'Alembert's article on theatres written for the *Encyclopédie*. He had already broken with its overall editor, Diderot, and now he broke with the circle of philosophers in Paris. At Montmorency in France he worked away at his novel *La Nouvelle Héloïse* (also called *Julie*), which was published in 1761. That was followed by *Du Contrat Social* and *Émile* in 1762: the latter being a treatise on education in the form of a novel. Both were critical of dogmatic Christianity and also of sceptical philosophy, and both were to bring trouble in their wake for their author. After Rousseau's arrest had been ordered he fled to Switzerland, only to renounce his Genevese citizenship in 1763. The trouble arose from the Petit Conseil having ordered the burning of *Émile* and *Du Contrat Social*. Like Voltaire in such a situation, he insisted on having the last word, and the following year he produced the *Lettres écrites de la Montagne*, a reply to the Petit Conseil's account of why it ordered the burning of *Émile*. Voltaire was not going to be left out, and wrote a venomous little pamphlet entitled *Le Sentiment des Citoyens*, which deeply upset Rousseau, and may have been a factor in his decision to write his autobiography, *Confessions*. In January 1766 he in his turn became an exile in England, leaving Geneva to the Calvinists, and Voltaire.

Already Voltaire had become something of a magnet at *Les Délices*, attracting visitors from all over Europe. Among the first was Mme d'Épinay, the banker's wife who had befriended Rousseau, and had come to consult Dr Tronchin. She missed nothing, and recorded everything in letters to her faithful Baron Grimm (their liaison lasted twenty-seven years). Of Voltaire she wrote:

> I again spent a day with Voltaire. I was received with a politeness and attention which I believe I deserve, but which I am not accustomed to receive. He asked me for news of you, of Diderot and of all our friends. He made every effort to be pleasant. And he succeeded. It is not hard for him.

Another visitor was the historian Edward Gibbon, who also had visited Voltaire when he first came to Switzerland, and when he was living for a short while in Lausanne. Another who came to *Les Délices* was Casanova. According to his *Memoirs*, he had the best of an argument over religion, which he claimed to have defended as being a necessity for the masses: that, in fact, was the view which Voltaire himself held.

There was much during 1755 and 1756 to occupy the philosopher. The publishers Cramer were bringing out a collected edition of his writings, which he was constantly amending and altering, especially at the last minute. At the same time that the *Poème sur le désastre de Lisbonne* was published, at the end of November 1755, Voltaire also allowed his *Poème sur la loi Naturelle* to be printed. Its principal theme was that beneath all religions was a natural law which gave men an inborn sense of justice and morality. Or, to put it another way, that religious precepts and instructions were not the sole fount of the better side of man's nature. Yet again he had piled fuel on the fire on which his enemies would like to see him roasted.

But from the point of view of posterity the most important event during 1756 was the publication of the *Essai sur l'histoire générale et sur les moeurs et l'esprit des nations*: the full title of the *Essay on Customs*. In the past many had attempted to write a history of the world, but such works were little more than a chronological list of events, seen from a strongly Christian standpoint. In the *Essai sur les Moeurs* Voltaire really did embrace world history, as it was then known, from an independent if not strictly neutral viewpoint. It was no mere catalogue of facts, but an analysis of what made nations live. Its breadth of view is indicated by the fact that two chapters each were devoted to China, India and the Arabs, and one to Persia. But the Jewish people, the springboard of Christianity and modern Europe itself, were seen as of minor importance. The work was the well-digested outpouring of all the knowledge he had absorbed during the years at Cirey.

The *Essai* was more than just a lengthy attack on religion. Analysis went hand in hand with scholarship, and if he never missed an opportunity to condemn what he considered to be Christianity's shortcomings, he also flayed all forms of injustice, cruelty and fanaticism, whatever their source.

In a world where religious persecution has been largely superseded by the intolerance of political extremists every bit as cruel and dogmatic, there is still much food for thought in the *Essai*.

Blood has run in wars and on scaffolds for five hundred years on account of theological disputes . . . because morality has always been sacrificed to dogma.

Substitute "political beliefs" for dogma and *tout passe mais rien change*.

There was inevitably a hostile reaction to the work when it was published, and Genevese tolerance was stretched to breaking point. All the while Voltaire was contributing to the *Encyclopédie*, and later 118 entries (together with the *Questions sur l'Encyclopédie*) would make up the *Dictionnaire Philosophique*, which, as has been pointed out, is neither a dictionary nor philosophical.

The range of subjects covered was remarkable, from Abraham to Virtue, and including such diverse subjects as China, Dreams, Flooding; Julian the Apostate; Madness; Motherland; Persecution; Pride; Self-respect; Tolerance and Torture. He also wrote an entry on Transubstantiation, which while not as savage as his attack in *L'Examen de Milord Bolingbroke* none the less contained passages which could not fail to be highly offensive to Catholics. To say that the *Encyclopédie* contains nothing objectionable on religious grounds is understating the case. For example, in the section on Tolerance Voltaire wrote:

Of all religions, Christianity is without doubt that which should inspire the greatest toleration, though up to now the Christians have been the most intolerant of men.

The year 1756 saw quite an important change in the composition of Voltaire's household. Largely through the instigation of Mme Denis, the secretary Collini was dismissed; or at least he preferred to terminate his employment with the philosopher, and go and live at the Court of the Elector Palatine. In his place was the Protestant Jean Louis Wagnière, who was to prove conscientious and loyal to Voltaire both during his lifetime and after his death.

In the past Voltaire had attempted to play the diplomat, with only limited success. Now, in 1757, he set out to mediate in the Seven Years War. England against France; France against

Prussia; Prussia against Austria. Nation after nation was becoming involved in yet another European war. If most seventeenth-century conflicts, like the Thirty Years War, were religious in origin, those of the eighteenth century were mostly dynastic, or else trade wars.

On 18 June 1757 Frederick the Great suffered a defeat such as he had never known at Kolin, east of Prague. He always carried poison on him, and now he declared that if his fortunes did not change he would use it. However, he rather spoilt the effect of the gesture by writing a poem about his desperate thoughts and sending it to his French polisher at *Les Délices*. Voltaire may not have taken the threat seriously, but he scolded his one-time friend and correspondent in a most sensible manner, and set about doing all he could to end the war between France and Austria.

Frederick had declared that he would die by his own hand, like Cato or Brutus, in the defence of liberty. "Nobody is going to look on you as a martyr to liberty," wrote Voltaire. "One must look facts squarely in the face. You must keep in mind how many Courts there are who see a violation of international law in your invasion of Saxony."

Over many years Voltaire had flattered Frederick the Great to a ridiculous and embarrassing degree: now he did not hesitate to tell him the truth. What was more, Voltaire wrote to the king's sister, the Margravine Wilhelmine of Bayreuth, to enlist her help as a go-between to end the war. But this came to nothing as she died soon after. On that same day, 14 October 1758, her brother suffered another defeat, at Hochkirche. Then Voltaire turned to his old friend the Duchess of Saxe-Gotha, writing her letters in which all names were changed, so that only she could recognise the identities of those mentioned. Frederick was "the flirt," while Voltaire signed himself "Jacques Sutamier," with an address not at *Les Délices* but at Nyon. Before then, he had written Frederick the most outspoken letter the monarch can ever have received:

You love glory, and today you place it in dying in a manner which men rarely choose and which none of the sovereigns of Europe has thought of since the fall of the Roman Empire. . . .

Moreover, though I do not meddle in politics in any way whatsoever, I cannot believe but that sufficient will always remain yours to make you a considerable sovereign. If you preferred to scorn all grandeur, like Charles V, Queen Christina, King Casimir and so many others, you could play the part better than all of them; and in you it would be a new grandeur. In short, every course might be fitting except the odious and deplorable course you wish to take. Will it be worth while being a philosopher if you were unable to live as a private man, or if, while remaining a sovereign, you could not endure adversity?

Eventually Voltaire did act as an unofficial intermediary. Both the Duc de Choiseul and Frederick wrote to him, though their letters were really intended for each other. In addition Frederick wrote Richelieu a letter which Voltaire also passed on. Richelieu wrote explaining that he had no authority to negotiate peace, but would give the letter to the King. But Mme de Pompadour hated the homosexual Prussian for the verses he had written at her expense, and he received no reply from Louis XV. Then, in a startling reverse, Frederick defeated the French on 5 November 1758 at Rossbach. His army was only half the size of that commanded by Soubise, but he routed it for the loss of only 550 men. On the French side the losses were very considerable, including 7,000 killed and 5,000 captured, among them five generals and three hundred officers.

Voltaire complained to Thieriot:

It is not pleasant to be a Frenchman in a foreign country now. We are ridiculed to our faces, as if we had all been adjutants of Monsieur Soubise.

The correspondence between the philosopher and the philosopher-king regained some of its old warmth, but while Frederick kept Voltaire up to date about his campaigns against the Austrians there was none the less an undercurrent of bickering in the letters. At a personal level Voltaire dragged up the episode of his and Mme Denis' arrest at Frankfurt, adding that the enemies of the philosophers had declared:

Philosophers cannot live in peace, and cannot live together. Here is a King who does not believe in Jesus Christ, he calls to his Court a man who does not believe in Christ either, and he ill-treats him; there is no humanity in these pretended philosophers and God punishes some of them by means of the others.

Frederick was becoming petulant. In June 1760 he blamed the French for rejecting his overtures of peace, adding:

I would rather be castrated than speak the syllable *peace* again to you Frenchmen. . . . I have no time to waste in these futilities; and, though I should perish, I would rather apply to the Great Mogul than to *Louis le Bien-Aimé* to escape from my labyrinth.

He was still smarting over the interference by Mme de Pompadour:

I do not think a King of Prussia owes any deference to a Miss Poisson, especially if she is arrogant and fails in the respect she owes to crowned heads.

The resumed correspondence between Voltaire and Frederick the Great was to prove short-lived. It was Mme de Pompadour and Peter the Great who indirectly brought it to a close for four years. In 1761 Voltaire dedicated his latest play, *Tancrède*, to Mme de Pompadour, tactlessly alluding to her as the king's mistress. Louis XV took great offence, for in addition to being well-beloved he also wished to appear home-loving. As for Frederick the Great, any form of flattery offered to his enemy Mme de Pompadour was bound to be taken as a personal affront. Also, he bore little love for the Russians, who had recently defeated his armies, and even captured Berlin for a few days. Now he had heard that Voltaire was writing a history of Peter the Great at the request of the Empress of Russia. Their correspondence ceased until 1765.

Another relationship which deteriorated during the late 1750s was between Voltaire and the inhabitants of Geneva. His fellow Encyclopedist d'Alembert had offended the citizens with his article on Geneva, and Voltaire had made matters worse by defending it in a letter in which he went so far as to describe

Calvin as "an atrocious soul". Even sex became a religious issue, when he defended a Protestant maidservant who had been seduced by a Catholic valet.

Voltaire was himself becoming disillusioned, and although he continued to make improvements to the garden at *Les Délices*, he now considered moving to Lorraine. But nothing came of the idea, and in 1758 he decided to remain in the area, and bought two properties. One was in France, and the other almost on the frontier itself, just inside the Republic of Geneva.

He explained in a letter to Thieriot:

> You are mistaken, old friend, if you think that I have only two legs. I am a quadruped. I have one leg in Lausanne, in a very nice little winter house, and one leg in *Les Délices* near Geneva, where the best people come to visit me. These are the two fore-legs. The hind legs stand in Ferney and Tournay, which I have purchased from President de Brosses.

Although nothing outrageous or sensational was happening at this time, many strands were being woven together which made up the complete picture: the death of optimism; work on his entries for the *Encyclopédie*; the final severance from France; the beginning of withdrawal from city life in Geneva and even Lausanne; work on his *Life of Peter the Great*; improvement of the gardens at *Les Délices*, and maintaining his correspondence.

Far away at Versailles *Louis le Bien-Aimé* was degenerating into an ageing voluptuary, as Mme de Pompadour realised. While he turned to young girls for satisfaction she for her part emulated Mme de Maintenon of three-quarters of a century earlier, and turned to religion. Since Voltaire had cut himself off from the French Court, that fact would have been of little interest to him except for a request from Mme de Pompadour that he should translate the Psalms into French verse. He did not act on her suggestion, but later—in 1759—he produced French translations or adaptations of two of the most starkly contrasting books in the Old Testament: the granite-like *Ecclesiastes* and the sensuous *Song of Solomon*. His versions had great merit, but his reputation was such that the Church promptly ordered the *Précis de l'Ecclésiaste* and the *Précis du Cantique des Cantiques* to be burnt.

Nor were these the only recent examples of his work to suffer at the hands of the hangman, *La poème sur la Loi Naturelle* met the same fate. With Catholic Paris on one side and Protestant Geneva on the other Voltaire really was between two fires. Diderot fared even worse, in what had become the war of the *Philosophes*. The spiteful elements among the less successful of the philosophers in Paris had started what amounted to a war against the *Encyclo-pédistes*. D'Alembert threw in his hand altogether in 1758, when his article in the seventh volume, on Geneva, was attacked. Sedition and atheism were the charges levelled at him. He was jailed in the fortress-prison at Vincennes, and the suppression of the *Encyclopédie* was ordered by the *Parlement de Paris*.

Its story began in 1745 when Diderot was first approached by the publisher André le Breton with a view to bringing out a French edition of Chambers' *Cyclopedia*. But soon the whole character of the enterprise changed under the guiding hands of Diderot and his co-editor d'Alembert. The *Encyclopédie* had as its main objective the explanation of the essential principles and applications of every art and science. The first volume appeared in 1751, and the last in 1772. It was a truly monumental work comprising seventeen volumes of text and eleven of plates: the latter beautifully engraved illustrations showing among much else exactly how various industrial processes were carried out. After only a few volumes had been published the *Encyclopédie* became the mouthpiece of the Age of Enlightenment: a useful name for a not very easily defined period of intellectual and political development in France, which was begun at the end of the previous century by such men as Pierre Bayle and later Montesquieu. From them sprang a whole generation of philoso-phers, such as Voltaire, Rousseau, and younger men like Diderot and d'Alembert, all of whom were religious sceptics.

Diderot made his personal views clear in the *Pensées Philoso-phiques*, published in 1746, though his opinions were to become even more extreme in later life. After d'Alembert's resignation from the project in 1758 it was Diderot who was left to manage the editorship almost single-handed, and also bear the brunt of the opposition the work aroused from Church and State. Official displeasure brought him a three-month jail sentence, but even after his release his troubles were still not at an end. In 1764 his own publisher, Le Breton, removed material which he considered might give offence (though to later eyes it seems innocuous enough) from no less than ten folio volumes, to Diderot's understandable chagrin.

The year 1758 brought personal sadness to Voltaire. Sir Everard Falkener died. For ten years between 1735 and 1745 he had been English Ambassador to the Sublime Porte, and very possibly it was he who gave Voltaire an additional interest in that great empire in decline. Perhaps he had his old friend in mind when he ended Candide's adventures on the shores of the Bosporus.

After returning from Constantinople, Falkener became private secretary to George II's son, the Duke of Cumberland, and after that he was appointed Postmaster-General, which he remained until the time of his death. Years before, Voltaire's attachment to Mme du Châtelet had caused him to decline an invitation to visit Turkey, and now both were dead. But in 1774 the Englishman's two sons came to visit him at Ferney, and with emotion he seated himself between them at dinner, exclaiming: "*Mon Dieu, que je me trouve hereux de me voir placé entre deux Falkeners.*"

The previous year had marked the death of Fontenelle, who, together with Bayle, had been one of the originators of the whole philosophical movement. Among his achievements was the stimulation of popular interest in science and astronomy. Also he was one of the first to reject the principle that man's destiny was shaped by supernatural intervention, with the inevitable reaction from the Church. Now, at the remarkable age of one hundred, he had died, and with him went the last of the names associated with the *Grand Siècle* into which Voltaire had been born.

By eighteenth-century standards Voltaire himself was an old man now. He kept contact with some of his contemporaries, such as the Duc de Richelieu, the Argentals and the less than admirable Thieriot. Then there were the second generation philosophers, who looked on Voltaire as a father-figure and a Grand Old Man of letters, rather than an active leader of the Enlightenment. Among them were Condorcet (1743–1794), a mathematician, philosopher, politician, and permanent secretary of the Academy of Sciences, who was later to be Voltaire's biographer; Turgot (1727–1781), economist and administrator, and future Finance Minister, contributor to the *Encyclopédie* and admirer of Voltaire;

Homage to the bust of Voltaire on the stage of the *Comédie Française*
drawn by *Moreau the Younger*, engraved by *Gaucher*

The 'Coronation' of Voltaire at the *Comédie Française*, March 30, 1778
(left) the Marquise de Villette (*Belle et Bonne*) (right) Mme Denis

Voltaire's triumphant funeral procession as it left the Hôtel of Villette, in Paris.

and Baron Paul d'Holbach (1723–1789), a German-born philosopher who chose to make his home in France and at whose house the *Encyclopédistes* were always welcome. Like the other philosophers he was opposed to the political and religious institutions of his adopted country.

This then was the changing world of which Voltaire was still a part. But now since he avoided the Courts and salons of Europe there was a certain detachment about him both physically and intellectually. While he kept up an endless stream of writing, much of it ephemeral, in the form of journalistic pamphlets, he was also continuing with his contributions to the *Encyclopédie*, and finding time to write his best loved tale, *Candide*.

Less is known about the genesis of *Candide* than of almost any other of his works. The Elector Palatine, who gave Voltaire a considerable pension or annuity, had invited him and Mme Denis to stay as his guest at Schweitzingen near Mainz, and *Candide* was written during the leisurely journey, which included a stay with the Margrave of Barden-Durlach.

Candide is a character to whom everything happens, without any active participation on his part. His naïve optimism lays him open to every imaginable disaster, and by means of these misadventures Voltaire was able to place under irrational philosophers and tyrannically dogmatic churchmen alike squibs which still fizzle and explode with delightful effect two centuries later. After the Lisbon earthquake, the effects of which were witnessed by Candide, Rousseau had attempted to exonerate Providence from blame for the disaster by saying that if man had not crowded together in cities such as Lisbon there would have been no great holocaust and loss of life. He chose to overlook the fact that the surrounding countryside with its scattered villages also suffered severely from the tremors.

Accompanying Candide is the ineffable Dr Pangloss, a worthy follower of Leibniz and exponent of the theory of optimism. On contemplating the ruins the philosopher comments: "Nothing could have been better [than the earthquake], for if there is a volcano under Lisbon, it could not have been elsewhere, since it is impossible that things should not be as they are, as all is well."

Voltaire goes on to other targets, in the next paragraph mocking the more rabid churchmen:

A little fellow dressed in black, a familiar of the Inquisition, who was seated at his side, politely took up the conversation, and said: "It would seem that the gentleman does not believe in original sin, for, if all is as good as can be, there can have been neither a fall of man nor divine punishment."

"I most humbly beg your Excellency's pardon," answered Pangloss still more politely, "for the fall of man and the subsequent curse necessarily entered into the scheme of the best of all possible worlds."

"Then, sir, you do not believe in free will?" asked the familiar.

"Excuse me, Your Excellency," said Pangloss, "free will is compatible with absolute necessity, for it is necessary that we should be free; for, in fact, the will being determined. . . ." Pangloss was in the middle of his sentence when the familiar gave a significant nod to his serving-man, who was helping him to a cup of the wine of Oporto, commonly called Port.

Such talk leads to the arrest of Candide and Pangloss, who find themselves participating in an *auto-da-fé*:

It was decided by the University of Coimbra that the spectacle of a few people roasted over a slow fire, with grand ceremonies, is an infallible specific for preventing earthquakes.

Candide escapes with a flogging, carried out in time to the music of an anthem, but Pangloss is hanged. The hanging is not fatal, however, since he reappears many chapters later as a Turkish galley-slave when all the principal characters are on their way to their final haven, a house with a large garden on the shores of the Bosphorus.

Before then, but after Candide has travelled to South America and visited El Dorado—a Utopian communistic paradise from which no one can escape, except for Candide and his companions —they adventure on, voyaging to England and into the scene which includes one of Voltaire's most famous quotations:

. . . they came in sight of Portsmouth; a multitude of people lined the shore, and had their gaze fixed attentively on a stout man, who was kneeling, with eyes blindfolded, on the deck of one of the men-of-war; four soldiers, stationed opposite this man, discharged three bullets each into his skull, in the calmest manner possible; and then the crowd returned home, very well satisfied with what they had seen.

"What is the meaning of this?" said Candide, "and what demon exerts dominion everywhere?"

In answer to his inquiry who that stout man was who had just been put to death with such ceremony, he was told that he was an admiral.

"And why do they kill an admiral?"

"Because," said his informants, "he has not caused enough people to be slaughtered; he gave battle to a French admiral, and it has been found that he did not come to sufficiently close quarters."

"But," said Candide, "the French admiral must have been as far from the English admiral as he was from the other!"

"That cannot be disputed," was the reply; "but in this country it is thought a good thing to shoot an admiral from time to time to encourage the others."

But, since they live in the best of all possible worlds, they eventually find peace on their little farm beside the Bosphorus, and whenever Dr Pangloss (who eventually recovers from his dejection at not being able to shine at some German university) comments that all events are inextricably linked in this the best of all possible worlds, Candide would agree, adding "but we must cultivate our garden."

Although it debunks the philosophy of optimism, *Candide* is not pessimistic (a word unknown in Voltaire's day). The theme underlying all the persiflage and fantasy is: if you want a better world, get up off your backside and do something about it, even if it is nothing more than cultivating your garden. At least you are doing something useful. Deeds, not words, are what count, especially if you are concerned for the welfare of your fellow-men; and that was certainly true of the Voltaire of recent years. In the future he would take up causes like the unjust punishment of Calas, Sirven and General Lally—a French equivalent of Admiral Byng.

In *Candide* the *conte philosophique* reached its peak, and as a literary form it has never been successfully emulated since; but it was written by a man who at an advanced age, and with a wealth of worldly experience behind him, had suddenly had his heart touched with compassion, even a love, for ordinary people. When he wrote it he was indeed *le rieur plein des larmes*.

Candide became an instant best-seller. Six thousand copies were sold within a few weeks in Paris, and people literally snatched it from each other's hands. While Europe howled with laughter at Candide's misfortunes the authorities stepped in and banned it, and of course before long the book was burnt by the hangman. But if that had not happened Voltaire would have considered that he had failed in his objective: to make people laugh, and then think seriously about the society in which they lived. The work was printed simultaneously in several different places, not under his name, and for a while it amused Voltaire to deny authorship. Of course, everyone knew there was only one man who could have written such a little masterpiece.

Chapter 18

WITHDRAWAL TO FERNEY

Words continued to flow from Voltaire's quill at a prodigious rate, and in a short space of time two plays were written and published. The first was the tragedy *Tancrède* and the second the comedy *L'Ecossaise*. *The History of Peter the Great and his times* was going through the presses, and there were two malevolently satirical pamphlets, aimed at the Jesuits. And yet at about this time Voltaire, who could be so anti-clerical, rebuilt the little church at Ferney, giving it a unique dedication: *Deo erexit Voltaire.*

Later, an English visitor, Richard Twiss, recorded him as saying, "This church which I have erected is the only one consecrated to God alone; all the others are consecrated to male or female saints."

In a letter in English to Lord Lyttelton he wrote: "As to religion, I think, and I hope, he thinks with me, that God is, neither a presbyterian, nor a Lutheran, nor of the low church, nor of the high church; but God the father of all mankind, the father of the noble author [Lord Lyttelton] and mine."

Having built a church dedicated to his concept of the Supreme Father, Voltaire then asked the Pope for a relic to place in it. He claimed that he had been sent the hair shirt of St Francis. Elsewhere he wrote that he had placed the relics sent by His Holiness on the chimney-piece. It is likely that he received a few bones of early Christians taken from the catacombs of Rome, which on occasions were given as presents to favoured churches or individuals by the Pontiff. But he was still the old and at times flippant Voltaire, and later he wrote: "I have built a church and a theatre; I have already celebrated my mysteries at the theatre but as yet I have not heard a mass in my church. On one and the same day I received relics from the Pope, and a portrait of Mme de Pompadour."

Little by little Voltaire was withdrawing from *Les Délices*, and therefore from Geneva itself, and concerning himself almost entirely with his properties at Tournay and Ferney. He described the privileges he enjoyed as the Seigneur of Ferney in his *Autobiography*:

> He likewise purchased two estates in the *Pays de Gex*, about a league from Geneva. His principal residence was at Ferney, which he made a present to Mme Denis, it was a Seignory [*sic*], which had been absolutely free from all royal duties and imposts from the time of Henry IV. In all the other provinces of the kingdom, there are not two which have the same privileges; the King confirmed these privileges to him by a warrant, which was an obligation conferred upon him by the interest of the most generous and worthiest of men, the Duke de Choiseul, to whom he had not even the honour of being personally known.

Voltaire's mysteries, as he described them, which had been celebrated at *Les Délices*, included the first performance of *L'Orphelin de la Chine*. Other plays had been given during his comparatively short stay in Lausanne, and now of course there were performances in his newly-built theatre at Ferney. In 1760, the comedy *L'Ecossaise* was staged at the Comédie Française. Its writing must have given much pleasure, because in it Voltaire levelled the score with the critic Fréron, who had set himself up as the defender of Church and State against the philosophers and the *Encyclopédistes*. Under the name of Frelon (Hornet) he had been lampooned for once and all. The public, if not the authorities, loved the piece.

After sixteen very successful performances *L'Ecossaise* had to make way for *Tancrède*, an historical tragedy set in Syracuse, with Lekain and Mlle Clairon in the leading roles. It too was successful, but pressure from outside may have been responsible for its withdrawal after thirteen performances, though more followed early in 1761, when it again filled the house.

The action of *Tancrède* takes place in eleventh-century Sicily. It is perhaps the most carefully written of all Voltaire's plays, though he is said to have finished it in a month. If his stage works are remembered at all today it is by the concert and opera-going public. At least ten plays were turned into operas, while several of the *contes* were also adapted. Verdi had one of his rare failures with *Alzire* (*Alzira*); Rossini was more fortunate with *Tancrède* (*Tancredi*), and *Sémiramis* (*Semiramide*); *Montezuma* (after *Alzire*) and *Mérope* were set by Graun with librettos by Frederick the Great; *Olympie* by Spontini, and *L'Ingénu* by Grétry. As recently as 1958 Leonard Bernstein made *Candide* into a lively opera.

It would not be quite true that a new and more compassionate Voltaire suddenly emerged as it were from a chrysalis about the year 1760. All his mature life he had detested and where possible opposed injustice and tyranny from any quarter. But now he was involved in the affairs of individual people, rather than abstract ideas. Two diverse and striking examples of his new attitude are, first, his championship of the rights of his tenants in the little Pays de Gex, before the ink was hardly dry on his contract of purchase; and, second, the very generous assistance he extended to a penniless collateral descendant of the playwright Corneille.

The estate at Ferney was run down and poverty-stricken. In the *Autobiography* he wrote:

... in the village of Ferney, which, at the time of his purchase, was only a wretched hamlet tenanted by forty-nine miserable peasants, devoured by poverty, scrofula, and tax-gatherers, very soon became a delightful place, inhabited by twelve hundred people, comfortably situated, and successfully employed for themselves and the nation.

Among his first actions was an attempt to induce the authorities to abolish the salt tax in the whole of the Pays de Gex, and to fall out with the local churchmen. For some years the villagers had refused to pay tithes to the priest of the nearby village of Moens, believing them to be an illegal imposition. The parliamentary court at Dijon, within whose jurisdiction the Pays de Gex was situated, and whose head was the President de Brosses, ordered the imprisonment of two non-paying farmers. Voltaire took action on their behalf, but when he found the taxes were in fact legal he paid them himself to obtain the farmers' release.

More trouble followed soon after, involving the priest at Moens, who seems to have been a man of extreme views. He heard that three local youths were having supper with a widow of doubtful reputation, and, according to the priest's informant, making fun of him. At this the priest gathered together a band of farmers and peasants with sticks. Together they went to the house and savagely beat the young men. One thought he was dying and exclaimed: "Shall I die without confession?" To which Ancian, the priest, replied: "Die like a dog; die like a Huguenot!"

That was enough for Voltaire, who rushed precipitately into the affair. Two of the young men feared the power of the priest, who was both rich and influential, and they refused to lodge a formal protest. At Voltaire's instigation the father of the third, De Croze, lodged a complaint. Voltaire wanted Ancian sent to the galleys for his murderous assault. Of course this never came about. The actual assailant disappeared, but the priest remained at Moens. President de Brosses wrote Ancian a stinging rebuke for his action, but at the same time reproached Voltaire for becoming involved in the affair. Nor would he take action against a Jesuit priest who had refused to give absolution to the sister of De Croze unless their father dropped the case.

"The case of the poor De Croze would be inconceivable in any other country than in France," Voltaire wrote to Cramer, his publisher.

In the end Ancian was ordered to pay 1,500 *livres* compensation to De Croze.

Voltaire's motives here were less anti-clerical than retaliatory, for Ancian had complained about the philosopher's actions at Ferney. First Voltaire had ordered the removal of a Calvary from the churchyard, referring to it as a gallows. Then he rebuilt the church itself, which the priest considered a desecration, and forthwith ordered the removal of the Host reserved within its walls to his own church at Moens.

A more successful encounter, from Voltaire's point of view, was with his neighbours the Jesuits. The trouble here stemmed from his championing the cause of six brothers, most of whom were still under age, whose family estate was mortgaged to creditors in Geneva. Adjoining the Du Crassi estate was land owned by the Jesuits. The Superior, who had understandably changed his name from Fesse (Buttock) to Fessi, arranged to buy the land from the creditors in Geneva, though since most of the brothers were still minors there was the risk that they might be able to reclaim the estate. This proposition Fessi waived aside, confident that they could never find the money. He was reckoning without Voltaire, who promptly went to the Clerk of the Precinct of Gex, and deposited a sufficiently large sum to pay off the creditors in Geneva. He commented on the eventual outcome of the episode with typical irony:

The best of the whole affair is, that a little time after, when France was delivered from the Reverend Jesuit Fathers, these very gentlemen, whose property the good fathers were desirous of seizing, purchased the lands of the Jesuits, which were contiguous to them. M. de Voltaire, who had always combatted the Atheists and Jesuits, wrote upon the occasion that we must acknowledge a Providence.

At the expense of the Church, Voltaire had endeared himself to his tenants, and it is to his credit that within his little kingdom, as he sometimes referred to his estates, Catholic and Protestant lived side by side in amity. Even before the inhabitants had had personal experience of his concern for their welfare, his arrival on Christmas Eve 1757 as the new Seigneur of Tournay was like a royal progress, with salutes by cannon and muskets, drums and whistles. On arrival baskets of oranges entwined with ribbons were presented by young girls, and the cannon were again fired, while his health was drunk.

Within six months he had spent 15,000 *livres* improving the estate, and ploughed back any income derived from it to help improve the condition of the worse-off tenants.

Such was the complexity of Voltaire's nature that he could even quarrel with President de Brosses, from whom he had bought the property, over something as trivial as a load of firewood left on the land after completion of purchase, which he thought belonged to him, but was in fact owned by a local woodseller. Voltaire took and used the wood, and then the woodseller presented him with a bill for it. The philosopher refused to pay, and blamed de Brosses for the whole episode. The President sued the woodseller, and the woodseller sued Voltaire. A very rude letter from Voltaire, in which he practically accused the President of sharp practice, earned him a rebuke. De Brosses informed him that had he asked he would have been given the firewood as a present, and enclosed a receipt for him to sign, to that effect.

I, the undersigned François Marie Arouet de Voltaire, Chevalier, *Seigneur de Ferney, Gentilhomme ordinaire du Roi*, hereby acknowledge that Monsieur de Brosses, President of the parliamentary court, has made me a gift of firewood to heat Tournay, to the value of 281 francs, for which I thank him.

Whether Voltaire ever paid the sum as a debt of honour is uncertain; but the sorry episode never came to a proper conclusion, and nine years later the philosopher was still nursing a grudge against de Brosses. So much so that when the President sought admission to the Académie Voltaire wrote to d'Alembert saying that he would use his influence to block the election. De Brosses never did become an Immortal.

An episode which shows Voltaire in a more favourable light concerned a relative of Corneille. In the *Grand Siècle* the name of Corneille had ranked second only to that of Racine. Now one of the few left to bear it was a near-illiterate son of a cousin, and his young daughter. The father was employed as a letter-carrier in a village near Evreux, while Marie-Françoise Corneille wove wicker baskets to be sold in the market of that city. This Jean François Corneille was unaware that he was even remotely related to the playwright until someone pointed it out to him, adding that he must also be related to Fontenelle, who was Corneille's nephew.

The father and daughter immediately went to Paris to seek Fontenelle's aid, but the ninety-seven-year-old man of letters repudiated them as impostors, and left them nothing in his will. After his death three years later his heirs did give a little financial assistance for a short while, and then Voltaire's old adversary

Fréron induced the Comédie Française to give benefit performances of two of Corneille's plays. This brought in 5,000 *livres*,
most of which went towards settling debts, but Marie-Françoise
was sent to a convent school, until the money had quite gone,
when she was removed by her father.

At this point the poet Denis Lebrun took an interest in the girl's
welfare, and wrote to Voltaire at Ferney seeking his help. With
the impulsive generosity of which he was capable, and under the
impression that she must be a granddaughter of Pierre Corneille,
he wrote back: "Send this child to me. It is right that an old
soldier of the great Corneille should be useful to his general's
grandchild."

By the same post he wrote to the d'Argentals, whom he described as his "angels," requesting them to see that the girl made a
safe departure from Paris. He also requested Dr Tronchin's
brother, who lived in Lyon, to take care of her when she was in
that city.

Voltaire and Marie Corneille set eyes on each other for the first
time in December 1760, and the philosopher was delighted with
what he saw. Marie was a lively little charmer, with a pug-like
nose, laughing eyes and beautiful teeth. What was more, she was
intelligent and anxious to please. In a sense Mme Denis had a
young rival, but Voltaire's interest and affection were only of a
fatherly nature, and in fact Mme Denis entered enthusiastically
into the girl's education and improvement, which included correcting her bad pronunciation.

To the pure all things may be pure, but literary Paris, headed
by Fréron, thought the worst, and said so aloud. With biting
sarcasm the man who had been satirised in *L'Ecossaise* as the
Hornet, now proceeded to sting his adversary.

One would not believe what a sensation Monsieur de Voltaire's
noblemindedness is causing in good society. It is the topic of
discussion in the periodicals and newspapers, and I am convinced that these reports are a real torture to the modest poet
who knows that the main merit of good deeds is to keep them
secret. . . . It must be admitted that Mademoiselle Corneille,
after leaving the convent, will come into good hands.

Voltaire's reaction to such insinuations was to rush into a lawsuit, but no one in Paris was anxious to support him, and in the end he contented himself with publishing *Anecdotes sur Fréron*. Now the Hornet stung Lebrun, the originator of the whole idea of enlisting Voltaire's aid, but he retaliated by showing up Fréron's shaky classical education, and Paris enjoyed a vitriolic quarrel.

For his part, Voltaire was behaving with extraordinary generosity. So that Marie Corneille should have a dowry when the time came for her to marry, he undertook the huge task of editing a complete edition of Corneille's plays, including a critical analysis. Such was his prestige now that Louis XV, Mme de Pompadour, the Empress Elizabeth of Russia, and Frederick the Great put their names down for two hundred or two hundred and fifty copies each. Also, he succeeded in interesting leading personages on both sides of the Channel, such as Lord Chesterfield and the Duc de Villars; while he put himself down for one hundred copies. Altogether this definitive version of Corneille's plays brought in about 100,000 francs, a truly generous windfall for Marie.

By 1760 the move to Ferney as Voltaire's permanent residence was complete. Geneva had failed him with what he considered was its narrow-mindedness and intolerance, culminating in the burning of *Candide* by the hangman. Despite the loving improvements which he lavished on the house and garden at *Les Délices*, that particular chapter was now ended. He ceased to be a citizen of Geneva, and became the sage of Ferney.

Being famous, sought-after, and the Seigneur of a delightful "little kingdom" was not without its drawbacks; as Voltaire himself declared with asperity, he had become "the tavern-keeper of Europe". Friends, acquaintances, correspondents, the celebrated and the merely curious all made their way to his door, to receive welcomes of varying degrees of warmth.

In addition to old friends, Voltaire found himself visited by the children—themselves now middle-aged—of those he had known and loved in a remote past when he himself had been a sophisticated meteorite flashing across the sky of Parisian society. Some forty years before he had made himself ill with unrequited love for the Maréchale de Villars; now her son, himself nearly sixty, and aged by a life of dissipation, came to Ferney. De Villars was the Governor of Provence, but his favourite occupation was acting. He insisted on taking the role of Genghis Khan in *L'Orphelin de la Chine*, though in view of his position in public life the performance took place behind closed doors.

In the *Autobiography*, Voltaire described the theatre:

> ... he built a handsome little theatre at Ferney, and, notwithstanding the bad state of his health, sometimes played himself; his niece, Mme Denis, who possessed uncommon talents for music and elocution, acted several characters there. Mademoiselle Clairon, and the famous Lekain, performed in some pieces on the stage, and people twenty leagues distant came to hear them. He had oftener than once had suppers of a hundred covers, and balls; notwithstanding his advanced age, and the appearance of a life of dissipation, he never discontinued his studies.

Another young visitor, who in fact was a welcome guest for several months, was the twenty-six-year-old Chevalier de Boufflers, son of the light-headed and charming Marquise who had formed one of the circle of friends at Lunéville not long before Emilie du Châtelet's death. A schoolfriend who came on what was little short of a state visit was Richelieu, who stayed with his retinue at Tournay, and passed his days at Ferney. All his life he had been a gallant, and now he wished to add Mme Cramer, wife of Voltaire's publisher, to his list of conquests. M. Cramer was sent off to have a laudatory poem by Voltaire printed overnight so that it could be presented to the Maréchal the following morning. But Mme Cramer was not as easily vanquished as Admiral Byng, and she laughed outright in her would-be seducer's face. Richelieu was so struck by the novelty of actually receiving a rebuff that when he returned to Paris he recounted the episode as a great joke.

Visitors of his own choosing were one thing, but those who arrived unheralded were another, which called forth the well known exclamation: "My God, save me from my friends; I'll deal with my enemies myself." Then there was the rebuke administered to the Abbé Croyer, who announced that he intended to stay for several months: "You, Monsieur l'Abbé, are a worthy counterpart of Don Quixote; he mistook inns for manors; you mistake manors for inns."

Chapter 19

THE CALAS AFFAIR

After his experiences with the Calvinists of Geneva, Voltaire had as little love for the more extreme forms of Protestantism as he had for Catholic fanaticism. He himself was a man of extreme emotions, not to say intellectual passions, but he almost invariably expected moderation in others. Consequently, when he first heard that a certain Calas, a Huguenot merchant in Toulouse, had been executed for murdering his son because the youth wished to become a Catholic he accepted the story at its face value. Although his first reaction was somewhat flippant, he eventually became sufficiently committed to arouse compassion and financial assistance from George III of England; Catherine the Great of Russia; the King of Poland, and many others. Presumably the only reason he did not enlist the aid of Frederick the Great was because at that time the two men were not corresponding with each other.

On 22 March Voltaire commented on the Calas affair, as it was soon to be known, in a letter. His attitude to the principal religious factions was impartial condemnation: "We [the Roman Catholics] are not worth much, but the Huguenots are worse than we are. They declaim against comedy."

But something stirred in his mind: a feeling which may have stemmed from his legal background that there must be two sides to the case. At the end of March Voltaire was visited at Ferney by a merchant from Marseille, Audibert by name, who had been in Toulouse when the trial and execution of Calas took place. "I told him [the merchant] that the crime of Calas was not probable; but it was still more improbable that disinterested judges should condemn an innocent man to be broken on the wheel."

In the previous week he had still been something of a detached spectator. "I am interested as a man, and a little as a philosopher. I want to know *on which side* is this horror and fanaticism."

Quick to anger and to let fly a barbed shaft, Voltaire could also react speedily when his compassion was aroused. Now, both compassion and a feeling that a terrible injustice had been committed moved him to action, though he still retained a certain detachment, and did not allow his emotions to run away with him. On 27 March he wrote to the Comte d'Argental: "Could you not induce M. de Choiseul to have this fearful case investigated?"

Thus he set in motion an investigation which would uncover a crime not committed by an elderly and respected merchant, but by the Church and Judiciary of the city in which he lived. The Calas affair would send a wave of horror and shame among real Christians, as opposed to religious fanatics, and the case could well be counted as a step along the road towards the French Revolution itself.

Two days after writing to d'Argental, Voltaire wrote to d'Alembert:

> France is becoming hated everywhere. Everyone says that we are as barbaric as any weak-minded nation which knows how to break someone on the wheel, but not how to win a fair fight, and which has progressed from the Massacre of Bartholomew to comic opera. We are arousing the terror and the contempt of Europe; it grieves me, since we are meant to be agreeable.

Less than a month later the youngest of the Huguenot's children, who had been an apprentice at Nîmes, sought refuge in Geneva when his whole family was brought to trial in Toulouse. And now, in April 1762, his presence was brought to the attention of Voltaire. Since Ferney was just inside France, Voltaire invited the fifteen-year-old Donat Calas to stay at *Les Délices* in the safety of the Republic of Geneva. Much later, in a letter to the philosopher Damilaville, dated 1 March 1765, he wrote:

> I had the young Calas come to my house, I expected to see a young fanatic of the sort that his upbringing sometimes produces. I found a simple, naïve child, quiet and attractive, who tried vainly to keep back his tears while he talked to me. He

told me that he was serving his apprenticeship in a manu-
factory at Nîmes, when he learnt from public announcements
that his entire family was about to be sentenced to death in
Toulouse. He had been told that nearly all Languedoc believed
the Calas family to be guilty. . . .

I asked him if his father and mother had been given to
violence; he answered that they had never struck any of their
children and that no parents could have been more indulgent or
loving.

By now Voltaire was completely committed to the cause of
exposing a terrible miscarriage of justice, and of rehabilitating the
surviving members of the family. In Switzerland there were many
sympathisers with these persecuted French Protestants, and a
fund was started to cover the inevitable legal expenses. Voltaire
pulled every string he could: the Duchesse d'Enville would use
her influence at Court; the Duc de Richelieu would speak with
Saint-Florentin, the Chancellor. Others went to work enlisting the
support of Chancellor Guillaume de Lamoignon, who would be
powerful enough to reverse the decision of the regional court at
Toulouse. The barrister Élie de Beaumont promised to obtain the
support of the lawyers in Paris, while Voltaire busied himself in
consultations with a Genevese lawyer. Also, he instructed a
lawyer in Montpellier to interview magistrates in the Toulouse
region and obtain such documents as would be relevant when the
case was laid before the authorities in Paris.

Voltaire was marshalling some very impressive forces with
which to annihilate the *Parlement de Toulouse*. He even enlisted
Mme de Pompadour to use her influence with the king. In August
she replied that the Calas affair was enough to make one shudder:
adding that although the victim was to be pitied for having been
born a Huguenot there was no reason for treating him like a
highwayman, or branding his family. She went on to say:

The kind heart of the King has suffered much at the recital of
this strange adventure and all France cries out for vengeance.

Perceptively, Mme de Pompadour put her finger on the root

cause of all the trouble. "These people at Toulouse are hot-headed, and have more religion of this kind than they need to be good Christians."

Languedoc had a reputation for excessive religious zeal, and Toulouse was a city where each August the anniversary of the Massacre of Saint Bartholomew was celebrated as a two-day festival and holiday.

The first difficulty which had to be overcome was to induce the widow of Jean Calas to leave her hiding place in the country and come to Paris. In June the penniless widow came, with all her expenses paid by Voltaire. In the capital it was the d'Argentals who took care of her, while advice was given by such as d'Alembert. Élie de Beaumont and the more senior barrister Mariette were briefed to act on her behalf. They refused a fee. When a request was made to the *Parlement de Toulouse* asking for copies of relevant documents, not only was permission refused but no one was even allowed to see the originals. Neither Louis XV nor Chancellor Saint-Florentin wanted an investigation to take place, which obviously would reflect great discredit on the whole French judicial system.

Now another son of Jean Calas had escaped from the monastery in which he had been virtually imprisoned, and he came to join his brother Donat at Geneva. He too was questioned by Voltaire, who wrote:

> I am passing my days and nights writing letters to all those who can exert their influence to right a wrong which has attracted the attention of the whole world, and it seems to me that the honour of France demands that it shall be cleaned up. We have Pierre Calas here. I have questioned him for four hours; I shudder and I weep. But the point is to act.

With the Calas affair Voltaire might be said to have discovered the power of public opinion, for he deliberately set about informing all Europe of what had happened at Toulouse, which many now wished to see hushed up.

On 5 July 1762 Voltaire wrote to the Comte d'Argental:

> We demand nothing more than to be told for what Calas was

sentenced to death. What a terror such a secret judgment is if it does not have to give its reasons! Is there any more dreadful tyranny than to be able to shed blood without having to account for it to anybody?

A number of pamphlets were published during the summer of 1762, under the collective title of *Pièces originales concernant la mort de Sieur Calas et le jugement rendu à Toulouse*. First came the contents of a letter written by Mme Calas, giving her account of the events of 13 October 1761, followed by one from Donat to his mother: written 22 July 1762, and ghosted by Voltaire. Next came a "Memoir by Donat Calas for his father, his mother, and his brother." In it the hand of an extremely clever Voltaire appeared, for Donat wrote without rancour about the religious persecution his family had suffered; in fact he spoke most respectfully of Roman Catholicism, and assured the reader of his loyalty to Louis XV.

One by one Voltaire was spiking his enemies' guns before they could be fired. The next pamphlet, *Déclaration*, was written in the name of Pierre Calas. In it the young man expressed the opinion that it was not just a question of clearing his father's name, but involved the important principle that the public should know the truth. The sting in the tail was his apparently naïve conviction that once the *Parlement de Toulouse* realised there had been a miscarriage of justice it would of its own accord do what it could to right a wrong.

The *Pièces Originales* were promptly banned in France, but translated into English and German. And they stirred the compassion of such influential figures as George III and Catherine of Russia to such an extent that they made contributions for the benefit of the Calas family. De Beaumont presented the Council with a petition signed by fifteen leading lawyers in which he exposed the weaknesses of the case for the prosecution, which had resulted in the conviction of Calas. No one, he declared, could be sentenced to death on the flimsiest of circumstantial evidence, and there should be a retrial.

In an attempt to damage Voltaire's standing in the affair, a letter from him to d'Alembert in Paris was published in which the philosopher was supposed to have vilified the king, his ministers and the *Parlement de Toulouse*. What had happened was that some-one acting on the instructions of a higher authority had removed the letter from the post, copied it out, adding offensive references, and then let the original continue on its way. When Voltaire was told, he asked d'Alembert to send the original to Choiseul, who could then read for himself that it had contained nothing objectionable.

Thanks to the pamphlets which made up the *Pièces Originales*, not even Louis XV and all his ministers could stifle the Calas affair any longer. That creation of Voltaire's, public opinion, had won its first victory. In May 1763, just over a year after he had first interested himself in the case, Voltaire heard that the *Parlement de Toulouse* had been ordered by the Council to hand over all documents relevant to the trial. "A great day in the calendar of the philosophers," declared Voltaire.

For the first time the truth started to emerge about what had really happened late on the evening of 13 October 1761, in the house of the Huguenot cloth-merchant, Jean Calas.

Toulouse was not a city for an ambitious Huguenot. In England no Catholic could hold public office, but in Languedoc the professions and many trades were barred to non-Catholics as well. None could become doctors, surgeons, apothecaries, lawyers, booksellers, printers or grocers. There, in the Rue des Filatiers, Jean Calas lived with his family over a shop where he sold his cloth. He was sixty-three, and looked older. The household consisted of himself, his wife of about forty-five; their four sons, two daughters and a maidservant. By law the servant had to be a Catholic, because no Huguenot was allowed to have an apprentice or a servant of his own faith.

The eldest son was Marc-Antoine, a difficult young man of twenty-eight; embittered by the fact that his religion barred him from becoming a lawyer; and now drifting through life, and talking incessantly of suicide. The second was Pierre, about twenty-five. Next came Louis, who became a Catholic of his own free will. His father certainly did not oppose the conversion, taking the line that he was old enough to make decisions for himself. The only one to object was in fact Marc-Antoine. The youngest boy, the fifteen-year-old Donat, was an apprentice at Nîmes, while the two daughters, Rose and Nanette, were in their early twenties. The maid, Jeanette Viguière, had been with the household for thirty years, and despite her different religion was treated like one of the family.

On the evening of 13 October 1761 those in the house were Jean Calas and his wife, Marc-Antoine, Pierre, the maid and a young friend named Gaubert Lavaysse, who visited them while passing through Toulouse, and was invited to stay to supper. His father was a prominent lawyer connected with the *Parlement de Toulouse*. Near the end Marc-Antoine got up and went into the kitchen. He did not join his parents, brother and their guest when they went into the living-room, where Pierre dropped off to sleep. At a quarter to ten Pierre was awakened to go and fetch a light, and to accompany Lavaysse downstairs to the street door. On the ground floor they found the door into the shop was open. What they discovered made them cry out.

Marc-Antoine had opened the doors of a tall cupboard, placed a piece of wood across the top and had hanged or rather strangled himself. His jacket and waistcoat were lying folded on the shop counter. The distraught father lifted his son down, and the piece of wood fell to the floor. The noose was removed, and Jean Calas and the others tried to revive Marc-Antoine, without success. Then Pierre was told to go and fetch a doctor. One came, by the name of Gorse, who declared that Marc-Antoine was quite dead. Then he noticed the bruising round the young man's neck.

Now there was one thought in the father's mind, to hide the fact that his son had committed suicide. For centuries it was the custom to treat barbarously the body of anyone who had taken his or her own life. The fate of Marc-Antoine Calas would have been to have his body dragged face down, naked, through the streets of the city, and then be hung up in chains to be stoned by the mob.

Pierre started out of the house again to get more help, and as he went his agonised father called after him: "Don't say anything about your brother having killed himself: at least save the honour of the family."

Pierre found Lavaysse at the house of a friend and neighbour, Cazing, and begged him to say nothing about Marc-Antoine having killed himself. Lavaysse agreed, but at the same time he felt it was his duty to report the incident to the Council. Within a few minutes an alderman and magistrate named Beaudrigue appeared with a guard of forty men, and promptly arrested Pierre, and at the same time sent for a doctor and two surgeons. By now all the comings and goings had attracted a large and excited crowd. Suddenly someone started the rumour: "These Huguenots murdered their son because he wanted to become a Catholic."

It spread through the crowd like wild-fire, reaching the ears of David Beaudrigue, who was himself as fanatical as any of those outside in the street. He promptly ordered the arrest of Jean and Anna Rose Calas, Lavaysse, and even the neighbour Cazing.

The body of Marc-Antoine was laid on a bier, and it headed a torchlit procession through the streets to the Hôtel de Ville. There a colleague suggested to Beaudrigue that he was rather jumping to conclusions; whereupon he was assured that this was a matter of faith. "I take all the responsibility. It is in the cause of religion."

Beaudrigue was so blunderingly cocksure that, contrary to an edict of 1670, he had removed nearly every piece of evidence, and by law the inquest should be held at the actual scene of the tragedy.

At the Hôtel de Ville, surrounded by hostile authorities, all those under arrest swore that they had found the body on the floor; though in fact this was only true for Mme Calas and the maid. For their part they were trying to cover up a suicide, while the authorities, and soon all Toulouse, were convinced that they were uncovering a murder committed for religious motives. The prisoners remained under arrest, their feet chained, during the remainder of October. When cross-examined separately they now all told the same story, that it was in fact suicide.

The body was embalmed, and laid out in the torture chamber of the Hôtel de Ville. There it remained until 7 November, when burial was suggested. Beaudrigue approached the priest of the parish in which Marc-Antoine had lived, and suggested that there should be a Catholic funeral. This was staged in a provocative, macabre manner calculated to inflame further everyone against Jean Calas and his family. It had been suggested, quite without evidence, that Marc-Antoine had been intending to join the Order of the White Penitents. Members of that order were at the service with candles in their hands and masks over their faces. On the coffin, which was mounted on a catafalque, lay a skeleton, representing Marc-Antoine. In one hand was a palm, a symbol of martyrdom, and in the other the pen he would have used had he lived to sign his renunciation of the Huguenot faith prior to embracing the Roman Catholic religion.

Before the trial Cazing was dismissed from the case, but on 9 March Jean Calas was brought before the court. One of the worst aspects of the judiciary in pre-Revolutionary France was the fact that some were able to buy their positions for life, regardless of the fact they had no legal qualifications whatsoever. The municipal court of Toulouse consisted of twelve members, of whom the two who had bought their positions completely dominated the remainder, who had been elected for a comparatively short period. One of these was the self-righteous David Beaudrigue.

The case for the prosecution rested entirely on hearsay evidence, and was so slight that, under the terms of the edict of 1670, an announcement was made in all the district's churches that anyone with any information must report it to the authorities on pain of excommunication. Sixty-five people now came forward, all but one of them hostile. Beaudrigue had said openly before the trial that he regarded Marc-Antoine as a martyr, so that supporters of the Calas family petitioned for his removal as a judge. But the petition was not even allowed to be filed.

First there were, in accordance with French judicial practice, the preliminary hearings: ten in number in this case. It was demanded that the parents and Pierre should be hanged, Lavaysse sent to the galleys and the maid imprisoned for five years. But because of the blatant irregularities in the conduct of the case it was referred to the *Parlement de Toulouse*, the highest legal body in the district. This consisted of the two judges, who had bought their positions for life, and eleven councillors. The findings of the trial stood, and for the *Parlement* it was only a matter of passing sentence.

On 9 March 1762 Jean Calas was taken to the Hôtel de Ville. Outside was a large pyre. The sight of it completely unnerved the old man, who thought it was for him. In fact it had been prepared for the burning of a book by a Protestant clergyman. His answers to the judges were so incoherent that they were convinced of his guilt, and by eight votes to five he was sentenced, first to be tortured and then put to death. Three voted for torture only, and only one for acquittal.

In the twentieth century torture is still carried on with nauseating sophistication for political ends. But in seventeenth- and eighteenth-century France it was carried out for both political and religious reasons, and with appalling cruelty. The three most notorious examples in France must be the seventeenth-century priest, Grandier of Loudun, accused among much else of demonic possession; the slightly weak-minded Damiens who made a futile attempt to assassinate Louis XV; and Jean Calas.

The Huguenot was sentenced to undergo the ordinary and the extraordinary torture, to discover the names of his supposed accomplices. First, in the *Question Ordinaire*, his limbs were dislocated on a form of rack, after which he was questioned by the magistrate and a priest. No confession was forthcoming, since Calas had none to make. Then he had to undergo the *Question Extraordinaire*. First an enormous quantity of water was forced down him until his body was distended to twice its normal size. Then his feet and the lower part of his legs were crushed in the Boot or Spanish Shoe, which was like a vice. Still no confession was forthcoming. After that Calas was taken first to a church, outside which he was supposed to do public penance, and then to the place of execution. Usually it took about fifty well-placed blows, and some unfortunates lived for as long as forty-eight hours, but after two hours Beaudrigue failed yet again to obtain a confession, and Calas was strangled by the executioner.

His steadfastness at least saved his family. Pierre was sentenced to banishment for life, though until he succeeded in escaping he was incarcerated in a monastery. Mme Calas and the maid were set free, though their freedom was worth little, since all of Jean Calas' property had been confiscated by the State. They sought refuge in the country. Gaubert Lavaysse was also freed, though his health was ruined, along with his reputation. Rose and Nanette, the daughters, were imprisoned in separate convents. Their brothers Louis and Donat, who were not in Toulouse at the time, did not suffer directly.

That was the story which, little by little, Voltaire succeeded in exposing to a horrified Europe. A Church and a State which could do such a thing to a man and his family on the strength of unsubstantiated rumour deserved to perish by revolution. The mobs who perpetrated the September Massacres of 1791 and the outrages on the Swiss Guards following the storming of the Tuileries the following August had been well taught by their spiritual and temporal leaders during the days of the *ancien régime*, for such scenes as those in Toulouse were all too common in the Place de la Grève in the heart of Paris.

At the end of the decade Voltaire would write with trenchant irony (in the entry *Torture* of the *Dictionnaire Philosophique*) of the solemn magistrate returning home to dinner, and of his wife being revolted the first time he recounted what had taken place. Then in time curiosity gets the better of her—since all women are curious by nature—until the day comes when the first thing she asks as she helps him off with his robes: "Sweetheart, haven't you put anyone to the Question today?"

While the *Parlement de Toulouse* and the Chancellor Saint-Florentin in Paris were too fanatical to be embarrassed by the outcome of the trial, it was none the less unsatisfactory. Could Calas have been innocent? Since he, the principal character in the case, was now dead, all that could be done was to put pressure on the remaining members of his family, the maid and Lavaysse, who at this time were still in prison. Pierre was informed by a monk that he would suffer his father's fate if he did not renounce his religion and become a Catholic. But within four months he had escaped, and eventually he joined his younger brother in Geneva. The mother and daughters went to live in Montauban, a Huguenot stronghold, where they were helped by their co-religionists. But they were not to remain in peace for long. Saint-Florentin was a lifelong enemy of the Huguenots, and through him two *lettres de cachet* were obtained against Rose and Nanette, who were confined in separate convents in Toulouse.

That was the situation regarding the Calas family when the news started to filter through to Voltaire at Ferney. Unexpected testimony came into his hands and his circle of friends in Paris. It took the form of a letter from one of the nuns charged with the conversion of Nanette. When the girl was freed, thanks to the Duchesse d'Enville, the nun gave the girl a letter to take to Paris in which she wrote that from what Nanette had said she was convinced the whole family was innocent. Copies were made and circulated widely, to the embarrassment of the authorities. But on 7 May 1763 the day came towards which Voltaire had been working: the Council in Paris ordered the *Parlement de Toulouse* to send the documents which previously the lawyers Mariette and Beaumont had not been allowed to see.

The law now moved more slowly than it had done when it had been a question of trying and sentencing Calas, and during the summer of 1763 Voltaire wrote the essay entitled *Traité sur la Tolérance à l'occasion de la mort de Jean Calas*. It was a call for tolerance and an end to the vicious religious persecution which was still going on in France. In the anonymous pamphlet Voltaire let facts speak for themselves, quoting examples taken from history.

Understandably, the pamphlet had to be smuggled into Paris, where it was only given to a trustworthy few. Among those were Choiseul and Mme de Pompadour. Towards the end of it the reader can almost hear the *Marseillaise*—or is it the *Ça Ira*?

> May all men remember that they are brothers! May they all detest the oppression of souls as they detest the robbery which deprives them of the fruits of their labour and peaceful industry! If the misfortune of war is inevitable, let us at least not hate and tear each other to pieces in the midst of peace, and let us make use of the brief moment we have to live, to bless equally in a thousand tongues. Your goodness which has given us this moment!

Voltaire was addressing directly the God for whom he had rebuilt the church at Ferney.

Twice deputies actually went to Paris from Toulouse to try to prevent the Council from reversing the original judgment on Calas. There the *Parlement* was behaving in a manner that was astonishing for a regional authority. Quite apart from its attitude over the Calas affair the *Parlement de Toulouse* had antagonised Louis XV in September 1763 by threatening to arrest the Duc de Fitz-James when he was sent as the king's agent to ensure the passing of new financial laws. Fitz-James had to flee, following

threats on his life. This infuriated the Council in Paris, who regarded it as a slight on their authority, and they decided to use the
Calas affair as a means of hitting back at these arrogant provincials.
Even if it were for the wrong reasons, they were at least espousing
the cause of justice.

In June 1764 the re-trial began, to the fury of the *Parlement de
Toulouse*, which regarded it as an attack on its independence. Also,
other regional *Parlements*, such as Dijon, looked on with anxiety,
for the outcome could affect them all. On 9 March 1765, three
years to the day since Jean Calas had been condemned to death,
his complete innocence was declared, together with that of his
family, Lavaysse and the maid. Forty judges deliberated the case
in six sittings, totalling twenty-eight hours, and then found them
all "perfectly innocent". During the period of re-trial, which lasted
nine months, Voltaire was bombarded with abusive letters—
anonymous of course—in which the writers declared that the
Calas family was guilty, and should all have been put to death, by
breaking on the wheel for preference. Others simply abused him
for having been instrumental in getting a re-trial.

At the re-trial, far from the atmosphere of religious hysteria
engendered in Toulouse, witnesses now came forward to testify
what an exemplary character Jean Calas had possessed, and for
the first time a letter was produced written by Marc-Antoine in
which he called his brother Louis an apostate for having become
a Roman Catholic. In February 1765 the fanatical David Beaudrigue, devoid of humanity or integrity, was dismissed.

On the last day of the same month all the accused were instructed to report as prisoners to the Conciergerie, where the
rehabilitation of Jean Calas was pronounced, and the acquittal
of all the others read to them.

Donat Calas was at Ferney when the news reached Voltaire of
the verdict. Both the eighteen-year-old boy and the seventy-one-
year-old philosopher wept tears of joy. As far as could be done, a
terrible injustice had been righted. That day saw what was perhaps
Voltaire's finest hour.

No order was made for compensation to be paid by the
Parlement de Toulouse, and since the King gave Mme Calas and
her daughters a reasonable sum of money Voltaire did not pursue
the matter. Earlier gifts to Mme Calas had been swallowed up in

legal expenses, so he set about raising more money to cover the debts that remained. The artist Carmontelle made an engraving of the accused people in the Conciergerie, listening to Lavaysse reading over his own *mémoire*, or brief, to them. Now Voltaire requested his numerous friends and acquaintances to subscribe generously for copies of the engravings. His own copy hung over his bed until the day he died. Pierre and Donat chose to make Geneva their home, where their well-being was looked after by Voltaire, and in 1770 they, their mother and Lavaysse, all visited him at Ferney, and in his own words he cried like a child.

It was not only the provincial *Parlements* who were outraged at the result of the re-trial. The *Parlement de Paris* itself felt endangered, and took refuge in petty spite. The sale of Carmontelle's engraving was banned on the grounds that it was good propaganda for the Protestants. In Toulouse itself the verdict of the re-trial was never printed officially, either in a gazette or as a poster.

That old enemy Fréron wrote a piece pretending to be a letter from a Protestant philosopher, which he published in his literary journal. In it he doubted the innocence of the Calas family, and sided with the *Parlement de Toulouse*:

> In the circumstances Monsieur de Voltaire's poetic head grew hot. He was not so much carried away by feelings of humanity as by the need to recall public attention to his existence and to do something to get himself talked about.

When this squalid individual died in 1776 his widow actually wrote to Voltaire suggesting that he should adopt their daughter as he had done Marie Corneille. Voltaire did not even find the suggestion funny.

The Calas affair was the first of a number of such cases in which he used his intellect and contacts to combat religious persecution or miscarriages of justice.

THE SIRVEN FAMILY

Logically, if not chronologically, the continued struggle against injustice should come first. Before the Calas affair had reached its conclusion, Voltaire found himself involved in a similar case, concerning a family by the name of Sirven. It, too, took place in the district of Toulouse, and involved a Protestant family accused of murdering one of their number for religious reasons. But in Voltaire's bitter expression "it lacked a scaffold." That no one was smashed to pulp in the cause of justice and religion was simply due to the fact that the Sirven family fled before they could be arrested.

It was the fate of our Recluse on the borders of Switzerland, to vindicate the innocence of those who were accused and condemned in France. . . . The whole family of *Sirven* condemned to death in a village near Castres, by a set of ignorant and cruel judges, fled for shelter to his estate. Though he was engaged eight years in procuring justice to be done them, he was never disheartened, and at last he succeeded.

The two cases, Calas and Sirven, actually overlapped, but Voltaire did not openly champion the latter until the day the Calas family was formally acquitted of all charges. He was guided partly by a sense of psychology and partly by an unerring theatrical instinct. That the latter should play a part in so serious a situation may seem frivolous or cynical, but he was right. After all, he had created public opinion, and he also knew human nature and the inevitable diminishing of interest caused by the repetition of a dramatic effect.

Paul Pierre Sirven lived with his family in Castres, no great distance from Toulouse. By profession he was a *feudiste*; one who specialised in all the complications and technicalities of feudal tenures, and who dealt with the fees and taxes due to various lords of the manor in the district. It was a system which had not changed since the Middle Ages. Sirven was fifty-one, with a wife and three daughters, the youngest of whom, Elizabeth, was weak-minded.

On 6 March 1760 Elizabeth disappeared. The others searched everywhere, but she was not to be found. Then in the evening Paul Pierre Sirven was summoned by the Bishop of Castres, who informed him that Elizabeth had expressed the strongest desire to become a Catholic, and that she had already been placed in the Convent of the Black Nuns where she would receive instruction.

Sirven knew whom he had to thank for this situation. It was the Bishop's sister, whose religious zeal was second to none. But whatever his personal feelings, Sirven concealed them, showing as much toleration as Calas had done when a member of his family had wanted to change his faith. Like many weak-minded people, Elizabeth was highly suggestive, and it was not long before the over-enthusiasm of her mentors resulted in hallucinations and delusions of hearing angelic voices. In her desire to mortify the flesh she asked for flagellation, and a servant girl whipped her. In October her condition was such that the Bishop ordered her return home, where Sirven saw the marks on her body, and complained. A contumacious act on his part, since he was a Protestant and a heretic, and one for which he would pay dearly.

Soon Elizabeth was afflicted with fits of violence, and had to be restrained, or even tied down. This was regarded by the convent as interference with one in the throes of divine experience. Complaints were made to the Bishop, who ordered Sirven to let his daughter return to the convent if she wished. There she was examined by doctors, and, as a result, was not received into the Catholic faith.

The following summer, July 1761, the family moved to the village of Saint-Alby, about fifty miles from Castres, so that Sirven could be near his work, which was for a certain M. d'Esperandieu. Until November all went peacefully, when the Abbé Bel (the local *curé*) visited Mme Sirven to inform her that Elizabeth should be allowed to hear Mass at the neighbouring village and receive religious instruction. When her husband heard of this he visited the *curé*, who said he was acting on orders. Sirven made up his mind that in due course he would take Elizabeth to see the Bishop. That same evening he and the Abbé Bel went to dine with M. and Mme d'Esperandieu, where Sirven spent the night.

The next morning a messenger came from Saint-Alby to say that Elizabeth had disappeared in the middle of the night. After much searching Sirven came to the conclusion that she must have returned to the convent. On that earlier occasion she had been taken without his knowledge, and since then she had been indirectly intimidated more than once, so now he did not pursue the question of her disappearance.

On 3 January the body of Elizabeth was found at the bottom of Sirven's well at Saint-Alby. The next morning a local magistrate, named Trinquier, was summoned from the nearby town of Mazamet. For four days the inhabitants of Saint-Alby were questioned, and all spoke favourably of Sirven and his family. They were convinced that his weak-minded daughter must have jumped down the well.

At that date, January 1762, the whole Calas family, together with Lavaysse and the maid, was in prison awaiting trial. At all costs the authorities wanted a conviction, and here in the same district was another case in which a Huguenot parent was thought to have murdered his child because the offspring wished to change her religion. The opportunity was too good to be missed. An identical story to that whispered about Jean Calas was whispered in Saint-Alby; that Sirven had murdered Elizabeth rather than let her become a Catholic. It spread rapidly, and soon the local authorities received word from Toulouse to act ruthlessly against the Sirven family.

Elizabeth had been a strong girl, capable of putting up considerable resistance to any attempt to drag her to the well. Furthermore, Sirven had a perfect alibi, since on the night of the alleged crime he was staying with M. d'Esperandieu. Mme Sirven was sixty-three, physically weak and of small stature. Their eldest married daughter was pregnant, so that the only possible culprit could have been the third sister, Jeanne. The tenants in the basement declared that they heard no sounds of a struggle and stated that only one person had left the house at about midnight.

The Procureur Trinquier, however, did not call any witnesses who could have substantiated Sirven's alibi, or those of his wife and daughters. Several physicians had carried out a post-mortem on Elizabeth, and now Trinquier heard that a local lawyer had offered them money for a copy of their findings. The original had been given to the authorities immediately after the post-mortem. This information convinced them of Sirven's guilt, and on 19 January his arrest was ordered. Later Voltaire was to write:

> It passes for fact among the Catholics of the *departement* that it is one of the chief principles of the Protestant religion that fathers and mothers should hang, strangle, or drown all their children whom they suspect of having any inclination towards the Roman faith.

Sirven was at Castres when the order was made, and as soon as his wife heard the news she and their two remaining daughters set out to warn him. They were none too soon. Just after they had left Saint-Alby a troop of mounted police came to the house and confiscated all their personal property. That night the Sirven family stayed with friends in Castres, and as soon as it was dark the following evening they set out on foot to flee to Switzerland. Paul Pierre Sirven separated from them, spending a month in the mountainous country near Castres, while the mother took one route, the eldest daughter took another, and her sister travelled by a third. In the mountains Marie-Anne fell eleven times from her horse, and somewhere "amid the glaciers" near the French-Swiss frontier she gave birth to a stillborn child. Two and a half months elapsed before the three women reached Lausanne and safety. By a different route Sirven also reached the city ahead of them, in April.

Meanwhile the law had been taking its iniquitous course in Mazamet. Three Declarations were issued, written in almost identical terms to those used against the Calas family. The lawyer who had offered the physicians money in return for a copy of their findings in the post-mortem report was asked by the judge how he, a Catholic, could undertake the defence of a Protestant.

The use, or rather, the abuse, of the doctors' evidence was to prove of great importance. In the *Avis au publique* Voltaire speaks scathingly of only one doctor, but in fact there were at least two. In their original report they offered no opinion as to the actual cause of death, but when pressed by the authorities they said it appeared Elizabeth had been strangled and then thrown down the well. Voltaire uses the verb *assommé*: overcome or overwhelmed; but that is a minor point. This conclusion was arrived at because they reported that no water was present in the stomach. Drowning is caused by water filling the lungs, cutting off oxygen from the blood, so that the victim suffocates. The doctors had apparently examined the girl's lungs, and found water there, but the evidence was suppressed on the orders of the prosecution, as it was contrary to what they wished to prove: that Elizabeth was dead before she went into the well. At least the Faculty of Medicine at Montpellier had the courage to point out the obvious, during the course of the trial.

Not only was the medical evidence deliberately suppressed; on the night of 5-6 January 1762 Elizabeth's body disappeared from the Hôtel de Ville. Sirven, it was said, had removed it for burial. As with the Calas trial the court allowed only hostile witnesses to be called. After that the hearings dragged on for more than a year, until February 1763. Then another year passed before the case was actually heard, Trinquier, the local magistrate, demanded that Sirven should be broken on the wheel, then burnt alive and his ashes scattered. He also wanted Mme Sirven hanged, with their two daughters present at the executions, after which they were to be sent into perpetual banishment.

On 19 March 1764 the presiding judge assessed the evidence, in less than an hour, and pronounced sentence. Both parents were to be hanged, in the presence of their daughters. But all four had fled to Switzerland, and to the authorities that in itself was proof of their guilt. So, on 11 September 1764 a macabre scene took place in the market square of Mazamet. On a scaffold two dummies were hanged, watched by two more dummies. Since the sentence had been given in the absence of the accused, ratification did not have to be sought by the *Parlement de Toulouse*, which meant that when Voltaire took up the case he would have to use different tactics to those used in the Calas affair. Of course, all property belonging to the Sirven family was confiscated to the king.

The four victims had been reunited in Lausanne in June 1762, and were living on financial assistance provided by the citizens of the Canton of Berne. Later Paul Pierre Sirven found employment in Geneva, and in due course the whole family was brought to Ferney. Voltaire was acquainted with the case, but at that time he was completely occupied by the Calas affair. Tragic though it was for them, at least the Sirven family had escaped with their lives. Also, he was grappling with the Council, as well as the somewhat hostile *Parlement de Paris,* and at the same time doing all he could to discredit the *Parlement de Toulouse.* Given half a chance the last named body would happily have seen Voltaire broken on the wheel for all the trouble he was causing them. If he and his lawyers took up the Sirvens' case they would have to appeal to the *Parlement de Toulouse* to reverse the verdict of the Mazamet court, which came within its jurisdiction.

The Sirven family besought his assistance, and he was won over, though not yet prepared to act openly. When a priest callously remarked that it would be better to let the dead bury the dead Voltaire replied:

I found an Israelite by the roadside: let me give him a little oil and wine for his wounds. You are the Levite: let me be the Samaritan.

9 March was a happy day for the Calas family. Their name had been cleared after a three-year fight by Voltaire. On the same day he openly began his fight for the Sirvens. Élie de Beaumont would also act as their council. Little could Voltaire have thought that this particular fight would take nine years. Worn out by worry and the effects of her journey across the Alps in winter, Mme Sirven died in June that year.

The case of the Sirven family was almost a repetition of the Calas case. Voltaire was well aware of this, and also of the fickleness of public opinion. Sirven wrote his account of the whole affair, which Voltaire forwarded to Beaumont in Paris with a covering letter.

The innocence of the Sirven family is even clearer than that of the Calas family: there is not the slightest indication of any guilt here. One is ashamed to be a member of the human species when, in the same country, one sees one place giving comic operas while in another fanaticism presses the sword into the executioner's hand.

The *Parlement de Toulouse* refused to deliver copies of relevant documents, exactly as it had done with Calas, but now Voltaire had one victory over them to his credit. Grudgingly it was agreed that if the Sirven family were innocent, they might be pardoned. But pardoned for what? They had done nothing. The concession made by the *Parlement* did not satisfy Voltaire. He wanted complete exoneration or nothing.

It took Voltaire two years to get hold of the documents relating to the hearings, trial and sentence at Mazamet, and that was probably only achieved by bribery.

Patience is often a gift which comes with increasing age, and Voltaire would need all his patience before the Sirven case was brought to a happy conclusion. But before then it would be overlapped by yet a third terrible miscarriage of justice, springing from wild rumour-mongering allied to religious fanaticism. This was the case of the young Chevalier de la Barre.

Elie de Beaumont completed his petition in January 1766, and sent it to Ferney. Voltaire considered it "the masterpiece of a genius," and when Sirven read it, it was soon wet with tears. Once again the philosopher mustered his battalions for the coming struggle, and an impressive list they were too. In that year Frederick the Great had resumed his correspondence with Voltaire, and he not only sent a contribution, but also offered the Sirven family a home in Prussia. Other royal contributors were Catherine the Great, the King of Poland, Christian VII of Denmark, the Duchess of Saxe-Gotha, the Margravine of Baden and the Princess of Damstart. In fact Voltaire seemed to have enrolled quite a sizeable portion of the Almanach de Gotha.

For his own part Voltaire wrote two particularly important pamphlets, first published in 1766, which were relevant to justice in general and the Calas and Sirven cases in particular. One, published under the pseudonym of "A Lawyer of Provence," was the *Commentaire sur le livre "Des Delits et des Peines"* (Commentary on the book "Of Crimes and of Punishments"), and it contained the following suggestion, very progressive for that time:

> It was said, a long time ago, that a hanged man is good for nothing, and that the punishments invented for the good of society should be useful to that society. It is evident that twenty brawny thieves, condemned to work at public projects all their lives, serve the state by their punishment, and their death is only good for the hangman, who is paid to kill these in public.

The other pamphlet, published in 1766, was the *Avis au Public, sur les Parricides imputés aux Calas et aux Sirven.* At that date the word "parricide" in French was not confined to the murder of a father, but the killing of any member within a family. In it Voltaire set forth the facts of both cases, commented on weaknesses in the law, and castigated fanaticism in general. If the *Avis* is journalism, it is crusading journalism of the best kind. But its effect on the lawyers working on the case in Paris was to throw them almost into a state of panic.

All the references to fanaticism and intolerance made them fear for their own safety. If Voltaire chose to antagonise the whole legal world, that was his affair, but they had no desire to have their names coupled with his. Also, Voltaire had frequently referred to Élie de Beaumont's *Pétition* as though it was about to be published, which was not what its author intended.

At last the *Pétition* was presented to the Council, in 1768, but now the case had entered the sphere of national politics. The Council was anxious about the reaction of the other regional *Parlements* if a case were taken away from the one at Toulouse to be dealt with in Paris, for they were exceedingly jealous of their rights. The *Pétition* was rejected. Five years' work on Voltaire's part had gone for nothing.

If the Council in Paris refused to reverse the verdict for fear of antagonising the regional *Parlements* it would mean that Sirven would have to go to Toulouse himself, and if the original verdict were upheld he would probably share the fate of Calas.

For months Voltaire pondered how to get round the difficulty.

Then he was informed that there had been a change in the attitude of ordinary people in Languedoc. After making sure that this was so, he found a member of the *Parlement de Toulouse* who was prepared to act as surety for the safety of Sirven in that city. In March 1769 the *feudaliste* returned to Languedoc, though his two daughters remained in Switzerland. He could not afford to wait any longer, because appeals had to be lodged within five years of the sentence. It was nearly five years since he and his wife had been hanged in effigy in the market square in Mazamet.

There was much work for Sirven to do, chiefly collecting evidence from witnesses. The most valuable came from the Medical Faculty at Montpellier. This organisation exposed the lack of integrity of the physicians who had examined Elizabeth's body and falsely declared that there had been no water in her lungs. Then Sirven gave himself up to the authorities at Mazamet, where he was so harshly treated that Voltaire lodged a strong complaint with the judiciary in Toulouse. Under French law the greater part of a trial was taken up by the preliminary hearings, when statements by witnesses and the accused were heard and recorded by the examining magistrates. All this material would then be assessed by the judge, and the trial itself would be quite short, before the verdict was given.

The principal judge at Sirven's first trial had been replaced, though the other two were members of that court. Trinquier made particular use of evidence given by witnesses now dead. For sixteen days the hearings dragged on, but at least Sirven had the satisfaction of demolishing the evidence of one of the physicians who had given the authorities only those facts he knew they wished to hear. The climax came on 10 November 1769. The Prosecutor demanded the death sentence for the murder of Elizabeth. The court dismissed the charge. Sirven was released, though it was not until 1771 that the *Parlement de Toulouse* finally made such amends as it could by declaring that the late Mme Sirven was guiltless of the "false and slanderous charge of murder".

"It took only two hours to sentence this family to death. But it took nine years for the courts to make official acknowledgement of their innocence," noted Voltaire at the conclusion of his second major victory over injustice.

In eighteenth-century France it was a capital offence for a

Protestant pastor to preach in public, and while the victims of the Calas affair were in prison in Toulouse awaiting trial a certain François Rochette was arrested, tried, and in February 1762 actually beheaded on that charge.

Voltaire was profoundly shocked at the fate of the pastor, but if nothing could be done to help him there were others who could be assisted: the Protestant Espinasse, for instance, also from Languedoc, who had been arrested for giving supper and a night's lodging to a pastor in 1740. In 1763 the story reached Voltaire, and he interceded successfully for the release of Espinasse, who came to join his almost destitute wife and children in Switzerland. The following year he obtained the release of another galley-slave, a man named Chaumont, who had been arrested for listening to a Protestant who was preaching in the open. A third for whom Voltaire obtained freedom was Paul Achard, after he had spent nineteen years chained to a galley bench. There were others that both Voltaire and Choiseul would have liked to see freed, but they were unable to obtain their release from that hater of heretics, Saint-Florentin. For them freedom did not come until the beginning of Louis XVI's reign.

Whatever one may think of Voltaire's attacks on Christianity as such, how could anyone defend a Church or State which perpetrated such injustice and fomented such hatred and intolerance? Many sneered at Voltaire, especially the less successful in his own profession, for the way that he had amassed a very large fortune not only by his writings but as a result of his shrewd business sense, which included investments and the actual lending of money to prominent people. Among the latter was the great Duc de Richelieu himself, whom he never embarrassed when the question of the payment of interest seemed somehow to have been forgotten. What Voltaire's detractors chose not to recall was that all the profits from his plays were given to the actors, and sometimes if the printers and publishers were themselves in difficulties they kept the monies which normally he would have received. Also, over the years he spent thousands of pounds improving the living conditions of his tenants at Tournay and Ferney. If rumour were true, and he was one of the richest private citizens in Europe, he was also the most generous with his money, his talents and his influence.

Chapter 21

CRUSADES AND QUARRELS

The little theatre at Ferney was completed at the end of 1761, and Voltaire undertook a programme of writing, supervision and rehearsals, and even participation in plays which would have been enough to occupy the time of a lesser man. Lekain and Mlle Clairon would come either to act or sit in the audience, both at *Les Délices* and at Ferney. *Olympe* was written in six days in October 1761, and then revised and rewritten for six months, before being performed for the first time on 25 March the following year at Ferney. It was a tragedy, and the audience wept most gratifyingly, and when staged in Paris in 1763 it was given a reception that was probably warmer than it merited.

Other plays written at this time included the unsuccessful *Triumvirat* (also called *Octave*), and the comedy in verse, *Le Droit de Seigneur*. If none was of the first quality it is hardly surprising in the light of the deeply serious work on which he was also engaged, quite apart from the Calas affair and a variety of less serious concerns.

The latter included verses and pamphlets, mostly anonymous arising from his feud with the Marquis de Pompignan. Of course there was malice in some of them, but also much humour, and in 1760 the salons of the intelligentsia were diverted by the funniest literary dogfight since the publication of *Dr Akakia*.

De Pompignan was a wealthy landowner from Montauban, and also a poet and playwright. In 1758 he came to Paris, feeling that only there would his talents be appreciated. For a start he wished to become an Immortal, but failed to gain election. The following year, however, Maupertuis died, and in 1760 de Pompignan was elected to his chair. Though extremely conformist in attitude, de Pompignan was ambitious, and his very orthodoxy was sufficient to win the approval of Louis XV. It was his hope that one day he might become tutor to the children of the Dauphin, a position which could lead to the wielding of great power. Also, he had been made Royal Historian in succession to Voltaire, which in itself was enough to ensure the philosopher's ill-will.

In his speech to the Académie de Pompignan began by paying the customary tribute to his predecessor. Then he went on to lambast philosophers and all he thought they stood for. The contents of the speech were forwarded to *Les Délices*, where at that time Voltaire was still living (he finally gave up the property in 1765). Although he was a philosopher, it took very little to rile him. How dare this self-important Marquis from the provinces attack him in a boot-licking speech that was obviously designed to win the approval of the king himself? It was not long before Paris was giggling over the inevitable retort, which took the form of an anonymous pamphlet entitled *Les Quands*, with the lengthy subtitle *Useful notes on a discourse pronounced before the Académie Française 10 March 1760*:

> When one has the honour of being received into a respectable company of men of letters it is not necessary to turn one's inaugural address into a satire against men of letters: that is to insult the company and the public.

In seven paragraphs all beginning "When" Voltaire punctured the pretensions of the Marquis, and implied that he was a cad for saying that penniless philosophers publicly despised wealth because they secretly envied it; and reminded the public that this now devout and orthodox man had, many years before, translated Pope's poem *The Deist's Prayer* into French; that he had taken his speech "to the foot of the throne," and suggested that the philosophers were undermining both throne and altar.

> But happily princes and ministers never read these discourses, those who have read them once never do so again.
>
> When one harangues an Academy in France it is not necessary to dismiss the philosophers produced in England: it would be better to study them.

When one is admitted into a respectable body one should in one's address hide under the veil of modesty the insolent pride, which is the prerogative of hot-heads and mediocre talents.

Voltaire planted his darts with all his old skill, and the philosophers in Paris soon joined in attacking their common enemy. More darts followed from Geneva, all starting with the words, *"Pour," "Que," "Quoi," "Oui"* and *"Non."* As a result de Pompignan became a laughing-stock. There was even a song composed at his expense, with words by Voltaire.

Injured pride sent the Academician hurrying to the king and queen to beg for their assistance, while reminding them how well they had received his discourse, the cause of all the trouble. As was so often the case, there was a serious purpose beneath the wit and wickedness. Voltaire felt that if someone did not ridicule time-servers like de Pompignan the Académie Française would become nothing more than the mouthpiece of official thought, with the exclusion of men of intellect, especially the philosophers. A year later de Pompignan again attacked the philosophers in what should have been a eulogy for the Dauphin's eldest son, who had just died. Voltaire replied by writing *Les Ah! Ah!*. Totally ridiculed, the Marquis disappeared from the world of literature.

Years before, Voltaire and Richelieu had discussed the idea of writing a treatise on tolerance. Now, as he became more and more deeply involved in the Calas affair, Voltaire's thoughts returned to the subject. Within the framework of that episode he set forth in some ninety pages the case for tolerance, and above all for religious tolerance. Although directly inspired by the miscarriage of justice which he was trying to right, the *Traité sur la Tolérance* was eventually to have a much wider effect. It is Voltaire whom Protestant minorities in predominantly Catholic countries have to thank for the toleration of their public worship.

At the time of its appearance, in 1762–3, the *Traité* could be rated as among the most inflammatory of his writings. At first it was not even published, but passed from hand to hand in manuscript form, and of course it was anonymous. Not that anyone could have doubted for a moment who its author was. By the end of 1763 it had been published, but for fear that it might prejudice the Calas re-trial copies were given only to a chosen few. With an engaging lack of modesty Voltaire described its genesis in the *Autobiography*:

> Several worthy men engaged Mr de Voltaire at that time to write his treatise upon tolerance, which is esteemed one of his best works in prose, and is become the catechism of all who have either good sense or moderation.

In 1757 Voltaire had begun his *History of Peter the Great* at the request of the Empress Elizabeth. Two years later the first volume was published, and in 1763 the second came from the presses a year after the German-born Catherine was rid of her unspeakable consort Peter III, who was killed by her lover, though he probably did it without her actual knowledge. After that she became Empress of Russia. If ever anyone could be described as an enlightened despot it was Catherine, one day to be called the Great. She was proud to acknowledge herself a pupil of Voltaire.

Time had to be found to revise the *Essai sur les Moeurs des Nations*, with *Additions*, which was not so much an appendix as a complete volume in itself. Voltaire was also at work on the definitive edition of the plays of Corneille, and the accompanying commentary was to be a masterpiece of its kind. Much of the work must have been deadly dull, and its completion says as much for Voltaire's powers of concentration as it does for his determination to ensure that Marie Corneille should have a reasonable dowry.

That any man could achieve as much as Voltaire did, particularly between the years 1760–5, would have been remarkable for a man half his age, but he was now approaching seventy. He was involved in yet another play: *Saul*. And as if all this were not enough (and it should be remembered that at the same time he was running the business side of his estates most competently, campaigning on behalf of the Calas and Sirven families, receiving a large number of visitors, and conducting a huge correspondence), he also undertook reviewing for the *Gazette Littéraire*, including volumes in English such as the *Letters of Lady Mary*

Wortley Montagu and Hume's *History of England*. All this was eventually overshadowed by the publication of the *Dictionnaire Philosophique*, perhaps the most important of all his publications.

The *Encyclopédie* was a wonderful achievement, but by its size and cost it was obviously limited to a very small public, who for the most part would be comparatively enlightened anyway. What Voltaire wanted to produce was an inexpensive little volume that the man in the street could carry about in his pocket. The *Dictionnaire Philosophique* covered a wide range of subjects, many of them adapted from the material supplied for the *Encyclopédie*. Some of the entries were not so much definitions as brief personal comments, while others read more like essays or reflections. What they all had in common was the fact that they were not written from a basically Christian point of view. While some were anti-Christian in tone others were neutral, and nearly all were shot through with that vein of irony which, together with clarity of expression, was the hall-mark of Voltaire's writing. As he pointed out, if the Gospel had cost 1200 sesterces, Christianity would never have been established. Now he was propagating the gospel of free-thinking.

The subsequent history of the *Dictionnaire* is somewhat involved. The first edition came out in 1764, consisting of 344 pages, and was printed in Geneva. An enlarged edition followed a year later, printed in London, on which most subsequent printings were based, with additions by Voltaire. In 1770 he began his *Questions sur l'Encyclopédie*, part of which later editions incorporated into the *Dictionnaire*. When Beaumarchais and Condorcet were attempting the almost impossible, by bringing out the complete Kehl Edition of his works (1784–87), in a mood of desperation they lumped together numerous unpublished writings, essays, pamphlets, entries for the *Encyclopédie*, and even the *Lettres Philosophiques*, under the general title of *Dictionnaire Philosophique*. The editions published between 1764–1770 under the title *Dictionnaire Philosophique portatif* are the authentic bombshells, which finally led to the major explosion of 1789.

The alphabetical entries of the 1764 edition began with Abraham, and ended with Virtue, and covered such a diversity of topics as Baptism, China, Circumcision, Criticism, God, Fanaticism, Fraud, Grace, Flooding, Liberty, Laws, Wickedness,

Prejudices, Resurrection, Dreams, Tolerance and Tyranny. A number of them, including those on God, Fraud and Liberty, are cast in the form of dialogues. Many of the entries, particularly those on Fanaticism and Tolerance, can still be read with great profit today.

Of course the *Dictionnaire Philosophique portatif* was promptly banned, burnt and placed on the Index at the Vatican. The *Parlement de Paris* took particular exception to the comment on Tyranny—"It is better to have to deal with a single tyrant than a whole flock of little tyrants"—and immediately ordered the book to be burnt by the hangman. Voltaire's first concern was always to find proof of hitherto unquestioned events or people. Facts first, and then personal observations and conclusions. Most active Christians of the day were fundamentalists at heart: that is, they accepted literally everything in the Bible, and here was this horrible philosopher asking impertinent questions and casting doubt on everything. To them he was the Spirit that Denies, or at least he indulged in destructive criticism while offering nothing in its place. They could not realise that what he was offering man was the freedom to think and act for himself.

1764 saw Voltaire's seventieth birthday, and also the death of Mme de Pompadour, his best and perhaps only friend in the king's immediate circle. That year also saw the death of the Venetian Algarotti, who had charmed Voltaire and Emilie du Châtelet at Cirey, before he moved on to Potsdam.

Now, after a break of some six years, the old friendship between Frederick and Voltaire was renewed. It was the philosopher who made the first move. He heard that the king had been ill, and wrote hoping that he was better. Soon they were corresponding once again with some of the old cordiality: "we philosophers" criticising the stupidity of others and discussing the baleful influence of *l'infâme*. The King of Prussia permitted himself still to regret the departure of his guest in unfortunate circumstances in 1753:

Scarcely had you left our country when imaginative literature began to decline; and I fear geometry may there stifle the few germs which might reproduce the fine arts. ... Whatever happens, I have been your contemporary. You will last as long as I have to live, and I care little about the taste, sterility or abundance of posterity.

Goodbye; cultivate your garden, 'tis the wisest thing to do.

But even so the friendship never quite assumed its old amiability. Certainly not the intimacy of those distant days when they had both indulged in writing uncharitable verses about Louis XV and others. A second reason for coolness on Frederick's side lay in the warm relationship which Voltaire had already established with the young Catherine of Russia. Before their correspondence had been broken off in 1760 Frederick had written to Voltaire about his *History of Peter the Great*:

> Please tell me, what is this I hear about you writing the history of Siberian bears and wolves? And what can you say about the Tsar that you have not already said in your *Histoire de Charles XII*? I do not want to read the history of these barbarians. I would prefer to ignore the fact that they ever lived in our hemisphere.

By October 1763, when Catherine began her correspondence with Voltaire she had left far behind the little German state of Anhalt-Zerbst where the court physician was also the local executioner. At fourteen she had been sent to Russia as the fiancée of the sixteen-year-old Grand Duke Peter. While she was extremely intelligent Peter was an imbecilic youth who liked making his valets march up and down like soldiers. Their marriage took place in 1745. Life for the new Grand Duchess was lonely, as her husband preferred to have affairs with the plainest women he could find in the Court (and regaling his wife with all the details), and she spent most of her time reading: Cicero, Plutarch, Tacitus and Bayle. First and foremost among living authors she chose Voltaire and Montesquieu.

Catherine took lovers from an early age, and in her *Memoirs* practically admitted that the father of the future Paul I was not her husband, though the child grew up to resemble him.

Within a short while of Peter coming to the throne in 1762 there was a palace revolution, engineered by two brothers, one of whom—Gregor Orloff—was Catherine's lover. Peter III was strangled on the orders of Alexix Orloff, though Catherine undoubtedly knew nothing of the plans for the murder.

As much as anything Catherine wanted the good esteem of the man she most admired: Voltaire. For his part, at first he believed her guilty of complicity. In the service of the Empress of Russia was a Genevese secretary who had known Voltaire before going to Russia. Now he wrote justifying the crime, explaining that it was committed for the good of the country. Voltaire's reply was not wholly satisfactory, and he did not dare show it to Catherine. But by October that year Voltaire had changed his opinion about the guilt of the Empress, and their celebrated correspondence began:

> ... I can assure you that, since 1746, when I became mistress of my own time, I have the strongest obligations towards you. Before then I only read novels; then by chance your works fell into my hands; and since then I have never stopped reading them. ... In any case, Monsieur, one thing is certain, that if I have any knowledge, I owe it to this man alone. ... Just now I am reading his essay on Russian history: I should like to learn every page of it by heart, while I am waiting for the book on the great Corneille for which, I hope, a note of exchange has been sent to cover my subscription.
>
> Katharina

Catherine had not made an auspicious entry on to the scene as the new ruler of a vast and little-known empire, and she was anxious to have the good opinion of the most progressive thinkers in Europe; and above all the high esteem of Voltaire himself. She succeeded. Before long Voltaire was completely under the spell of the "Semiramis of the North". Not only was he convinced that Catherine was not involved in the murder of Peter III, but for the rest of his life he sang the praises of the Empress of Russia, and all that she claimed she was doing in the name of progress and enlightenment. It would not be the only time when the ruler of a totalitarian state has duped a famous intellectual in the West into believing all that he had been told, in the knowledge that the good opinion of that person was invaluable propaganda for his or her régime. But it is a matter of surprise that someone as shrewd as

Voltaire should have been taken in so completely. Could it have been due to the fact that in the recent past he had suffered much at the hands of the authorities, and was prepared to overlook the failings of a powerful ruler who so obviously wished to be his friend and ally?

Catherine's good-will did not stop with Voltaire. All the philosophers in Paris had her blessing and, as a way of assisting Diderot, she bought his personal library for 15,000 *livres*. He would retain it for his lifetime, and she even paid him 1,000 *livres* a year to act as its curator. It was a most tactful way of offering financial assistance to the Editor of the *Encyclopédie* without appearing patronising.

The Empress invited Diderot to St Petersburg, where this awkward genius from time to time quite forgot who she was, and treated her with unintentional familiarity. Catherine only pushed her chair back a little when in his enthusiasm Diderot slapped her on the thigh to emphasise a point. Such was his regard and liking for Catherine that on his last evening in St Petersburg he actually burst into tears, and it was all she could do to control her own emotions. Later she widened her circle of correspondents among the philosophers in France to include d'Alembert, Holbach and Baron Grimm; the last being an expatriate German.

In addition to corresponding with many of the most celebrated people of his day, Voltaire did not forget old friends who today are only remembered because their paths crossed those of the great man. One was plump, cheerful and kindly Mme Champbonin, whom he had known at Cirey.

Voltaire's circle of correspondents had been widened even more when he was seeking subscribers for the edition of Corneille's plays. Now he had added Maria Theresa, Queen Charlotte (George III's consort), the Duc de Choiseul, Lord Chesterfield, and William Pitt, the future Earl of Chatham, among many others.

The adoption of Marie Corneille was one of the most attractive and innocent episodes in Voltaire's life. Ever since her arrival he had found time to educate the girl, and made learning a pleasure. From being an ignorant girl who had only had a brief and superficial convent education, he turned her into a charming and desirable wife for someone. She had not the intellect which could absorb and understand such works as the *Essai sur les Moeurs* or the *Dictionnaire Philosophique*, and Voltaire did not try to turn her into a blue-stocking. At *Les Délices* and Ferney she was everyone's favourite: with Mme Denis, with the secretary Wagnière, and with the servants. Voltaire, the septuagenarian Church-baiting free-thinker, even accompanied her to Mass on Sundays, making no attempt to undermine her faith with his destructive logic.

The innuendoes in Paris, largely circulated by "the hack" Fréron, really stung him, but there was nothing Voltaire could do, except retaliate with ridicule. But one result of the malicious gossip was to frighten off prospective bridegrooms for Marie Corneille. On 12 February 1763, however, she married a neighbour at Ferney, Pierre Dupuits, a cornet in the dragoons, aged twenty-three. Voltaire could not have been more involved if it had been his own grandchild, who was married in the little church at Ferney at midnight. The young couple lived at the château, and became part of the diverse household which soon would include Father Adam, an exiled Jesuit with whom Voltaire used to play chess in the evenings, and Mlle Dupuits, Marie's sister-in-law.

Visitors of many nationalities came in an unending procession, either as guests or as thrusting sightseers. Among the former was Boswell, who had asked Mme Denis if he might call. On arrival at Ferney he was ushered into a salon by two or three footmen while his letter of introduction was taken in to the sage. Back came the reply that M. de Voltaire was very sorry to inconvenience him, but he was in bed. Boswell was prepared to wait, and at last he was rewarded.

He had a slate-blue, fine frieze great-coat, Night-gown, and a three-knotted wig. He sat erect upon his chair, and simpered when he spoke. He was not in spirits, nor was I.

Boswell asked if he still spoke English.

"No. To speak English one has to put one's tongue between one's teeth, and I have lost all my teeth."

After further polite conversation Voltaire withdrew, and

although Boswell stayed to dinner, and was made much of by Mme Denis, he did not see the philosopher again.

Another visitor was Edward Gibbon, already familiar to Voltaire from his visits to Lausanne. He found Voltaire in better health than he had been for years, "tho' very old and lean." That same evening in August 1763 there was a performance in the theatre of *L'Orphelin de la Chine*, but now Gibbon did not consider Voltaire as good an actor as he had done in 1758.

> Perhaps I was too much struck with the ridiculous figure of Voltaire at seventy acting a Tartar conqueror with a hollow broken voice, and making love to a very ugly niece of about fifty.

Voltaire used to claim that Mme Denis was almost the rival of Mlle Clairon, an opinion which others—including Gibbon—did not share. He disarmed criticism of himself by declaring: "I was the best old fool in any troupe. I had rage and tears—attitudes and a cap."

Mlle Clairon had acted at *Les Délices*, to the delight of the theatre-starved Genevese and the anger of the Calvinist City Fathers. At Ferney Mlle Clairon took the leading female role in *L'Orphelin de la Chine*, while the same part was taken by Mme Denis at Ferney. When Mlle Clairon had come to act Voltaire had been almost prostrated with sciatica, as well as an affliction of the eyes. Although he had to use crutches, he insisted on going through his part. With such as she, the show had to go on.

In addition to sciatica, a lifelong weak digestion, and various real or imaginary ailments, Voltaire now suffered from snow blindness each winter. He really was frail, and by his own admission a toothless old man; but still he was the possessor of the shrewdest brain in Europe. The quiet settled life of a country gentleman concerned with his estates had had a mellowing effect on this man who for so long had been, in Byron's words, "fire and fickleness."

The roots of the quarrel between Voltaire and Rousseau, who were as opposite in character, aspirations and likes as it is possible to imagine, went back a number of years. The clergy in Geneva had taken exception to Voltaire's *Poème sur le désastre de Lisbonne*, which was both compassionate and despairing, and Rousseau replied with the curious observation that it was man's fault for crowding together in cities. Voltaire still admired his fellow philosopher, and only gave a good humoured if frivolous reply.

The next stage towards open hostility came when the volume of the *Encyclopédie* appeared which contained d'Alembert's entry on Geneva, to which Voltaire had added his own opinion of the City Fathers for their attitude towards theatres.

The drama is not permitted in Geneva for fear of the passion for finery, diversion and levity, which is said to engender immorality. But Geneva ignores the obvious fact that strict laws could be enacted against that sort of thing, and that the theatre could remain as a good influence on public taste.

By then Rousseau's persecution mania had become more pronounced, and he began to hate Voltaire, as much as anything for his worldly success, whilst he, Rousseau, remained poor and, in his own eyes at least, unappreciated. Tragedy, he declared, was pernicious, because it encouraged people to waste their emotions on fictitious situations, while comedy was equally obnoxious because it taught people how to indulge in immorality without getting caught.

Some while later Rousseau asked if he might publish Voltaire's letter on destiny. Since he did not wish to be drawn into a controversy, Voltaire declined. But in 1760 it appeared in print in Berlin. By then Rousseau's persecution mania had reached the point when he imagined that Voltaire was actively plotting against him, and wrote a letter which today appears pathetic, but at the time only succeeded in arousing Voltaire's contempt. "I do not like you," wrote the unbalanced Rousseau:

You have inflicted on me, your most enthusiastic disciple, the deepest grief. You have polluted Geneva [with the theatre at *Les Délices*] as a reward for the refuge it gave you. You make residence in my own native country impossible for me and you force me to die abroad, while every honour a man can achieve is bestowed on you in my native country. I hate you because you want me to do so.

Over the years Voltaire's writings had been burnt by the public hangmen in France, Switzerland, Holland, and several of the German states, including Prussia. In 1762 the authorities in Paris ordered the burning of *Émile*, Rousseau's treatise on education in the form of a novel, and the magistrate seriously suggested that its author should be burnt as well. Soldiers were sent to arrest him at Montmorency. He fled, and at once Voltaire's sympathy for a fellow victim of intolerance was aroused, and he offered a refuge in his own house. Rousseau answered with another offensive letter:

I have no love for you, because you corrupt my republic with your comedies, and in return for the sanctuary it has given you—I hate you.

There was a warrant out for his arrest in France, and soon after both *Émile* and *Le Contrat Social* (in which Rousseau preached the equality of all men of all races) were condemned to be torn up and burnt by the hangman in Geneva.

Neither Paris not Geneva was safe for Rousseau now, and he retaliated against his native city by writing the *Lettres écrites de la Montagne*. In it he attacked Geneva's Protestant inhabitants. From being the persecuted, he declared, they had themselves become the persecutors. Everywhere he imagined that Voltaire's hand was raised against him. To get his own back he disclosed that Voltaire was the author of the anonymous pamphlet *Serment des Cinquante*, as well as being the author of the *Dictionnaire Philosophique portatif*.

This was serious. The *Serment des Cinquante* was a pamphlet of about fifteen pages full of destructive anti-Christian writing. In it fifty worthy people take it in turn to preach the Sunday sermon, and in the pamphlet Voltaire sets forth what purports to be a prayer and one of the sermons. This maintains that Christianity owes its origins to a scheme by priests to bestow divinity on Christ for their own ends.

Now there was even talk in Paris of having Voltaire imprisoned in the Bastille for the remainder of his life, and the news was quickly relayed to Ferney. To his fellow philosopher Helvétius he wrote: "As soon as any immediate danger threatens me I ask you please to inform me, so that I can deny everything with my usual frankness and innocence."

At the same time he wrote to deny Rousseau's exposure of him as the author: "The King is too good and just to condemn me on the strength of careless denunciations. He will not chastise a weak, sickly old man of seventy-one upon so vague a charge."

Rousseau had hit below the belt by giving away a fellow philosopher as the author of proscribed writings, and Voltaire retaliated by washing Rousseau's personal linen in public. For years the self-styled "Savoyard Vicar" had been living with the illiterate servant Thérèse Lavasseur, who claimed he was the father of her five children. As they were born, Rousseau literally placed them at the door of a foundling home. Now the fact had come to light he declared that as a philosopher who believed in the simple life in which no one was corrupted by money and material possessions he had acted in the best interests of the children, who would grow up to become farmers and farm workers, instead of being corrupted by the things he most professed to despise.

Voltaire was one of the very few people who knew about these five children in an orphanage. Another pamphlet came from the presses, apparently the work of a citizen of Geneva. Entitled *Le Sentiment des Citoyens*, it contained a paragraph which was to prove fatal to the reputation of the "Savoyard Vicar":

> Can a native of our city scoff in this way at our priests? With reluctance we are forced to admit that he is a man who still bears the marks of his excesses, a mountebank who drags with him from town to town the poor woman whose children he has left at the doors of a foundling home.

In rapid succession the doors of Europe closed to Rousseau. Some forty years previously Voltaire had sought asylum in England: now it was Rousseau who crossed the Channel. In England he was befriended by the Scottish philosopher David Hume, becoming fashionable in London society. But Horace Walpole carried on where Voltaire had left off by writing a letter to the philosopher purporting to be from Frederick the Great. In view of his mental condition it was a somewhat cruel joke, because Rousseau took it seriously, and soon became a laughing-stock. In his confused state of mind Rousseau thought that Hume must have been opening his correspondence, and attacked him on that supposition, whereupon Hume rounded on him as an ungrateful wretch. Voltaire now wrote the *Lettre á Docteur Pansophe*, which demolished Rousseau's reputation in London to such an extent that he returned to France, where at last he was allowed to live unmolested either by the authorities or his fellow philosophers.

With hindsight there is little to admire in the prospect of two great men trying to destroy each other's reputation. Quite separately, and in different ways, they were to do more than any-one to change the face of eighteenth-century society. Rousseau, who believed in a natural religion that owed nothing to Christianity, made people look at society with new eyes, largely through reading his *Du Contrat Social*; while Voltaire undermined irrevocably the authority of the Church as it existed in his day.

Chapter 22

THE LA BARRE CASE

Almost before the Calas affair had ended, and while the Sirven case was to drag on for several years yet, further miscarriages of justice were brought to Voltaire's notice. In February 1765 the Calas family had been declared innocent of the criminal charges that had cost Jean Calas his life. In August the same year an even more shocking affair began, which was to develop into a peculiarly vicious example of ecclesiastical vindictiveness.

On the night of 8–9 August a wooden crucifix on the Pont-Neuf in Abbeville was damaged, while another in a local cemetery had been defiled with filth. That much was fact, though the cross on the Pont-Neuf might just possibly have been damaged by a passing cart. Naturally, the inhabitants of Abbeville were distressed, and they requested that the Bishop of Amiens should come and do penance on their behalf. He came, and in solemn procession walked barefoot and with a halter round his neck to pray for the town's forgiveness before the desecrated crosses. He described the unknown culprits as being men who, though not beyond the reach of God's mercy, had rendered themselves worthy of the severest penalty of this world's law. Feelings were running high in the town, and monitories were read in the churches instructing anyone with information to come forward. A certain Belleval, a tax official, declared that three young men had recently been rebuked for using blasphemous language, and for not baring their heads and genuflecting as the Corpus Christi procession passed by, including as it did the Host carried in a monstrance.

On 26 August warrants were issued for the arrest of the three young men, all of whom were under twenty-one. The eldest was

the Chevalier de la Barre, aged nineteen; the second was D'Etallonde de Morival, and the third a youth of about sixteen named
Moisnel. D'Etallonde had already fled to Prussia, but the other
two were arrested.

Belleval, who lodged the first complaint, was Moisnel's guardian, and he visited the youth in prison where he encouraged him
to save his own neck by indicting la Barre. His friend had something of a reputation as a rake, educated by a country *curé*, but
largely under the influence of his aunt. She herself was a character
who could only have existed at that particular period. The Abbess
de Willancourt did not take her duties particularly seriously, and
her nephew had her own rooms in the grounds of the convent.
The wild parties she gave were well known locally, and la Barre
and his friends were always welcome. What was more, the Abbess
knew about the books which her nephew had in his room, some
of which were merely indecent, while others were dangerous to
possess. In the latter category were such works as Bayle's *Dictionnaire historique et critique*, and Voltaire's *Dictionnaire Philosophique
portatif*. La Barre's interest in the last two probably stemmed
from the fact that they were banned, and therefore exciting to
own, rather than for the knowledge they contained.

When la Barre was arrested on 1 October 1765 the Abbess
ordered a monk to burn any books which might be considered
incriminating. But the ones that really mattered were not destroyed. Moisnel, interrogated by the magistrates, inculpated la
Barre to save himself. According to him the Chevalier had spat
on pictures of the saints, and, together with the now-vanished
D'Etallonde, the three of them had sung obscene songs. Much
more damning was his statement that la Barre had lent him the
Dictionnaire Philosophique portatif and also a copy of the *Epître à
Uranie*, and that he had seen D'Etallonde hitting at the crucifix on
the bridge, and daubing the other in the cemetery with filth.

Next, la Barre was questioned on the strength of Moisnel's
testimony. First he declared he had no idea who might be responsible for the outrages against the two crucifixes, but then
changed his statement to admit that D'Etallonde told him he had
struck the one on the Pont-Neuf with the scabbard of his sword.
He also admitted that he and D'Etallonde had not genuflected or
removed their hats as they passed the Corpus Christi procession.

He said that if he had used irreverent words it might have been that he was quoting from *La Pucelle* or *L'Epître à Uranie* when drunk. Among the remarks he had made which were now used against him was the statement that he had been accustomed to genuflect before his bookcase, because it contained the sacrament which he adored. It must have come as a bombshell when he discovered that a number of the books kept there had not been destroyed, and were in the possession of the authorities.

At that date the possession of banned publications was severely punished, unless one was influential enough to be beyond the reach of the authorities. The *Dictionnaire* of Bayle, the *Dictionnaire Philosophique portatif* of Voltaire, and *De l'Esprit* by Helvétius had all been burnt by the hangman in numerous European cities.

As the trial neared its end Moisnel retracted his evidence against la Barre and D'Etallonde, saying that it had been made under pressure from his guardian, Belleval. But it was too late. The authorities wanted blood. First to be sentenced was the absent D'Etallonde. He should do public penance before the main portal of Saint-Wulfran, with a placard round his neck bearing the words "Damned and despised Blasphemer and violator." Then his tongue should be torn out, a hand cut off, and he should be burnt alive, his ashes scattered to the winds and his property confiscated. Voltaire gives full details of exactly how the sentence should be carried out. But since D'Etallonde was abroad it was ordered that the sentence should be executed on an effigy, as had been done with the Sirvens.

Significantly, when the judges came to sentence la Barre no mention was made of his having had any part in the desecration of the two crucifixes. He was found guilty of failing to uncover his head or to genuflect when the Host was carried past him; of having blasphemed and sneered at the tenets of the Church; of having sung two blasphemous songs, and worshipped foul and blasphemous books by genuflecting before his bookcase. By the standards of the day he might have merited a spell of "corrective detention," to cool his hot head. The sentence passed on him was appalling. He must undergo the torture; do public penance outside Saint-Wulfran; have his tongue torn out; be beheaded, and have his body burnt and with it Bayle's *Dictionnaire* and Voltaire's *Dictionnaire Philosophique portatif*.

The sentence had to be reviewed by the *Parlement de Paris*. This was done with the minimum of publicity, and the *Conseiller de Parlement*, Pasquier, demanded confirmation of the sentence, despite la Barre's youth. He declared that an example should be made of him to counteract the godless influence of the philosophers, headed by Voltaire. In his eyes it was the Sage of Ferney who was responsible for all the trouble at Abbeville. There was also a political motive: recently the *Parlement de Paris* had been responsible for the expulsion of the Jesuits from France, and the la Barre case would be an excellent opportunity to show that they were as anxious as anyone to spring to the defence of the Faith. By a majority of fifteen to ten they voted in favour of the death penalty. By now most ordinary people wanted and expected the king to step in and reprieve the youth. Even the coach taking la Barre back to Abbeville travelled as slowly as possible by an indirect route. But no pardon came, and the victim showed remarkable courage to the end.

On 1 July 1766 he was put to the Ordinary and Extraordinary Torture, similar to that inflicted on Calas. Then he was taken to Saint-Wulfran, but there he refused to go through with the charade of penance, and a deputy had to be found. "The worst part about this day," exclaimed la Barre, "is that I can see people in the windows whom I believed to be my friends." As part of the public example demanded by Pasquier, five executioners had been sent for from five different cities to carry out the sentence; but even they only made a pretence of tearing out la Barre's tongue. When one of them finally cut off his head most skilfully there was a round of applause from all the spectators. After that it only remained to burn the body and the books.

In Paris a brave lawyer, Linguet, declared that the trial had been defective because the warrant for la Barre's arrest was illegal, and since the youth Moisnel had retracted his statement there had been no real evidence against the prisoner. The *Parlement de Paris* tried threatening Linguet, but he had the backing of most of the legal profession in the capital. Linguet printed a petition, but the *Parlement* bought up nearly all the copies to prevent them reaching the public.

When news of the atrocity reached Ferney, Voltaire felt, apart from the cruelty of it all, indirectly responsible for the tragedy because of the prosecution's use of the fact that la Barre owned a copy of his *Dictionnaire Philosophique portatif*. Fearful for his own safety, he moved a few miles to Rolle in the Canton of Vaud, whence he wrote to Elie de Beaumont, asking if there was in fact a law by which a person could be sentenced to death for uttering impieties. There was not, and the magistrates in their blind fury had only assumed there must be one, without bothering to check. The death sentence could only be imposed for sacrilege coupled with witchcraft, as Voltaire was to point out.

At the same time he wrote a pamphlet, under a pseudonym: *Relation de la Mort du Chevalier de la Barre*. If anything, it was an even finer piece of humanitarian journalism than anything he had composed about Calas and Sirven. In the *Relation* he brought out a curious detail about Belleval, the man who originally made the accusations leading to the arrest of la Barre and his companions. He gave the Abbess de Willancourt a good character (*sage sans superstition*); adding, however, that Belleval, who dealt with some of the convent's affairs, was on terms of considerable intimacy with her, to the point of being in love with the Abbess. For her part the Abbess made it quite plain that his attentions were unwelcome. In 1764 she took young la Barre—a grandson of a Lieutenant-General—under her wing after his father had run through a fortune of 40,000 *livres*. La Barre lived outside the actual convent, but was a frequent guest at her parties, from which Belleval was excluded. La Barre knew of Belleval's infatuation, and treated him with lordly contempt.

Not long afterwards came the occasion when the young man behaved disrespectfully towards the Corpus Christi procession, followed a month later by the damage and sacrilegious treatment of the crucifixes. As Voltaire pointed out, there was no connection between the two episodes. Belleval set out to discover what he could about la Barre's mode of life; questioning servants, and impressing on them that he was a highly placed official (albeit to do with taxation), and that after the monitories delivered in the churches it was everyone's duty to repeat all that they knew about the young man. But no one had heard anything about him having been responsible for the damage to the crucifix on the bridge. For his part, Belleval was telling people that even if they were not sure that la Barre had mutilated the crucifix as he passed over the bridge, it was certain that he had passed within thirty paces of a religious procession without taking off his hat. Also it was known that he had sung licentious songs, and that was a mortal sin. (Voltaire described these as "barrack-room songs" which had been current for a century.) Belleval was indulging in character assassination by insinuation, motivated by personal spite. It was to succeed only too well. He had started the avalanche, and, as with the Calas case, wild rumour and unfounded gossip would do the rest, carrying witnesses along on a wave of hysteria. But then something went wrong for Belleval. Witnesses named Moisnel as one of la Barre's companions.

Voltaire put in a personal word against the use of monitories in the churches; pointing out that they gave people a chance to make accusations about others more successful in life than they themselves "of whom they are always jealous." In the *Relation* Voltaire refrained from using violent language or excessive irony, and the piece is all the more effective for his restrained style. Facts first, then comment, and finally a brief summing up. He knew that the truth was the most deadly weapon of all.

The effect of la Barre's fate on Voltaire was so strong that he seriously considered leaving Ferney and settling at Cleves, just inside Prussian territory. His plan was to found a colony for philosophers, including Diderot, d'Alembert, Damilaville and Holbach. Frederick was surprised, but assured Voltaire of a welcome. But despite all the advantages the philosophers and encyclopedists preferred to stay in Paris, which, judging by the jealousy which had existed between Voltaire and Maupertuis at Potsdam, was perhaps as well.

Voltaire never succeeded in obtaining the same judicial rehabilitation for la Barre that he did for Calas and Sirven, but he did draw the nation's attention to an act of injustice. He would comment in a letter, "the spirit of la Barre cries out in vain for vengeance against his murderers."

Another case which Voltaire took up in 1770 was that of the Montbailly family in Saint-Omer, near Arras. The family consisted of a drunken mother, a son and a daughter-in-law. By calling they were snuff-makers, a trade carried on by a licence which would expire when the mother died. The old woman despised her daughter-in-law, and obtained a court order for the expulsion of the young couple from the house. The son tried to pacify his mother, who was in bed, drunk. Finally she fell asleep.

The next morning he could not rouse her. She had died from a stroke. All was set for the funeral when someone started the rumour that the young couple had killed the old woman to avoid being turned out of the house—a most unlikely story—since of course the licence to make snuff (and therefore their livelihood) expired with her. But it was believed, the husband and wife were arrested, and both were sentenced to death. But since the wife was pregnant her execution was postponed until after the birth of her child. Meanwhile, her unfortunate husband was taken back to Saint-Omer, where he was tortured to make him confess. He said nothing, even when threatened with eternal hell-fire by the priest who was present. Then his right hand was cut off and he was broken on the wheel.

The woman's relatives appealed to Voltaire, who took up the case with Chancellor Maupeou, and at the same time wrote the pamphlet *La Méprise d'Arras*. In it he pointed out that there had been no outcry against the sentences imposed on the Montbailly family, because they were people of no influence and unable to defend themselves adequately. His protest was successful: the Council ordered a re-trial, and Mme Montbailly was found not guilty. Also, for what it was worth, her late husband was declared innocent of any crime. The fickle town of Saint-Omer received the young widow back like a conquering heroine.

At the end of the 1760s and the beginning of the 1770s Voltaire's attacks on the Christian religion decreased somewhat. Largely because of his concern for justice he turned his attention to attacking the judiciary, where high office could still be bought regardless of qualifications or merit. His particular target was the *Parlement de Paris*, the Jansenist rival to the authority of the Crown.

In 1768 he wrote the short piece *L'Homme aux quarante écus*. The pill was sugared to make it entertaining reading, but the message was there none the less: France was in dire need of a government which understood economics, and an overhaul of the whole system of taxation. The point was not lost on the *Parlement de Paris*, who inevitably ordered the pamphlet to be burnt by the hangman. Later the episode was repeated on the orders of the authorities in Rome.

The danger Voltaire was running by daring to criticise the state in the slightest degree may be illustrated by the following episode. In lieu of money an apprentice accepted some books for settlement of a debt, which he then sold to a bookseller. The books included *L'Homme aux quarante écus*, by Voltaire, *Le Christianisme dévolié* (Christianity unveiled), possibly by Damila- ville, and a play by Fontenelle. The authorities found out. The books and the play were ordered to be burnt. The apprentice and the bookseller were ordered to be branded, and placed in the pillory for three days, while the former was sentenced to the galleys for nine years, and the latter for five. Even the book- seller's wife suffered. She was sentenced to be imprisoned in the Salpêtrière—the women's prison in Paris—for five years. The apprentice died after being exposed in the pillory and before he could be sent to the galleys. That was in September 1768. On 5 October the *Parlement de Paris* issued a warrant for the arrest of Voltaire himself, as the author of a "wicked book which menaces good morals."

L'Homme aux quarante écus was milk and water compared to *Le Diner du Comte de Boulainvilliers*, published the year before, which Voltaire chose to attribute to the poet Saint-Hyacinthe, who had in fact died as long ago as 1746. In the distant past he had been unwise enough to criticise the *Henriade*. *Le Diner* was a series of dialogues over dinner carried on by real characters. Religion was the subject. The argument of the piece, as revealed at the end, is a variation on the remark "If God did not exist, it would be necessary to invent Him." In this case the conclusion drawn was that man needed a religion, but one from which the thinkers had removed all traces of superstition.

There was no end to the awkward and pertinent questions Voltaire posed in his pamphlets, written either anonymously or else under far-fetched pseudonyms. *Les questions de Zapata* consisted of sixty-nine questions put by a spurious seventeenth- century theologian of Salamanca University. Many of his ques- tions concerned the persecution of the Jews: not that Voltaire was himself free from anti-Semitism. Zapata starts off by asking how he can explain away the fact that the Jews, who in his day were being burnt alive in their hundreds, were for four thousand years God's chosen people:

> If God is the God of Abraham, why do you burn Abraham's children? And if you burn them, why do you recite their prayers, even when burning them? How, if you adored the book of their faith, can you put them to death for their faith?

If some of the questions were pertinent, others had a typically Voltairian flippancy:

> ... why was the Pharaoh's daughter bathing in the Nile, where no one bathes because of the crocodiles?

By a mixture of wit, erudition and bad taste Voltaire was achieving his aim: the undermining of the whole rotten fabric of society in France. Those he did not scandalise and infuriate he made laugh. Either way he made people think as they had never thought before, instead of blindly accepting what was handed down to them from above.

When it came to righting wrongs and correcting evils the most useful lesson Voltaire taught future generations was to let the truth speak for itself, and if certain persons were confounded in the process so much the better. This was particularly true in 1769, when he even risked publishing the *Histoire du Parlement de Paris, par M. l'Abbé Big*. ... In it he did nothing but print facts, and in so doing completely destroyed the credibility of the *Parlement*. The severest punishment was threatened against anyone daring to sell the infamous work, imported from Amsterdam. To throw the *Parlement* off his scent as the true author, Voltaire declared that he could not possibly have written it, as he did not have access to the official archives in Paris which were quoted in the piece. No, but a number of his friends had that right of access.

The Attorney-General Séguier actually visited Voltaire at Ferney, and informed him in the course of a casual conversation that his colleagues in the *Parlement* kept wishing that he would order the burning of the *Histoire*, so that he, Séguier, would have to set about discovering the identity of the author. Blandly Voltaire commented that he thought the *Parlement* should be grateful that such a truthful and balanced work had been written. Then, in 1770, the *Parlement de Paris* had other matters to occupy its time, and the threatened investigation never took place.

Chapter 23

THE OLD MAN OF FERNEY

At Easter 1768 Voltaire had a strong desire to receive Communion, as he had done at Colmar after leaving Potsdam. Almost casually he asked a priest who was a guest at Ferney if he could receive absolution. "Willingly," said the priest, and there the matter rested. Accompanied by a disapproving Wagnière he went to church on Easter Sunday. There he mounted the pulpit and delivered what was probably a good sermon, which at least had the merit of brevity. What happened reached the ears of the bishop. He was cast in a finer mould than many of his contemporaries, and he wrote Voltaire a reasonable letter, hoping that his future life would prove the sincerity of his act. The news also reached the philosophers in Paris, and they were scandalised. Voltaire tried to save his face by claiming that he was only following the principle of "when in Rome, do as the Romans do." But the upshot was that the bishop forbade any of the clergy in the diocese of Annecy to administer the Sacrament to Voltaire.

Always at the back of his mind was the fear of having his body thrust unceremoniously into a hole in the ground, sprinkled with quicklime, and then stamped into oblivion. A year later, in March 1769, Voltaire felt the need to insure himself against such a fate, and indulged in some highly discreditable chicanery to gain his end. He got his doctor (not Tronchin, who had moved to Paris) to agree that he was ill with a high fever, and a certificate was sent to the local *curé*, saying that he wished to be fortified by the Sacraments of the Church. The *curé* delayed, and contacted the bishop, who sent a profession of faith for Voltaire to sign. The patient lectured the *curé* on morality and tolerance, and demanded immediate absolution. What was more he received it, and then rose and went for a walk. Even those gentlest of friends, the Argentals, took him to task for his almost childlike waywardness. But he had had his own way, and in Paris the philosophers all blamed the age in which they lived which made such expedients necessary, and not the perpetrator of the ruse.

In Paris the old *Parlements* were dissolved, not without intense opposition, and six new Supreme Courts set up in their place. The minister Maupeou had Voltaire's moral support, and he hoped the philosopher would publish anonymous pamphlets praising his action. Here was the rare and extraordinary sight of a minister of the crown encouraging Voltaire to write pamphlets, and actually inserting inflammatory statements from other sources to suit his own purpose. The members of the old *Parlement de Paris* who had confirmed the death sentence on la Barre had been exiled by *lettres de cachet* to the country, and scornfully Voltaire wrote:

Do the murderers of la Barre deserve pity because they now have to live in the country? I have had to live in the country for seventeen years, and I have murdered nobody.

But Maupeou was doing the right things for the wrong reasons when he ordered the new *Parlement de Toulouse* to vindicate the Sirven family, and in Paris saved Mme Montbailly from execution only just in time. By ordering such re-trials or reversals of verdicts by the old courts he achieved personal popularity, and the goodwill of the public for the new *Parlements*, which were his creation. From Ferney, Voltaire saw the change that had come about as the beginning of a new and more enlightened era. But it was to prove a false dawn.

Soon the new *Parlement de Paris* was to show by the trial of Beaumarchais how little had really changed. Beaumarchais is today best remembered as the author of two plays later turned into operas: *The Marriage of Figaro* and the *Barber of Seville*. But when it was first written *Figaro* was considered such political dynamite—for making fun of the aristocracy and the *ancien régime*—that it was banned in Paris and Vienna.

The episode which was to discredit the new *Parlement* started as an action brought by Beaumarchais against the Comte de la Blanche, the heir of one of the four Pâris-Duverney brothers. In the past Beaumarchais had put good business in the way of the third of the banker brothers, and in recognition received credit to further his own financial speculations. He had in his possession a document signed by Pâris-Duverney giving the details of the loan. Now it had been repudiated by the Comte de la Blanche. He claimed that a balance of 15,000 *livres*, together with a further 75,000 *livres* interest-free for eight years, was a forgery. The Comte declared that Beaumarchais had obtained a sheet of paper, blank save for Pâris-Duverney's signature and filled in the details himself. He refused to honour the terms, but to his chagrin the document was declared legal. In February 1772 he appealed to the *Parlement de Paris*.

The case was heard the following March, but by then Beaumarchais was in prison, following a quarrel with the Duc de Chaulnes. To blacken Beaumarchais' reputation, the Comte was putting it around Paris that his opponent had poisoned three wives. Beaumarchais had in fact only been married twice. *Parlement* found in favour of the Comte, and fined Beaumarchais a crippling sum.

In May 1773, when he was released from prison, Beaumarchais at once sought an interview with Goëzman, the judge who had presided at the trial he had been unable to attend in person. It was common knowledge that anyone wishing to have such an interview would first have to bribe Mme Goëzman. Beaumarchais was advised by Lejay, the judge's publisher, that one hundred *louis d'or* should be sufficient. It gave him an interview, but only for a very few minutes.

The price of a second audience was a diamond-studded watch, plus a further hundred *louis d'or*. This time it was said that the money was for the judge's secretary. But there was no interview, and Mme Goëzman returned all the money except for fifteen *louis d'or*, which she claimed were to be given to the secretary. Unfortunately for her Beaumarchais heard they had never been received by the secretary, and he wrote accusing Mme Goëzman of misappropriating the sum. She retaliated by declaring that he had tried to bribe her.

Using Voltaire's own weapon of an appeal to public opinion, Beaumarchais let the facts be widely known. Goëzman was frantic to save his own reputation, and asked the police commissioner to obtain a *lettre de cachet*. The request was refused, but he put pressure on Lejay to declare that Beaumarchais had requested him, Lejay, to try to bribe Mme Goëzman on his behalf. On the strength of that he started libel proceedings against Beaumarchais before the *Parlement de Paris*. It was the beginning of a four-year fight to clear himself of being indicted and convicted of forgery.

A neat epigram circulated in Paris. Louis XV had overthrown the old *Parlement*, and now *quinze louis* were overthrowing the new. Beaumarchais wrote four *Mémoires* with the object of influencing public opinion, and the tenor of them was that private citizens who lacked influence had no redress against biased courts of law.

Beaumarchais also somehow discovered that Goëzman had forged a birth certificate to hide the paternity of a child of which he was the real father. And he also exposed Marin, another member of the *Parlement*, in all his hypocritical rottenness. Marin's unofficial duty was to provide pamphlets supporting Maupeou. But at the same time he was distributing pamphlets blackening the Chancellor's reputation at a considerable profit to himself. Also, Marin added to his income by the resale of banned books which had been confiscated by the authorities from booksellers, who, like as not, had been condemned to the galleys for their offence.

At Ferney the *Mémoire* was read by an admiring Voltaire, who could not have done better himself in similar circumstances.

What a man! In himself there is intellect, reason, wit and energy. He knows how to appeal to the feelings. In short, he is successful in every kind of eloquence. He destroys his opponents and routs his judges. I can excuse all his carelessness and all his violence.

Beaumarchais was staking everything on one throw of the dice. If his case went against him, *Parlement* would show no mercy, and he would be sent to the galleys for life. In the event he received a curious and medieval-sounding punishment: he was sentenced to receive the "severe rebuke." Under it Beaumarchais would forfeit any offices and titles he might hold, and be deprived of his rights of citizenship. When the judgment was delivered there was such a demonstration from the public gallery that the judges fled incontinently from the hall.

As with the Calas affair, public opinion had scored a victory over a dishonest and biased judiciary. The "severe rebuke" was never carried out, and *Parlement* had to content itself with petty spite: the tearing up and burning by the public hangman of Beaumarchais' four *Mémoires* in the Cour de Mai of the Palais de Justice.

Indirectly the victory was as much Voltaire's as it was Beaumarchais'. Both had used the truth, set forth in readable terms, as their only weapon. And now it was plain for all to see that the new *Parlement de Paris* was as corrupt as the one it had replaced.

Just as Voltaire could pursue a vendetta or a literary quarrel for years, in his old age he could pursue a fight for justice, or help others. So it was with D'Etallonde, who had fled to Prussia to avoid the fate of his friend la Barre. The youth was well received by Frederick the Great, and given a commission in the army. In 1774, by which time he had become a responsible adult, he came to Ferney. For some time he had been corresponding with Voltaire on the subject of a royal pardon, and he had come on leave of absence to discuss the best method of approach.

The situation was difficult. If Louis XV granted him a pardon, that in itself was an admission that the sentence passed on la Barre had also been unjust. Frederick saw that obstacle, and in a letter written in February 1774 doubted whether Voltaire had sufficient influence at Court now to obtain the pardon which would lead to the restitution of D'Etallonde's rights as a French citizen. As it was, even his inheritance from his mother had been confiscated.

Voltaire was agreeably surprised when he met D'Etallonde, finding him sensible, with good manners, and enthusiastic about his career in the Army:

> I cannot recover from my surprise when I see what his fault was and his sentence. He is only charged legally with having passed quickly, and with his hat on his head, forty yards from a procession of monks, and with having sung with several other young men a bawdy song written more than a hundred years ago.

Frederick the Great took a gloomy view of the chance of a pardon:

> Regardless of what progress philosophy may make, stupidity and bigotry will always find their roots in the Church, and the name of superstition will always remain the trumpet that assembles the weak-minded and those who have been bitten by the passion to save their neighbours' souls.

In May 1774 Louis the well-beloved died, from smallpox contracted from a milkmaid, and the new sovereigns were Louis XVI and Marie Antoinette. Turgot was appointed Prime Minister. He belonged to the second generation of philosophers, and counted himself a pupil of Voltaire. He was the one man at that date who could have cured France's financial ills. All too soon, however, he was removed from office at the instigation of Marie Antoinette, who was influenced by her pernicious circle of friends who resented his proposed tax reforms. On the eve of the Revolution history was to repeat itself when the Swiss banker Necker (whose daughter, the future Mme de Staël, was personally known to Voltaire) suffered the same form of dismissal.

Many in Paris and at Versailles were shocked at one of the *Encyclopédistes* being given high office. The well-meaning young king commmented: "All the same, he is an honest man, and that's all I ask."

Full of hope, Voltaire wrote to Maupeou asking him to take up the case of D'Etallonde. But in August the Minister was forced from office, and in October the old *Parlements* were recalled. It was a triumph for the reactionaries. Once again the position of judge could be bought, regardless of capabilities or qualifications, and plans for the abolition of torture were abandoned.

But Voltaire did not give up hope. Frederick the Great gave D'Etallonde an excellent reference, and the Duchesse d'Enville promised to speak with the Minister Maupeou. But no Parisian lawyer would touch the case, for fear of antagonising *Parlement*. All Voltaire could do was write another pamphlet: *Cri du Sang innocent*. Whether the pamphlet was ever read by Louis XVI, who at that time was quite obsessed by hunting, is not known. At all

events, it was not until Voltaire had been dead for ten years that
D'Etallonde was finally pardoned, in 1788.

Now yet another miscarriage of justice claimed the philosopher's attention. Years before he had met General Lally,
through the Duc de Richelieu. The general was descended from
an Irish Jacobite family which followed James II into exile after
that king's defeat at the Battle of the Boyne. During the Seven
Years War Europe was not the only scene of conflict between
the French and English. A struggle for supremacy took place in
southern India between the French, with the assistance of Hyder
Ali, and the British under Clive. General Lally, who had inherited a hatred of the British, was sent to India in 1758, and at
first he inflicted a number of defeats on his enemies. But he
had to contend with dissension and jealousy among his senior
officers.

Apart from driving the British from southern India, Lally also
had instructions to stamp out corruption among the officials of
the *Companie des Indes*. The hatred this stirred up, aided by his
naturally quick temper, led to his eventual downfall. Madras
was captured, but while the ill-disciplined troops were thieving
in the city, the English counter-attacked. Senior French commanders failed to come to Lally's assistance, and he was forced
to retreat to Pondicherri. There he was captured, and it was the
British who had to defend him from the rage of his own countrymen.

Lally was sent as a prisoner of war to England. In London he
heard that his enemies were ruining his reputation in Paris, and
he was allowed to return home on parole to confront his slan-
derers. If he succeeded in exposing the corruption of high
officials in the *Companie des Indes* (the French equivalent of the
East India Company) they would be ruined. It was a question of
who could destroy whom first.

Like Warren Hastings at a later date in England, he was
accused of extortion and the misappropriation of public funds.
But Lally was also accused of high treason. According to his
enemies he had betrayed Pondicherri to the British. The trial
itself was a farce. Lally was allowed no counsel, and the judges
were wholly ignorant of anything concerning India. The general
wrote his own brief, but in order to scotch any sympathy among

those who might read his defence the trial proceeded with indecent haste. He was found guilty on all counts, and sentenced to death, while his property was sequestered to the king. Not only did he go to his execution in a cart with his hands tied behind his back like an ordinary criminal but he had a gag in his mouth to prevent embarrassment to the authorities by a last-minute speech to those around the scaffold. For his part, Louis XV shut himself away so that he would not have to distress himself by so much as considering the question of a pardon.

At Ferney Voltaire was shocked at the news, and in his *Précis du Siècle de Louis XV* (1768) he practically described the execution as legalised murder. Seven years passed, and then the general's son, Comte Lally-Tollendal, approached him in the hope that he would take up the case. By then the new *Parlements* had been called, and Voltaire felt that a direct attack on the *Parlement de Paris* would be the wrong method. Instead he decided to use the weapon which he had made his own: public opinion. In August 1773, four months after Comte Lally-Tollendal had first approached him, Voltaire published his *Fragments historiques sur l'Inde et sur le général Lally*. Sandwiched between interesting information about India, its people and customs, Voltaire gave a detailed account of General Lally in India, his campaigns, misfortunes, return to France, and his trial and execution. He made no comment himself and drew no conclusions, being content to let the facts speak for themselves.

Five more years were to elapse before General Lally's post-humous rehabilitation was complete. After the accession of Louis XVI and the recalling of the old and reactionary *Parlements* the reopening of the case was bitterly opposed, despite the petition presented to the Council, in which it was pointed out that Lally had been denied any defence counsel. But the President, Pasquier, deliberately blocked any chance of a pardon being granted by the king.

There the matter rested until Voltaire paid his final visit to Paris in the spring of 1778, when the Council and *Parlement* could not hold out against the extraordinary wave of enthusiasm brought about by the old man's return to the capital. The sentence passed on General Lally was quashed by the Council, and on 26 May Voltaire, by then on his death-bed, dictated his last letter to

Count Lally-Tollendal, congratulating him on the clearing of his his father's name.

At the end of his long and turbulent life it was not political or religious polemics which occupied his thoughts, but the fact that he had succeeded in obtaining justice for a young man who could have meant nothing to him personally.

Voltaire was ready to speak out on behalf of anyone whom he considered was a victim of injustice whether from Church or State, and it was through him that the inhabitants of an area in the Jura were freed from being the serfs of the Church authorities at Saint-Cloud. Also he obtained relief for the inhabitants of the Pays de Gex from the very heavy taxes which for centuries had crippled the district.

"Doing good" today often carries the association of well-meaning but inept meddling. But at Ferney Voltaire "did good" to a remarkable degree. He set up local industries such as watch-making and stocking manufacture. While Rousseau preached an impractical philosophy, calling for a return to nature and the simple life, Voltaire set about giving practical assistance and a reasonable standard of life to as many as possible of his fellow creatures.

From being run-down and poverty-stricken, Ferney under Voltaire became something of an agricultural showplace. Fields were properly tilled; crops harvested and stored in well-built barns and granaries. There was good pasturage for the sheep and cattle; trees were planted, and Voltaire obtained the latest agricultural implements, including a seed drill of which he was particularly proud. Even the gardens contributed to the general weal. The grass on the walks was not scythed until it was tall enough to be gathered as hay for the animals.

Until 1772, when he reached the age of seventy-eight, there was one field which no one else was allowed to touch, and which Voltaire ploughed and sowed himself. The farm animals too were well cared for. There were two great barns, one for the cows and calves, the other for horse and oxen. Each had its own allotted place, and fodder for the mangers was provided by hoppers from the granaries above.

Silk-weaving was second only to watch-making at Ferney as an industry, and Voltaire used his illustrious connections to further his business interests. To the Duchesse de Choiseul he wrote in 1769:

> It is from my own silkworms that I have made the material for these stockings; it is with my own hands, aided by a son of Calas, that they are made at my place; these are the first stockings that have ever been made in this country.
>
> Be so kind as to put them on, Madame, just one time; then show your legs to whomsoever you please; and if it is not admitted that my silk is stronger and more beautiful than that of Provence or Italy, I shall give up the manufacture.

He used the same direct methods when it came to selling his watches, made by workers who lived in specially-built houses. In 1770 he circularised all the ambassadors in Paris that the Royal Manufactory of Ferney was producing watches ranging in price from three *louis* to forty-two *louis* for a repeater. At this time his friendship with Catherine the Great was as cordial as ever, and she gave an order for watches costing an unspecified sum. For her part she sent him numerous gifts, including her portrait set with diamonds, a wrap of sable, and a snuff box made by herself. It was on Voltaire's advice that she had introduced inoculation against smallpox into Russia, a system which he had advocated half a century before in his *Lettres Philosophiques* (*sur l'insertion de la petite vérole*). Other consignments of watches were sent all over Europe, to Turkey, to America, and even to China. Frederick the Great took not only watches but gave homes and employment (which would be tax-free for twelve years) in Berlin to eighteen watchmakers and their families who had been forced to leave Geneva because of the civil disturbances then bedevilling the city.

In 1772 a third industry was added at Ferney: that of lace making. Such was the paradox of the philosopher and Deist that he rejoiced at the religious toleration he saw about him as Catholic and Protestant lived side by side in good neighbourliness. "Is this not better than Saint Bartholomew?" he asked. "When a Catholic is sick, Protestants go and take care of him."

By now many of Voltaire's old friends had died, including the *Encyclopédiste* Damilaville, and in 1768–9 Mme Denis had returned to Paris for a while after she had been suspected, rightly, of helping steal manuscripts of part of *La Pucelle* from his desk drawer.

At Ferney the house was shared by Marie Corneille and her husband and his sister; together with the husband that Voltaire had found for her too. Then there was Wagnière, his wife and family. The children used to play in the room while Voltaire was dictating to his secretary. Last of all, there was old, lame Father Adam, the Jesuit who had been given shelter by Voltaire after the expulsion of his order from France.

But for all that the philosopher was lonely, and he lavished his care and concern on all his children, the tenants of Tournay and Ferney. If the crops failed he would import grain and sell it to them at less than cost price, and rejoice that their prosperity rested on "freedom of trade and freedom of conscience."

From time to time Voltaire continued to give annoyance to the City Fathers in Geneva, as when he championed one Robert Covelle, who was charged with immoral conduct with a young unmarried woman, and with being the father of her child. Anyone found guilty by the Consistory Court, which was in fact a court of morals, had to kneel before its members to be reprimanded and then forgiven. Covelle refused, and was imprisoned. Voltaire stepped in, writing a pamphlet showing that the Court had no case in law for trying to make the offender kneel and beg for forgiveness. In the end he succeeded in having the decree abolished. He had his own personal resentment against the City Fathers, who it will be remembered had banned his theatre at *Les Délices*. It all came out in *La Guerre civile de Gènève ou les amours de Robert Covelle*. It was a thoroughly bawdy epic, containing more personal malice than wit.

Within everyone's hearing at Ferney, including the servants, Voltaire used to refer to Robert Covelle as *Monsieur le fornicateur*. Covelle looked on Voltaire as his friend and saviour, and paid numerous uninvited visits to the château. Under the impression that Voltaire was speaking of him by an official title (such as *Monsieur le Procureur*), the bewigged footmen invariably threw open the salon doors to announce loudly the arrival of "*Monsieur le fornicateur!*"

The civil strife in Geneva, which was largely a class struggle, reached such proportions that in January 1767 the French sent troops to blockade the city and bring it to its senses by starvation and the disruption of trade. Voltaire and his little colony suffered, until Choiseul sent an order to Ferney exempting it from the blockade. The Colonel of the Prince de Conti's regiment stayed at the château, while three companies of men were billeted in the village. Such was Voltaire's concern for their welfare that he made sure they had blankets against the bitter winter nights. During their stay *Semiramis* was performed at the theatre (later Voltaire gave the robes to the church he had rebuilt, to be used as vestments), and a number of grenadiers had walk-on parts as guards. In return they were to be given supper and whatever fee they chose to ask. One spoke for all: "We won't accept any reward. We have seen Voltaire, and that is reward enough."

They had probably never heard of the *Henriade* or the *Essai sur les Moeurs*, but they had heard of Calas and Sirven, and it was their privilege to help this sprightly little old man with hardly a tooth in his head but always a twinkle in his eye. After that they were welcome for a meal, or to help by doing odd jobs about the place.

Later, when the "Civil War of Geneva" had run its course, Voltaire suggested that Gex and the surrounding area, which was French territory, should have some means of direct access into France, from which it was cut off by the mountains, instead of all its commerce having to pass through Geneva with its customs and restrictions. It was only after the map of Europe had been redrawn in 1815 that the extreme north-western shores of Lake Geneva became Swiss, and in 1768 Voltaire suggested that the French should build a port at Versoix, which would make Gex independent of Geneva. Work actually started, thanks to Choiseul, but when he fell from office in 1770 the whole project was abandoned.

Perhaps the best known description of Voltaire during these last years is that written by Martin Sherlock, chaplain to the Bishop of Bristol, in April 1776. The clergyman described the industries at Ferney, and then Voltaire himself in his famous dressing-gown:

He caused the first houses to be built, and gave them for a perpetual quit-rent; then he lent money, by way of annuities, to those who would build themselves; to some on his own life, to others on the joint lives of himself and Madame Denis.

His sole object seemed to me to have been the improvement of this village, that was his motive for asking an exemption from taxes; that was the reason why he endeavoured every day to inveigle workmen from Geneva to establish a manufactory for clock-making. I do not say that he did not think of money; but I am convinced that it was only a secondary object.

On the days I saw him, he wore white cloth shoes, white woollen stockings, red breeches, with a night-gown and waist-coat of blue linen flowered and lined with yellow: he had on a grizzle wig with three ties, and over it a silk night-cap embroidered with gold and silver.

Earlier, in 1770, Mme Necker had suggested that the sculptor Pigalle should be commissioned to produce a statue of the philosopher. A subscription list was opened, and among those who contributed were Richelieu and Frederick the Great. Pigalle made the journey to Ferney, but Voltaire was so active and vivacious that it was not until the seventh and last day of his visit that he could obtain a sitting. Mischievously Voltaire had written to Pigalle that he should emulate Pygmalion and his Galatea by sculpting him in the nude. Pigalle took him at his word, but since Voltaire in a state of nature looked more like a *memento mori* than any living person has a right to do it was not a happy idea.

More edifying was the statue Frederick the Great commissioned from the royal porcelain factory in Berlin:

He caused a statue of his old servant to be made in his fine manu-factory of porcelain and sent it to him with the word *Immortal* inscribed upon the pedestal. Mr de Voltaire wrote under it,

> *Vous êtes généreux. Vos bontés souveraines*
> *Me font de trop nobles présens.*
> *Vous me donnez sur mes vieux ans*
> *Une terre dans vos domaines.*

You're generous. Your royal bounty deigns
To croud too noble presents on the past;
Worn out with age, and breathing now my last,
You grant me an estate in your domains.

In the spring of 1777 Joseph II, son of Maria Theresa, visited his sister Marie Antoinette at Versailles. He was expected to stop at Ferney on his way home. Voltaire made preparations, and even had the road to Versoix repaired. A procession of carriages approached. But when the coachman called out that they had reached Ferney Joseph II ordered him to whip up the horses and drive on, and without stopping they moved off.

Joseph was himself something of a philosopher, and co-ruler of the Austrian Empire. But he was also the son of the self-appointed guardian of Viennese morals, and a staunch Catholic. Was he fearful of what his mother would say when she heard that he had visited the free-thinking philosopher, who, to make matters worse, was a friend of the Empress Maria Theresa's arch-enemy Frederick the Great? But, quite equally, in the past Voltaire had corresponded with Maria Theresa. Strangely enough, Joseph stopped at Versoix to see the harbour which had been inspired by Voltaire, and begun by Choiseul. But he left a saddened old man at Ferney, for though Voltaire put a good face on the episode, he felt in his heart that he had been deliberately snubbed or disgraced.

A newcomer now entered the life of the household at Ferney, and before long she had endeared herself to everyone by her ingenuous charm and innocence. Her name was Reine-Philiberte de Varicourt, the daughter of an army officer. She came in 1775. Her chances of finding a suitable husband were poor because her parents could not afford to give her a dowry. The only alternative was to enter a convent. But this was averted by coming to live at Ferney as companion to Mme Denis, who showed no jealousy at the affection lavished on the girl by Voltaire. Before long he had nicknamed her *Belle et Bonne*, and they were like grandfather and granddaughter.

How, the old man wondered, could one so young and fair bring herself to give a morning kiss to an old death's-head like him when she brought in his coffee? If he were out of sorts or in a difficult mood *Belle et Bonne* could be relied upon to jolly him out of it. At eighty-three he was not too old to teach her how to dance. Already he had married off Marie Corneille and her sister-in-law Mlle Dupuits. Now the Marquis de Villette returned to stay at Ferney (his family lived in the district), which he had last visited eleven years before. His reputation in Paris was that of a middle-aged rake who could produce charming light verse. But he had left the capital for the peace and quiet of Ferney after an affair which had involved a duel.

At the château he first caught sight of *Belle et Bonne* as she walked in a procession in honour of St Francis of Assisi, which was also Voltaire's own name-day. Philosopher, free-thinker, Deist, undogmatic Christian—whatever he may have been at heart, Voltaire always celebrated such occasions with processions: his household in their best clothes, and all the villagers taking part in holiday mood. When Villette saw *Belle et Bonne* for the first time she was carrying a pair of white doves in a basket. On that same day he also saw Voltaire sitting in the garden, correcting proofs, and surrounded by a flock of grazing sheep, as he wrote to d'Alembert:

> In the middle of the group [of young people bringing presents] and worthy of the pencil of Poussin, there appeared the beautiful adopted daughter of the Patriarch. She carried, in a wicker basket, two doves, with white wings and rosy beaks. Her shyness and blushes enhanced the charm of her face. . . .
>
> I must tell you that he gave his tenants a superb meal, and that he made two hundred of them sit at his table. Afterwards there were illuminations, songs, dances. In the morning it had been a demonstration of filial affection: in the evening it was all enthusiastic joy, and old men flinging their hats in the air.

Now Voltaire set about reforming Villette, and in November 1777 he and *Belle et Bonne* were married at midnight in the church dedicated to God. Voltaire, huddled in the wrap given by Catherine the Great, gave her away.

Still the visitors came in an unending procession: the welcome and the unwelcome, the celebrated, the genuine and the merely curious. One such was Mme de Genlis, herself to become a writer, and, through her connections with the household of the Duc d'Orléans, a cool onlooker at the Court of Versailles. She came to Ferney ready to criticise, but ended by writing of Voltaire's eyes "which have in them an inexpressible sweetness."

It was an expression which Houdon was to capture soon after in his celebrated statue of the seated philosopher. Another visitor was Mme Saint-Julien, who had suggested starting the lace industry, and who invited herself for long visits to the little kingdom. It was largely thanks to her influence that the crippling tax of 40,000 *livres* a year on the Pays de Gex was finally lifted.

An earlier guest was Dr Burney, on the occasion of his celebrated visit to Italy in 1770, when he was compiling his *History of Music*.

We drove to Ferney through a charming country, covered with corn and vines, in view of the Lake, and mountains of Gex, Switzerland and Savoy. On the left hand, approaching the House, is a neat Chapel, with this inscription:

Deo erexit Voltaire MDCCLXI

I sent to inquire whether a stranger might be allowed to see the House and Gardens; and was answered in the affirmative. A servant soon came, and conducted me into the cabinet where his Master had just been writing: this is never shown when he is at home; but since he had walked out, I was allowed that privilege.

Then Dr Burney caught sight of Voltaire in the grounds.

He was going to his workmen. My heart leapt at the sight of so extraordinary a man. He had just then quitted his garden, and was crossing the court before the House. . . . It is not easy to conceive it possible for life to subsist in a form so nearly composed of skin and bone as that of M. de Voltaire. He complained of decrepitude and said he supposed I was anxious to form an idea of the figure of one walking after death.

However, his eyes and whole countenance are still full of fire; and though so emaciated, a more lively expression cannot be imagined.

Few of Voltaire's old friends were still alive now. There were Richelieu and d'Argental, but most of the others had gone. One, who was indeed like a voice from the past, was Saint-Lambert, by whom Emilie du Châtelet had borne the child which had killed her all those years ago at Lunéville. He sent his old and secret rival his poem *The Seasons*, and received a most amiable and courteous reply, as one poet to another.

That life at Ferney bored Mme Denis was no secret to her uncle, and it was decided that a lengthy visit to the capital, for business and health reasons, would be a good idea. She longed for the salons, and what she considered was a life suited to her intellectual achievements. Several years before Dr Burney's visit (in fact in 1768) Mme Denis, La Harpe—a young writer Voltaire had befriended, and who repaid the hospitality he received by stealing several of the philosopher's manuscripts, including *La Guerre civile de Gèneve* and memoirs not intended for publication during the author's lifetime—together with Marie Dupuits and her husband, all left for Paris. No sooner had they gone than Voltaire had the whole château cleaned from top to bottom.

Nearly fifty years before, Voltaire, in his flush of enthusiasm for things English, had championed Shakespeare, barbarian though he was, in a France which only recognised the genius of Corneille and Racine. Now a translation of Shakespeare had appeared in Paris, which described the playwright as the god of the theatre, but made no reference to Corneille, Racine *or* Voltaire. At Ferney the old man was furious. It was he who had shown that there were riches in Shakespeare, if you looked hard enough, and now Letournier had thrust into what he regarded as his own literary preserve. In the past he had been derided for defending Shakespeare. Now, in a fit of perversity, he wrote a long letter to the Académie Française in which he declared that Shakespeare was no more than an indecent buffoon who had "ruined the taste of England for two hundred years." He translated a number of the coarser passages to try to prove his point. It was the regrettable action of an eighty-two-year-old man who felt that someone else had stolen his glory.

But there was still work to be done. He wrote two more plays, *Irène* and *Agathocle*: neither among his best works for the theatre. Above all, it was a time for summing up the thought and experience of a long lifetime, and for setting his affairs in order. His pen was as busy as ever. There was the *Commentaire historique sur les oeuvres de l'auteur de la Hendriade* (1775–6), which includes the quaint little *Autobiography*, the English translation of which has been quoted on a number of occasions. A lifetime of unbelief found its way into *La Bible enfin expliquée*, while his defence of the French theatre was given permanent form in the *Lettre à l'Académie Française*.

He may have been temporarily blinded to reason through irritation at Letournier, but all that was best in him showed through in the summing-up of his views on law reform. In February 1777 the *Gazette de Berne* carried an announcement that a philanthropist, who wished to remain anonymous, had offered the Economic Society of Berne a prize of fifty *louis d'or* for the best essay on the administration of criminal justice, bearing the following points in mind: the ratio between crime and punishment; the efficiency of proofs and surmises; the need to ensure a speedy trial resulting in conviction or aquittal so that the safety of society as a whole was preserved, and at the same time freedom and humanity were respected.

Voltaire offered another fifty *louis d'or* to the prize, but one cannot help wondering whether he was not the originator of the whole idea. It has the touch of deviousness that might be expected from him. Within eight months he had published his own views on the subject. They were intended, or so he said, as a useful guide for would-be competitors. In the piece he said all that he wanted to say about the French judicial system.

In place of arbitrary verdicts handed down without explanation by the *Parlements* he wanted trial by jury; and an end to the concept of an eye for an eye and a tooth for a tooth. Instead of having savage laws for crimes against property it would be much better to eradicate poverty, and a distinction should be made between serious and trivial crimes, both of which could carry the death penalty. If there were no extreme penalty for the most serious crimes there was nothing to deter the hardened criminal from committing the ultimate crime, murder, in further-ance of theft. But it should only be used in serious cases. Voltaire reasoned that a criminal was tempted to steal 10,000 francs and not just ten, because if caught he would probably be executed anyway. Nor did Voltaire hesitate to condemn the idea that heresy was a crime against God worthy of death by burning, and cited the fact that when the burning of necromancers and sorcerers was finally abolished the interest in witchcraft declined.

Voltaire had clearly defined views on a wide range of topics. In matters of sex he held the opinion that what adults chose to do was the business of no one but themselves. All his life he had been persecuted one way or another, because of his writings, and naturally he wanted to see freedom of speech and freedom for the written word. Ecclesiastical informers, inspired by the monitories read in the churches which promised hell-fire for anyone who did not come forward with information, however meagre or circumstantial, merited his particular anger. It was such people who had brought about the deaths of Calas and la Barre. Thanks to the writings of Voltaire, Catherine the Great had banned torture in Russia as a means of extracting confessions. Nor—at least until Nazis came to power—was it used in Prussia and what later became the German Empire. The same was true in Maria Theresa's Austria, while in Britain torture had long since been abandoned, though flogging as a punishment would remain legal until 1948.

The idea that the Church in France should use or condone torture was particularly obnoxious to him, and he found it hypocritical that while a wife's adultery was severely punished, any misconduct on her husband's part was regarded as little more than an amusing escapade. Nor did he find it admirable that if a Roman Catholic were of sufficient importance, grounds could usually be found for the annulment of a marriage.

Obviously, the cases of Calas and Sirven were in Voltaire's mind when he wrote about the fallibility of witnesses who, then as now, will see what they want to see, regardless of the facts. He quoted the case of a well-to-do woman, a Mme de Chauvelin, who was accused of murdering her husband. Two maids declared they had seen the murder take place; others said that they had seen blood-stained linen, and the daughter of the house claimed that her father had called out: "*Mon Dieu*! have pity on me!" Then the victim returned home, after having gone on an unexpected journey.

The *Prix de la justice et de l'humanité* was one of the most worthwhile pieces Voltaire ever wrote (and is among the least known), and although not as devastating in its effect as the *Dictionnaire Philosophique portatif* (which might be decribed as the slow fuse of the French Revolution), it was yet another nail in the coffin of the *ancien régime*.

Physically, Voltaire might be old and afflicted by every ailment, real or imaginary, but his mind was as active as ever. A few months later that most fickle of cities, Paris, was to proclaim: "At eighty-four he wrote *Irène*." But the tragedy was not wholly successful, and when he first sent it to Paris Condorcet told him outright that it was not worthy of his genuis. By then he had already written *Agathocle*, which was no masterpiece either. But at the beginning of January 1778 *Irène* had been accepted by the Comédie Française for production. La Harpe, who had left Ferney under a cloud, now made amends for his past conduct by insisting that a play of his own should be postponed so that nothing should delay *Irène*. Another playwright, Nicolas Barthe, acted similarly, writing to the Comédie Française to say that the tradition by which plays were performed in order of acceptance should be broken in favour of Voltaire.

Meanwhile, at Ferney, Voltaire was filled with an urge to return to Paris. He had never actually been exiled from the capital by any written directive. It was as though his life were coming full circle, and Voltaire longed to see the city again: its buildings, its streets and its people. Above all he wanted to see old faces, especially those he had known when he had been a schoolboy at Saint-Louis le Grand. But now there were so few left. Both Richelieu and d'Argental were in their eighties, and who remained who had welcomed him into their salons during the Regency and the early years of the reign of Louis XV?

Ferney was Voltaire's kingdom, but Paris was his world. He wanted one last look at that world, and then to return content to his colony near the shores of Lake Geneva. He was not alone in the idea. Bossy, superficial Mme Denis, ever ready to offer an instant opinion on whatever was under discussion, detested Ferney. While she might be the niece and housekeeper of the most celebrated man in Europe, and act as hostess to a stream of distinguished visitors, she found life there almost insupportable. Snow, ice and boring industries were all she could see. She, who had received music lessons from Rameau himself, and had her own salon of rather dim luminaries, felt far more an exile from Paris than her uncle ever did. But if they went back, and Voltaire could be induced to remain there, she would have the best of both worlds: an unending social life, and the interest and importance which would centre on her as the niece of such a celebrity. He must be encouraged in the scheme.

Lovingly Voltaire had created the colony out of his own brain and his own pocket, and he was father to all the tenants, whether their work was agricultural or industrial, and he took the responsibility for their welfare most seriously. But his absence would only be for a few weeks, six at the most, and then he would be back, to spend his last years peacefully in their midst. Even so, he had his reservations. Voltaire must have lost count of the number of times the hangman had burnt his writings in public in Paris alone: and had not one official suggested quite recently, and in all seriousness, that he as well as his writings should be burnt?

"Don't you know that there are forty thousand fanatics who would bring forty thousand faggots to burn me? That would be my bed of honour," he commented plaintively.

But it was pointed out to him that there would be eighty thousand friends who would wish to put out the fire, and drown the fanatics as well, if that were his wish.

Mme Denis could hardly wait for her uncle to make up his mind, and together with the Marquis de Villette and *Belle et Bonne* she set out for Paris on 3 February 1778. By a coincidence, the town house of the Marquis had once belonged to M. and Mme de Bernières, and fifty-five years before Voltaire had rented an apartment there, which he shared with the undeserving Thieriot. Now the house was being prepared in readiness for his coming.

It was 5 February, and time for Voltaire to depart with Wagnière. Swathed in the sable wrap given by Catherine the Great, he paused before getting into his carriage to speak to the little company waiting outside the château. Many were in tears, and all were uneasy. They had nothing to worry about, he assured them, In six weeks he would be back with his children. In fact Voltaire had not even tidied up his desk. Soon he was gone, with tears in his own eyes.

Word spread along the route to Paris: "Voltaire's coming!" After a self-imposed exile of more than thirty years he was returning to Paris: if not against the command of king or *Parlement*, at least against the pleasure of Louis XVI and the Church. While the young king was not as stupid as many of his critics have asserted, he was without imagination, curiosity or real culture, Voltaire's name was abhorrent to him because he attacked the Church whose faith he unquestioningly followed, and because he was no respecter of kings or the privileges of the class whom God in His wisdom had seen fit to set to rule over the French nation. When asked what play he would like to see performed at Versailles, his answer was anything so long as it was not by Voltaire. Marie Antoinette was better disposed towards him. While she was thoughtless, and surrounded by friends who were a bad influence, she at least had some degree of curiosity about what went on beyond the confines of the Palais de Versailles and the Petit Trianon. It is said that until the Revolution she never read a book to the end. But she loved the theatre, and took part in amateur productions, permitting Lekain (her favourite actor) to go and visit Voltaire at Ferney, and she was curious about this old man who wrote beautiful tragedies which made everyone cry.

In the past Voltaire's spirits had soared when he kept up the fiction of not knowing who was responsible for some outrageous pamphlet or book bearing a highly unlikely pseudonym. Now he was supposed to be travelling incognito, and when he was not reading he was entertaining Wagnière with his inimitable stories. At Nantua, the first overnight stop, Voltaire had to lock himself in his room in the posting-house to escape from the crowd. At Bourg-en-Bresse half the town gathered to watch the horses being changed, and cheered when the posting-master ordered the postilions to drive as fast as they could, even if it killed the horses. "You are carrying M. de Voltaire!"

At Dijon the town dignitaries came to pay their respects, and the curious bribed the staff in the hotel to leave the door open, while the more enterprising tried to pass themselves off as waiters: anything to have a good look at the famous old man. As the party reached Paris the axle broke, and there was a delay while Villette's coach was sent to fetch him.

All round the city on the main roads were the *barrières*: customs posts where all who entered were checked for dutiable goods. The coach drew up at half-past three, 10 February, and Wagnière got out. Two officers entered and asked the occupant if he had anything to declare. "I believe there is nothing contraband here except myself," came the answer. "*Mon Dieu!*" exclaimed one of the officers, tugging at his colleague's coat. With a mixture of awe and admiration they descended from the coach, and Paris' most unruly son returned home.

Chapter 24

CORONATION

The carriage drew up outside the Hôtel de Villette on the Quai des Théatins, and although he had been travelling for five days, Voltaire at once started to walk round to see the Argentals. At the same time the Comte set out for the Quai des Théatins, by another route. After a while Voltaire returned, and at last the two old schoolfriends were united. "I have interrupted my death-agony to come and embrace you," exclaimed Voltaire with all his old flippancy. It was to turn out to be true.

For half the night the two old men sat up discussing where improvements could be made to *Irène*. But Lekain would not be appearing in it. He had died two days earlier.

Years before it had been said that Louis XV reigned but Voltaire was king. Now it would certainly be true to say that Voltaire was king in Paris. Nearly everyone came to do homage at the Hôtel de Villette, and Voltaire received all personally, as many as three hundred in one day. That in itself would have been sufficient to undermine the constitution of a man half his age, and Mme Denis did nothing to check the flow of visitors. In fact she was in her element. At Ferney she had considered herself to be buried alive, but here everyone who was anyone was crowding into the salons of the Hôtel de Villette, while all day and every day a large crowd waited outside, hoping for a glimpse of her uncle. Not even a visit by the Marquis de Jaucourt to inform her of the grave displeasure at Versailles caused by Voltaire's return to Paris could cause Mme Denis' selfish euphoria to evaporate. When Louis XVI asked: "Has the order forbidding M. de Voltaire's return to Paris ever been annulled?" nothing could be found, for the simple reason that no order had ever been committed to paper.

Even before his return the Church had begun its campaign against him. Its principal mouthpiece was the Abbé Beauregard, a popular preacher before the royal family at Versailles. In Notre Dame he declared:

The philosophers direct their blows against kings and against religion! In their hands are the hatchet and the hammer! They are only waiting for the favourable moment to overthrow the throne and the altar. Yes! Thy temples, O Lord, will be desecrated and destroyed. The feast days abolished, Thy name blasphemed, Thy worship banned and Thy ministers massacred!

The tragic fact was that much of what he said was to come true, not, as he envisaged, through the triumph of the hated philosophers, but in the horror of the September Massacres and the guillotine in the Place de la Révolution. From what had been a long overdue cleansing of the state, the Revolution of 1789 accelerated downhill into wholesale slaughter in which one form of fanaticism was replaced by another even more horrible. The day would come when priests were murdered, and a prostitute would dance on the High Altar of Notre Dame, which would be turned into a Temple of Reason.

Once, despite intense lobbying and influential friends, Voltaire had been refused admission to the ranks of the Immortals. The day after his return to Paris a deputation of three members came to the house to pay their respects. Next it was the turn of the Comédie Française to send a deputation. Between the two groups came Gluck, who was in France to supervise performances of his operas, followed by his almost forgotten rival, Piccini.

Another visitor was Mme Necker, wife of the Swiss financier and mother of the future Mme de Staël, who was still not quite sure whether she approved of Villette as a husband for one so innocent as *Belle et Bonne*. When Benjamin Franklin, the lion of Paris society, was announced, Voltaire paid him the compliment of speaking in English. This irritated Mme Denis, who had to know everything that was being said. "I could not refrain from indulging myself in the vain satisfaction of speaking the same language as Dr Franklin," was Voltaire's reply.

The two talked of the new American republic, and Voltaire

assured his visitor that if he were forty he would go and settle in his "happy country." Accompanying Franklin was his young nephew, and according to legend Voltaire raised his hands over the boy's head in a gesture of benediction and said in English: "My child, God and Liberty. Remember those two words."

Thanks to the hostile influence of Marie Antoinette, or rather her circle of friends, Voltaire's self-confessed disciple Turgot was forced from office before he could put through financial reforms which might have saved the French economy. He too was among the visitors, and one whom Voltaire was genuinely delighted to welcome. "When I see M. Turgot," he remarked to his eager audience in Villette's salon, "I think I see the statue of Nebuchadnezzar." Back came the retort from Turgot: "Yes, the feet of clay." "And the head of gold," parried Voltaire. "And the head of gold."

In view of his later career, there is an element of surprise in learning that as a young man Talleyrand was a priest, and, in the early days of the Revolution, Bishop of Autun. Now, at the age of twenty-five, he insinuated his way into the house to have a look at the celebrated Sage of Ferney.

To receive Voltaire's confession and bring him to a state of repentance for all that he had written against the Church was the ultimate spiritual trophy which Paris in February 1778 could offer to an ambitious clergyman. Whether such a person had any real concern for Voltaire's salvation is another matter. But the most genuine of them was undoubtedly Father Gaultier, who contacted him on 21 February. In addition to the spiritual healers, however, there was Dr Tronchin, who had lived in Paris for ten years. After Voltaire's arrival he wrote reproaching him for his silence during that time. But soon he came to see his old patient, anxious about the strain to which he was being subjected.

D'Argental was also anxious about Voltaire's health, but what could he do against Mme Denis, who was at the centre of so much bustle and excitement? As it was, the eighty-four-year-old was complaining of pains in the abdomen, and serious overtiredness. Even his patience was tried too far by the sycophantic poet Saint-Ange, who, for the benefit of the perpetual crowd of onlookers, introduced himself like the public orator.

"Today, Monsieur, I have seen Homer. I shall call another day to see Euripides and Sophocles; and then Tacitus and then Lucan...."

"Monsieur," interrupted Voltaire, "I am very old. Couldn't you pay all these visits today?"

Dr Tronchin evidently realised that a quiet word with Mme Denis or Villette was useless, so he administered what amounted to a public rebuke and a warning, through the medium of the press. A letter appeared over his signature in the *Journal de Paris* for 20 February:

I should very much like to tell M. le Marquis de Villette in so many words that while M. de Voltaire is in Paris he is living on the capital of his strength whereas all his true friends must wish that he would only live on his income. The way things are going, his strength will soon be exhausted; and we shall be accomplices in the death of M. de Voltaire.

It was after reading the *Journal de Paris* that the Abbé Gaultier wrote to Voltaire, requesting an interview:

Many admire you; from the bottom of my heart I wish to be numbered among them. If you so decide, that honour is mine, but it depends on you. There is still time; if you allow me to talk to you I shall explain my meaning. Although I consider myself the most unworthy of all ministers, I shall not say anything unworthy of my ministry, nothing that should give you anything but pleasure. Though I shall not flatter myself that you will give me so great a happiness, I shall not forget you in the sacrifice of the Mass. With the utmost seriousness I shall pray to the just and compassionate God for the salvation of your immortal soul, which perhaps is on the point of being judged upon all its actions.

All his life Voltaire had had a fear of dying, or of what lay beyond. But almost stronger was the fear of what would happen to his body. Would the Church treat it as it had done the beautiful and generous Adrienne Lecouvreur: burial at dead of night in an unmarked grave on wasteland? The older he grew, the more obsessed he became with that fear. But if he made some sort of peace with the Church he might escape that fate.

The Abbé Gaultier came immediately he received a favourable reply. Voltaire was surrounded by the admiring and the curious, but he ended what amounted to a reception, and retired into a private room with the Abbé, to the surprise of Wagnière. Already the *curé* of Saint-Sulpice, in which parish the house was situated, had called in vain. A certain Abbé Marthe had put on ordinary clothes to gain access to Voltaire's bedroom, and as soon as they were alone together he had commanded: "Confess at once to me! No delay! Quickly!" He was forcibly ejected by Wagnière.

Gaultier told Voltaire of his ministry: first a Jesuit, then a *curé* in a parish near Rouen, and now he was the chaplain at the Hospital of the Incurables in Paris, where he said Mass every day. The old man asked if he had been sent by the Archbishop or the *curé* of Saint-Sulpice. He was gratified to find he had come of his own free will. According to one version the conversation was interrupted three times: by the Marquis de Villeville, by Voltaire's nephew, the Abbé Mignot, together with Wagnière, and finally by Mme Denis, who begged her uncle not to become overtired. Gaultier was invited to call again, and, according to Wagnière, after he had gone Voltaire described him as *un bon imbécile*. Coming from him that was an affectionate compliment.

On 25 February, while dictating to Wagnière from his bed, Voltaire had a violent fit of coughing which ruptured a blood-vessel, causing blood to spurt from his nose and mouth. The philosopher's first reaction was not to send for Dr Tronchin, but for the Abbé Gaultier. The message was not passed on by Wagnière, but instead the doctor was called. Despite the fact that the patient must already have lost a considerable amount of blood Dr Tronchin bled him, removing three cups. More useful was his refusal to allow any visitors, and he installed a nurse in the house to see that his instructions were obeyed. On and off, the haemorrhage lasted for three weeks.

The following day Voltaire passed a message to Gaultier, asking him to come as he had promised, though it was not until 2 March that he actually saw him. When he did come Wagnière eavesdropped outside the door, and heard Voltaire say he wanted to make Confession. But the Abbé replied that he must repudiate everything he had ever written. Such was his fear of suffering Adrienne Lecouvreur's fate that three days before Voltaire had written a form of confession on a slip of paper:

> I am dying in the worship of God, loving my friends, without hatred of my enemies and with contempt for superstition. February 28, 1778, Voltaire.

Now he gave it to the Abbé, asking him to have it published in the Paris newspapers. But Gaultier took it to the Archbishop, who did not consider it sufficient. There was an undeniable ambiguity about it. Which God? The God of the Deists, or the God of professing Christians?

Back he went to the house. Voltaire was prepared to bend the truth to obtain what he wanted:

> The undersigned states that for the last four months he has suffered haemorrhages [eight days in fact] and that at his age of eighty-four years he was unable to drag himself to a church. As the parish priest of Saint-Sulpice has added to his other good deeds the kindness of sending the Abbé Gaultier to me, I have confessed to him and I am now dying in the Catholic faith in which I was born, and I hope that God in his mercy will consider me worthy of forgiveness of all my faults and if I have ever offended the Church, I ask God and it forgiveness.
> March 2, 1778, in the house of the Marquis de Villette.
>   Voltaire.

Then the Abbé offered to give the Sacrament, but Voltaire declined, saying that because of his continual haemorrhages he had no wish to mix his blood with that of God.

Later, La Harpe called to inform Voltaire that the Académie Française had just passed a resolution that a messenger should be sent every day to inquire about his condition for as long as he was ill. Voltaire replied that he had tried to repay this courtesy by fulfilling his Christian obligations: this would allow the Académie to have a Mass said for the repose of his soul by the Franciscans, as was customary following the death of an Academician.

Till that time he had particularly wished to attend the first performance of *Irène*, but now, as he told another physician, all he desired was to return to Ferney:

> I do not want to be thrown into the carrion pit. These priests annoy and bore me, but they have me in their hands. . . . As soon as I can I shall depart. The frantic zeal of these priests cannot follow me to Ferney. Had I stayed there this would not have happened.

Ever self-contradictory, Voltaire now started to recover. He had more important things to do than die; like altering and revising *Irène*, and trying to infuse a little fire into Mme Vestris, who was playing the female lead. After she came to his room to recite her lines with bovine complacency he commented to Mlle Clairon that things had been different with Mlle Duclos when he had been young.

"Ah!" exclaimed Mlle Clairon, "but where will you find anyone to render them like that? The effort might kill her [Vestris]."

"So much the better. I should be only too glad to offer the public such a service."

Obviously Voltaire was feeling much better.

The first night drew near, and since the rehearsals were actually taking place in the house Dr Tronchin insisted that Voltaire must stay in bed. With him safely out of the way d'Argental and La Harpe cut and altered *Irène* as they thought fit. On 16 March the curtain rose at the Comédie Française, before a house which included Marie Antoinette and the king's youngest brother the Comte d'Artois. But Louis XVI refused to attend, and Voltaire was too ill to be present.

It was an indifferent play, but it received a tumultuous reception, and during the actual performance Marie Antoinette copied down what she considered were the more edifying passages to show to her prejudiced husband. Afterwards Voltaire's bed was surrounded by congratulating friends and admirers, all assuring him what a success it had been.

But sunshine was followed by storm. Voltaire discovered that the text of *Irène* had been altered without his knowledge or consent. He flew into a temper which lasted for twelve hours, rounded on Mme Denis, La Harpe and d'Argental, and then forgave them all most humbly.

Still the visitors continued to come, both individually and in deputations. Among the latter were representatives of the Freemasons' Lodge of the Nine Sisters, which was largely composed of writers and artists. At a meeting they had made him an honorary member, in recognition of his love of people and his hatred of fanaticism.

Again and again there were episodes of a theatrical nature during the course of Voltaire's life, whether by accident or design; and now on 30 March came the climax. He was going first to the Académie Française, and then to the theatre to attend a performance of *Irène*. As he put it, "It would be sad if I had only come to Paris to be confessed and to be hissed."

It all began at four in the afternoon, when the waiting crowd on the Quai des Théatins saw a bright blue carriage spangled with gold stars drive up. When he appeared, Voltaire looked no less striking. His grey powdered wig was of the type which had been all the mode forty years before. On it he wore a square cap, while over his coat and breeches he wore an ermine-lined red coat, and over that Catherine the Great's sable wrap. His thin legs were clad in white silk stockings made at Ferney. For support he held a cane topped with a handle in the form of a crow's beak.

All the way to the Louvre the crowd acclaimed him. At the Académie Française he was accorded an honour which not even royalty could command. Instead of waiting in their places all the members (with the exception of a few clergymen who chose to stay away) had crowded into the entrance hall to welcome him there. Ceremonially he was ushered into the Presidential Chamber, and unanimously elected president for the next term of office. Then d'Alembert, the Permanent Secretary, read his Eulogy of Boileau, which was in fact a eulogy of Voltaire himself. After comparing Boileau, Racine and Voltaire, he ended:

I am naming the last although he is still living; why should we forgo the pleasure of putting a great man in the place he will be granted by posterity, whether we do so or not?

As Voltaire returned to the coach everyone jostled to catch sight of the unique M. de Voltaire. To some he was the author of noble tragedies; to others the author of the *Dictionnaire Philosophique*. There were others again who saw him as the defender of Calas and la Barre, someone with the courage to stand up to the entrenched tyranny of the State. While to those who stayed away he was a mocking atheist with no respect for the laws of God or man; one of the accursed philosophers, who tried to undermine the old order with dictionaries and pamphlets and, in Voltaire's particular case, the most deadly of weapons, ridicule.

With Voltaire in the coach was *Belle et Bonne*. According to Wagnière one admirer jumped on the footboard of the coach in order to shake the great man's hand, but in error grabbed that of *Belle et Bonne*. "In truth, this is a very plump hand for a man of eighty-four years!" he exclaimed.

Outside the Comédie Française the crowd was in a state bordering on hysteria. Some even plucked out handfuls of fur from Catherine the Great's sable wrap as souvenirs. Inside the theatre he was ushered to the box usually occupied by Court officials, where Mme Denis and *Belle et Bonne* were already waiting. He wanted to sit behind them, but the audience insisted he must place himself between the two ladies, so that everyone had him clearly in sight. Now the audience started shouting.

"The wreath! The wreath!"

The actor Brizard entered the box and placed it on Voltaire's head. But the old man removed it and put it on *Belle et Bonne*, exclaiming: "You will kill me with glory."

The audience shouted to the Marquise to put it back where it belonged. Finally the Prince de Beauvau succeeded in replacing it. For twenty minutes the applauding and stamping continued in the packed theatre, and even the actors and actresses came before the curtain to join in the homage.

At last the performance got under way. Not that anyone, except perhaps Voltaire, paid much attention to the tragedy. At the end there was another storm of applause, and all the audience stretched up their hands towards the box, as though greeting or supplicating some deity. The curtain rose and fell. Then it rose to reveal the bust of Voltaire, brought on to the stage from the foyer of the theatre for the occasion. At the back stood soldiers who had been recruited to take the part of Imperial Guards. Around the bust were grouped the actors and actresses, still in costume, and holding palm leaves or garlands of flowers. Brizard stepped forward and crowned the bust with a laurel wreath, to the sound of trumpets and drums. Then it was the turn of Mme Vestris to recite an ode by the Marquis de Saint-Marc which included the lines:

> Voltaire, receive the crown
> Which has just been presented to you;
> To merit it is beauteous,
> When it is given by France herself.

The lines had to be repeated. Then the cast filed past the bust, each adding his or her own wreath. At the end of the evening, unparalleled in the history of the French theatre, both the audience and Voltaire were moved to the point of tears.

Then the same clamorous and over-excited audience, swelled by the crowd waiting outside the theatre, escorted Voltaire by the light of torches back to the Hôtel de Villette. Behind its closed doors the old man broke down and wept.

"If I had known people would commit such follies I would never have gone to the Comédie," he declared.

Next morning there was a question which had to be answered. When was he going back to the peace and quiet of Ferney?

Voltaire would be glad to be gone, but neither Mme Denis nor the Marquis de Villette wished even to consider the idea. Although nearing seventy, Mme Denis was flirting vigorously with a dull young man named Duvivier, whose general effect on conversation was such that behind his back he was known as "the extinguisher". On Voltaire's side were *Belle et Bonne*, who wanted what must be best for her guardian; Wagnière, who wished to return to his own family; M. and Mme Dupuits, such old friends as d'Alembert, and above all Dr Tronchin.

"Go in a week," was his advice, and he assured Voltaire that he was fit to travel. He even wrote to Ferney for his patient's own coach and coachman to come and fetch him home.

Angrily Mme Denis tried to argue with the doctor, but to no avail. Was it the Hôtel de Villette that her uncle did not like?

First she tried to buy a house in the Fauborg Saint-Honoré, and when that came to nothing she talked Voltaire into negotiating the purchase of another in the Rue Richelieu. But his heart was set on returning to Ferney.

He had received an unprecedented ovation at the Comédie Française, but he knew how fickle his countrymen could be, and commented to Wagnière that they would do as much for Rousseau. And in fact Jean-Jacques Rousseau had received almost as enthusiastic a reception, only to have it followed by a *lettre de cachet* ordering his arrest. Also, it was said that Marie Antoinette had actually set out for the theatre on the evening Voltaire was present, only to be recalled on the king's orders. What was more, there had been a calculated snub when *Irène* was given at Versailles only a few days later, and he was not invited.

On the other hand, how could Voltaire go when he had just been elected to a three months' presidency of the Académie Française? Mme Denis clinched the matter by making the unfounded statement that if he left Paris he would be forbidden to return.

Now one of the servants brought a dog from Ferney. It was delighted to see Voltaire, and he exclaimed: "You see I am still beloved at Ferney." But it was never allowed near him again.

Dr Tronchin was in despair.

"I have seen a great many fools, but never such an old fool as he is," he said on 6 April, the day Voltaire went on foot to the Académie Française, surrounded by an admiring crowd. The following day he was received as a guest of honour by the Freemasons at the Lodge of the Nine Sisters.

Two visits which he paid to old friends were particularly poignant. One was to the Comtesse de Ségur, practically on her death-bed. She hoped that he had made his peace with the Church, and before a room full of eavesdropping spectators the two old people nearly quarrelled. But the subject was changed, and they reminisced about the past. Then the conversation turned to their respective ailments. As he was about to leave Voltaire recommended to the Comtesse a diet which included egg-yolks mixed with potato flour. Standing close by was a dim-witted fellow who assumed that everything uttered by Voltaire must be witty. Beaming, he turned to the old Comte and exclaimed:

"Potato flour! What a man! What a man! Not a word without a shaft!"

Sixty years before Voltaire had known and adored Suzanne de Liviry, daughter of the Mayor of Sully. After she became the Marquise La Tour du Pin du Gouvernet she had severed relations, and her footmen had closed the doors of her new town house in his face. Now the two old people, deeply moved, were together again in her salon. On the wall hung the portrait of himself which had been painted by Largillière for her: a young man of twenty-four in a green coat and fashionable wig, with brilliant, intelligent eyes and a faintly whimsical expression playing about his mouth. Voltaire still had his brilliant eyes, but of the Suzanne de Liviry whom he had gently chided for her snobbishness in the poem *Les Vous et Les Tu* nothing remained in the old lady in her eighties.

Back once again at the Hôtel de Villette he exclaimed in a mood of great sadness: "I return from the other side of the Styx." Soon after the Marquise sent him the portrait, which he gave to *Belle et Bonne*.

Now, as spring returned to the Gardens of the Tuileries, and the trees came into bud on the Champ de Mars, another figure from the past appeared: Longchamp, the footman-cum-secretary who had been the brother of Emilie du Châtelet's maid. It was he who, long before, had copied manuscripts without permission, and been forgiven for it. He even wrote his own gossiping account of life at Cirey. Now he was welcomed as a friend from another age.

The evening of 30 March had been the conscious apotheosis of Voltaire's career. Now it was as if he were tying up the loose ends of his life. In between seeing old friends and remembering other days he was busy on a major project. What France needed was a new dictionary, and when he again visited the Académie during a session on 27 April he expounded his plan. The French language, he declared, was like a poor but proud woman, who had to be given alms against her will. Years before he had settled the spelling of *Anglais* for once and all. Before his time it had usually been spelt *Anglois*. Now he suggested that an actor who played a tragic role should be called a *tragédien*.

When he returned for another visit on 7 May he had worked out how the dictionary should be produced. The Academicians should each take a letter of the alphabet, and for his part he would provide the material for the letter A.

"Gentlemen, I thank you in the name of the alphabet," ended Voltaire.

"And we thank you in the name of literature," was the reply he received.

The Académie Française was not the only institute of learning to honour Voltaire. On 29 April he was invited to attend a session of the Académie des Sciences where he was the guest of honour. As the novelty of his being in Paris began to wear off, so the crowds began to diminish, but the papers assiduously printed all his utterances, real and imaginary.

Two institutions which were never to come to accept his presence in the capital were the Church and State. At Versailles the preacher Beauregard kept up his denunciations, and criticised the Chancellor for not taking action against him, or at least forbidding any expressions of public admiration or esteem. Louis XVI thoroughly approved of the sermon.

Mme Denis was more determined than ever to remain in Paris. She could not forbid Dr Tronchin to enter the house, but she could get Wagnière out of the way. On 29 April the devoted secretary was sent off to Ferney, ostensibly to fetch papers required by his employer. Now there was no one in the house to restrain Voltaire, and if possible he worked harder than ever on his new dictionary, keeping himself going with endless cups of coffee.

One evening he made an incognito visit to the theatre to see *Alzire*, but at the end of the fourth act the audience discovered he was in their midst, and there was a repetition of the scene which happened during the performance of *Irène*.

What now worried Dr Tronchin was the almost obsessive intensity with which he worked, continuing in bed when he felt too ill to get up.

On 12 May Voltaire went for a walk, and, declaring on his return that he felt unwell, retired to bed. There he was visited by an old friend, Mme Saint-Julien, who realised that he was seriously ill, and urged Mme Denis to send for Dr Tronchin. The niece declined to do so, but later Villette went to the local apothecary for medicine, which had no beneficial effect whatsoever. In the evening Voltaire was visited by the Duc de Richelieu, who suggested that he should try the medicine which he took for his gout, and which contained laudanum. Whether or not Voltaire took any of it is uncertain, but that night he became worse.

Dr Tronchin was called in, but there was little he or anyone could do. In spite of himself, Voltaire was starting to die. His worn-out body wanted to return to dust, but his mind would not let it go. He was to fight death for eighteen days. Beside Mme Denis and his nephew, the Abbé Mignot, Villette and *Belle et Bonne* were constantly on hand; as well as Dr Tronchin and a servant named Morand.

One last victory remained to Voltaire. On 26 May news was brought that the king had annulled the judgment passed against General Lally, and that his name had been cleared of the charges which resulted in his execution. At once his son, Lally-Tollendal, had sent word to the Hôtel de Villette. Voltaire roused himself from the coma into which he was slipping, sat up in bed, and dictated his last letter:

> The dying man revives on hearing the good news; he affectionately embraces M. de Lally; he sees that the King is the defender of justice; he will die content.

At his instruction a large notice was pinned to the curtains which surrounded his bed:

> On 26th May the judicial assassination, committed by Pasquier upon the person of Lally, was avenged by the King's council.

It remained there until after his death.

Evidently the Abbé Mignot discovered that the Church intended to pursue its feud to the graveside, and deny Voltaire decent burial. He went to the *curé* of Saint-Sulpice, asking him to come to the Hôtel de Villette. De Tersac said there was no point if Voltaire was wandering in his mind, and that the old man could not expect Christian burial on the strength of the profession of faith which he had already made.

Mignot threatened to apply to the *Parlement* (of which he was Clerk) for justice. De Tersac told him to do as he pleased, knowing that Voltaire was far too ill ever to be able to make another and fuller confession. Mignot went to the Archbishop. On 30 May the Abbé Gaultier called, hoping that Voltaire would sign a further retraction, which might satisfy the *curé*. The three clergymen entered Voltaire's room. The dying man was rambling in his mind. De Tersac came to the bedside and demanded loudly:

"M. de Voltaire, you are at the end of your life; do you recognise the divinity of Jesus Christ?"

Feebly Voltaire pushed him away, saying: "In the name of God, let me die in peace."

Accounts differ as to the last two or three hours of Voltaire's life. The philosophers declared that he died with fortitude. The Calvinist Dr Tronchin regretted his lack of orthodox Christian faith; while before long the Church in Paris was circulating the story that he died in abject terror, believing that the Devil was sitting on the end of his bed. A story *pour encourager les autres*. *Belle et Bonne*, who was likely to be the most truthful witness, gave her account years later to Lady Morgan, who recounted it in a book.

"Until the last moment," she [*Belle et Bonne*] told me, "all breathed the benignity and goodness of his character; everything showed forth his tranquillity, peace, resignation, save only the slight movement of exasperation he showed to the *curé* of Saint-Sulpice when he asked him to withdraw, saying: 'Let me die in peace.'"

Somewhere after eleven o'clock on the evening of 30 May Voltaire took the hand of his servant, saying: "Farewell, my dear Morand. I am dying." Ten minutes later he was dead.

Chapter 25

THE FINAL TRIUMPH

A race against time and the Church began. It was obvious that the profession of faith made by Voltaire (and still preserved in the Bibliothèque Nationale, Paris) would not satisfy the *curé* of Saint-Sulpice. The Abbé Mignot and his half brother, Dompierre d'Hornoy (son of Voltaire's elder sister, Marie Marguerite, by her first marriage), had already been to the Minister of the *Département de Paris*, and to the Police Commissioner. But any chance of burial in consecrated ground was out of the question. The Archbishop of Paris had expressly forbidden it. But at least they had permission to remove the body from the capital. The old philosopher's wish had been to be buried at Ferney, but since it was the obvious place to which the family would try to take the body, such a move was too risky. Also, the Bishop of Annecy was sure to raise the same objections there as had the *curé* of Saint-Sulpice in Paris.

If they moved swiftly there was one place where Voltaire could receive decent burial: Mignot's own Abbey of Scellières, in Champagne. The rest of the night of 30–31 May was taken up with the task of embalming the body.

When Voltaire had entered Paris on 10 February he had jokingly commented to the customs officers that he was the only contraband in the carriage. Now the jest had become a ghastly truth. While it was still dark the body was clad in a dressing-gown, with a nightcap on its head, carried downstairs and placed in a carriage. There it was propped up, to look as though the great man was asleep, with a servant sitting beside him. Already the Abbé Mignot had left for Scellières to warn the Prior what was coming. Behind the carriage was another, containing Dompierre d'Hornoy and two of his cousins.

By noon, 1 June, the carriages reached the Abbey, where the body was put in a simple pine coffin, and placed in the choir of the church, after which the Vespers for the Dead were sung by the monks. The following day Voltaire was buried with the rites of the Catholic church.

On 3 June an order came from the Bishop of Troyes, in whose diocese Scellières was situated, forbidding the Prior to give burial to the hated philosopher. It was too late, but to mollify the fanatics Voltaire's relatives put the story into circulation that he had been buried under two feet of quicklime. The Bishop dared not attack the Abbé Mignot, who was Clerk to the *Parlement de Paris*, so instead he dismissed the Prior.

By the time Mignot returned to Paris the news of Voltaire's death was circulating by word of mouth, for the authorities had forbidden any mention of it in the press. The *Journal de Paris*, which printed the obituary notices, was specifically forbidden to insert anything referring to Voltaire. Nor were the Franciscan monks at the Cordeliers permitted to celebrate the Mass which was customary after the death of a member of the Académie Française.

D'Alembert wrote to Frederick the Great telling him of the rejection of the Académie's request to have a Mass celebrated. He added that in his opinion no one was likely to be elected quickly to the chair left vacant by Voltaire's death. It was the free-thinking Prussian king who arranged for a Mass to be said for him in Berlin.

In his will Voltaire had left small legacies to those in his employment. No special provision was made for Wagnière, who deserved a handsome reward, because he was confident that Mme Denis would see that he was generously provided for. But that was not to be the case. She disliked the Swiss for his loyal solicitude towards his employer, and gave him nothing. Years before she had quite wrongly blamed him for making trouble when she and La Harpe had been sent off to Paris after the misappropriation of several of Voltaire's manuscripts, including part of the *Civil War in Geneva*. It was left to Catherine the Great to make provision for him.

All Mme Denis wanted to do was to be rid of Ferney and return to Paris, to marry M. Duvivier. By December she had completed the sale to the Empress of Russia of all Voltaire's library, with the exception of his books in English, which had not been left for her to dispose of as she pleased. As well as 6,210 volumes there were all his personal papers, including letters and documents relating to such trials as Calas and la Barre. All were catalogued and set in order by Wagnière, and when Catherine heard how badly off he was she gave him a pension for life. Later he visited Frederick the Great, and then returned to spend the rest of his life at Ferney.

The pious might thank God that such a wicked man had been removed from this world, but there were those who remembered him differently. In August d'Alembert selected Voltaire as the subject for a prize-winning poem for the members of the Académie, and later La Harpe delivered his own eulogy. In the past he had behaved shabbily to the man who had taught him so much and made him so welcome at Ferney, but now he redeemed himself with an unexpected nobility of phrasing:

> Let those who have been alarmed by his attacks trust to the mighty balances in which time weighs all things; time will retain what is good and reasonable in those works of genius, and discard everything that human passions have intermixed with them. The evil that you fear is transitory. The good will endure.

> Voltaire was at least one of the most steadfast worshippers of the Godhead. "If God did not exist, it would be necessary to invent Him." That fine utterance was one of the thoughts of his old age, and it is the utterance of a philosopher. . . . His villagers who had lost him; their children, the heirs of the blessings he had bestowed, would say to the traveller who turned aside to see Ferney: "This numerous and flourishing colony was born under his auspices, in a place where there was once a wood. . . . It was here that the carriage arrived bringing the desolate family of Calas; and there all those unfortunate people surrounded him, embracing his knees. See that tree, untouched by the axe, under which he was sitting when a number of poverty-stricken came to implore his help; help which he gave with tears in his eyes, which gave them renewed life.

In his biography written in 1910 Tallentyre summed up Voltaire in one paragraph:

Who has done the more good for the world—the stainless anchorite, be his cloister a religious one or his own easy home; or this sinner, of whom it was said at his death, with literal truth, that the history of what had been accomplished in Europe in favour of reason and humanity was the history of his writings and of his deeds?

Frederick the Great now occupied the President's chair in the Berlin Academy, and in November 1778 he delivered his own eulogy at a specially called session. First he castigated those who had tried to deny him decent, let alone Christian, burial. Then he declared:

Which is the more truly Christian: the magistrate who drives a family into exile, or the philosopher who welcomes and supports it; the executioner of Calas, or the protector of his desolate family?

These things have endeared the memory of M. de Voltaire for ever to all who are born with tender hearts, and are capable of being moved to compassion. However precious may be the gifts of the mind and imagination, or exalted genius, and wide knowledge, those rare gifts can never outweigh acts of humanity and beneficence. The former may be admired; but the latter are blessed and venerated.

And so it still is. While the world has long since passed away which needed the *Dictionnaire Philosophique* or trenchant attacks on a Church, so that eventually it corrected its failings from within, his plea for tolerance, compassion and a love for humanity is as valid today as ever it was. Much may have changed, but much in human nature remains the same.

Voltaire was a genius, but a flawed genius. So much time and talent was squandered on feuds and personal ill-will. In the extreme anger which followed the arrest of himself and Mme Denis at Frankfurt he eased his spleen by writing the *Mémoires pour servir à la vie de Monsieur de Voltaire*, which were not intended for publication. In them he referred to Frederick the Great's homosexuality with biting cruelty, which came oddly from one who at other times spoke of the need for tolerance and understanding, whether moral, religious or political. In fairness to him he did throw the manuscript into the fire after ending his quarrel with Frederick the Great in 1760, but what he did not know was that two copies had been made by Wagnière. One was stolen by La Harpe in 1768. If he got over his hatred of the Prussian king, Mme Denis never did; nor for that matter did Catherine the Great, whose troops had suffered severe losses during the Seven Years War. Each now possessed a copy of the objectionable *Mémoires*.

In 1784 Beaumarchais began the great task of bringing out a complete edition of the works of Voltaire, and Mme Denis gave him permission to include the *Mémoires*. Because of the political repercussions which could arise Beaumarchais was secretly advised to omit them, and they remained unprinted until the last volume came out in 1790, after Frederick's death. But by 1784 manuscript copies were circulating in Paris. Obviously they were shown to Frederick the Great. He never so much as looked at the bust of Voltaire by Houdon when it arrived from Paris. It was a sad end to a unique friendship.

Any kind of monument to Voltaire was banned in France, and that included a memorial over his grave in the Abbey of Scellières. The edition by Beaumarchais of his writings was denounced by the clergy, and the Archbishop of Vienne declared that anyone in his diocese who subscribed to it was committing a mortal sin. The edition brought little but worry and bankruptcy to Beaumarchais. An important section was the correspondence with Catherine the Great, but now she wanted to edit the letters; making such alterations and omissions as she thought fit, which enormously increased the cost of printing. By 1785 thirty of the seventy volumes had been published (incidentally, the correspondence alone, edited by Theodore Besterman, the leading authority on Voltaire, runs to no less than 108 volumes, and includes some 12,000 letters). That same year the Archbishop of Paris denounced the edition, and the Council banned its sale in France. Because of official disapproval the printing had not taken place on French soil, but at Kehl, just across the Rhine from Strasbourg. As a result of the ban the number of subscriptions was only 2,000 and 15,000 copies had been printed. The fact that posterity and the publishing houses of the world were to make ample amends would have been of little consolation to Beaumarchais, who was ruined by the enterprise.

Mme Denis had no intention of returning to Ferney. All those years she had only tolerated the place and its inhabitants. So she sold the estate to Villette, stayed on in Paris and married M. Duvivier. Astonishingly, it was he who turned out to be the dominant partner, and not the woman whose only claim to fame (apart from the recently discovered correspondence between her and her uncle) was the fact that she was Voltaire's niece, as Frederick the Great put it with some degree of truth.

Villette and *Belle et Bonne* made their home at Ferney. They were reasonably happy, but neither had the business instinct to maintain the industries which were the life-blood of the village. One by one the watch-makers, silk-weavers and lace-makers moved away. Before long Ferney, once a model of its kind, had dwindled into little more than a château with a cluster of houses nearby. The Villettes were not destined to remain at Ferney for many years. Somehow the Marquis was involved in the bankruptcy of the Prince de Guéménée (whose wife was governess to the royal children), and he was forced to sell the château. When Voltaire's body had been embalmed his heart had been removed and placed in a silver vase which Villette set in a place of honour in the old man's study. Now it and many other personal relics were taken back to Paris, where the couple continued to live.

In July 1789 a crisis erupted with the rumour that M. Necker had been dismissed as Finance Minister, and that Swiss and German mercenary troops would soon be cutting the throats of the "patriots." Two days later the Bastille fell, and the Revolution had begun.

The following year all Church property, including the Abbey of Scellières, was taken over by the State. Voltaire's republican plays were all the vogue, and in November 1790 Charles Villette, as he now preferred to be known, took the opportunity after a performance of *Brutus* to make a plea that Voltaire's body might be brought back to the capital and interred in a manner befitting a national hero. It can be imagined how willingly Louis XVI signed the decree presented to him on 1 July 1791 by the National Convention. Apart from anything else he was preoccupied with plans for the escape of the royal family from the Tuileries to the

Austrian Netherlands, and from there to join Marie Antoinette's relatives in Vienna. As history knows, that ended with their capture at Varennes, only thirty miles from the frontier.

One of the acts of the revolutionaries had been to convert the church of Sainte-Geneviève (the patron saint of Paris) into a secular shrine, the Panthéon, for the nation's illustrious dead. It was there that Voltaire's body would be taken in a procession which became an act of homage.

The triumph of the last visit to Paris had been remarkable enough, but that which came thirteen years after his death was astonishing. An enormous funeral car of classic design was prepared, and set out for Scellières at the beginning of July. The people of the nearby village of Romilly-sur-Seine, unwilling to lose so famous a personage, asked that they should be allowed to keep the head and right arm. But this request was rejected, because it smacked of the custom of the Catholic Church with the relics of saints. It was even feared there might be trouble with the villagers when the time came to remove Voltaire. But the philosopher's body, accompanied by a detachment of the National Guard, was placed on the funeral car without incident.

Between the Abbey and the village itself the route was lined by villagers with cypress branches in their hands, and mothers held up their children to kiss the vehicle as it passed. The slow journey from Romilly-sur-Seine to Paris continued from 6 to 11 July, and it was more like a Roman triumph than a funeral cortège. Every town and village added its wreaths and garlands of flowers to those already covering the sarcophagus, which had on its front: "To the shade of Voltaire," while on one side was the inscription, "If man is born free, he ought to govern himself," and on the other, "If man has tyrants he ought to dethrone them."

At 10 a.m. on 11 July the body of Voltaire re-entered the city out of which it had been smuggled in the guise of a sleeping man thirteen years before. Preceded by a squadron of cavalry the sarcophagus passed under triumphal arches and through the city gates. Flowers were strewn in its path, and young girls in classical robes danced on either side, while the men of the National Guard had decorated their guns with sprigs of oak leaves or laurel.

That night the sarcophagus was set on a temporary altar on the site of the Tour de la Bazinère, where Voltaire had been imprisoned, amid the rubble of the demolished Bastille. A torch-light vigil was kept, and then the next day came this strange second apotheosis. For the people of Paris it was a great occasion, but not a solemn one. The mood was that of a happy, though emotional festival. Throughout the night the sarcophagus had lain on an altar with the inscription: "On this spot, where despotism chained thee, receive the homage of a free people."

The final procession was quite remarkable. Taking part were workmen who had helped demolish the Bastille, bearing trophies such as cannon balls and chains. In their midst was the harpy who claimed to have led the mob on that first Bastille Day. Then there were the elected members of the Estates General called in 1789, and also from the later National Assembly. Next came school-children, members of political clubs, engineers, writers and soldiers on foot and on horse. Many carried flags or standards copied from those of ancient Rome. At the head of the main part of the column came a group in togas bearing a gilded replica of Houdon's statue of the seated Voltaire. Then came the funeral car. At least thirty feet high, it was in the form of an altar set on three steps which were mounted on the funeral car itself, which had four large wheels of bronze. Two pairs of mourning genii were placed on either side, while on top of the porphyry sarco-phagus lay the carved figure of Voltaire as though asleep on a couch, a broken lyre at his side, and at his head a winged Victory holding a wreath of stars. The inscription declared:

He avenged Calas, la Barre, Sirven and Montballi. Poet, philosopher, and historian, he gave mankind the greatest gifts. He prepared us to be free.

Twelve horses, three abreast, drew the funeral car. Behind walked *Belle et Bonne* and Citizen Villette, together with a nurse carrying their infant daughter. Following were the Deputies from the National Assembly, judges and municipal authorities, and Mayor Bailly, who seemed under the impression that the applause from the crowd—estimated at 600,000—was for himself.

The first stop after the Bastille was the Opéra. There the pro-cession halted while singers emerged and rendered a chorus from *Samson* by Voltaire (music by Rameau, never published): *Peuple, éveille-toi, romp tes fers!* Until the advent of the *Marseillaise* in the summer of 1792 it was the battle-hymn of the Revolution.

Now the procession of 100,000 people passed the south end of the Tuileries, before crossing the Pont Royal to reach the Quai des Théatins, recently renamed the Quai Voltaire. All but one of the palace windows which looked on to the quay were crowded with spectators. Behind the drawn blinds of that one window sat Louis XVI and Marie Antoinette.

A stand had been set up outside the Hôtel de Villette on which some fifty girls in white dresses were waiting, with flowers to strew in the path of the procession. With them, in deep mourning, were the two daughters of Calas.

First the copy of Houdon's statue was set in a place of honour under an arch of branches. *Belle et Bonne* approached, kissed it and to great applause held out her infant daughter, as though dedicating the child to reason and freedom. Another song was sung, with words by André Chénier, who would himself be guillotined during the Terror, for no other reason than that his name had been confused with that of another person.

As rain threatened, the procession moved forward again, to the Comédie Française and the Théâtre de la Nation. Outside the former was the bust which had been crowned with laurel leaves during that performance of *Irène* in March 1778. Now it bore the inscription: "He wrote *Oedipe* at seventeen." Outside the Théâtre de la Nation were the words: "He wrote *Irène* at eighty-four."

Rain started to fall as the sarcophagus was borne into the Panthéon, and placed not far from the tombs of Descartes and Mirabeau.

The Revolution grew more extreme, but with the overthrow and deaths of Robespierre and Saint-Just the Terror ended, and before long Napoleon was directing the nation's affairs. He remained in power until his exile to Elba in 1814. Back to the throne came the Bourbons, in the form of Louis XVIII, the younger brother of Louis XVI.

Then came the reckoning for the Bonapartists and also—even indirectly—for those who had helped touch off the events of 1789. The Revolutionaries had themselves unceremoniously removed Mirabeau from the Panthéon after it came to light that he had had double dealings with the royal family shortly before his death in

1791. Now it was Voltaire's turn. A number of reactionaries, forerunners of the "Ultras" whose excessive conservatism would eventually cost Charles X the throne in 1830, broke open the coffin, threw the bones into a sack and took them to waste ground outside one of the *Barrières* of the city. There a hole had already been dug, and the sack emptied into it. The earth was shovelled over and stamped down, and in the middle of the night all that Voltaire had ever feared concerning his remains had happened. But something was left: his heart. Charles Villette had died in 1791, and during the remainder of her life *Belle et Bonne* did all she could to keep her guardian's memory alive. But in 1864 the direct line died out, and it was decided that Voltaire's heart, which had become the property of the nation, should be placed in the tomb in the Panthéon. Not till then was the theft of fifty years discovered. But whatever had been the fate of his body, the name of François Arouet, known to posterity as Voltaire, was by now immortal.

SELECTED BIBLIOGRAPHY

VOLTAIRE. *Correspondence*. Edited by Theodore Besterman. 102 volumes. Genève, Institut et Musée Voltaire, 1953–1965. General Index Volumes 103–107. Genève, Institut et Musée Voltaire, 1965.

Voltaire. Theodore Besterman, Longmans, 1969.

Select Letters of Voltaire. Translated and edited by Theodore Besterman, Nelson, 1963.

Voltaire. (2 volumes) Georg Brandes, Tudor Publishing Co., New York, 1930.

Voltaire's Visit to England. Archibald Ballantyne, John Murray, 1919.

Voltaire. H. N. Brailsford. O.U.P. (paperback), 1968.

Voltaire. Gustave Lanson; translated by Robert A. Wagoner, published Wiley.

The Living Thoughts of Voltaire. André Maurois, Cassel, 1939.

Voltaire in Love. Nancy Mitford, Hamish Hamilton, 1957.

Voltaire. Alfred Noyes, Faber and Faber, 1936.

Voltaire. Richard Aldington, G. Routledge and Sons, 1925.

The Romances of Voltaire. Edited by Manuel Komroff, Tudor Publishing Co., New York, 1936.

Lettres sur les Anglais. Edited by A. Wilson-Green, C.U.P. (also available in English: *Letters Concerning the English Nation*, Davies, London, 1926).

Mélanges (very comprehensive, including the best of Voltaire's essays, pamphlets, etc.). Bibliothèque de la Pléiade, Gallimard, Paris, 1961.

Voltaire et l'Encyclopédie. Raymond Naves, Édition des presses Modernes, 1938.

Voltaire: *Dictionnaire Philosophique*. Éditions Garnier Frères, Paris, 1936.

Letters of Voltaire and Frederick the Great. Translated by Richard Aldington, Routledge and Sons, 1927.

Candide. Available in many editions, both in French and English.

Candide and other stories. Translated by Joan Spencer, introduction by Theodore Besterman, London, O.U.P., 1966.

INDEX